T0243093

The Spoken Language Translator

This book presents a detailed description of the Spoken Language Translator (SLT), one of the first major projects in the area of automatic speech translation. The SLT system can translate among English, French, and Swedish in the domain of air travel planning, with an accuracy of about 75 percent. The greater part of the book describes the language processing components, which are built on top of the SRI Core Language Engine and which use a combination of general grammars and techniques that allow them to be rapidly customized to specific domains. Speech recognition is based on Hidden Markov Model technology and uses versions of the SRI DECIPHER ^{TM} system.

This account of the Spoken Language Translator is an essential resource both for those who wish to know what is achievable in spoken language translation today, and for those who wish to understand how to achieve it.

Manny Rayner joined SRI International in 1991. He is currently a Senior Computer Scientist at SRI's Artificial Intelligence Center at Menlo Park, California, where his work focuses on spoken language interface technology. He has published more than 50 papers, including articles in journals such as *Artificial Intelligence* and *Computational Linguistics*.

David Carter worked as a computer scientist at SRI International for 12 years, and is now a Senior Scientist with Speech Machines in Malvern, England. He recently served on the editorial board of *Computational Linguistics*, and has published extensively on natural language processing.

Pierrette Bouillon has been a researcher at ISSCO/TIM, University of Geneva for the past 10 years, with particular interest in lexical semantics and machine translation. She has numerous publications in international conferences, journals, and books, and has served on the programme committees of several international conferences.

Vassilis Digalakis is currently an Assistant Professor in the Department of Electronics and Computer Engineering at the Technical University of Crete. He received his PhD in Electrical Engineering in 1992 from Boston University. He is the author of more than 60 publications on speech recognition.

Mats Wirén has been at Telia Research since 1995, where he has acted as leader on several projects, including the Spoken Language Translator. He received his PhD in Computer Science from Linköping University, and has numerous publications in conference proceedings and books in the areas of parsing, translation, and dialogue management.

Studies in Natural Language Processing

Series Editor: Branimir Boguraev, Apple Computers Inc.

Also in the series:

The Spoken Language Translator

Manny Rayner
SRI International

David Carter
Speech Machines, Malvern, England

Pierrette Bouillon
University of Geneva, ISSCO/TIM

Vassilis Digalakis
Technical University of Crete

Mats Wirén
Telia Research

CAMBRIDGE
UNIVERSITY PRESS

CAMBRIDGE UNIVERSITY PRESS
Cambridge, New York, Melbourne, Madrid, Cape Town, Singapore, São Paulo

Cambridge University Press
The Edinburgh Building, Cambridge CB2 8RU, UK

Published in the United States of America by Cambridge University Press, New York

www.cambridge.org
Information on this title: www.cambridge.org/9780521770774

First published 2000
This digitally printed version 2007

A catalogue record for this publication is available from the British Library

Library of Congress Cataloguing in Publication data
The spoken language translator / Manny Rayner . . . [et al.].
    p.   cm. – (Studies in natural language processing)
    Chiefly in English; includes examples in Danish, French, and Swedish.
    Much material in this report is based on published papers.
    Includes bibliographical references.
    ISBN 0-521-77077-7 (hb)
    1. Machine translating.   2. Speech processing systems.   I. Rayner, Manny, 1958–   II.
Series.
    P309 .S68   2000
    418'.02'0285 – dc21   99-054619

ISBN 978-0-521-77077-4 hardback
ISBN 978-0-521-03882-9 paperback

Contents

Preface

Automatic recognition of human speech and automatic translation among natural languages have been two long-term goals of computer technologists almost since the dawn of the digital age. Substantial efforts were put into machine translation in the 1950s and early 1960s, until the U.S. National Academy of Sciences published a report by its Automatic Language Processing Advisory Committee (ALPAC) in 1966. The ALPAC report concluded that more basic research was needed before practical machine translation could be achieved.

The first major attempt to produce automatic recognition of continuous speech was the Speech Understanding Research (SUR) program sponsored by the Advanced Research Projects Agency (ARPA) of the U.S. Department of Defense in the early 1970s. The program failed to produce practical speech recognition technology at that time for a number of reasons, not the least of which was the fact that the computers of the day were far too small and slow for the task. Nevertheless, the most successful system, Carnegie Mellon University's HARPY, was one of the first to be based on the hidden Markov model (HMM) concept that later provided the foundation for almost all successful speech recognition technology.

Following these early efforts, research on both machine translation and speech recognition went through a dormant phase. Research on computer processing of natural language indeed turned from attempts to produce immediately useful translation systems to exploration of the underlying basic linguistic and computational issues. This change in focus was reflected in the change of the name of the leading professional society in the field from the Association for Machine Translation to the Association for Computational Linguistics. Work on the basic problems of computational linguistics progressed, and in the mid-1980s a number of related research threads came together into a family of feature-based grammar formalisms under the general description of "unification grammar." This approach quickly became widely adopted in North America, Europe, and Japan.

About the same time unification grammar was taking off as the dominant approach to natural-language processing, speech recognition research once more began attracting the attention of funding agencies. ARPA (by this time renamed

DARPA) initiated a new speech recognition program in 1985, which within a few years came to be dominated by the HMM approach, inspired at least in part by the increasing success IBM's speech recognition research group had with the approach. Progress was rapid both in the DARPA-funded program and among groups in Europe. By the late 1990s, continuous speech dictation products for PCs were available from such companies as Dragon Systems, IBM, Lernout and Houspie, and Philips; and server-based speech recognition technology for telephony applications was fielded by established companies like AT&T, as well as startups like Nuance Communications (a spinoff from DARPA-funded research at SRI International).

With this record of progress in both computational linguistics and speech recognition, activity in machine translation began to revive in the 1980s, with the added twist that spoken language translation began to receive significant attention. In Japan, the Advanced Telecommunications Research Laboratories (ATR) were founded with spoken language translation as a major goal; AT&T Bell Laboratories demonstrated speech-to-speech translation at the 1992 Olympic Games in Barcelona; and in 1993 the German government began a high-profile spoken language translation project called VERBMOBIL.

This is the context in which the work described in the present book sits. Begun in 1992, the Spoken Language Translator was founded on a combination of state-of-the-art unification-based natural-language processing technology developed by SRI International in Cambridge, England, and state-of-the-art HMM-based speech recognition technology developed by SRI in Menlo Park, California. In the course of the project, a number of significant results were obtained through the development of novel techniques. In computational linguistics, these include grammar specialisation through explanation-based learning and discriminant-based statistical preferences for language processing. In speech recognition, perhaps the most important result is the development of discrete-mixture HMMs, leading to two to three times faster recognition than with state-of-the-art continuous HMMs having similar recognition accuracy. Perhaps the greatest achievement of the project, however, is that these results, as well as overall performance that appears to be comparable to any in the world, were obtained with far fewer resources than some other research efforts. This account of the Spoken Language Translator is an essential resource for both those who wish to know what is achievable in spoken language translation today and those who wish to understand how to achieve it.

Robert C. Moore
Microsoft Research, Redmond, Washington

Acknowledgements

The main Spoken Language Translation project was funded by the Telia Networks Division and by Telia Research. We would particularly like to thank Bengt Hagström and Conny Björkvall in this connection. The work was carried out by Telia Research, SRI International, the Technical University of Crete, and, during the first phase of the project, the Swedish Institute of Computer Science (SICS). Work involving French was mainly carried out under a separate project that involved SRI International and ISSCO/TIM, under internal funding from SRI and Suissetra. Work on Danish was carried out by SRI and Handelshøjskolen i København under a third project, under internal funding from both parties. The work described in Chapter 7 was partly funded by the Defence Research Agency, Malvern, UK, under Strategic Research Project AS04BP44, and the work in Section 16.5 was partly supported by a DARPA-sponsored Spoken Language System project.

Björn Gambäck and Jussi Karlgren, while at SICS, took part in the SLT-1 project; together with Mikael Eriksson, Björn also took part in the initial stages of the SLT-2 project. They made valuable contributions to the Swedish version of the CLE and helped write the first version of the English-to-Swedish transfer rule set. During the same period, Hiyan Alshawi implemented the first versions of the transfer rule compiler, and the speech-language interface, while Marie-Susanne Agnäs wrote the first version of the English ATIS lexicon and helped develop the first English ATIS grammar. Manolis Perakakis and Stavros Tsakalidis contributed to the implementation of the discrete-mixture HMM described in Chapter 15. Vassilis Diakoloukas contributed to the Dialect Adaptation work described in Chapter 18. Nikos Chatzichrisafis assisted in the development of the SLT-3 Swedish recogniser. Harry Bratt provided the English ATIS training and test data for the grammar induction experiments in Section 16.5. Martin Keegan judged nearly the whole of the English treebank, a task requiring impressive reserves of patience and fortitude; Maria Arnstad, Tove Matthis, and Maria Kronberg were responsible for its Swedish counterpart. Maria Kronberg also provided valuable user feedback for the acquisition tools described in Chapter 6. Eleonora Beshai developed word-to-word transfer rules and Sara Rydin contributed to the evaluations of the composed Swedish-to-French system described in Section 13.5.

xviii *Acknowledgements*

Many people helped translate ATIS material into Swedish, including Anita Andersson, Martin Eineborg, Malin Ericson, Eva Lindström, several graduate students at Stockholm University, and a large number of employees at Telia Research and Telia Mobitel. Gunnel Källgren and Britt Hartmann, Department of Linguistics, Stockholm University, kindly gave us permission to use texts from the Stockholm-Umeå corpus. People involved in collecting the Swedish speech data described in Chapter 17 included Anita Andersson, Johanna Etzler, Qina Hermansson, Inge Karlsson, Carin Lindberg, Janne "Beb" Lindberg, Jaan Pannel, Curth Svensson, and Tomas Svensson. Camilla Eklund and Nils Meinhard were instrumental in organising and carrying out the Wizard-of-Oz simulations described in Chapter 8. Beata Forsmark and Rósa Guðjónsdóttir carried out annotations of disfluencies of the WOZ1 material described in Chapter 8.

The English-to-French and English-to-Swedish tests in Chapter 20 were evaluated by Sophie Lavagne and Jens Edlund, respectively, and the Swedish-to-French tests in Chapter 13 by Nathalie Kirchmeyer and Thierry Reynier. Other people who helped with evaluation work included Malin Ericson, Beata Forsmark, Carin Lindberg, Janne "Beb" Lindberg, Don Miller, Sara Rydin, Jennifer Spenader, John Swedenmark, and Matilda Wernström.

We would like to thank Steve Pulman for useful comments on the material in Chapters 4 and 13, Elisabet Engdahl and Lars Ahrenberg for insightful discussions of the issues relating to Swedish word order discussed in Chapter 11, and Eva Lindström for comments on Swedish verbal -s- forms in the same chapter. Robert Eklund executed the task of correcting, restructuring, and formatting the set of references with great diligence and care. The diagrams and graphs in Chapter 3 were all prepared by Ralph Becket, who kindly made available to us his skills with Tgif and Gnuplot. We have almost certainly forgotten to thank some people, and if so, we beg their forgiveness.

Much of the material in this report is based on published papers. Permission to reuse parts of those papers is gratefully acknowledged. Chapters 2 and 4 draw on Rayner and Carter (1996), and Appendix A uses Carter (1995), which are both © Association for Computational Linguistics; Chapter 10 is an edited version of Rayner, Bouillon, and Carter (1996); Section 1.4 is based on Rayner and Carter (1997) and Section 8.2 on Bretan, Eklund, and MacDermid (1996), both © IEEE; Section 1.5 uses Rayner and Bouillon (1995); Section 13.3 uses Rayner et al. (1996) and Carter et al. (1997). Section 19.2 uses Carter et al. (1996), © IEEE; Section 19.3.1 uses Sautermeister and Lyberg (1996); Sections 20.1–20.3 use Carter et al. (1997); and Section 20.5 uses Rayner et al. (1994), © IEEE.

Manny Rayner and David Carter
SRI International, Cambridge

Pierrette Bouillon
ISSCO/TIM, Geneva

Vassilis Digalakis
Technical University of Crete

Mats Wirén
Telia Research, Stockholm

1   Introduction

MANNY RAYNER, DAVID CARTER,
PIERRETTE BOUILLON, MATS WIRÉN,
AND VASSILIS DIGALAKIS

1.1   What This Book Is About

Automatic translation of spoken language has long been a cherished dream of science fiction writers and futurologists, but it has been only during the last decade that serious implemented systems have started to emerge. This book presents a detailed description of Spoken Language Translator (SLT), one of the first major projects in speech translation. SLT started in the second half of 1992 under sponsorship from Telia Research, Stockholm, and with a few interruptions continued until the middle of 1999. To be exact, there were three distinct projects. SLT-1 ran from mid-1992 to mid-1993. The partners were Telia Research, SRI International, and the Swedish Institute of Computer Science (SICS). SLT-2 began in mid-1994 and ended in late 1996. In this second project, SICS dropped out of the consortium, and ISSCO/TIM (University of Geneva)[1] and TUC (Technical University of Crete) joined it. SLT-3 began shortly after the end of SLT-2, with the same partners, and continued until mid-1999.

We will start this introductory section by looking at the most basic questions: why we want to build spoken language translation systems at all, what the basic problems are, what we can realistically attempt today, and what we have in fact achieved. Later in the chapter, we present an overview of the main system architecture (Section 1.2) and an example illustrating the processing of a typical utterance (Section 1.3). Sections 1.4 and 1.5 discuss at a high level of generality our reasons for adopting the hybrid processing architecture we have chosen, Section 1.6 presents an overview of the issues addressed in developing the speech recogniser used in the SLT system, and Section 1.7 summarises the basic properties of the corpus material we have used. The remainder of the book describes the technical aspects of the SLT system in extensive detail.

---

[1] ISSCO/TIM participated under independent funding from Suissetra.

1.1.1   Why Do Spoken Language Translation?

The SLT project represents a substantial investment in time and money, and it is only natural to ask what the point is. Why is it worth trying to build spoken language translation systems? We think there are several reasonable answers, depending on one's perspective: one can consider it as a short-term or as a long-term task, and one can focus on the practical or the theoretical aspects. Naturally, all these viewpoints overlap to some extent.

In the long term, it seems clear to us that a readily available, robust, general-purpose machine for automatic translation of speech would be extremely useful. It is in fact difficult to talk about the commercial value of such a device: it would probably transform human society as much as, for example, the telephone or the personal computer. However, it is realistic to admit that we are still at least twenty years from being able to build a system of this kind. To be able to maintain credibility, we also want to point to closer and more tangible goals, which are partly theoretical in nature.

In the medium term, it is uncontroversial to state that the field of speech and language technology is growing at an explosive rate. Spoken language translation is an excellent test bed for investigating the issues, both practical and theoretical, that arise when trying to integrate different subfields within this general area. It involves attacking most of the key problems, particularly speech recognition, speech synthesis, language analysis and understanding, language generation, and language translation. By its very nature, spoken language translation also requires a multilingual approach. These are exactly the reasons that have prompted the German government to organise its whole speech and language research programme around the VERBMOBIL spoken language translation project (Bub, Wahlster, and Waibel 1997).

In the short term, spoken language translation is one of the most accessible speech and language processing tasks imaginable. Technical explanations are not necessary: one just has to pick up the microphone, say something in one language, and hear the translated output a few seconds later. We know no simpler way to convey to outsiders the excitement of working in this rapidly evolving field, and to quickly demonstrate the increasing maturity and relevance of the underlying technology. We have been pleased and surprised by the media interest attracted by the SLT project and by other speech translation projects around the world. If people are this curious about what we are up to, we feel that, at the very least, our research must be asking the right questions. We hope that the rest of the book will help convince the reader that we are making good progress towards identifying acceptable answers.

1.1.2   What Are the Basic Problems?

We will now take a step backwards and spend a few paragraphs evaluating where we are with respect to our long-term goals in spoken language translation. Although many of these goals are clearly still distant, it is nonetheless important to satisfy ourselves and our critics that we are moving in the right direction.

To fully realise our long-term goals, then, we would need to solve nearly every major problem in speech and language processing. On the speech side, we would need to be able to recognise continuous, unconstrained, spontaneous speech in a large number of languages, using an unlimited vocabulary and achieving a high level of accuracy. It would be desirable to be able to do this over the telephone, or using a hand-held device, or both. We would want recognition to be speaker independent (no previous training on a given speaker should be necessary), and robust to many kinds of variation, particularly variation in dialect and in environmental conditions. We would also have to synthesise high-quality output speech. Recognition and synthesis would have to take into account not only the words that are spoken, but also the *way* that they are spoken (their prosody), since this often conveys an important component of the meaning.

On the language side, we would need to be able to produce accurate, high-quality translations of unconstrained, spontaneous speech, again including both the actual words and their prosody. In practice, this would probably involve being able to analyse arbitrary utterances in the source language into some kind of abstract representation of their meaning, transforming the source-language meaning representation into a corresponding structure for the target language, and generating target-language translations annotated with the extra information (emphasis, punctuation, etc.) needed to allow synthesis of natural-sounding speech. All of the above processing would, in general, need to be sensitive to the context in which the utterance was produced.[2] It is also highly desirable that the techniques used to perform the various processing stages be domain independent, or at least easily portable among domains.

Spontaneous speech is frequently ill-formed in a variety of ways. In particular, speakers can and often do change their minds in midsentence about what it is that they are going to say, and speech recognition is certain to fail at least some of the time. Thus, translation must be robust enough to deal with ill-formed input. One would also prefer translation to be simultaneous, in the sense that it should lag only a short distance behind the spoken input. This implies that processing for both speech and language should work incrementally in real time, rather than waiting for the end of the utterance.

The requirements outlined above are well beyond the state of the art in automatic spoken language translation, and would indeed tax the capabilities of even the most skilled human interpreters. (Anyone who has listened to the simultaneous translation channel at a bilingual conference will testify to this.) Some compromise

---

[2] The above assumes use of a transfer-based architecture. Essentially similar considerations apply in an interlingual framework, except that the source- and target-language representations will then coincide. It seems to us implausible that purely surface-oriented translation methods would be capable of producing the kind of high-quality context-dependent translations we require here.

with the current limitations of speech and language technology is necessary. This leads to our next question.

1.1.3   What Is It Realistic to Attempt Today?

If we are to cut the problem down to a size where we can expect to show plausible results using today's speech and language technology, we must above all limit the variability of the language by confining ourselves to a specific, fairly concrete domain. Partly because of the availability of recorded data, we have chosen the domain of airline flight enquiries for the SLT project. Other groups working on similar projects have chosen conference registration and meeting scheduling (Bub et al. 1997; Waibel et al. 1996). Domains like these have core vocabularies of about 1 000 to 2 500 words. In view of the nontrivial effort required to port speech and language technology to a new language, it is also sensible to start with a small number of languages.

The speech technology we are using is speaker independent and can be run on high-end personal computers, either directly or via a telephone connection. Recognition performance is most simply measured in terms of the *word-error rate* (WER), roughly the proportion of input words incorrectly identified by the recogniser. Current technology places a lower limit of about 3 to 10 percent on the WER for tasks of the type considered here, depending on various factors, particularly, the extent to which speech is spontaneous as opposed to planned, the nature of the communication channel (close-talking microphone versus telephone), the degree to which the system is optimised for speed as opposed to accuracy, the language in question, and the amount of training data available. Of these factors, the spontaneous-speech/planned-speech opposition is the most important.

As an interface, speech adds the highest possible value on systems operating on wearable or hand-held devices, where it is often the only alternative. Continuing advances in hardware will, in the near future, make it possible to package sufficiently powerful processors in these environments, permitting use of speech-enabled applications. In the latter stages of the SLT project we have investigated a client-server architecture for computationally demanding applications (Digalakis, Neumeyer, and Perakakis 1999) that can be implemented in the immediate future: the clients, deployed on heterogeneous environments, such as personal computers, smart devices, and mobile devices, capture speech and, after some local processing, send the information to the server, which then recognises the speech according to an application framework and sends the result string or action back to the client. Another important goal that we have actively pursued and that seems quite feasible, is to aim for systems that permit a high level of dialectal variation (see Chapter 18).

Speech synthesis technology has made great progress over the last few years, and with today's technology it is possible to produce speech of fairly high quality. The challenge is now to incorporate natural-sounding prosody into the synthesised output; this is a hot research topic. When determining the correct prosody for the output, it is feasible, though challenging, to try to take account of the prosody of the input signal.

With regard to language processing, it appears that high-quality translation requires some kind of fairly sophisticated grammatical analysis: it is difficult to translate a sentence well without precisely identifying the key phrases and their grammatical functions. However, all grammars constructed to date *leak*, in the sense of only being able to assign reasonable analyses to some fraction of the space of possible input utterances. The grammar's performance on a given domain is most simply defined as its *coverage*, the proportion of sentences that receive an adequate grammatical analysis. It is feasible in restricted domains of the kind under discussion to construct grammars with a coverage of up to 85 to 90 percent. Going much higher is probably beyond the state of the art. Similar coverage figures apply to the tasks of converting (*transferring*) a source-language representation into a target-language representation, and generating a target-language utterance from a target-language representation.[3]

Achieving this kind of high-quality, robust performance using domain-independent techniques is once again feasible but challenging. There are a number of known ways to attempt to make language processing robust to various kinds of ill-formedness, and it is both feasible and necessary to make efforts in this direction (Frederking and Nirenburg 1994; Gavaldà et al. 1995; Jackson et al. 1994; Stallard and Bobrow 1993). Simultaneous translation, in contrast, still appears to be somewhat beyond the state of the art.

The preceding paragraphs sketch the limits within which we currently have to work. In the next section, we give an overview of what we have achieved to date during the SLT project.

1.1.4   *What Have We Achieved?*

The current SLT system is capable of good speech-to-speech translation between English and Swedish in either direction within the air travel information systems (ATIS) domain (see Section 1.7). Translation from English and Swedish into French is also possible, with nearly the same performance. There is an initial version of the system which translates from French into English.

English speech recognition is carried out using a previously developed version of the SRI DECIPHER^{TM} system (Digalakis, Monaco, and Murveit 1996; Murveit et al. 1993); a Swedish version of DECIPHER^{TM}, and also an initial French version, have been constructed during the project. All three versions of the recogniser are essentially domain independent, but are tuned to give high performance in the air travel information domain. DECIPHER^{TM} is based on continuous-distribution

---

[3] Note, however, that the coverage of a system consisting of N components with coverage c is usually better than the c^N one might initially assume: see Section 20.5.

hidden Markov models (CDHMMs) with *genonic* (state-clustered) mixtures of Gaussian densities (see Chapter 15) that achieve a very good speed-recognition performance tradeoff. The main version of the Swedish recogniser is trained on the Stockholm dialect of Swedish, and achieves faster than real-time performance with a word-error rate of about 7 percent. Techniques described in Chapter 18 have also made it possible to port the recogniser to other Swedish dialects using only modest quantities of training data. Speech synthesis is carried out in Swedish by the Telia Research Liphon system (Bäckström, Ceder, and Lyberg 1989), and in English and French by commercially available third-party systems.

Language processing is performed using a multi-engine architecture, which combines two processing engines: a complex grammar-based system intended for deep analysis and high-quality output, and a simple word-to-word system intended for shallow processing, speed, and robustness. The grammar-based translation subsystem consists of three versions of the SRI Core Language Engine (CLE) (Alshawi 1992) equipped with grammars and lexica for English, Swedish, and French, respectively. Grammatical coverage for each language within the chosen domain is around the 85 to 90 percent mark, and there are high-coverage sets of translation rules for five of the six possible language pairs. (As we will see in Chapter 20, it is not straightforward to assign simple coverage figures to translation tasks.) The sophisticated grammar-based system essentially translates as much of the input utterance as possible; if anything is left over, the word-to-word translation system fills in the gaps (cf. Sections 2.1 and 4.5).

The language-processing modules are all generic in nature. They are based on large, linguistically motivated grammars, and can fairly easily be adapted to give adequate performance in new domains. Much of the work involved in the domain-adaptation process can be carried out by nonexperts using tools developed under the project (see Chapters 5 and 6).

Formal comparisons between systems are problematic, in view of the different domains and languages used and the lack of accepted evaluation criteria. Nonetheless, the evidence at our disposal suggests that the current SLT prototype is comparable with the German VERBMOBIL demonstrator (Bub et al. 1997), in spite of a difference in project budget of more than an order of magnitude.

1.2   Overall System Architecture

The previous section gave a thumbnail sketch of the SLT system, which we will now flesh out in more substantial detail; in Section 1.3, we present an illustrative example. Here, we describe the basic SLT architecture, shown in Figure 1.1. Source-language speech enters the recogniser at the top left and target-language speech is produced by the synthesis process at the top right; the rest of the diagram is concerned with language processing.

Reading first from left to right, there are three stacks of components. On the left, we have monolingual source-language processing, and on the right, monolingual

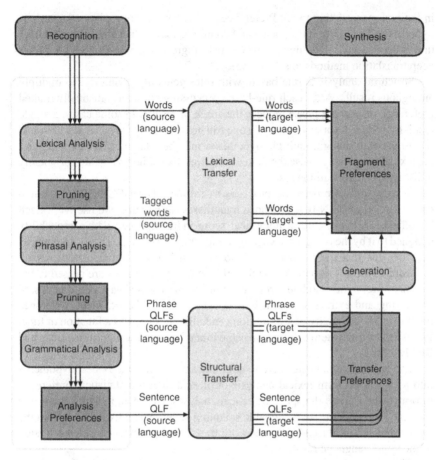

Figure 1.1. Basic architecture of the Spoken Language Translator.

target-language processing. These are linked by the two bilingual translation modules, respectively dealing with word-to-word or lexical translation and Quasi Logical Form (QLF) or structural translation.[4]

If we now read from top to bottom, we see four different processing paths, crossing from left to right at increasingly deep levels of linguistic processing. These correspond to four different ways of translating the input: as raw words produced by the recogniser, as a sequence of lexical items marked by part-of-speech tags, as a sequence of phrases, and as a single grammatical utterance. Each of these levels adds further structure to the preceding one. In general, each processing path produces a lattice of possible translated fragments. The four processing paths meet

---

[4] An overview of Quasi Logical Form translation is presented in the next chapter.

in the box marked "Fragment Preferences"; this component receives the various hypothesised translation fragments and combines them into a single result. Other things being equal, it attempts to use as few fragments as possible, and to prefer deep translation methods to surface ones.

Structural analysis is rule based, with rules generally giving rise to multiply ambiguous results. After each rule-based processing phase, a statistically trained preference or pruning phase reduces the space of results. In some cases, a single result is produced; for example, only one full grammatical analysis is sent to transfer. In general, though, multiple hypotheses may be retained; for example, after the lexical-processing phase the system removes lexical items that are sufficiently unlikely, and leaves all the rest.

In more detail, processing proceeds as follows. The DECIPHER^{TM} system delivers a list of its N-best utterance hypotheses; in practice, we use N=5. Each hypothesis is tagged with a numerical score indicating the relative probability assigned to it by the recogniser's acoustic and language models. The top hypothesis (i.e., the one that the recogniser considers most likely) is immediately sent to the word-to-word translation module, and the translated results are passed to the fragment-preference module. From this point onward, it is always possible to stop processing and extract a current best translation from the fragment preference module, with the quality of the solution generally improving as a function of time. In this sense, the system exhibits the behaviour of an anytime algorithm (Dean and Boddy 1988).

The next processing steps are to combine and conflate the N-best hypotheses into a lattice, perform lexical analysis on it, and then use statistical-preference information to prune the space of lexical analyses. At the end of this phase it is possible to extract the most probable spanning set of lexical hypotheses from the lattice, and send it through word-to-word translation to produce a second version of the target-language result.

When lexical analysis is complete, the system applies all possible phrasal grammar rules, and then performs another statistical pruning phase. Once again, the best spanning set of fragments is extracted. However, since the phrasal analyses have grammatical structure, translation at this stage consists of transfer using structural rules, followed by application of the target-language grammar to generate phrases from the transferred representations.

In the final processing phase, the source-language processor uses its full grammar to combine the lexical and phrasal analyses so far produced. Ideally, the result will be a set of grammatical analyses, each of which spans the entire utterance, though if none can be found that span the whole utterance, analyses of fragments are used. Another application of the preference module picks out the most probable analysis; this is again sent through structural transfer and target-language generation to the fragment-preference module, in order to produce the final version of the translation.

1.3   An Illustrative Example

This section presents an English-to-French translation example illustrating the flow of top-level processing in the system.[5] The original speech input is the English utterance "When will the cheapest flight leave?", and the recogniser produces the following N-best list. Each sentence hypothesis is shown with its associated acoustic cost.[6]

Cost	Sentence hypothesis
0	what will the cheapest flight leave
20	what will cheapest flight leave
92	when will the cheapest flight leave
112	when will cheapest flight leave
114	what will do this flight leave

Language processing starts by performing word-to-word translation on the (incorrect) top recognition hypothesis, producing the following result: in this and subsequent figures, we divide up the source and target utterances into portions that have been translated as single units.

English	what	will	the	cheapest	flight	leave
French	quel		les	le moins cher	vol	partir

Even with considerable good will, it is hard to say that this represents an intelligible translation: there are just too many mistakes. To start with, the important word "when" has been misrecognised. Also, the article is incorrectly duplicated (*"les"*, *"le"*), the adjective phrase *"le moins cher"* is incorrectly placed before the noun rather than after, and the verb *"partir"* is in the infinitive form instead

---

[5] This is a genuine example logged during system interaction, although it has been carefully selected to display an unusual number of interesting features.

[6] By *acoustic cost* we mean the shortfall from the score of the top hypothesis; thus, the higher the acoustic cost of the hypothesis, the less likely the recogniser considers it to be. In fact, the term "acoustic" is a slight oversimplification, as the scores the recogniser assigns are influenced by its language model as well as by the properties of the speech signal.

of the future. In most of these cases, the fundamental difficulty is that a word is being translated without reference to its surrounding context: for example, "leave" could become any one of *"pars"*, *"part"*, *"partent"*, *"partira"*, and so on. Lacking further information, the surface translation method simply chooses the most frequently occurring alternative, which in this domain happens to be the infinitive. In the succeeding versions of the translation produced by the deeper translation methods, we will see that these problems are all eventually resolved.

The next processing step is to convert the N-best hypothesis list into the following word lattice.[7]

0	what	will	the	cheapest	flight	leave
20				cheapest		
92	when					
114			do	this		

After this conversion, lexical processing is called to associate each word with one or more lexical entries and thus transform the word lattice into an initial version of the analysis chart. Immediately afterwards, statistical pruning is applied to remove unlikely constituents. In the following representation, each constituent has been marked with a symbol indicating its syntactic category. It will be seen that the words introduced in the fifth speech hypothesis, "do this", have been removed altogether, because their poor acoustic score is reinforced by their being unlikely in their immediate context.

0	what:NP	will:V	the:DET	cheapest:ADJ	flight:N	leave:V
20				cheapest:ADJ		
92	when:PP					

In some cases, lexical processing will enable a better word-to-word translation to be produced, since the part-of-speech information may block unsuitable rule

---

[7] Word lattices have been a very popular interface between the speech and natural language modules, especially since the SRI group (Murveit et al. 1993) introduced the progressive-search methodology. The word lattice presented in this example has a much larger number of hypotheses than those contained in the original N-best list. For example, it includes the hypothesis "When will do this flight leave" that was not part of the 5-best list.

applications. This, however, is fairly uncommon and does not happen in the current sentence.

The next step is to carry out phrasal analysis, which adds constituents to the analysis chart representing small phrases; immediately afterwards, statistical pruning is applied to remove unlikely constituents. The result is a new version of the analysis chart:

0	what:NP	will:V	the cheapest flight:NP	leave:V
20			cheapest flight:NP	
92	when:PP			

Note that all the lexical constituents contributing to the noun phrases "the cheapest flight" and "cheapest flight"[8] have been removed from the chart, since the results of system training (see Chapter 5) suggest that the probability is low that they can be used in any other way in a unified analysis of the utterance.

The new version of the translation produced after the phrasal parsing phase is:

English	what	will	the cheapest flight	leave
French	quel		le vol le moins cher	partir

This is still far from being good French, but at least the noun phrase "the cheapest flight" is correctly rendered, which corrects about half of the errors present in the initial version.

In the final processing stage, the full grammar is applied, yielding four different analyses corresponding to the possible input sentences "what will the cheapest flight leave", "when will the cheapest flight leave", "what will cheapest flight leave", and "when will cheapest flight leave". There are thus two choices to make: whether the first word is "what" or "when", and whether or not there is an article before "cheapest".

The second choice is the easier one. The noun phrases "the cheapest flight" and "cheapest flight" have similar syntactic properties, but the second one has a lower recogniser score, without any compensating advantages. The choice

---

[8] English singular noun phrases with count noun heads normally require a determiner, but determinerless phrases such as "cheapest flight" are so common in the ATIS domain that we extended the grammar to cover them.

between "what" and "when" is more interesting. In this domain, the verb "leave" can certainly be used transitively in a suitable context, for example, in a sentence like "When does the flight leave Boston?". However, the preference statistics reveal that all the analyses in the training data where "leave" potentially takes the noun phrase "what" as its object have been marked as incorrect. So, although "what" occurs ahead of "when" in the N-best hypothesis list, there is strong evidence that "when" is the more plausible analysis, and this hypothesis is consequently preferred.

The selected analysis is passed to QLF translation, which is now able to treat the whole utterance as a single unit and produce the result

English	when will the cheapest flight leave
French	quand partira le vol le moins cher?

This, at last, is entirely adequate French; the verb has been put into the future tense and moved to its correct place before the subject, and the mis-recognition at the start of the sentence has been fixed. Running on a Sun Ul-traSparc20, the whole translation process requires on the order of five to seven seconds.

1.4   In Defence of Hand-Coded Grammars

The alert reader will already have noticed that the SLT system makes extensive use of hand-coded grammars. There is at the moment widespread disenchantment with this idea. Critics generally offer some variant of an argument that can briefly be summarised as follows:

1. Grammars take too long to develop.
2. They always leak badly.
3. They need substantial manual tuning to give reasonable coverage in a new domain.
4. Even after doing that, processing is still very slow.
5. At the end of the day, performance is anyway no better than what you would get from a surface processing method.
6. So why bother?

We are well aware of these objections, and we do not think them unreasonable; they are based on many people's painful experience, including our own. However, we do not believe that the problems listed above are insurmountable. This section gives an overview of the methodology we have developed for attacking them. In equally brief form, our response is:

1. We keep our grammars, lexica, and other linguistic descriptions as general as possible, so that the large development cost is a one-off investment.
2. We make sure that the grammar contains all, or nearly all, of the difficult core constructions of the language; then most coverage holes are domain specific, and relatively easy to locate and fix (see Chapters 7, 9, 10, and 11).
3. Nontrivial tuning is needed when adapting the grammar for use in a specific domain. However, a large portion of this tuning can be performed semiautomatically with supervised training procedures usable by non-expert personnel (see Chapters 5 and 6). The remaining work can be organised efficiently using balanced corpora to direct expert attention where it will be most productive (see Section 8.6).
4. Automatic corpus-based tuning of the language description by grammar specialisation and chart pruning makes grammar-based language processing acceptably efficient (see Chapters 3 and 4).
5. Bottom-up processing strategies can intelligently combine the results of deep linguistic processing and fall-back processing using shallow surface methods (see Sections 2.1 and 4.5).
6. The results show a clear improvement over those produced by the surface methods alone (see Chapter 20).

Much of the remainder of the book can be seen as an extension of the above sketch argument; in this section, we will content ourselves with describing in a little more detail what we regard as the central issues. The biggest problem with an unconstrained general grammar is its extreme ambiguity. Even the most innocent-looking sentence generally gets at least three or four different analyses, and this can easily multiply out to tens or hundreds of possibilities, leading to impractically slow and inefficient processing. However, experience tells us that for many domains it is quite feasible to write domain-specific grammars that do not suffer from massive ambiguity.

Thus, the most urgent question is how we can transform an inefficient general parser into an efficient domain-specific parser. Our work here is a logical continuation of two specific strands of research aimed in the same general direction: focussing the search on only a small portion of the space of theoretically valid grammatical analyses.

The first is the popular idea of *statistical tagging* (Church 1988; Cutting et al. 1992; DeRose 1988). Here, the basic idea is that a given small segment S of the input string may have several possible analyses; in particular, if S is a single word, it potentially may be any one of several parts of speech. However, if a substantial training corpus is available to provide reasonable estimates of the relevant parameters, the immediate context surrounding S will usually make most of the locally possible analyses of S extremely implausible. For example, in the ATIS domain, "list" can be either a noun or a verb, but in the context "please list the . . . " it is unlikely to be a noun. In the specific case of part-of-speech tagging, it is well known (DeMarcken 1990) that a large portion of the incorrect tags can be eliminated safely, that is, with very low risk of eliminating correct tags. We generalise the statistical tagging idea to a method called *constituent pruning*; this acts on local analyses (constituents) for single words and of larger phrases. Constituents are pruned out if, on the basis of supervised training data, they seem unlikely to contribute to subsequent parsing operations leading to an optimal analysis of the full sentence. Pruning decisions are based both on characteristics of the constituents themselves and on the tags of neighbouring constituents. From each constituent and pair of neighbouring constituents, a *discriminant* (abbreviated description of the constituent or pair) is extracted, and the number of times this constituent or pair has led to a successful parse in training is compared to the number of times it was created (see Chapter 4). Constituents that are never or very seldom successful on their own, or that only participate in similarly unpromising pairs, are pruned out, unless this would destroy the connectivity of the chart.

The second idea we use is that of *explanation-based learning* (EBL) (van Harmelen and Bundy 1988; Mitchell, Kedar-Cabelli, and Keller 1986). Here, we aim to exploit the fact that grammar rules, in any specific domain, tend to combine much more frequently in some ways than in others. Given a sufficiently large corpus parsed by the original, general grammar, it is possible to identify the common combinations of grammar rules and *chunk* them into macrorules. The result is a specialised grammar; this has a larger number of rules, but a simpler structure, allowing it in practise to support much faster parsing using an LR-based method. The coverage of the specialised grammar is a strict subset of that of the original grammar; thus, any analysis produced by the specialised grammar is guaranteed to be valid in the original one as well. The practical utility of the specialised grammar is largely determined by the loss of coverage incurred by the specialisation process. We show later in Chapter 3 that suitable chunking criteria and a training corpus of a few thousand utterances can in practice give a good speed-up while reducing the coverage loss to a level that does not affect the performance of the system to a significant degree.

The two methods, constituent pruning and grammar specialisation, are combined as follows. The rules in the original, general grammar are divided into two sets, called *phrasal* and *nonphrasal*, respectively. Phrasal rules, the majority of which define fairly simple noun-phrase constructions, are used as they are; nonphrasal rules are combined using EBL into chunks, forming a specialised grammar, which is then compiled further into a set of LR tables. Parsing proceeds bottom-up by interleaving constituent creation and deletion. First, the lexicon and morphology rules are used to hypothesise word analyses. Constituent pruning then removes all sufficiently unlikely edges. Next, the phrasal rules are applied bottom-up, to find all possible phrasal edges, after which unlikely edges are again pruned. Finally, the specialised grammar is used to search for larger constituents, ideally, full analyses of the utterance.

Specialising the grammar in the way described above makes processing much faster, but still leaves a grammar loose enough that ambiguity is an important problem. It is, in general, necessary to choose between a number of possible interpretations of an utterance, taking into account criteria that include the scores assigned by the speech recogniser to the different input utterance hypotheses. Extra information needs to be supplied in some way to allow the system to make these decisions. In a domain-specific grammar, this information can often be hard-coded into the rules. When we start from a general grammar, we would again prefer to extract the relevant facts from a domain corpus.

We have already indicated how discriminants (properties that distinguish alternative analyses) are used at run time to decide which constituents should be pruned. Similar discriminants are also used to choose between alternative analyses for a sentence. However, deriving discriminant statistics involves selecting the correct analysis for each sentence in a corpus. This requires human intervention, and we would prefer the human in question not to have to be a system expert; but even for an expert, inspecting all the analyses for every sentence would be a tedious and time-consuming task. There may be dozens of quite detailed analyses that are variations on a small number of largely independent themes: choices of word sense, modifier attachment, conjunction scope, and so on.

It turns out that some kinds of discriminant can be presented to nonexpert users in a form they can easily be taught to understand. For training to be effective, we need to provide enough such *user-friendly* discriminants to allow the user to select correct analyses, and as many as possible *system-friendly* discriminants that, over the corpus as a whole, distinguish reliably between correct and incorrect analyses and can be used for this purpose at run time, either in constituent pruning or in preferring one analysis from a competing set. Ideally, a discriminant will be both user friendly and system friendly, but this is not essential.

We have developed an interactive program, the TreeBanker (described in full in Chapter 5), that maintains a database of the discriminants that apply to the different analyses of each sentence in a corpus. It presents discriminants to the user in a convenient graphical form. Among the most useful discriminants are the major categories for possible constituents of a parse; thus, for the sentence "Show me the flights to Boston" the string "the flights to Boston" as a noun phrase discriminates between the correct reading (with "to Boston" attaching to "flights") and the incorrect one (with "to Boston" attaching to "show"). Additional discriminants describe semantic triples of head, modifier, and dependent (for example, "flight+to+Boston", which is correct, and "show+to+Boston", which is incorrect), and other information about analyses such as the sentence type or mood. Using the TreeBanker, we have found that nonexperts can disambiguate sentences at a rate of several hundred a day, making it possible to train preference functions quickly and efficiently.

In summary, we claim that our architecture adequately addresses the key problem: using simple supervised training methods, we can convert an inefficient general grammar into an efficient specialised one.

1.5   Hybrid Transfer

Many of the considerations that applied to linguistic analysis also motivate our approach to transfer. For similar reasons, we combine unification-based rules and trainable discriminant-based preferences: in this sense, we have a *hybrid* transfer architecture (Brown et al. 1992; Carbonell, Mitamura, and Nyberg 1992; Grishman and Kosaka 1992).

In the rest of the section, we present examples of English → French translation in the ATIS domain to motivate this division of knowledge sources, and describe how they interact. We will begin with examples where it is fairly clear that the problem is essentially grammatical in nature, and thus primarily involves the rule-based part of the system; later, we give examples in which the problem mainly involves the preference component, and examples in which both types of knowledge are needed.

1.5.1   The Need for Grammatical Knowledge

An obvious case of a grammatical phenomenon is agreement, which is considerably more important in French than in English; the rules for agreement are rigid and well defined, and easy to code in a feature-based formalism. Quite frequently, however, they relate words that are widely separated in the surface structure, which makes them hard to learn for surface-oriented statistical models. For example, there are many instances in ATIS of nouns that in French are postmodified both by a prepositional phrase (PP) and by a relative clause, for example,

> Flights from Boston to Atlanta leaving before twelve a m
> → *Les vols de Boston à Atlanta qui partent avant midi*

Here, the verb *"partent"* has to agree in number and person with the head noun *"vols"*, despite the gap of five surface words in between.

Many problems related to word order also fall under the same heading, in particular those relating to question formation and the position of clitic pronouns (cf. Chapter 10). For example, French yes-no (Y-N) questions can be formed in three ways: by inversion of subject and main verb, by prefacing the declarative version of the clause with the question particle *"est-ce que"*, or by *complex inversion*, fronting the subject and inserting a dummy pronoun after the inverted verb. If the subject is a pronoun, only the first and second alternatives are allowed; if it is *not* a pronoun, only the second and third are valid. Thus for example,

> Does it leave after five p m?
> → *Part-il après dix-sept heures?*
> → *Est-ce qu'il part après dix-sept heures?*
> → **Il part-il après dix-sept heures?*

> Does that flight serve meals?
> → **Sert ce vol des repas?*
> → *Est-ce que ce vol sert des repas?*
> → *Ce vol sert-il des repas?*

Embedded questions constitute another good example of a mainly grammatical problem. Just as in English, French embedded questions normally have the uninverted word order, for example,

> Tell me **when these flights arrive in Boston**
> → *Dites-moi **quand ces vols arrivent à Boston***

However, if the main verb is *être* with an noun phrase (NP) complement, the inverted word order is obligatory, for example,

> Tell me **what the cheapest fares are**
> → *Dites-moi **quels sont les tarifs les moins chers***
> → **Dites-moi **quels les tarifs les moins chers sont***

In ATIS, embedded questions occur in about 1 percent of all corpus sentences; this makes them too frequent to ignore, but rare enough that a pure statistical model will probably have difficulties finding enough training examples to acquire the appropriate regularities. The relevant facts are, however, quite easy to state as grammatical rules. Moreover, they are domain independent, and can thus be reused in different applications.

1.5.2 The Need for Preferences

In contrast, there are many phenomena, especially involving word choice, that are hard to code as rules and are largely domain and application dependent. The simplest examples of transfer rules are those used to translate individual words; here it is immediately clear that many words can be translated in several ways, and thus that more than one rule will often apply. For instance, the English preposition "on" can be translated as any of the French prepositions *"avec"* ("fly to Boston on Delta"→ *"aller à Boston avec Delta"*); *"sur"* ("information on ground transportation" → *"des renseignements sur les transports publics"*); *"à bord de"*

---

* As is customary, we use asterisks to indicate incorrect usages.

("a meal on that flight" → *"un repas à bord de ce vol"*); *"pour"* ("the aircraft which is used on this flight" → *"l'avion qu'on utilise pour ce vol"*); or omitted and replaced by an implicit temporal adverbial marker ("leave on Monday" → *"partir le lundi"*). In each of these cases, the correct choice of translation is determined by the context.

To take a slightly more complex example, which involves some grammar, there are a number of transfer rules that list possible ways of realising the English compound nominal construction in French. Among these are noun+adjective ("economy flight" → *"vol économique"*); noun+PP ("arrival time" → *"heure d'arrivée"*; "Boston ground transportation" → *"transports publics à Boston"*); or in special cases simply a compound noun ("Monday morning" → *"lundi matin"*). Again, the individual lexical items and the context determine the correct rule to use.

In our framework this means that, in cases like those just discussed, the information used to decide on an appropriate translation is primarily supplied by the transfer preferences. In more detail, the preference given to a transfer candidate is a combination of discriminants on transfer rules and discriminants from target-language semantic triples (see Section 5.4.1). The transfer rule discriminants make transfer rules act more or less strongly as defaults. If a transfer rule R is correct more often than not when a choice arises, it will have a positive discriminant, and will thus be preferred if there is no reason to avoid it. If use of R produces a sufficiently strong negative target-language discriminant, however, the default will be overridden.

Let us look at some simple examples. The English indefinite singular article "a" can be translated in several ways in French, but most often it is correct to realise it as an indefinite singular (*"un"* or *"une"*). The discriminant associated with the transfer rule that maps indefinite singular to indefinite singular is thus fairly strongly positive. There are, however, several French prepositions that have a strong preference for a bare singular argument; for instance, "flights without a stop" is almost always better translated as *"les vols sans escale"* than *"les vols sans une escale"*. In cases like these, the "a"-to-*"un"* rule will be wrong, and the less common rule that takes indefinite singular to bare singular will be right. This can be enforced if the negative discriminant associated with the semantic triple "vol+sans+indef_sing" has a higher absolute value than the positive discriminant associated with "a"-to-*"un"*, and is thus able to overrule it.

Similar considerations apply to prepositions. In the ATIS domain, most prepositions have several possible translations, none of which is strongly preferred. For example, the discriminants associated with the transfer rules "on"-to-*"sur"* and "on"-to-*"avec"* both have low absolute values; the first is slightly negative, and the second slightly positive. Target-language triples associated with these prepositions are, however, generally more definite: the triples "aller+avec+⟨airline⟩" and "renseignement+sur+transports" are both strongly positive, while "aller+sur+⟨airline⟩" and "renseignement+avec+transports" are strongly negative. The net result is that the target-language discriminants make the decision, and as desired we get "fly on Delta" and "information on flights" translated as *"aller avec Delta"* and *"des renseignements sur les vols"* rather than *"aller sur ... "* and *"des renseignements avec ... "*.

In general, therefore, a combination of rules and collocational information is needed to translate a construction. Another good example of this is the English implicit singular mass determiner, which is common in ATIS. Grammatical rules are used to decide that there is a singular mass determiner present, following which the correct translation is selected on collocational grounds. An elementary French grammar will probably say that the normal translation should either be the French partitive singular determiner, for example,

> I drink **milk**
> → *Je bois **du lait***

or else the definite singular, for example,

> I like **cheese**
> → *J'aime **le fromage***

In the ATIS domain, it happens that the nouns that most frequently occur with mass singular determiner are "transportation" and "information", both of which are conventionally singular in English but plural in French. Because of this, neither of the standard rules for translating mass singular gets a strong positive discriminant score, and once again the target-language model tends to make the decision. For instance, if the head noun is "transportation", it is most often correct to translate the mass singular determiner as a definite plural, for example,

> Show me **transportation** for Boston
> → *Indiquez-moi **les transports** pour Boston*

This is captured in a strong positive discriminant score associated with the target-language triple "def_plur+det+transport". Note that the translation "transportation" to *"les transports"* is only a preference, not a hard rule; it can be overridden by an even stronger preference, such as the preference against having a definite plural subject of an existential construction. So we have, for example,

> Is there **transportation** in Boston?
> → *Y a-t-il **des transports** à Boston?*
> → **Y a-t-il **les transports** à Boston?*

The above discussion has been informal and anecdotal; our aim has been to supply examples supporting our claim that good translation requires both grammatical and statistical knowledge sources. In Chapters 4 and 5, we will fill in the details, and in particular explain how the TreeBanker can be used to train the transfer preferences.

1.6   Speech Processing

This book is directed mainly at an audience interested in the natural-language processing aspects of a speech translation system. This is only natural since, as we saw in Section 1.2, most of the structural components of the system lie on the language processing side. SLT, however, is a *speech-enabled* system. Its speech-recognition front end constrains the range of applications it can tackle and limits the overall system performance. We believe, therefore, that it is important to also present in this book the issues addressed in developing the speech recognisers used in the SLT system, both for completeness and to allow the reader to gain some insights into the capabilities of the technology today and in the years to come. To help the language-processing reader to follow the speech material presented in Part III of the book, we keep our description of the speech issues self-contained and at a high level.

In developing the speech recognition components of SLT, there were several important issues that we had to keep in mind, and that perhaps distinguished our research from other work in the field. The objective of the SLT project was, at every stage, to build and enhance experimental prototypes. Unlike the speech recognition research funded during this period by the U.S. Defence Advanced Research Projects Agency (DARPA), which never considered processing time and was solely driven by recognition performance, we had to build systems that would run at or near real time. The DARPA philosophy was that fundamental processor and algorithm improvements would eventually yield real-time performance. The SLT philosophy was that we should always look at the speed-performance tradeoff and develop systems with good speed-performance characteristics (cf. Chapter 15). Our approach was justified by the fact that speech recognition has matured significantly in the last decade, and has recently crossed the threshold above which a number of very interesting applications can be commercially deployed.

Another important dimension of a speech translation system is multilinguality. To have the ability to support multiple languages and dialects, the speech recognition module must satisfy a number of design requirements. It must be easily and economically portable to new languages and dialects. During the course of the SLT project, DECIPHER^{TM} was ported to French and to Swedish, including a number of Swedish dialects, and recognition performance had to be maintained at comparable levels to the English system, which was developed over a period of years and with large speech training databases available. This infrastructure cannot be created within a single project for multiple languages and dialects, and we addressed the issue by developing techniques for the efficient porting of the acoustic models[9] of the recogniser to new languages, performing multilingual recognition and efficiently adapting a recogniser to a new dialect. These techniques are described in Chapter 18.

---

[9] An overview of the various components of a speech recogniser, including the acoustic and language models, will be given in Chapter 14.

When porting recognisers to a new domain and language, which is the typical scenario in the SLT project and in most real-world applications, there will normally be very little data for training not only the acoustic models, but also the language model the recogniser uses during the search. In Chapter 16, we deal with the issue of training language models from sparse data, and adapting a general language model to a new domain using little or no domain-specific data.

1.7   Corpora

The SLT system is trained on Air Travel Information System (ATIS) data. We began with the ATIS2 and ATIS3 English data sets, collected at six different sites in the United States in the early 1990s (Hemphill, Godfrey, and Doddington 1990; Hirschman et al. 1993).

In this original ATIS data, speakers make spontaneous enquiries to a prototypical speech understanding system in order to obtain timetable information about flights between North American cities (ten in ATIS2 and forty six in ATIS3). Together, the two corpora contain approximately 22 200 utterances recorded from around 600 subjects at six sites. All utterances have been transcribed, and most were collected using partially or fully automated data collection systems. As part of the transcription process, all utterances were classified as one of *A* (utterance

- Show all flights on Thursday morning.
- What's the ground transportation like at Pittsburgh?
- Show all those nonstop flights from E W R to Cleveland.
- Flights from Cleveland to Miami.
- First class please.
- Please list fare under two hundred dollars.
- List flights arriving between one P M and five P M.
- All Northwest and United Airlines flights with stopovers in Denver.
- I'd I want to leave Boston at eight thirty eight and arrive in Denver at eleven ten in the morning.
- What time did you say the Continental flight serving lunch leaves?
- What meals are available on these flights?
- I need an evening flight from San Francisco to Memphis on the twenty eighth of September.
- I'm looking for a nonstop flight between Saint Petersburg and Charlotte that leaves in the afternoon and arrives as soon as possible after five P M.
- Which airlines?
- Where does flight eight thirteen stop?
- Show me a flight on US West from Toronto to San Diego that stops in Salt Lake City.
- What United Airlines flights leave in the afternoon?
- Which airline has the most coach class flights available?
- How many are there?
- List flights between Kansas City and Minneapolis with airfares below one thousand dollars round trip.

Figure 1.2. Sample ATIS utterances.

can felicitously be interpreted as a database query without reference to preceding context), *D* (utterance can felicitously be interpreted as a database query, but only given preceding context), or *X* (utterance cannot be interpreted as a database query). We will occasionally make reference to the official ATIS categories; the only important point is that X utterances are basically outside the domain, and hence as a rule, are more challenging.

These ATIS utterances have an average length of nine words. Some examples, selected at random, are shown in Figure 1.2.[10]

Swedish ATIS material was collected using the methods described in Chapter 8. A small amount of French ATIS material was produced by hand translation of English and Swedish ATIS sentences.

---

[10] The transcriptions are the official ATIS ones, but punctuation and casing have been added for readability.

PART I

Language Processing and Corpora

2 Translation Using the Core Language Engine

MANNY RAYNER, DAVID CARTER,
PIERRETTE BOUILLON, AND MATS WIRÉN

2.1 Introduction: Multi-Engine Translation

The previous chapter gave an impressionistic picture of the SLT system. We now present a more formal description of the individual components, and how they fit together.

As already indicated, the top level of the system is a *multi-engine hybrid architecture* which combines deep processing and surface processing. The basic notion of multi-engine machine translation stems from the work of Frederking and Nirenburg (1994); as with many good ideas, it is in essence extremely simple. Any given translation architecture will represent a tradeoff between various competing requirements: it will have certain weaknesses, and other compensating strengths. In particular, a knowledge-based architecture aimed at producing high-quality output tends to be both slow and brittle; conversely, a surface-based method is typically fast and robust, but unable to deliver high-precision results.

Frederking and Nirenburg made the suggestion, obvious in retrospect, that there is no need to commit to a hard choice between these alternatives. Several different translation engines can generally cooperate in a constructive way, producing partial translation results and entering them into a chart structure indexed by the words in the source sentence. Some kind of dynamic programming algorithm can then walk through the chart and extract a near-optimal combination of the results from the two translation engines.

In the SLT system, a straightforward version of this idea is used. There are two translation engines. The first, which is described in Section 2.2, uses a minimal word-to-word surface algorithm. The second, and by far the more complex part, is the subsystem responsible for structural translation via Quasi Logical Form (QLF) transfer.[1]

Each method is called twice. The word-to-word translation engine is first run on the raw output from the recogniser, and then on a version in which words have

---

[1] The idea of Quasi Logical Form transfer was first described in Alshawi et al. (1991).

been marked with part-of-speech tags; the deep translation method, first on partial constituents corresponding to small phrases, and then on the output produced by the full grammar. Both sets of results from both translation engines are entered into a single chart, and a preference method is used to extract an optimal sequence of translated fragments (cf. Section 4.5).[2]

2.2   Word-to-Word Translation

The word-to-word translation engine is intentionally designed as a minimal surface algorithm. A word-to-word rule associates a source-language phrase of one or more words with a target-language phrase of zero or more words; source-language words may be tagged with part-of-speech labels. The following are typical examples of word-to-word rules for the English → French language pair:

```
trule_ww([eng, fre], from >= ['en partance de'])
```

(translate "from" to *"en partance de"*.)

```
trule_ww([eng, fre], [to/p] >= [à])
```

(translate "to" to *"à"* if it is a preposition.)

```
trule_ww([eng, fre], [is] >= [est])
```

(translate "is" to *"est"*.)

```
trule_ww([eng, fre], [there/pp] >= ['là-bas'])
```

(translate "there" to *"là-bas"* if it is a PP.)

```
trule_ww([eng, fre], [is, there] >= [y, 'a-t-il'])
```

(translate "is there" to *"y a-t-il"*.)

During processing, all possible rules are applied, and the target-side fragment preference component decides which translated fragments to include in the final target-language result (cf. Section 4.5). Other things being equal, this will prefer word-to-word rules with longer left-hand sides: so for example "is there" will normally be translated as a unit into *"y a-t-il"* rather than compositionally into

---

[2] Technically, we in fact have three translation engines; as a final fall-back, we always allow a source-language word to be translated as itself. As explained in Section 4.5, these "identity translations" are for obvious reasons heavily dispreferred. In practice, they only appear as a result of clear system bugs, most commonly due to the recognition vocabulary and the word-to-word translation rule set getting out of step.

"est là-bas". The methodology used to acquire word-to-word transfer rules is outlined in Section 6.2.

The rest of this chapter will be concerned with translation through Quasi Logical Form transfer. We start in the next section by describing the QLF formalism itself.

2.3   Quasi Logical Form

2.3.1   Introduction

Quasi Logical Form is a function/argument representation that is intended to be useful for a wide variety of language-processing tasks. Like logical form, it is based on the idea of representing semantic relationships in terms of predicates, quantifiers, and bound variables. The crucial property, however, that distinguishes it from logical form is that it is scope neutral. So, for instance, a logical-form representation of "every man loves some woman" will schematically look like one of the following two alternatives, depending on the relative scope of the quantifiers "all" and "every":

```
every(X,                       some(Y,
      man1(X),                       woman1(Y),
      some(Y,                        every(X,
          woman1(Y),                       man1(X),
          loves1(X,Y)))                    loves1(X,Y)))
```

A QLF representation will instead have a top-level structure roughly of the form

```
loves1(term(every,X,man1(X)),
       term(some,Y,woman1(Y)))
```

This is a simplified representation; examples of full QLF representations will appear shortly. For the moment, the main point we want to make is that QLF encodes the predicate/argument structure common to the two possible logical forms, but leaves the scopes of the quantifiers undetermined.

The point of using QLF as a transfer formalism is that the predicate/argument level of representation removes many of the surface irregularities in the source and target languages, so that transfer rules can be fairly general. QLF is in particular a significantly deeper level of representation than a surface constituent tree. For example, transformation of an English declarative sentence into a question will normally change the constituent structure considerably; compare "John loves Mary" with "Does John love Mary?" or "Whom does John love?". At the level of QLF, however, all these variants will be structurally similar: schematically they will, respectively, look something like

```
declarative_sentence(
  loves1(term(name,X,name_of(X,john)),
         term(name,Y,name_of(Y,mary)))))
yn_question(
  loves1(term(name,X,name_of(X,john)),
         term(name,Y,name_of(Y,mary)))))
wh_question(
  loves1(term(name,X,name_of(X,john)),
         term(wh,Y,person(Y)))))
```

In general, there is always a tension present in developing a transfer formalism. The deeper the level of representation, the closer it becomes to the ideal of language-independent meaning or *interlingua*, and the easier it is to formalise the transfer process. The drawback is that conversion between surface form and interlingua becomes correspondingly harder. In particular, analysing an utterance into a full interlingual representation will require decisions to be made concerning the scope of quantifiers and the resolution of anaphora and ellipsis, processes which typically require complex domain knowledge and are hard to make robust. Conversely, a shallow representation makes the analysis and generation steps easy, but places a greater burden on the transfer component. In practice, shallow-transfer systems can be simple and robust, but are unable to produce high-quality output.

QLF attempts to steer a middle way between these two extremes. It essentially only represents grammatical relations: some domain knowledge is still needed to resolve attachment ambiguities and similar phenomena, but, at least in ATIS, this kind of knowledge can adequately be captured in the form of simple statistical facts. The grammatical relationships are, however, represented at a deep enough level that they are, to a large extent, independent of surface constituent structure. The examples in Sections 2.3.2 and 2.3.3 will make these general reflections clearer.

2.3.2   Structure of QLF

We have so far shown QLFs only in a simplified form. We will now define the concrete QLF syntax used in the SLT system, presenting a series of examples which illustrate the central features of the QLF formalism.[3]

---

[3] In fact, we have throughout the book rationalised the representation of both QLFs and grammar rules in the interests of expositional clarity. The concrete notation used in the implemented system, and its relationship to the rationalised representation, are defined in Appendix B.

```
[dcl,
  form(verb(past,no,no,no,yes),E,
      [[book1,
        E,
        term(ref(pro,i,sing),X,[person,X]),
        term(q(a,sing),Y,[and,[flight1,Y],
                              [early1,Y]])]])]


[ynq,
  form(verb(no,yes,no,will,no),E,
      [[book1,
        E,
        term(ref(passive_agent),X,[entity,X]),
        term(q(a,sing),Y,[and,[flight1,Y],
                              [early1,Y]])]])]
```

Figure 2.1. QLFs for "I booked an early flight" and "Will an early flight have been booked?".

To start, the top half of Figure 2.1 shows the QLF for the English sentence "I booked an early flight". This has roughly the structure of the initial examples shown in Section 2.3.1, but there are some significant differences. Most importantly, we have added tense and aspect information: the subterm

```
verb(past,no,no,no,yes)
```

indicates that the tense is past, the aspect is neither perfect nor continuous (the first and second occurrences of no), there is no modal auxiliary verb (the third no), and the voice is active (the final yes). By way of contrast, the bottom half of Figure 2.1 shows the QLF for "Will an early flight have been booked?". Here, the verb subterm conveys the information that there is no explicit tense inflection (the first no), the aspect is perfect but not continuous (the yes and the next no), there is a modal auxiliary will, and the voice is passive (the final no).

The second thing to notice about the QLFs in Figure 2.1 is the form(...) construct which in each case wraps around three pieces of information: the verb(...) construct we have just discussed, the main predicate/argument construct [book1, ...], and the event variable E. The wrapper form(...) says that these three objects are semantically related at the same level, but that the explicit logical relationship is left unresolved. The verb relation [book1, ...] is enclosed in a list construct, which would also contain verb phrase (VP) modifiers if any were present; examples will appear shortly.

Looking at the bottom of the two QLFs, we see that the term(...) construct corresponding to "an early flight" again wraps around three pieces of structure. These are, in order, a representation of the article/quantifier information

```
[dcl,
 form(verb(no,no,no,will,yes),
     E,
     [[on1,E,term(q(bare,sing),X,
                  [tuesday1,X])],
      [fly1,E,term(ref(pro,i,sing),Y,
                   [personal,Y])]]])]
```

Figure 2.2. QLF for "I will fly on Tuesday".

(q(a,sing)); the object variable Y; and the restriction

```
[and,[flight1,Y],
     [early1,Y]].
```

Simple though these initial examples are, they contain all the key elements of the QLF formalism. terms represent NPs and semantically similar constructs, like the implicit agent of "have been booked" in the lower half of Figure 2.1. Properties and relations are represented either by predications enclosed in brackets ([early1, ...], [book1, ...]), or else by the form construct. They can be combined by logical operators, of which the most important is conjunction ([and, ...]). This simple and uniform syntax makes it easy to write code that recursively traverses QLFs.

Nonlocal dependencies between pieces of QLF structure are mediated by the variables associated with terms and forms. A common example is a PP acting as a VP modifier: in Figure 2.2, we have a QLF for the sentence "I will fly on Tuesday", where the PP "on Tuesday" modifies the verb phrase "will fly". Here, the event variable E appears in the representation of the PP [on1,E, ...], indicating that it is linked to the verb phrase associated with E. Similar considerations apply to relative clauses: Figure 2.3 shows a QLF fragment representing the NP "a flight

```
term(q(a,sing),
     X,
     [and,
      [flight1,X],
      form(verb(pres,no,no,no,yes),
          E,
          [[in1,E,term(proper_name,
                       Y,
                       [name_of,Y,boston])]),
           [stop1,E,X]])])
```

Figure 2.3. QLF fragment for "a flight that stops in Boston".

```
[dcl,
 form(verb(no,no,no,will1,yes),E,
      [[soon1,E],
       [leave1,E,
        term(ref(pro,i,sing),X,[personal,X])]]))]

[dcl,
 form(adv(maybe1),_,
      form(verb(no,no,no,will1,yes),E,
           [[leave1,E,,
             term(ref(pro,i,sing),X,[personal,X])]]))))]
```

Figure 2.4. QLFs for "I will leave soon" (verb-phrase adverb) and "I will maybe leave" (sentential adverb).

that stops in Boston". Here, the second (subject) argument to stop1 is the variable X, which is associated with the term "a flight. . .".

Some other aspects of QLF notation will be relevant in later chapters of the book, but for completeness we deal with them now. Verb-phrase adverbs are represented similarly to verbal PPs, while sentential adverbs are forms that wrap around the whole clause representation. Figure 2.4 illustrates this with two contrasting examples.

Control arguments occur with verbs taking VP or sentential complements, and are represented at QLF level by variables. For example, in the sentence "I want to fly with Delta", the implicit subject of "fly" is "I". The QLF representation is shown in Figure 2.5: the term X appears as the second (subject) argument of fly1 and the link to the term representing the subject "I" is represented by the shared variable.

Finally, a slightly unusual feature of the QLF formalism is its treatment of PP sequences, which are viewed both syntactically and semantically as constituents, grouped at QLF level using the form construct (cf. Sections 9.3.4 and 12.4). Figure 2.6 shows an example.

```
[dcl,
 form(verb(pres,no,no,no,yes),E,
      [[want1,A,
        term(ref(pro,i,sing),X,[personal,X]),
        form(verb(to,no,no,to,yes),E1,
             [[on1,E1,term(proper_name,Y,
                                [name_of,Y,delta1])],
              [fly1,E,X]])]]))]
```

Figure 2.5. QLF for "I want to fly with Delta" illustrating control argument.

```
term(q(bare,plur),X,
    [and,
        [flight1,X],
        form(pp_sequence,_,
            [[from1,X,term(proper_name,Y,
                            [name_of,Y,boston1])],
             [to1,X,term(proper_name,Y,
                            [name_of,Y,denver1])]])])
```

Figure 2.6. QLF for "flights from Boston to Denver" illustrating representation of PP sequence.

2.3.3   QLF as a Transfer Formalism: Examples

The point of QLF is to represent the structure of an utterance at a level deep enough that differences in surface form between the source and target language are reduced, thus simplifying the transfer process. Some examples will now make this claim more concrete.

A simple case is adjectival modification in the language pair English → French. In English, an adjective used as a nominal modifier normally comes before the noun ("a small airplane"; "red wine"). In French, the adjective may appear either pre or postnominally (*"un petit avion"*; *"du vin rouge"*). At QLF level, the differences in surface word order disappear. All four noun phrases will be represented by expressions of the general form

```
term(<Det>,
    X,
    [and, [<N>, X],
          [<Adj>, X]])
```

where <Det>, <N> and <Adj> are suitable fragments representing the determiner, noun, and adjective, respectively. Since the representation is uniform, the same adjective transfer rules may be used, irrespective of whether the French adjective appears before or after the noun.

Less trivial problems occur with clauses; as we will see in Chapter 10, there are several important differences in clausal structure between French and English. For instance, particle verbs like "take off" or "find out" are frequent in English, but do not occur in French: conversely, French has lexically reflexive verbs like *"s'arrêter"* ("stop") and *"se rendre"* ("go"), which English lacks. English often expresses tense by an auxiliary ("I will leave"), while French uses a verb inflection (*"je partirai"*). French has clitic pronouns (*"je le veux"*), while English doesn't ("I want it"). Finally, the French word order for questions and negation often differs substantially from the English one. All of the above phenomena interact: consequently, French and English surface strings often

```
[whq,
  form(verb(no,no,no,will1,yes),E,
      [[where1,E,term(q(wh,_),X,[place,X])],
       [stop1,E,term(ref(def,the,sing),Y,
                    [plane1,Y])]])]

[whq,
  form(verb(fut,no,no,no,yes),E,
      [[où1,E,term(q(wh,_),X,[place,X])],
       [se_arrêter1,E,term(ref(def,le,sing),Y,
                    [avion1,Y])]])]
```

Figure 2.7. QLFs for "where will the plane stop?" and *"où l'avion s'arrêtera-t-il?"*.

look quite different. However, at the level of QLF, these divergences are greatly reduced.

Figure 2.7 shows a typical example, contrasting QLF representations for the English sentence "where will the plane stop?" and a plausible French translation *"où l'avion s'arrêtera-t-il?"*. It is clear that the structures of the two QLFs are virtually identical, despite the numerous differences in surface syntactic form.

There is of course no such thing as a free lunch; considerable work is required to construct a grammar that can reliably map surface strings into their QLF representations, and vice versa. However, our experience is that it is a much more feasible task to attempt than that of defining a mapping of surface strings into a full-blown interlingua, and the payoff is still very substantial. Essentially, the point of introducing the QLF level of representation is to modularise the translation relation between the source and target languages into three pieces: the relation between source-language surface form and source-language QLF, the relation between source and target QLFs, and the relation between target-language surface form and target-language QLF. Although the second (transfer) relation is not trivial, we will present evidence in Chapter 12 suggesting that it is, at any rate, comparatively easy to define. Also in Chapter 12, we will return in more detail to the issues we have just discussed.

2.3.4   *Head-Head Relations in QLF*

QLFs are complex, nested structures. This is an intuitively reasonable way to represent the meanings of natural-language constructions, and, as we shall see in the next section, makes it easy to write unification grammar rules which build up QLF structure in a compositional fashion. Sometimes, however, computational requirements dictate not nested structures, but flat ones. In particular, for the trainable algorithms used in the preference components described in Chapters 4 and 5, we

```
[whq,
  form(verb(pres,no,no,no,yes),E,
        [[in1,E,term(ref(def,the,sing),X,
                            [morning1,X])],
          [leave1,E,
           term(q(wh(which),plur),Y,
                  [flight1,Y]),
           term(proper_name,Z,
                  [name_of,Z,boston1])]]]]
```

Triples:

```
    leave1+tense_and_aspect+verb(pres,no,no,no,yes)
    leave1+agent+flight1
    leave1+agent+q(wh(which),plur)
    q(wh(which),plur)+det+flight1
    leave1+object+boston1
    leave1+in1+morning1
    leave1+in1+ref(def,the,sing)
    ref(def,the,sing)+det+morning1
```

Figure 2.8. QLF for "which flights leave Boston in the morning?" with associated semantic triples.

need to represent a QLF by extracting a set of fixed-format elements that more or less describe it.

We have adopted the following solution to this problem. Since QLF is a predicate/argument representation, we identify each piece of structure with a substructure, which we can call its "head".[4] We can then describe the structure of the QLF in terms of relationships between heads; we call these relationships *semantic triples*, or simply, *triples*.

Figure 2.8 presents an example showing the QLF and its associated semantic triples for the English sentence "which flights leave Boston in the morning?". The heads are constants corresponding to the verb "leave", the nouns "flight", "Boston", and "morning", and the determiners "which" and "the". The triples encode the information that the tense of "leave" is present; that its subject argument is an NP whose head is "flight" and whose determiner is "which"; that its object argument is an NP whose head is "Boston"; and that it is modified by a PP whose preposition is "in", and whose NP has head "morning" and determiner "the". It should be clear

---

[4] This idea derives its inspiration from the classical linguistic notion of "head" used, for example, in Head-driven Phrase Structure Grammar (HPSG; Pollard and Sag 1994), but does not strictly coincide with it.

that the information in the triples is essentially sufficient to provide a complete description of the QLF.

The basic idea of semantic triples is extremely simple, but we have found it worthwhile to implement a nontrivial extension for the case in which triples are used to distinguish between two possible QLFs for the same utterance (cf. Chapters 4 and 5). In these situations, it often happens that a phrase, most commonly a PP, can attach to two different heads; it is well known (Hobbs and Bear 1990) that there is a strong default preference towards low attachment, that is, attachment to the closest head.

For example, in the utterance "Show me flights on Wednesday", the PP "on Wednesday" can attach either to "flights" (low) or to "show" (nonlow). In order to make the concept of low attachment directly available in the triples, a postprocessing step applied during analysis marks nonlow attachments specially; so in the example above, the triples relevant to the attachment of "on Wednesday" would actually be `flight1 + on1 + wednesday1` and `show1 + -on1 + wednesday1`, with the additional minus sign in the second triple indicating a nonlow attachment. Further examples of this notation appear in Section 5.4.1.

2.4 Unification Grammar and QLFs

In the previous section, we described the QLF formalism. We now go on to explain how the CLE performs linguistic analysis (turning surface strings into QLFs) and linguistic generation (turning QLFs into surface strings). We begin by describing the rule sets that define the declarative relationship between strings and QLFs; these are structured as a type of unification grammar (Gazdar and Mellish 1989). We will assume familiarity with the basic concepts, and concentrate on explaining the aspects that distinguish the version of unification grammar used in the CLE. In particular, we will present our sample grammars in a variant of the well-known Definite Clause Grammar (DCG) formalism (Pereira and Shieber 1987).

The central point is the role played by QLF. We write our unification grammars using a feature-value notation; there is a distinguished feature, present in every category, that represents the QLF value associated with that category. We turn a surface string S into a QLF by finding a derivation of S, and then reading off the value of the QLF feature from the root node. Conversely, we turn a QLF Q into a surface string by finding a derivation such that Q is the value of the QLF feature associated with the root node, then reading off the string from the fringe of the tree. In the rest of this section, we define the grammar notation and provide some examples of small CLE grammars.

2.4.1 The CLE Unification Grammar Formalism

The notation we use in the remainder of the book to present CLE unification grammars is built on top of Prolog syntax: basically, it is Definite Clause Grammar

```
% Grammar

np:[qlf=term(Det, X, Nbar)] -->
    det:[qlf=Det],
    nbar:[qlf=Nbar, arg=X].

nbar:[qlf=[and, Nbar, Adj], arg=X] -->
    adj:[qlf=Adj, arg=X],
    nbar:[qlf=Nbar, arg=X].

% Lexicon

det:[qlf=ref(def,the,sing)] --> [the].
det:[qlf=q(a,sing)] --> [a].

nbar:[qlf=[armchair1, X], arg=X] --> [armchair].
nbar:[qlf=[table1, X], arg=X] --> [table].

adj:[qlf=[big1, X], arg=X] --> [big].
adj:[qlf=[small1, X], arg=X] --> [small].
adj:[qlf=[black1, X], arg=X] --> [black].
adj:[qlf=[white1, X], arg=X] --> [white].
```

Figure 2.9. Minimal unification grammar fragment for core English NPs.

with features.[5] More specifically, we use standard DCG notation, except that non-terminal symbols are written as *categories* of the form

```
<CategoryName>:<FeatureList>
```

where <CategoryName> is an atom, and <FeatureList> is a list of *feature-value assignments*. A feature-value assignment is written as an equality of the form

```
<Feature> = <Value>
```

where <Feature> is an atom, and <Value> is an arbitrary term. Every category must specify the value of the distinguished feature qlf; features not explicitly specified are assumed bound to anonymous variables. There is an obvious translation into standard DCG notation. Figure 2.9 shows an illustrative CLE grammar fragment for English NPs that covers a few simple phrases like "a white table" or "the big black armchair". Figure 2.10 presents a sample derivation using the

---

[5] The grammar notation used here is a simplified version of the implemented one. See Appendix B for the details.

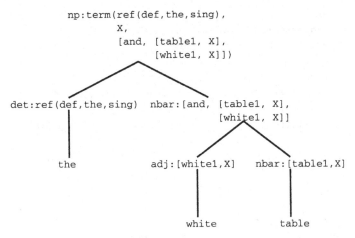

```
np:term(ref(def,the,sing),
        X,
        [and, [table1, X],
              [white1, X]])
```

```
det:ref(def,the,sing)    nbar:[and, [table1, X],
                                     [white1, X]]
```

the

```
adj:[white1,X]    nbar:[table1,X]
```

white   table

Figure 2.10. Derivation of "the white table".

grammar, where each nonterminal node has been labelled with its associated category symbol and QLF.

2.4.2   Unification Grammar Example: French Noun Phrases

The example fragment we have just seen in the preceding section is about as trivial as it is possible for a grammar to be. In order to display some of the other features of the CLE grammar formalism, we will now redo it for French. We will also make it a trifle more realistic by demanding that it cover both singular and plural nouns.

French adjectives and articles agree with nouns in number and gender, and adjectives may either precede or follow nouns. In general, an adjective is marked for feminine gender by adding the suffix *"e"*, and for plural by adding the suffix *"s"*, though spelling rules may cause the surface form to vary. We will return to this topic in detail in Chapter 7. For the moment, we will ignore the spelling rules: it then makes sense to represent utterances not as lists of words, but rather as lists of morphemes (stems and affixes). So, for example, we will write *"une petite souris brune"* ("a small brown mouse") as

> *une petit e souris brun e*

Taking this step allows us to extend the grammar to include rules that combine stems and affixes; we call these *morphology rules*. Figure 2.11 presents our new grammar fragment. The features num and gen encode number (singular or plural) and gender (masculine or feminine); the feature position on adjectives determines whether they can pre or postmodify. The three morphology

```
% Grammar rules
np:[qlf=term(Det, X, Nbar), num=N, gen=G] -->
   det:[qlf=Det, num=N, gen=G],
   nbar:[qlf=Nbar, arg=X, num=N, gen=G].


nbar:[qlf=[and, Nbar, Adj], arg=X, num=N, gen=G] -->
   nbar:[qlf=Nbar, arg=X, num=N, gen=G],
   adj:[qlf=Adj, arg=X, position=post, num=N, gen=G].


nbar:[qlf=[and, Nbar, Adj], arg=X, num=N, gen=G]) -->
   adj:[qlf=Adj, arg=X, position=pre, num=N, gen=G],
   nbar:[qlf=Nbar, arg=X, num=N, gen=G].


% Morphology rules
nbar:[qlf=Nbar, arg=X, num=p, gen=G] -->
   nbar:[qlf=Nbar, arg=X, num=s, gen=G],
   [s].

adj:[qlf=Adj, arg=X, position=Pos, num=p, gen=G] -->
   adj:[qlf=Adj, arg=X, position=Pos, num=s, gen=G],
   [s].

adj:[qlf=Adj, arg=X, position=Pos, num=s, gen=f] -->
   adj:[qlf=Adj, arg=X, position=Pos, num=s, gen=m],
   [e].


% Lexicon
det:[qlf=ref(def,le,sing), num=s, gen=m] --> [le].
det:[qlf=ref(def,le,sing), num=s, gen=f] --> [la].
det:[qlf=ref(def,le,plur), num=p, gen=_] --> [les].

nbar:[qlf=[fauteuil1, X], arg=X, num=s, gen=m] -->
   [fauteuil].
nbar:[qlf=[table1, X], arg=X, num=s, gen=f] -->
   [table].


adj:[qlf=[petit1, X], arg=X, position=pre, num=s, gen=m] -->
   [petit].
adj:[qlf=[noir1, X], arg=X, position=post, num=s, gen=m] -->
   [noir].
```

Figure 2.11. Minimal unification grammar fragment for French NPs.

rules define feminine forms of adjectives, and plural forms of both adjectives and nouns.

In order to demonstrate in detail how this grammar can be used in the generation direction, suppose that we want to find a string of morphemes realising the QLF (1):

```
(1) term(ref(def,le,plur),
         X,
         [and, [table1, X], [noir1, X]])
```

To produce the required string, we need to find a derivation of an NP category whose QLF feature unifies with the one above; the derivation will as usual have the structure of a tree. We will construct this tree recursively, starting from the root and working outward to the leaves. At each step, we will be trying to find a derivation for a new category *C*. There are only two ways to do this. Either *C* unifies with a lexical entry (a leaf in the derivation tree), or else *C* unifies with the mother of a grammar or morphology rule, which forms the root of a subtree attached to *C*.

So, let's start by considering the root category (1). There is no lexical entry whose pair unifies with this, and only one rule whose mother does, namely np -> det nbar.[6] Performing the unification, we now need to find derivations of the categories (2) and (3):

```
(2) det:[qlf=ref(def,le,plur), num=N, gen=G]
(3) nbar:[qlf=[and, [table1, X], [noir1, X]],
          arg=X, num=N, gen=G]
```

(2) is the easier one of these, since again there is only a single possibility that unifies: the lexical entry for the word *"les"*. Performing the unification, we have now instantiated N (the grammatical number feature) to the value p(lural).

There are two possible first steps for deriving (3): we could use either of the rules nbar -> nbar adj or nbar -> adj nbar. Suppose that we choose the first of these. (Later on, we will consider the consequences of making the other choice.) After unifying, we need to derive two new categories,

```
(4) nbar:[qlf=[table1, X],
          arg=X, num=p, gen=G]
(5) adj:[qlf=[noir1, X],
          arg=X, position=post, num=p, gen=G]
```

---

[6] In the rest of this section, it will be convenient to write, as here, np -> det nbar to mean "the grammar rule of the form np:[...] -> det:[...], nbar:[...]".

There is only one possibility for (4), namely the morphology rule `nbar ->` `nbar s`. This gives us two more items:

```
(6) nbar:[qlf=[table1, X],
          arg=X, num=s, gen=G]
```

followed by the terminal symbol s. Similarly, (6) can only be derived in one way, by unifying with the lexical item for the noun *"table"*, which completes the derivation of (5). Note that in the course of carrying out this unification, G (the grammatical gender feature) is instantiated to the value f(eminine).

We still have to derive (5), which thanks to the instantiation of G has now become

```
(5') adj:[qlf=[noir1, X],
          arg=X, position=post, num=p, gen=f]
```

The only possibility is the morphology rule `adj -> adj s`, yielding the category (7)

```
(7) adj:[qlf=[noir1, X],
         arg=X, position=post, num=s, gen=f]
```

followed by the terminal symbol s.

(7) only unifies with the rule `adj -> adj e`, giving (8)

```
(8) adj:[qlf=[noir1, X],
         arg=X, position=post, num=s, gen=f]
```

followed by the terminal e. Finally, (8) unifies with the lexical entry for the adjective *"noir"*. The complete derivation tree is shown in Figure 2.12, where again nonterminal nodes have been labelled with their associated category symbols and QLF fragments.

Reading off the lexical items from the fringe of the tree, we obtain the morpheme sequence

> *les table s noir e s*

If we combine stems and affixes, this yields the surface form

> *les tables noires*

We can now see what would have happened if we had chosen the rule `nbar ->` `adj nbar` when attempting to derive (3). The rest of the derivation would have proceeded in essentially the same way, until we reached step (8); however, the feature `position` would have been instantiated to `pre`. Consequently, (8) would not unify with the lexical entry for `noir`, and it would have been impossible to

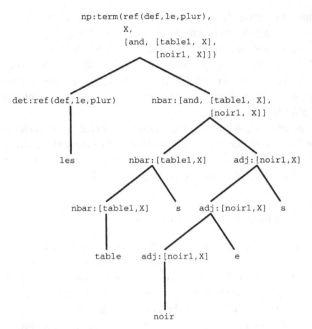

Figure 2.12. Derivation of *"les tables noires"* in minimal French NP fragment.

complete the derivation. Since this was the only step that presented a choice, it follows that no other morpheme sequence realises the original QLF.

2.4.3   Example 2a: Clauses in Swedish

The previous section illustrated the way QLFs are used in the CLE's unification grammars, integration of syntax and morphology, and the basics of the NP grammar. In this section, we present another minimal grammar that gives the core of our treatment of clauses. We do this in two stages. The first installment, in this section, presents a fragment for Swedish declarative clauses; in Section 2.4.4, we extend it to cover the simplest types of relative clause. Swedish clauses may use one of two possible word orders (cf. Chapter 11); here we will only consider the uninverted one, which is similar to that for English. Thus for example "Anna sleeps" is *"Anna sover"*, and "Anna loves Sven" is *"Anna älskar Sven"*.

Swedish verbs do not inflect either by person or number, so "I sleep" is *"jag sover"*, "you sleep" is *"du sover"*, "she sleeps" is *"hon sover"*, and so on. For the very simple examples we consider here, it will thus be possible to ignore agreement between subject and verb phrase. Swedish does however have several different conjugations of verb: conventionally, the base form is the imperative. So, for example, the first-conjugation verb *"älska"* (love) has present tense *"älskar"* and past tense *"älskade"*, while the second-conjugation verb *"åk"* (travel) has present tense *"åker"* and past tense *"åkte"*. This introduction should provide enough background to understand the fragment presented in Figures 2.13 and 2.14.

The grammar contains three rules: the s -> np vp rule which forms a clause from a subject NP and a VP, and two sample rules which form core VPs for intransitive and transitive verbs, respectively.[7] The single morphology rule combines the base form of the verb with a tense affix; the feature conjugation ensures that the appropriate affix is used.

An example derivation for the sentence *"Hon älskar mig"* ("She loves me") is shown in Figure 2.15. Note that the semantic value of the clause is passed up from the head verb, via the VP. This is typical for CLE grammars, and has consequences for generation which are briefly touched on in Section 2.7.3.

2.4.4   *Example 2b: Relative Clauses in Swedish*

Our primary motivation for presenting this second grammar fragment is to illustrate the CLE's treatment of movement phenomena. These are handled by means of the well-known idea of *gap threading* (Alshawi 1992, 70–74; Karttunen 1986; Pereira 1981). We describe movement by positing an empty constituent (gap) at the place from which the constituent has notionally been moved; the feature system is used to link the moved constituent and the gap in a way that enforces the relevant syntactic and semantic constraints. Figure 2.16 extends our Swedish grammar fragment to cover simple relative clauses using the gap threading mechanism: thus, for example, the surface structure of the relative clause *"som hon älskar"* ("that she loves") will be *"som hon älskar _"*, where the object-position gap (represented as "_") is linked to the relative pronoun *"som"*.

The basic technical idea is to use a pair of list-valued features gapsin, gapsout in order to link gaps to their associated moved constituents. If a constituent contains a gap, the values of gapsin and gapsout will be different: the value of gapsin will be that of gapsout with a representation of the gap added to the front. By unifying the gapsin and gapsout features of the mother category in a rule with those of its daughters, gaps can be linked to constituents higher in the derivation tree; by unifying the gapsout feature of one daughter with the gapsin feature of an adjoining one, gaps can also be linked to constituents on their left or right.

In our fragment, gaps are introduced into the gapsin feature through the s -> np s rule, which captures relative clauses consisting of an NP with rel=y followed by a clause containing a gap. The S and VP rules thread the gap through successive unifications of gapsin and gapsout features until it arrives at the gap NP, which is derived using the empty production np -> [ ]. By construction, this rule removes the gap from the gapsin list, leaving an empty gapsout. The basic

---

[7] The features rel, gapsin, and gapsout will be discussed in Section 2.4.4.

```
% Grammar rules

s:[qlf=VP, rel=Rel, gapsin=In, gapsout=Out] -->
  np:[qlf=NP, rel=Rel, case=subject,
      gapsin=[], gapsout=[]],
  vp:[qlf=VP, subject=NP,
      gapsin=In, gapsout=Out].

vp:[qlf=V, gapsin=In, gapsout=In]) -->
  v:[qlf=V, verbform=finite,
     subject=Subj, complements=[],
     gapsin=In, gapsout=In].

vp:[qlf=V, gapsin=In, gapsout=Out]) -->
  v:[qlf=V, verbform=finite,
     subject=Subj,
     complements=[np:[qlf=NpQ, case=object,
                      rel=NpR, arg=NpX,
                      gapsin=In, gapsout=Out]]
     gapsin=In, gapsout=Out],
  np:[qlf=NpQ, case=object,
      rel=NpR, arg=NpX,
      gapsin=In, gapsout=Out]

% Morphology rule

v:[qlf=form(TenseAndAspect, E, [Body]) -->
   verbform=VForm, conjugation=Conj,
   subject=Subj, complements=Comps,
   gapsin=In, gapsout=Out]) -->
  v:[qlf=Body, verbform=base,
     subject=Subj, complements=Comps,
     gapsin=In, gapsout=Out]),
  affix:[qlf=TenseAndAspect,
         conjugation=Conj, verbform=VForm].
```

Figure 2.13. Minimal unification grammar fragment for Swedish clauses: grammar and morphology rules.

pattern of alternating rules for introduction and absorption of gaps is repeated, in different forms, to handle the much more complex cases of movement that we will consider later in the chapters on English, French, and Swedish grammar coverage. Figure 2.17 illustrates the derivation of a relative clause.

```
% Some personal pronouns
np:[qlf=term(ref(pro,jag,sing), X, [person,X]),
    rel=n, case=subject,
    arg=X, gapsin=G, gapsout=G] --> [jag].
np:[qlf=term(ref(pro,hon,sing), X, [person,X]),
    rel=n, case=subject,
    arg=X, gapsin=G, gapsout=G] --> [hon].
np:[qlf=term(ref(pro,jag,sing), X, [person,X]),
    rel=n, case=object,
    arg=X, gapsin=G, gapsout=G] --> [mig].
np:[qlf=term(ref(pro,hon,sing), X, [person,X]),
    rel=n, case=object,
    arg=X, gapsin=G, gapsout=G] --> [henne].

% Intransitive verb
v:[qlf=åka1, Subj],
    vform=base, conjugation=2,
    subject=Subj,
    complements=[],
    gapsin=In, gapsout=In] --> [åk].
% Transitive verb
v:[qlf=[älska1, Subj, Obj],
    vform=base, conjugation=1,
    subject=Subj,
    complements=[np:[qlf=Obj, case=object,
                     gapsin=In, gapsout=Out]],
    gapsin=In, gapsout=Out] --> [älska].

% Affixes for present and past verb inflections
affix:[qlf=verb(pres,no,no,no,yes),
       conjugation=1, verbform=finite] --> [r].
affix:[qlf=verb(pres,no,no,no,yes),
       conjugation=2, verbform=finite] --> [er].
affix:[qlf=verb(past,no,no,no,yes),
       conjugation=1, verbform=finite] --> [de].
affix:[qlf=verb(past,no,no,no,yes),
       conjugation=2, verbform=finite] --> [te].
```

Figure 2.14. Minimal unification grammar fragment for Swedish clauses: lexicon.

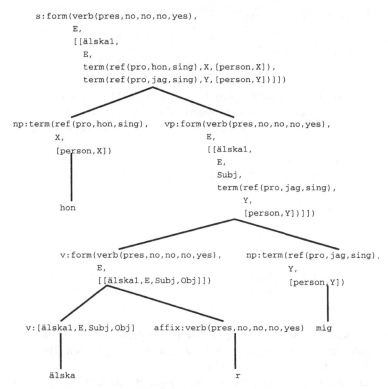

```
s:form(verb(pres,no,no,no,yes),
    E,
    [[älska1,
        E,
        term(ref(pro,hon,sing),X,[person,X]),
        term(ref(pro,jag,sing),Y,[person,Y])]])
```

```
np:term(ref(pro,hon,sing),          vp:form(verb(pres,no,no,no,yes),
    X,                                   E,
    [person,X])                          [[älska1,
                                             E,
                                             Subj,
                                             term(ref(pro,jag,sing),
                                             Y,
    hon                                      [person,Y])]]])
```

```
v:form(verb(pres,no,no,no,yes),          np:term(ref(pro,jag,sing),
    E,                                       Y,
    [[älska1,E,Subj,Obj]])                   [person,Y])
```

```
v:[älska1,E,Subj,Obj]   affix:verb(pres,no,no,no,yes)   mig

älska                                    r
```

Figure 2.15. Derivation of clause *"Hon älskar mig"* in Swedish unification grammar fragment.

2.5   Orthographic Analysis and the Lexicon

As described in the immediately preceding sections, the grammars used in the QLF-based processing path operate on strings of morphemes. It is consequently necessary to include rules that convert between surface form and morpheme strings. The task is not trivial, since morphemes may change their forms when combining into surface words. The declarative rules that govern these transformations are called *orthographic* or *spelling* rules and the process of applying them is called *orthographic analysis*.

We divide spelling rules into *intraword* rules, which combine morphemes within a word, and *interword* rules, which combine morphemes across word boundaries. A typical intraword rule in English is the one that describes the conditions under which consonant doubling occurs when an affix is added to a stem, for example, "getting" = "get+ing". English has only a few interword spelling

```
% Grammar rules

rel:[qlf=S, arg=X]) -->
  s:[qlf=S, rel=y, gapsin=[], gapsout=[], arg=X])]).

s:[qlf=S, rel=y, gapsin=[], gapsout=[], arg=X] -->
  np:[qlf=NP, rel=y, gapsin=[], gapsout=[], arg=X])
  s:[qlf=S, rel=n, gapsin=[(NP, np:[])], gapsout=[]].

np:[qlf=NP, rel=n,
    gapsin=[(NP, np:[])], gapsout=[]] --> [].

% Lexicon

np:[qlf=X, rel=y,
    arg=X, gapsin=G, gapsout=G] --> [som].
```

Figure 2.16. Minimal unification grammar fragment for Swedish clauses, continued: grammar rules and lexicon for simple relative clauses.

rules – mainly those governing the alternation between "a" and "an" – but they are common in some languages, a prime example being French. The spelling rule mechanism is described in detail in Chapter 7.

The lexicon associates one or more categories with each morpheme. We have already seen examples of lexicon entries in the grammar fragments presented earlier: in our DCG-like notation, they have all been of the general form

```
<CategoryName>:<Features> --> [<Morpheme>].
```

Since many content words have similar categories, it is possible to share structure in the lexicon, rather than duplicate it in each one of a set of related entries. This is accomplished through the use of parameterised lexical macros; a macro definition is of the form

```
macro(<MacroName>(<Parameters>), <Body>).
```

following which all occurrences in lexical entries of expressions unifying with

```
@<MacroName>(<Parameters>)
```

are replaced with occurrences of <Body>, with the values of <Parameters> substituted in. For example, going back to the Swedish grammar fragment in

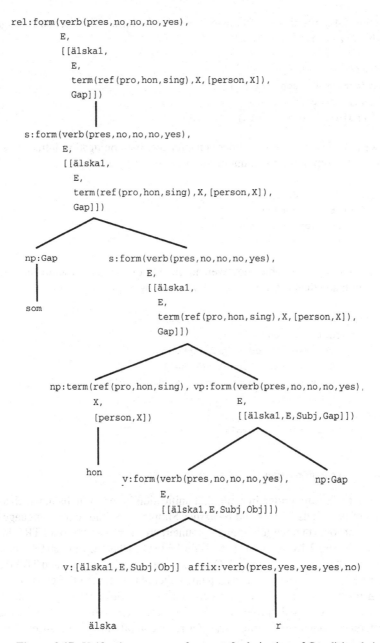

Figure 2.17. Unification grammar fragment 2: derivation of Swedish relative clause "*som hon älskar _*".

Section 2.4.3, we have the following entry for the intransitive second-conjugation verb *"åka"* (travel):

```
v:[qlf=[åka1, Subj],
   vform=base, conjugation=2,
   subject=Subj, complements=[],
   gapsin=In, gapsout=In] --> [åk].
```

If we now wished to add another entry for the first-conjugation intransitive verb *"sova"* ("sleep"), we could duplicate the structure by writing

```
v:[qlf=[sova1, Subj],
   vform=base, conjugation=1,
   subject=Subj, complements=[],
   gapsin=In, gapsout=In] --> [sova].
```

It is evidently preferable, however, to encode the shared structure in a macro definition and then call it in each entry, as follows:

```
macro(verb(Surface,intrans,Conj,QLFConst),
      v:[qlf=[QLFConst, Subj],
         vform=base, conjugation=Conj,
         subject=Subj, complements=[],
         gapsin=In, gapsout=In] --> [Surface]).
```

```
@verb(åk,intrans,2,åka1).
@verb(sova,intrans,1,sova1).
```

2.6   Transfer Rules

Transfer rules are written in a minimal unification-based formalism, which allows rules of two kinds: *simple* and *recursive*. Simple rules map source-language QLF fragments onto their target-language counterparts. For example, rules TR1 through TR3 in Figure 2.18 are of this type. Rule TR1 states that the English QLF constant flight1 maps into the French QLF constant vol1; rules TR2 and TR3 that the English QLF constant on1 can map into either of the French QLF constants sur1 or avec1. Note that the choice between the two different ways of translating on1 is not expressed in rules TR2 and TR3 themselves, but is left to the transfer preference component. Simple transfer rules compile into unit clauses: thus rule TR1 compiles into the unit clause TR1'.

Recursive transfer rules use *transfer variables* to express transfer of a QLF expression in terms of transfer of one or more of its subexpressions. For example, rule TR4 in Figure 2.18 is a slightly simplified version of the rule which can be

```
(TR1) trule([eng, fre], flight1 >= vol1).
(TR2) trule([eng, fre], on1     >= sur1).
(TR3) trule([eng, fre], on1     >= avec1).


(TR1') transfer([eng,fre], flight1, vol1).


(TR4) trule([eng, fre],
            [need1, E, tr(ag), tr(obj)]
            >=
            [il_qq_faut1, E, <il>, tr(obj), tr(ag)])


(TR4') transfer([eng,fre],
                [need1, E, X1, Y1]
                [il_qq_faut1, E, <il>, Y2, X2])
       <-
       transfer([eng,fre], X1, X2),
       transfer([eng,fre], Y1, Y2).
```

Figure 2.18. Some transfer rules.

used to translate the English transitive verb "need" (e.g., "I need a Delta flight") into French impersonal verb *"falloir"* (*"Il me faut un vol Delta"*).

Transfer variables are terms of the form tr(Id) or tr(Id,Pat), where Id is an identifier and Pat is an optional pattern. The expression matching the transfer variable tagged Id on the left-hand side of the rule is transferred into the expression matching the variable with the same identifier on the right-hand side; if a pattern is supplied on either side, the matching expression on that side is unified with the pattern. So rule TR4 compiles to the Horn-clause rule TR4'.[8]

Transfer rules have much in common with lexical entries (consider the similarities between ordinary monolingual and bilingual dictionaries); for reasons similar to those outlined in the preceding section, it is often possible to express transfer rules more compactly by using macros to encode shared structure. There are several ways to do this. Most simply, it can be the case that a whole class of rules have identical structure, except for variation in individual lexical constants: for example, when translating from English to French, there will be many rules that translate English compound nominals ("hire car", "weekday") into French expressions of the form "NOUN1 *de* NOUN2" (*"voiture de location"*, *"jour de semaine"*). In this case, we can introduce a single parameterised transfer macro which covers the class.

---

[8] We will find it convenient to write Horn clauses in a Prolog-style notation, with implicit wide-scope universal quantification over free variables. The Horn-clause interpretation of transfer rules will be required later in Chapter 13.

```
trule(@nn_compound(Day, DayPart, X)
    ==
    [and,
      [@ef_weekday(Day), X],
      @pp(temporal_np, X,
          @bare_sing(@ef_daypart(DayPart)))]).

macro(ef_weekday(monday1), lundi1).
macro(ef_weekday(tuesday1), mardi1).
...

macro(ef_daypart(evening1), soir1).
macro(ef_daypart(morning1), matin1).
...
```

Figure 2.19. Transfer rule using nondeterministic transfer macros. The rule translates English expressions of the form "Monday morning" in French expressions of the form *"lundi matin"*. The macros nn_compound, pp and bare_sing are deterministic and defined elsewhere.

When it is not possible to generalise the whole rule using a macro, it is still often useful to separate out pieces of QLF structure common to many rules, and represent these by macros. Finally, we can sometimes exploit the fact that macro expansion is allowed to be nondeterministic: a transfer rule that is meant to generalise over the words in a given limited class (for example, the class of days of the week) may be written using a macro that expands out to any member of this class. An example is presented in Figure 2.19.

Chapter 12 contains numerous examples of transfer rules.

2.6.1 Pre- and Posttransfer

Ideally, we would like to say that unification-based rules and trainable transfer preferences constituted the whole transfer mechanism. In fact, we have found it necessary to bracket the unification-based transfer component between pre and posttransfer phases. Each of these two phases consists of a small set of rewriting rules that are applied recursively to the QLF structure. It would in principle have been possible to express these as normal unification-based transfer rules, but efficiency considerations and lack of implementation time persuaded us to adopt the current solution.

The pretransfer phase implements a simple treatment of reference resolution or coercion, which at present only deals with a few cases important in the ATIS domain. Most importantly, QLF constructs representing bare code expressions used as NPs are annotated with the type of object the code refers to. Code expressions are frequent in ATIS, and the type of referent is always apparent from the code's syntactic structure. The extra information is necessary to obtain a good French translation: flight codes must be prefaced with *"le vol"* (e.g., "C O one three three" → *"le vol C O cent trente-trois"*) while other codes are translated literally.

The posttransfer phase reduces the transferred QLF to a canonical form (cf. also Section 12.4); the nontrivial aspect of this process concerns the treatment of nominal and verbal PP modifiers. In French, postnominal PP modifier sequences are subject to a default-ordering constraint: locative PPs should normally be first and temporal PPs last, with other PPs in between. For example, a literal French translation of "Monday flights from Boston to Denver" is *"les vols le lundi de Boston à Denver"*; by reordering the PPs, we can produce the distinctly better version *"les vols de Boston à Denver le lundi"*. In the limited context of the ATIS domain, the PP ordering requirements can be implemented fairly robustly with a half-dozen simple rules.

It is worth noting that the structure of the pre and posttransfer rule sets currently implemented is determined more by the idiosyncrasies of the QLF formalism than by properties of particular transfer pairs. The greater part of the rules is used to handle the posttransfer canonicalisation phase, and are independent of the source language.

2.7   The QLF-Based Processing Path

The treatment so far in the chapter has been in terms of declarative representations and rules. In this final section, we will now present an overview of the computational mechanisms that make up the QLF-based processing path. The three top-level phases are linguistic analysis (conversion of source-language input to source-language QLFs); transfer (conversion of source-language QLFs to target-language QLFs); and linguistic generation (conversion of target-language QLFs to target-language output).

2.7.1   Linguistic Analysis

The linguistic analysis process is organised around a directed graph structure called the *chart*. The basic purpose of the chart is to maintain a record of the constituents output by preceding phases of analysis, which are to be made available as input to following stages. Lexical analysis and parsing phases put constituents into the chart; pruning phases remove constituents from the chart that do not appear to be useful for downstream processing; and preference phases choose the best path through the chart, when one is required.

Conceptually, the flow of processing during the initial stages of analysis is to use spelling rules to recover morphemes from surface words, look up the categories for each morpheme in the lexicon, and then combine these categories as required using morphology rules. In practice, efficiency considerations mean that these three steps are conflated to some extent: for instance, legal spelling rule and affix combinations are precompiled for speed, and lexicon macros are expanded only when required, in order to economise on space. At the end of this phase, the chart will contain an arc for each lexical category that has been identified.

For numerous reasons, it is convenient to have these surface-processing methods work on both written and spoken input. The problems involved in doing so are not entirely trivial, since the output produced by a speech recogniser can differ in important ways from standard written language. In particular, languages like Swedish and German write nominal compounds without intervening spaces, while our recogniser treats the individual components of a compound as separate words. The principled linguistic approach used by the CLE makes it fairly easy to resolve the issues cleanly; the details are presented later in Section 19.2.

Following the surface-processing phase, parsing is, as usual, the activity of finding a grammatical derivation tree whose fringe matches (a portion of) the input. The CLE uses three different parsers: these are, respectively, the *phrasal parser*, the *left-corner parser*, and the *LR parser*.

The phrasal parser applies a simple bottom-up partial parsing algorithm, using only the subset of the grammar rules (the *phrasal rules*) that specify constituents guaranteed not to contain gaps. In practice, the majority of these rules define various kinds of small NPs. During the parsing phase, the phrasal parser is called first. It finds all the small gap-free phrases occurring in the input, and enters the resulting categories into the chart. After phrasal parsing is complete, either the left-corner parser or the LR parser is called to complete the parsing process; the left-corner parser is described in (Moore and Alshawi 1992), and the LR parser in Section 3.3.

As explained in detail in Chapters 3 and 5, the left-corner parser is used during the training phase, in order to build up a *treebank* of parsed sentences; these are then used to compile a more efficient grammar, which can be parsed using the LR parser. Each of these two parsers operates with a set of grammar rules that is essentially the complement of the one used by the phrasal parser, using these rules to combine the categories entered into the chart by the lexical and phrasal parsing steps. The new categories produced are once again entered into the chart. At the end of the parsing phase, the chart contains all the possible categories (including their associated QLFs) that can be derived from contiguous portions of the input.

Words and phrases are often ambiguous in a domain, but unambiguous in a local context. In situations like this, it pays us to prune sufficiently unlikely constituents from the chart as early as possible in the parsing process, as time then will not be wasted in creating spurious analyses involving them. Pruning, described fully in Section 4.2, is carried out after both morphological analysis and phrasal parsing. The creation of some constituents during phrasal parsing may provide the context to allow us to determine that others are incorrect; furthermore, there may be edges that are correct in that they have been used to form part of a larger constituent, but can be "hidden" from further parsing as they are unlikely to be useful directly as the input to it. A pruning decision for a lexical edge will take into account the word itself and the major category assigned to it by the edge. The word may be abstracted to a class of similar words to overcome the problem of sparse training data: for example, all city names in ATIS are abstracted to the same class name. For a phrasal edge, similar decisions are made using the name of the rule directly used to create it, as well as its major category and other information.

Although such pruning can rule out many incorrect parsing paths, parsing will still in general produce multiple analyses of multiple fragments of the input. At the end of the parsing phase, the analysis preference module is responsible for choosing an optimal path through this lattice, as described fully in Section 4.3. The selected path represents the final result of the source-language analysis process. The criteria used to determine the best path include minimising the number of distinct fragments, selecting fragments built from words with good recogniser scores, and preferring common head-head relations to uncommon ones.

The pruning and preference components are both statistical in nature, and make decisions based on the results of supervised training (see Chapter 5) on substantial domain corpora, from which the required information can be extracted with acceptable reliability and efficiency.

Figure 2.20 presents an example showing the state of the chart at various points during analysis of the input utterance "flights before three p m show me return fares". After the initial lexical analysis phase, the chart contains three lexical ambiguities. "Before" can be either a preposition or an adverb, "p m" can be either a time-of-day marker or a sequence of two characters, and "return" can be either a noun or a verb. The immediately following lexical pruning phase is able to eliminate all of these ambiguities on local statistical grounds: for example, analysis of the treebank reveals that "p m" after a number is always a time-of-day marker.

Phrasal parsing adds six NP edges and one PP edge to the chart, but phrasal pruning calculates that it is safe to discard all but seven of the edges so far accumulated. For example, the newly created NP edge for "return flights" is sufficiently probable that all the NBAR and NP edges dominated by it can be removed. Consequently, the size of the search space for the LR parsing phase is greatly reduced.

LR parsing, using the full grammar, adds three more edges: one for the NP "flights before three p m", and two for the imperative clauses "show me" and "show me return fares". Finally, the preference component determines that the best path through the chart is the one consisting of the NP "flights before three p m" followed by the S "show me return fares".

2.7.2 *Transfer and Transfer Preferences*

QLF transfer is similar in spirit to QLF analysis. A set of unification-based rules are applied top-down and nondeterministically to each source-language QLF. In general, this produces many possible target-language QLFs. Following QLF

After lexical analysis:								
nbar	p	number	timesuffix		v	np	nbar	nbar
flights	before	three	p	m	show	me	return	fares
	advp		char	char			v	
	before		p	m			return	
After lexical pruning:								
nbar	p	number	timesuffix		v	np	nbar	nbar
flights	before	three	p	m	show	me	return	fares
After phrasal parsing:								
nbar	p	number	timesuffix		v	np	nbar	nbar
flights	before	three	p m		show	me	return	fares
np		np					np	np
flights		three					return	fares
		np					np	
		three p m					return fares	
	pp							
	before three p m							
After phrasal pruning:								
	p	np		v	np	np		
	before	three p m		show	me	return fares		
np		pp						
flights		before three p m						
After full (LR) parsing:								
	p	np		v	np	np		
	before	three p m		show	me	return fares		
np		pp		s				
flights		before three p m		show me				
	np			s				
	flights before three p m			show me return fares				
Preferred path through chart:								
	np			s				
	flights before three p m			show me return fares				

Figure 2.20. Contents of chart at various points during processing of the utterance "Flights before three p m show me return fares". Each constituent is tagged with its category type.

transfer, a statistically trained preference module picks out the optimal transferred target-language QLF. The training method used is similar to that for source-language analysis; the criteria trade off preferences on transfer rules (by default, some rules are more likely than others) and preferences on the structure of the target-language QLF (by default, some target-language QLFs are more likely than others). Transfer preferences are discussed in more detail in Sections 1.5 and 4.4.

The basic philosophy of the transfer component is to make the transfer rules context independent, and to take account of context by filtering the results through the numerical transfer preferences. The positive side of this is that the transfer rules are robust and simple to understand and maintain. The negative side is that nondeterministic transfer choices multiply out, giving a combinatorial explosion in the number of possible transferred QLFs.

To alleviate this problem, transferred QLFs are *packed*, in the sense of Tomita 1986; lexical transfer ambiguity is left unexpanded, as a locally ambiguous structure in the target QLF. It is possible, as we will see in Section 4.4, to compute preference scores efficiently on the packed QLFs, and only unpack the highest-scoring candidates; this keeps the transfer phase acceptably efficient even when several thousand transferred QLFs are produced.

2.7.3   Generation

The final processing stage in the QLF-based processing path is the generation of a target-language string from the preferred transferred QLF. The problem is to use the target-language grammar to find a grammatical derivation whose root node has a specified QLF value; the method used is the Semantic Head Driven (SHD) algorithm (Alshawi and Pulman 1992; Shieber et al. 1990).

A proper description of the SHD algorithm is beyond the scope of this book, but the central idea is easy to explain. Looking at the structures of the grammar fragments presented earlier in the chapter, it is clear that there are many rules in which the value of the qlf feature in the mother is identical to that of the qlf feature in one of the daughters: we call rules of this type *chain rules*. By distinguishing chain and nonchain rules, much of the inefficiency inherent in a naive top-down generation algorithm can be eliminated.

Since chain rules keep the value of the qlf feature unchanged, a top-down algorithm can, in general, pass it down a sequence of such rules without any possibility of their blocking a derivation; the algorithm is only forced to backtrack when it reaches the end of the sequence, and finds that there is no unifying nonchain rule. Because of this, we risk exploring multiple combinations of chain rules, none of which have any possibility of being continued. The SHD algorithm addresses the problem by reversing the search order: it first looks for a possible nonchain rule to terminate the sequence, and only later attempts to fill in the chain rules leading up to it. Further optimisations are implemented by suitable compilation of the grammar rules and use of a well-formed substring table. The figures presented in Chapter 20 show that the implemented SHD algorithm yields quite acceptable generation times for typical ATIS domain sentences in all three main system languages.

2.8   Summary

We have presented an overview of the language-processing modules in the SLT system. The central idea has been the use of Quasi Logical Form to represent linguistic meaning. Parsers driven by tables derived from source-language unification grammars convert strings of source-language morphemes into source-language

QLFs, which are then transferred through unification-based bilingual rules into target-language counterparts. Strings of target-language morphemes are generated from the transferred QLFs by running the target-language unification grammars backwards. At each end of the process, spelling rules convert between morpheme strings and surface form. All the rule sets involved typically produce multiple possible outputs. Statistically trained preferences filter the space of results, both to increase efficiency and to decide on the final output of the translation process.

In the following chapters, we will reexamine in detail many of the points we briefly touched on here. We describe spelling rules in Chapter 7, unification grammars in Chapters 9, 10, and 11, and transfer rules in Chapter 12. Chapters 3, 4, and 5 cover the corpus-based mechanisms used to derive the preference and pruning statistics and the specialised version of the analysis grammar. Chapter 20 presents a comprehensive evaluation of the system.

3 Grammar Specialisation

MANNY RAYNER, DAVID CARTER,
AND CHRISTER SAMUELSSON

3.1 Introduction

In this chapter and the next one, we show how a general grammar may be automatically adapted for fast parsing of utterances from a specific domain. This chapter focuses on grammar specialisation based on explanation-based learning (EBL), while the next describes constituent pruning.

As sketched in Section 1.4, the original grammar rules are subjected to two phases of processing. In the first, EBL learning phase, a parsed training corpus is used to identify chunks of rules, which are combined by the EBL algorithm into single macro rules. In the second phase, the resulting set of chunked rules is converted into tables that drive a type of LR parser. By chunking the grammar rules into larger units, the search space is reduced, and parsing can be made faster. The downside is that some analyses are inevitably lost, resulting in decreased coverage.

There are two main parameters that can be adjusted in the EBL learning phase. Most simply, there is the size of the training corpus; a larger training corpus means a smaller loss of coverage due to grammar specialisation. Secondly, there is the question of how to select the rule chunks that will be turned into macro rules. At one limit, the whole parse tree for each training example is turned into a single rule, resulting in a specialised grammar all of whose derivations are completely flat. These grammars can support extremely quick parsing, but our experience indicates that the coverage loss is in practice unacceptably high, even with very large training corpora. At the opposite extreme, each rule chunk consists of a single rule; this yields a specialised grammar identical to the original one.[1] The challenge is to find an intermediate solution, which specialises the grammar nontrivially without losing too much coverage.

---

[1] In a preceding domain-adaptation step, any grammar rule that was not used to parse the training corpus was pruned from the grammar. This effect would otherwise be achieved by the latter rule-chunking strategy.

The rest of the chapter is structured as follows. In Section 3.2, we describe the version of EBL used in our system. Section 3.3 describes the LR parsing method applied to the specialised grammar. Finally, Section 3.4 describes a series of experiments that investigate the relationship between size of training corpus, choice of chunking criteria, coverage loss due to grammar specialisation, and parsing speed.

3.2   Explanation-Based Learning for Grammar Specialisation

3.2.1   A Definition of Explanation-Based Learning

The basic idea of EBL, as used here, is an elaboration of the notion of *macro rules* (Fikes and Nilson 1971). Suppose that we have some kind of general problem which is specified by means of a set of Horn clauses Γ. If we have a solution to some specific instance of the problem, then that solution will be a correct derivation tree T composed out of instances of the Horn clauses in Γ. In the specific case that will interest us later in the chapter, Γ will be a DCG encoding of a grammar, and derivation trees will correspond to parse trees; all of this section is, however, applicable in the wider context of a general Horn-clause theory.

Roughly speaking, what we are going to do is take a part of a derivation tree corresponding to a correct solution, and turn it into a single rule by recursively sticking together all the rules of which it is composed. It turns out that the resulting rule is in a strong sense equivalent to the original piece of derivation tree used to form it. Many people will be quite happy with this level of detail and should probably skip to the beginning of Section 3.2.2, but those who want a little more insight into the theoretical basis for EBL may read on.

There are several different ways to think about what derivation trees are, but the following will give us a good handle on the EBL idea. We label each node of the tree with a copy of the Horn clause used, renaming variables if necessary so that no two distinct Horn clauses share a common variable. We now say that the tree represents a correct derivation if the following two conditions are met:

- The body literals B_i in the Horn clause at each node N are in one-to-one correspondence with the nodes N_i immediately dominated by N. (This means that the leaf nodes must be labelled by unit clauses). We say that the Horn clause labelling N_i is "under" B_i. Intuitively, the tree rooted in N_i provides a proof of B_i.
- There is a variable substitution ϕ such that for every body literal B_i in every node N, $\phi(B_i)$ is equal to $\phi(H_i)$, where H_i is the head of the Horn clause labelling node N_i. Intuitively, this just says that we can unify all the variables in the obvious way, matching body literals with the heads under them.

The unification theorem (Robinson 1965) states that either (i) no such substitution ϕ exists, or else (ii) there is a substitution θ, unique up to variable renaming, such that any other substitution ϕ is the composition $\theta \circ \phi'$ for some ϕ'. We call such a θ a *most general unifier*.

Suppose that T is a derivation tree, S is a subtree of T, S is a correct derivation, and θ is a most general unifier for S. Then the *derived rule S'* formed from S is defined to be the Horn clause whose head literal is $\theta(H)$, where H is the head of the Horn clause labelling the root node of S, and whose body literals are the $\theta(B_i)$, where the B_i are all the literals occurring as body literals in the Horn clauses labelling the leaves of S.

We can now state the sense in which the subtree S and the derived rule S' are equivalent: the derivation tree T is correct if and only if the derivation tree T' formed by replacing S with S' is correct. The result is not difficult to prove with full rigour, but since the details are unlikely to be of interest except to people working in theorem proving or logic programming, we will only give a sketch.

Consider the sets of equalities that must hold for S, T, and T', respectively, to be correct derivations, starting with those required for T. These fall into three groups (see the left-hand side of Figure 3.1):

1. Equalities only involving terms in the subderivation S: write a typical element of this set as $S_{i1} = S_{i2}$
2. Equalities only involving terms in T, but not in S: write a typical element of this set as $T_{i1} = T_{i2}$

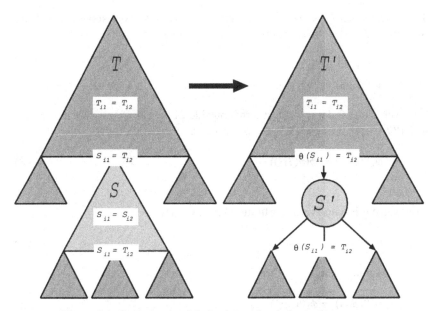

Figure 3.1. Replacing a subderivation with a derived rule.

3. Equalities between two terms, of which one comes from S, and the other does not: write a typical element of this set as $S_{i1} = T_{i2}$

Summing up, T is a correct derivation if the following equalities can be satisfied:

$$S_{i1} = S_{i2} \tag{3.1}$$
$$T_{i1} = T_{i2} \tag{3.2}$$
$$S_{i1} = T_{i2} \tag{3.3}$$

Recall that S is by hypothesis a correct derivation with most general unifying substitution θ; now look at the right-hand side of Figure 3.1 and consider the equalities that must hold in order that T' should be a correct derivation. We have replaced the subtree S by a single rule S', so all the equalities (3.1) disappear. Also, since the variables in each Horn clause are unique, we have that $\theta(X) = X$ for any term X that is not inside S, and hence the equalities (3.2) stay the same. Finally, we have the third group, (3.3). θ will affect the part that is in S, but not the part that is outside, so these become $\theta(S_{i1}) = T_{i2}$.

In summary, the derivation T' is correct if we can satisfy the following equalities:

$$T_{i1} = T_{i2} \tag{3.4}$$
$$\theta(S_{i1}) = T_{i2} \tag{3.5}$$

Suppose now that T' is a correct derivation, and that ϕ is a corresponding unifying substitution. Then we have from (3.4) and (3.5) that

$$\phi(T_{i1}) = \phi(T_{i2}) \tag{3.6}$$
$$\phi(\theta(S_{i1})) = \phi(T_{i2}) \tag{3.7}$$

However, since θ doesn't affect terms outside S, we can if we wish replace T_{i1} with $\theta(T_{i1})$. So (3.6) and (3.7) can be written as

$$\phi(\theta(T_{i1})) = \phi(\theta(T_{i2})) \tag{3.8}$$
$$\phi(\theta(S_{i1})) = \phi(\theta(T_{i2})) \tag{3.9}$$

Also, since θ is a unifying substitution for S, we have

$$\theta(S_{i1}) = \theta(S_{i2}) \tag{3.10}$$

and, thus, of necessity

$$\phi(\theta(S_{i1})) = \phi(\theta(S_{i2})) \tag{3.11}$$

Hence $\theta \circ \phi$ satisfies (3.1) through (3.3) and is a solution to T, so we have proved that the correctness of T' implies the correctness of T.

Conversely, suppose that T is a correct derivation, and that ϕ is a unifying substitution. Then ϕ must also be a unifying substitution for S. But since θ is by hypothesis a most general unifying substitution for S, there is some ϕ' such that $\phi = \theta \circ \phi'$.

Since $\phi = \theta \circ \phi'$ satisfies (3.2) and (3.3), we have

$$\phi'(\theta(T_{i1})) = \phi'(\theta(T_{i2})) \tag{3.12}$$
$$\phi'(\theta(S_{i1})) = \phi'(\theta(T_{i2})) \tag{3.13}$$

Also, since $\theta(X) = X$ for all the terms outside of S, these reduce to

$$\phi'(T_{i1}) = \phi'(T_{i2}) \tag{3.14}$$
$$\phi'(\theta(S_{i1})) = \phi'(T_{i2}) \tag{3.15}$$

But this means that ϕ' satisfies the equations (3.4) and (3.5), and hence T' is a correct derivation. So the correctness of T also implies the correctness of T', and the two are thus equivalent. QED.

3.2.2   *Explanation-Based Learning on Unification Grammars*

Rules in a unification grammar can be viewed as Horn clauses (Pereira and Shieber 1987), and consequently all the remarks made in the preceding section hold *a fortiori* for unification grammars too. Thus, any subtree of a derivation in a grammar G can be transformed into a composed rule, or macro rule, of G; the question now becomes how to select suitable subtrees. To make the discussion more concrete, we will present some examples.

A simple approach is to derive our rule from the portion of the derivation tree that consists precisely of the grammar rules, discarding the lexical entries. For example, consider the derivation shown in Figure 2.10, which uses the minimal unification grammar defined in Figure 2.9. We present it again in Figure 3.2, this time in a format consistent with the one used in this chapter. Nodes of the tree are labelled with Horn clauses, and the shaded portion marks the subtree consisting of the grammar rules. (The nodes excluded are the fringe, which consists of nodes marked with unit clauses representing lexical entries.) There are only two grammar rules; we form the derived rule by unifying the nbar daughter of the first rule with the head of the second. The result is

```
np:[qlf=term(Det, X, [and, Nbar, Adj])] -->
    det:[qlf=Det],
    adj:[qlf=Adj, arg=X],
    nbar:[qlf=Nbar, arg=X].
```

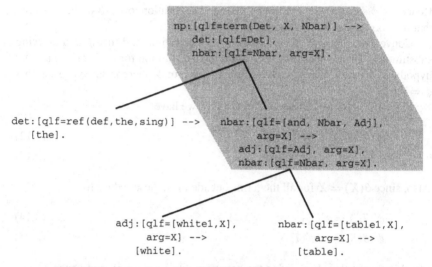

```
          np:[qlf=term(Det, X, Nbar)] -->
              det:[qlf=Det],
              nbar:[qlf=Nbar, arg=X].


det:[qlf=ref(def,the,sing)] -->      nbar:[qlf=[and, Nbar, Adj],
    [the].                                 arg=X] -->
                                       adj:[qlf=Adj, arg=X],
                                       nbar:[qlf=Nbar, arg=X].


      adj:[qlf=[white1,X],          nbar:[qlf=[table1,X],
          arg=X] -->                    arg=X] -->
          [white].                      [table].
```

Figure 3.2. Extracting a derived rule from the grammar rules of a simple derivation tree.

Our basic approach will be to start with a corpus of derivation trees created using the original grammar. We will then cut the trees up into pieces, each of which will be turned into a composed rule; in general, we will cut each tree into several pieces, and thus extract more than one rule from each example. For instance, a slightly more complex strategy than the one we used in our first example above would be the following: we remove lexical rules as before, and also cut the derivation tree at the maximal NP nodes. This yields one rule for each maximal nonlexical NP, and one for the whole tree.[2] Figure 3.3 shows an example in which a sample derivation tree is cut in this way, producing a total of three derived rules.

One of the key questions, then, is to determine the method we use to cut up the derivation trees in the training corpus. The experiments in Section 3.4 compare empirically a number of strategies for choosing these cutting-up criteria; the most complex of these is described in Section 3.2.4. In order to define it, we must first however introduce a refinement to the basic macro rule idea.

3.2.3   *Category Specialisation*

If coverage loss is to be controlled, we prefer grammars not to be too coarse grained. However, natural ways of cutting up derivation trees may yield subtrees which have the same mother category, but occur in very different contexts. For example, in the

---

[2] This strategy was first investigated in Samuelsson and Rayner (1991).

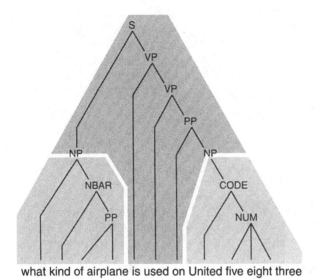

what kind of airplane is used on United five eight three

Figure 3.3. Cutting up a derivation tree into an S rule and two NP rules.

ATIS domain there are at least two kinds of VP which occur commonly enough that we may want to create derived rules for them. First, we have imperative VPs like "show me fares from Boston to Denver" or "tell me which flights serve a meal". Second, we also have nominal VP modifiers like "arriving after three p m" or "leaving Denver tomorrow morning". It is certainly not implausible to consider forming chunked macro rules to cover both of these kinds of constituents.

The two types of VP, however, intuitively are fairly different, and there is no particularly good reason to expect rules valid for one to resemble rules valid for the other. It makes sense in situations like this one to be able to derive rules not just for a particular category, but for a particular category occurring in a particular type of context.

It is in fact easy to extend our framework so as to achieve this goal. Viewing the problem for the moment in terms of Horn clauses rather than grammar rules, what we have done so far is to change our rule set by chunking rules into macro rules, and then replacing the original rules with the chunked ones. The set of predicates used in the rules, however, remains the same; if we are thinking in terms of grammar rules, predicates will correspond to grammatical categories.

Continuing to think in terms of Horn clauses, suppose now that P is some predicate. If we uniformly change all occurrences of P in the rule set by adding to P an extra argument arg_i whose value is an anonymous variable, then the status of any derivation with the old set of rules will be unaffected in the new set. Suppose further that instead of using anonymous variables, we assign values to arg_i in a systematic way, intended to codify the context in which predicate P is being used;

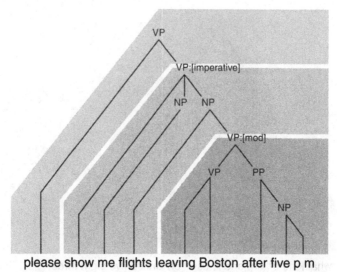

please show me flights leaving Boston after five p m

Figure 3.4. Cutting up a derivation tree using category specialisation. Rules derived from chunks with a VP head are labelled as either imperative or mod depending on whether the chunk appears as an imperative or a nominal modifier.

for example, say that we can have either $arg_i = c_1$ or $arg_i = c_2$, representing two possible contexts c_1 and c_2 in which P can occur. Then rules for P will be separated into two different classes; conversely, occurrences of P in the bodies of rules will make reference to one or the other class. If we switch to viewing the problem in terms of grammar rules, there is an obvious way to conceptualise the transformation we have just carried out: we have added a new feature arg_i with possible values c_1 and c_2 to the grammatical category P.

Let us see what this means in the context of the initial example with the two types of VP. (Figure 3.4 illustrates the process.) We have a predicate vp which represents VP constituents. If we have a training example involving, say, a nominal VP modifier, then we cut up the derivation tree so as to include a number of pieces, including a subtree S_1 corresponding to the VP modifier, and a second subtree, S_2, immediately dominating S_1. When we form derived rules from the two sub-trees, vp will be the predicate of the head goal in S_1' (the rule formed from S_1) and the predicate of one of the body goals in S_2' (the rule formed from S_2). Now we can add an extra argument ebl_type to vp in both S_1' and S_2', with value mod. Conversely, if the VP subtree in question is an imperative VP, the value of ebl_type in both derived rules is set to imperative. By systematically assigning values to ebl_type in the way indicated we build up two sets of derived rules for nominal VP modifiers and imperative VPs, respectively; we also ensure that other derived rules whose daughters are VP rules specify VP rules of the appropriate type.

A minor complication arises if we want to perform category specialisation on categories that can also appear as lexical entries. Suppose that we want to distinguish between two kinds of NPs, for example, recursive[3] and non-recursive. This might be a sensible thing to do if we wished to introduce some internal structure to the rules for NPs in the derived grammar without allowing full recursion. In such cases, it may well be desirable to consider lexical instances of the category as part of one of the specialised subclasses; in the example under consideration, we might want to say that lexical NPs are a kind of nonrecursive NP, so that derived rules with nonrecursive NP daughters can also take lexical NP daughters. We do this by adding extra rules to the derived grammar: here, the relevant rule would be of the form

```
np:[...ebl_type=non_recursive...] -->
  np:[...ebl_type=lexical...]
```

3.2.4   Elaborate Cutting-Up Criteria

This section defines our currently most elaborate set of cutting-up criteria; its utility is investigated empirically in Section 3.4. In this scheme, rule chunks are trees of rules whose roots and leaves are categories of the following possible types: full utterances, utterance units, imperative VPs, NPs, relative clauses, VP modifiers, and PPs. The resulting specialised grammars are forced to be nonrecursive, with derivations being a maximum of five levels deep. This is enforced by imposing the following dominance hierarchy between the possible categories:

```
utterance > imperative_VP > NP > rel, VP_mod > PP
```

There are six types of nonphrasal constituents in the specialised grammar. We start by describing each type of constituent through examples (see also Chapter 9).

> **Utterance** The top category.
> **Imperative_VP** Since imperative verb phrases are very common in the corpus, we make them a category of their own in the specialised grammar. To generalise over possible addition of adverbials (in particular, "please" and "now"), we define the `imperative_vp` category so as to leave the adverbials outside. Thus the bracketed portion of the following utterance is an `imperative_vp`: "That's fine now [give me the fares for those flights]".
> **Non_phrasal_NP** All NPs which are not produced entirely by phrasal rules. The following are all `non_phrasal_NPs`: "Boston and Denver", "Flights on Sunday morning", "Cheapest fare from Boston to Denver", "The meal I'd get on that flight".

---

[3] By "recursive NP", we mean an NP which contains at least one proper NP constituent.

Rel Relative clauses.

VP_mod VPs appearing as NP postmodifiers. The bracketed portions of the following are VP_mods: "Delta flights [arriving after seven p m]" "All flights tomorrow [ordered by arrival time]".

PP The CLE grammar treats nominal temporal adverbials, sequences of PPs, and A-to-B constructions as PPs (cf. Section 9.3.4). The following are examples of PPs: "Tomorrow afternoon", "From Boston to Dallas on Friday", "Denver to San Francisco Sunday".

We can now present the precise criteria that determine the chunks of rules composed to form each type of constituent. For each type of constituent in the specialised grammar, the chunk is a subtree extracted from the derivation tree of a training example; we specify the roots and leaves of the relevant subtrees. The term *phrasal tree* will be used to mean a derivation tree all of whose rule applications are phrasal rules.

Utterance The root of the chunk is the root of the original tree. The leaves are the nodes resulting from cutting at maximal subtrees for imperative_vps, nps, and pps, and maximal phrasal subtrees.

Imperative_VP The root is the root of a maximal subtree under an application of the S→VP rule whose root is not an application of an adverbial modification rule. The leaves are the nodes resulting from cutting at maximal subtrees for non_phrasal_np, and pp, and maximal phrasal subtrees.

Non_phrasal_NP The root is the root of a maximal nonphrasal subtree for a constituent of type np. The leaves are the nodes resulting from cutting at maximal subtrees for rel, vp_mod, and pp, and maximal phrasal subtrees.

Rel The root is the root of a maximal subtree for a constituent of type rel. The leaves are the nodes resulting from cutting at maximal subtrees for pp, and maximal phrasal subtrees.

VP_mod The root is the root of a vp subtree immediately dominated by an application of the NP→NP VP rule. The leaves are the nodes resulting from cutting at maximal subtrees for pp, and maximal phrasal subtrees.

PP The root is the root of a maximal nonphrasal subtree for a constituent of type pp. The leaves are the nodes resulting from cutting at maximal phrasal subtrees.

Two approaches have been attempted at automatically selecting the cutting-up criteria using statistical information derived from the training corpus (Samuelsson 1994b; Sima'an 1999). These, however, have failed to produce grammars as appropriate as those extracted using the hand-coded criteria described here.

3.3   An LR Parsing Method for Specialised Grammars

The reason why a specialised grammar is interesting is that it allows fewer analyses than the original one; hence it is reasonable to hope that it can be used to parse more · efficiently as well. In this section, we will describe a parsing algorithm suitable for exploiting the structure of a grammar that has been produced by specialisation according to the scheme we have defined above. In particular, we want to utilise the fact that many rules overlap totally or partially on the context-free level by using prefix merging and abstraction to handle groups of grammar rules at the same time. The technical tool we will use is the LR parsing method, which we first review.

3.3.1   Basic LR Parsing

The success of LR parsing lies in handling a number of grammar rules simultaneously, rather than attempting one at a time, by the use of prefix merging. LR parsing in general is well described in, for example, Aho, Sethi, and Ullman (1986), and its application to natural-language processing in Tomita (1986).

Basically, an LR parser is a finite-state automaton augmented with a push-down stack. The stack content consists of alternating grammar symbols and internal states. The current state is simply the state currently on top of the stack. At each parsing step, a nondeterministic LR parser has four different action options.

The first option is to *shift* the current input symbol, which is a preterminal symbol, onto the stack and transit to a new state. The new state is uniquely determined by the current state and the thus-consumed input symbol. The second option is to *reduce* the stack content using some grammar rule. In this case, the appropriate number of items are popped off from the stack and matched against the right hand side (RHS) of the grammar rule. After this, the current state (i.e., the one now on top of the stack) and the new symbol (i.e., the left hand side (LHS) of the grammar rule) uniquely determine what new state to transit to. This is done by pushing the LHS symbol and the new state onto the stack. The third option, when the current state is a final state, when the stack is empty apart from this state, and when there is no more input, is to *accept* the input string, that is, to halt and signal success. In addition to this, the parser always has the fourth option of failing and backtracking.

What actions are possible at any given point are determined by the grammar, and this information is compiled into the so-called action table. The state transitions accompanying reduce actions are also determined by the grammar, and compiled into the so-called goto table.

3.3.2   Prefix Merging

Prefix merging is accomplished by each internal state corresponding to a set of partially processed grammar rules, so-called *dotted items*, containing a dot (here shown as •) to mark the current position. For example, if the grammar contains the following two rules,

$NP \rightarrow Det\ N$

$NP \rightarrow Det\ Adj\ N$

there will be a state containing the dotted items

$NP \rightarrow Det \bullet N$

$NP \rightarrow Det \bullet Adj\ N$

This state corresponds to just having found a determiner (*Det*). Which of the two rules to apply in the end will be determined by the rest of the input string; at this point no commitment has been made to either of the two rules.

Prefix merging of unification-grammar rules is not, however, as straightforward as it might seem at first. As we have seen, prefix merging means that rules starting with similar phrases are processed together until they branch away. The problem with this scheme in conjunction with a unification grammar is that it is not at all obvious what "similar phrase" means. The choice made here is to regard phrases that map to the same context-free symbol as similar. The mapping of phrases of the specialised grammar to context-free symbols used was the naive one, where phrases were mapped to their syntactic category, for example, where np: [qlf=Det] is mapped to np. We thus resorted to using a context-free backbone grammar.

3.3.3   *Abstraction*

For efficiency reasons, parsing is split into two phases. The first phase is the LR parsing phase, and the grammar used here is the merged unification grammar to be described shortly. The output of this phase is an implicit parse tree indicating how the merged grammar rules were applied to the input word string and what constraints were associated with each word. The second phase applies the full constraints of the specialised grammar and the lexicon to the output parse tree of phase one.

The merged unification grammar used in phase one is constructed as follows. The specialised grammar rules all map to context-free backbone rules. Each context-free rule will have exactly one representative in the merged grammar. Consider the set of specialised grammar rules that map to some particular context-free rule. The merged grammar rule representing this context-free rule is simply the generalisation over this set of specialised rules. Now, if there is only one such specialised rule, the full constraints of the specialised grammar are applied already in phase one.

Similarly, the grammar symbols of the action and goto tables are not context-free symbols; they are the generalisation of a set of phrases of the specialised grammar. The grammar symbols of the shift and goto entries correspond to those that immediately follow the dot in the set of dotted items constituting the state from which the action transits. If several of these map to the same context-free symbol, the grammar symbol of the shift or goto entry will be the generalisation of them.

Lexical ambiguity in the input sentence is handled in the same way. For each word a generalised phrase is constructed from all phrases that it can be analysed as that map to the same context-free symbol. Again, if there is no lexical ambiguity within this context-free symbol, the full constraints are applied already in phase one. Nothing is done about lexical ambiguities outside of the same context-free symbol, though.

Generalisation is accomplished through the use of antiunification. Antiunification is the dual of unification – it constructs the least general term that subsumes two given terms – and was first described in Plotkin (1970). This operation is often referred to as generalisation in the computational-linguistics literature (see, for example, Gazdar and Mellish 1989, 232). If T is the antiunification of T_1 and T_2, then T subsumes T_1 and T subsumes T_2 and if any other term T' subsumes both of T_1 and T_2 then T' subsumes T. Antiunification is implemented efficiently as a built-in predicate of SICStus Prolog, called term_subsumer/3.

Each rule referred to in the output parse tree of phase one may be a generalisation over several different rules of the specialised grammar. Likewise, the constraints associated with each word can be a generalisation over several distinct lexicon entries. In phase two these different ways of applying the full constraints of the specialised grammar rules and the lexicon are attempted nondeterministically.

Using the original specialised grammar, instead of the merged version, for the LR parsing phase led to an increase in parsing time by a factor of five. Using purely context-free symbols was even worse, and led to an increase in parsing time by a factor of 100. Thus, using the merged grammar is an important ingredient of the scheme.

The SLT LR parser is normally run in a fragment-parsing mode (cf. Section 2.7) which attempts to find all possible analyses of all possible connected paths in the chart. The methods described in Section 4.5 are then invoked to select the most preferred sequence of fragments; among other things, this involves minimising the number of fragments in the sequence.

3.4   Empirical Results

3.4.1   *Experimental Setup*

This section reports the results of an empirical investigation of the relationships among the various factors involved in building and using specialised grammars. All experiments were carried out using a basic training corpus of 22 180

English-language ATIS utterances. These were analysed by the CLE using the left-corner parser (Moore and Alshawi 1992) and judged by human judges using the TreeBanker tool (cf. Chapter 5). There were 18 123 utterances that were judged to have at least one correct analysis, and only these derivation trees were actually used. Testing was performed on a set of 400 utterances of held-out data, specifically on 5-best speech hypothesis lists produced from these utterances by a version of the DECIPHER^{TM} recogniser.

We have two input parameters: the cutting-up criteria used to derive the specialised grammar, and the number of training examples used. We used the following three basic methods for cutting up derivation trees:

> **Flat** The simplest method: we extract a single rule from each derivation tree.
>
> **Two-level** The method used in the example from Figure 3.3: we extract one rule from each maximal NP, plus one for the top-level derivation.
>
> **Multilevel** Our current most elaborate method, described in Section 3.2.4.

Each of the above methods was used in two different forms. Our normal processing strategy treats phrasal rules specially (see Section 2.7.1). Consequently, derivation trees produced by the cutting-up criteria were by default pruned from the leaf nodes upwards, so that all nodes corresponding to phrasal rules were removed. In order to investigate the extent to which this special treatment of phrasal rules affected performance, we also compiled a second set of derived rules, in which phrasal rules were left inside the cut-up trees; when using these sets phrasal parsing was bypassed, since it now becomes part of the main parsing phase. We thus compare a total of six different types of derived grammars.

We also investigated two distinct strategies for limiting the number of training examples. The first simply used an initial segment of the full training corpus, discarding the rest: we ran tests using data sets of 500, 1 000, 2 000, 5 000, 10 000 and the full 22 180 examples. The second strategy extracted a set of derived rules from the full 22 180-utterance corpus, keeping count of the number of times each individual derived rule appeared; it discarded low-frequency rules before passing the remainder to the LR table compilation process (cf. Section 3.3). We tried setting the frequency threshold to the value 5 (rules need to occur five or more times to be retained), then to 4, 3, 2, and finally 1 (all rules retained). By default, we set the minimum frequency to 2, since retaining singleton rules in several cases resulted in rule sets so large that they broke the LR compilation process.

The output parameters used to evaluate performance were the following:

> **Rules** Number of rules in the derived grammar.
>
> **Single fragments** Proportion of utterances producing single-fragment analyses.

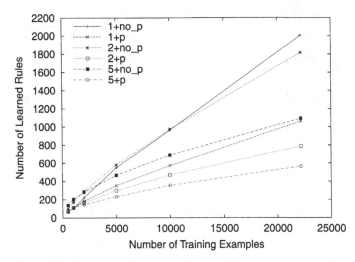

Figure 3.5. Relative performances of six specialised grammars: number of rules learned against number of training examples.

Number of fragments Average number of fragments in the most preferred analyses.

LR parsing time Average time spent on the main LR parsing phase, that is, parsing using the specialised grammar.

Analysis time Average time spent on all phases during linguistic analysis (cf. Section 2.7.1). Note that this is at least partially dependent on what happens during the parsing phase; for example, if more distinct analyses are produced, then more time needs to be spent on the preference phase that attempts to select the best one.

Figures 3.5 through 3.14 summarise the results. Timing figures refer to performance on a 450 MHz Pentium II processor running SICStus Prolog. The grammar types are identified according to a key in which 1 = flat, 2 = two-level, 5 = multilevel, p = special treatment of phrasal rules and no_p = no special treatment of phrasal rules.

3.4.2   *Discussion of Results*

The most obvious measure of grammar coverage is the proportion of utterances receiving a single-fragment analysis. Ideally, we would have preferred to measure the proportion of utterances receiving a *correct* single-fragment analysis, but time constraints made it impossible to judge the whole of 66 test sets, each consisting of 400 analyses.

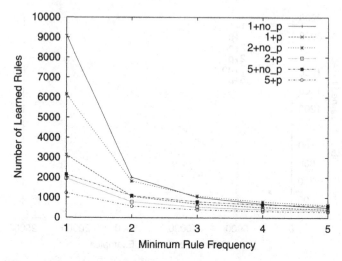

Figure 3.6. Relative performances of six specialised grammars: number of rules learned against minimum rule frequency.

The most significant differences among the different results clearly depend on whether or not a special treatment of phrasal rules was used (the "p/no_p" distinction). With small numbers of training examples or use of the flat or two-level cutting-up criteria, treating phrasal rules specially can more than double the proportion of utterances receiving a single-fragment analysis (Figure 3.7), without

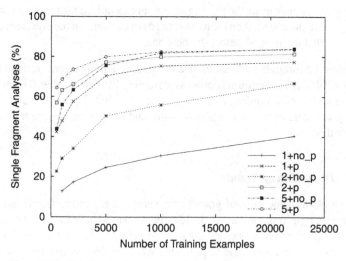

Figure 3.7. Relative performances of six specialised grammars: proportion of single-fragment analyses against number of training examples.

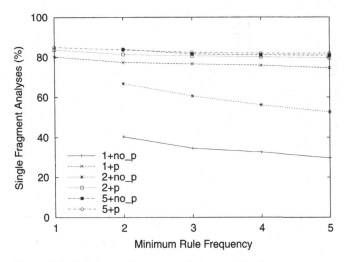

Figure 3.8. Relative performances of six specialised grammars: proportion of single-fragment analyses against minimum rule frequency.

greatly affecting processing speed (Figure 3.11). In fact, processing speed usually displayed a slight improvement. The differences in both coverage and speed resulting from special treatment of phrasal rules more or less disappear, however, for the multilevel cutting-up criteria and for large numbers of training examples. In all cases, though, the special treatment of phrases greatly reduces the number

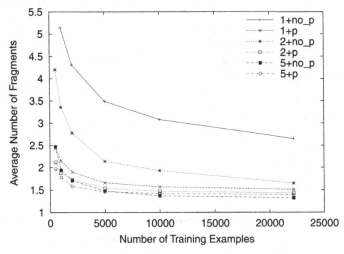

Figure 3.9. Relative performances of six specialised grammars: average number of fragments per utterance against number of training examples.

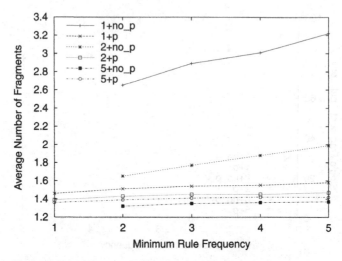

Figure 3.10. Relative performances of six specialised grammars: average number of fragments per utterance against minimum rule frequency.

of derived rules (Figures 3.5 and 3.6); without it, the very large number of derived rules produced sometimes exceeded the resource limits of the LR compiler, which explains the missing data points in some of the graphs.

Sensitivity of coverage to number of training examples varied greatly with basic grammar type. At one extreme, coverage of the flat grammar without special

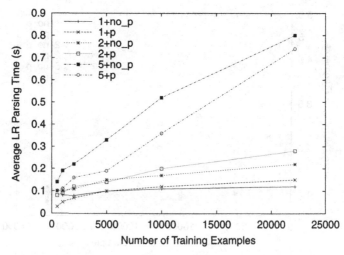

Figure 3.11. Relative performances of six specialised grammars: average LR parsing time against number of training examples.

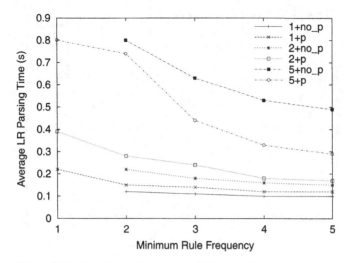

Figure 3.12. Relative performances of six specialised grammars: average LR parsing time against minimum rule frequency.

treatment of phrasal rules (1+no_p) improved from 30 percent to 40 percent when the number of training examples was increased from 10 000 to 22 180; at the other extreme, the multilevel scheme with special treatment of phrasal rules (5+p) only improved from 82.5 percent to 83.5 percent for the same increase in size of training set. In general, coverage curves for the grammars using a special treatment of

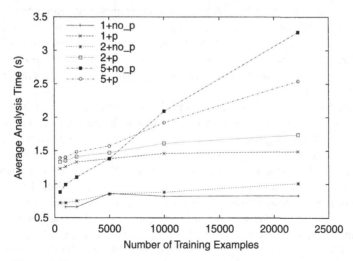

Figure 3.13. Relative performances of six specialised grammars: average analysis time against number of training examples.

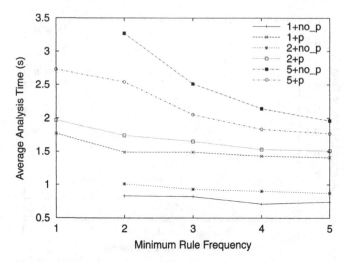

Figure 3.14. Relative performances of six specialised grammars: average analysis time against minimum rule frequency.

phrasal rules had all flattened out by the time the number of training examples had reached 10 000 (Figure 3.7). The dependency between parsing speed and number of training examples worked in the opposite direction: average parsing time for the simple grammars increased slowly as the number of training examples went up, while there was a marked effect for the complex grammars (Figure 3.11). For example, parsing time for 1+no_p only went up from 0.11 secs/utterance to 0.12 secs/utterance as the number of training examples increased from 10 000 to 22 180, while the corresponding figures for 5+p were an increase from 0.36 secs/utterance to 0.74 secs/utterance. Removing low-frequency rules had remarkably little effect on coverage (Figure 3.8), especially for the grammars that treated phrasal rules specially, though it did substantially reduce average parsing times (Figure 3.12).

In earlier work (Rayner and Carter 1996; Rayner and Samuelsson 1994; Samuelsson 1994a), we made efforts to compare the performance of a derived grammar and the original one in terms of coverage and processing speed. For example, Rayner and Samuelsson (1994) evaluated the CLE left-corner parser against a version of the LR parser on the task of finding full parses of ATIS utterances in text form, and reported an improvement in speed of a little less than two orders of magnitude against a loss of coverage of around 5 percent. We considered trying to run similar tests here, but our conclusion was that it would be essentially meaningless. The problem is that we have invested considerable effort in improving the LR parser, without any corresponding investment in the left-corner parser. In consequence, we can no longer carry out a proper comparison: the left-corner

Table 3.1. *Number of new derived rules found for different grammar types during last 1 000 utterances of a 22 180-utterance EBL training run*

Grammar type	Number
Flat, no special treatment of phrases	364
Two-level, no special treatment of phrases	210
Flat, special treatment of phrases	118
Two-level, special treatment of phrases	67
Multilevel, no special treatment of phrases	62
Multilevel, special treatment of phrases	35

parser is not capable of performing the task we have considered here – fragment parsing of lattices derived from 5-best speech hypothesis lists – without frequently exceeding reasonable resource bounds.

In order to obtain some indication of the absolute loss of coverage, Table 3.1 shows the number of new derived rules acquired for each type of grammar during the last 1 000 utterances, when training on the full 22 180-utterance set. Making the reasonable assumption that most of the new rules learned will only occur once, these results suggest that the best scheme (multilevel grammar with special treatment of phrases) involves an absolute coverage loss of less than 4 percent, while two other schemes (two-level grammar with special treatment of phrases, multilevel grammar without special treatment of phrases) lose between 6 percent and 7 percent. In actual fact, the phenomenon of *pipeline synergy* (cf. Section 20.5) means that, in the context of an integrated speech translation system, the real coverage loss due to grammar specialisation is even lower than these figures would suggest.

3.5   Conclusions

This chapter has presented a theoretical basis for the idea of using Explanation-Based Learning to perform corpus-based specialisation of unification grammars. We have described a number of concrete instantiations of the idea, and compared their performances on the task of performing fragment parsing of lattices derived from 5-best speech hypothesis lists.

Our overall conclusion is that the best versions of the method are fully adequate for tasks of this kind, assuming the availability of sufficiently large training corpora. For the ATIS domain, a corpus of between 5 000 and 10 000 utterances appears to be enough, with further training data yielding only marginal improvements.

4   Choosing among Interpretations

DAVID CARTER

I DEALLY, grammar specialisation, as described in Chapter 3, would result in only one analysis – the correct one – being found for each utterance. However, it would be unrealistic to hope for that; the main reason is that the choice of correct analysis depends at least as much on lexical as on grammatical factors. This chapter, therefore, looks at the way linguistic (mainly lexical) information is applied during parsing to rule out or prune certain constituents, and after parsing to choose the correct analysis from among the many output by the parser. Because these operations depend crucially on characteristics of the domain, we focus on customisation issues.

The chapter first introduces, in Section 4.1, the idea of the *discriminant* and the way discriminants are used in SLT. These considerations are fundamental to the use of customised data in constituent pruning, described in Section 4.2; in analysis choice, dealt with in Section 4.3; in translation choice, Section 4.4; and in choosing the best sequence of translation fragments, Section 4.5.

4.1   Properties and Discriminants

The constituent pruning, analysis choice, and translation choice algorithms used in SLT are all based on the idea of discriminants (Dagan and Itai 1994; Yarowsky 1994), which can be characterised and motivated as follows.

Any interpretation I of a piece of language (from a word up to an utterance, in SLT) can, by definition, be described by the *properties* that do or do not hold for it. Some examples of properties used in SLT are:

P1 I involves a verb occurring immediately after a determiner.

P2 I was created by using (among others) the grammar rule advp_det_ Sup.

P3 I mentions flights on a particular day of the week.

P4 I is an interpretation of (part of) the word sequence deemed most likely by the speech recogniser.

P5 *I* (a partial translation) was produced by the word-to-word translation rules.

Properties can be useful for making choices only when they are *discriminants*: that is, when they discriminate between interpretations, by being true of some interpretations and not of others. A discriminant that is reliably true of correct interpretations is useful. For example, P3 is true of the obvious reading of "show me flights to Boston on Wednesday", and not of the reading that could be paraphrased "show me flights to Boston, and do it on Wednesday", so if the system somehow knows P3 tends to characterise correct interpretations then it can use this information to prefer the first option here. We call discriminants such as P3 *positive*.

Negative discriminants, that is, ones that are reliably *un*true of correct interpretations, can be equally useful. For example, P1 would characterise a possible tagging of the string "show me a list of flights" where "list" was incorrectly labelled as a verb, so if the system knows P1 is strongly negative, it can safely rule out this part of speech for "list".

Other discriminants may be less strongly positive or negative; for example, P4 is mildly positive, because while the hypothesis at the top of the N-best list tends to be better than lower hypotheses, there are many exceptions. P5 is also likely to be mildly positive, because when it is a discriminant, it indicates a contrast with a probably less reliable partial translation produced at QLF level. Still others may give very little indication of correctness; P2 may be true of about as many incorrect as correct interpretations, and therefore provide little basis for any decision.

It can be seen that a wide range of discriminants can be defined, describing, among other things, syntactic structure, lexical association, and acoustic quality. If a discriminant can easily be extracted from a structure, and is either strongly positive or strongly negative, then it can be used to make choices at run time. Furthermore, if correct interpretations can be identified for the sentences in a training corpus (in the SLT system, this is done by the TreeBanker; see Chapter 5), then the strength and polarity of discriminants can be estimated, based on how often they characterise correct interpretations, and how often incorrect.

However, if discriminants are to be used to make choices, we need to decide how to combine them. Different discriminants may incline us toward selecting different interpretations, and it is not immediately clear how to arbitrate among them. In the absence of other information, a strong discriminant should clearly override a weaker one, but what if one interpretation is supported by two strong discriminants and another by three slightly weaker ones?

The approach most often taken in this kind of situation is to assume statistical independence among the different indicators, and add together (possibly using scaling factors) the log probability estimates associated with each indicator to derive overall estimates for the log probability of each interpretation. This was essentially the approach adopted in an earlier version of SLT (Alshawi and

Carter 1994). However, it suffers from several disadvantages:

D1 The assumption of statistical independence can be hard to justify, especially when we are working with dozens or even hundreds of different indicators.

D2 If scaling factors are to be used, we need to calculate them, adding to the complexity of the training process and perhaps making it slower. In practice, this puts quite a severe limit on the number of (separately scaled) indicators that can be used, so that similar indicators may need to be bundled into the same scaled indicator (cf. the use of a few dozen different preference functions by Alshawi and Carter (1994)). The bundling may of course be suboptimal.

D3 If different numbers of indicators apply to different interpretations, we may need to normalise the scores to make them comparable. This can be a particular problem when comparing paths of different lengths.

D4 If we are choosing among interpretations that are presented in packed form, rather than explicitly enumerated, it is far from clear how to identify reliably the highest scoring interpretation without unpacking them all; and in SLT, transfer can produce thousands of such interpretations, so unpacking would be very time consuming.

D5 If the system makes a wrong choice of interpretation at run time, it is seldom clear why, that is, whether the fault lies with individual mistrained indicators (and, if so, which), or whether some indicators are missing, or whether the scaling factors are wrong. Thus, it can be hard to correct training errors and to debug and improve the system.

For all these reasons, we have switched, both for constituent pruning and for the choices of analysis and transfer output, to algorithms that make the opposite fundamental assumption, that of maximal statistical dependence. Our algorithms are inspired by that of Yarowsky (1994). For the simplest case, that of analysis choice, we proceed as follows:

- Extract from each possible interpretation all the properties (known to the system) that hold for it.
- Discard those properties that are not discriminants (i.e., that happen to hold for all the interpretations).
- Look up the strength and polarity of each discriminant (the way these values are derived is discussed later).
- Discard any discriminants with a zero score; most of these will be ones that have not been seen at all in training.
- Order the discriminants by strength, with the strongest (either positive or negative) first.
- Apply each discriminant in turn to rule out some interpretations, unless to do so would rule out *all* the surviving interpretations. If the discriminant

is positive, rule out interpretations for which it does not hold. If negative, rule out ones for which it does hold.
- Stop when there is exactly one interpretation left, or when there are no more discriminants (in which case an arbitrary choice must be made – usually a sign of insufficient training).

This algorithm can, if desired, be modified to extract a ranked list of interpretations rather than just to choose the best one. The modification is that, when we apply a discriminant, we use it to partition the interpretations into a favoured and a disfavoured set; all members of the former will rank above all members of the latter. We apply the algorithm recursively and separately to the two sets thus created to determine the ranking within them. If we require only the best N interpretations rather than an exhaustive ranking, we can modify the algorithm to process a disfavoured set only if the corresponding favoured set does not contain enough members.

One way to view all variants of this algorithm is that they create (part of) a decision tree, where the choice at each level of the tree corresponds to a discriminant, with the strongest at the root. Favoured sets branch to the left and disfavoured to the right. The interpretations are to be found along the fringe of the tree, with the ranking going from left to right. We apply the algorithm to create as much of the tree as is needed to extract one, N, or all ranked interpretations.

Our algorithm addresses the disadvantages D1 to D5 of the sum-of-scores approach as follows:

D1 Assuming maximal statistical dependence is as much an approximation as assuming full independence; but it is arguably a better approximation, because, in practice, if there are many different discriminants there will be a lot of redundancy, with some of them describing the same choice in different ways.

D2 No scaling factors are required, because discriminant scores can be directly compared. Consequently, no bundling of discriminants is necessary.

D3 No normalisation is required either, for similar reasons.

D4 If interpretations are packed, unpacking is only required for the ones forming part of the (partial) ranking. Thus, the time required for the best-N ($N \geq 1$) algorithm is proportional to the total size of the packed structures rather than their unpacked equivalents. This claim will be substantiated in Section 4.4.

D5 When a wrong choice of interpretation is made, we can easily see the discriminant that rejected the right interpretation and, usually, another, weaker discriminant that could have rescued it had it been stronger. This can point us to possible judging errors in training, or, less often, the need to extend the set of discriminants we work with.

Points D2 and D5 are dealt with more fully in Section 4.3.2.

4.2   Constituent Pruning

As we saw in Section 2.7.1, before each of the CLE's parsing stages, the constituent table or chart can be examined to locate edges that are relatively unlikely to make any further contribution to correct analyses – that is, edges that are very likely either to be wrong or only to be correct as daughters of other existing edges, and not to be directly useful as input to further parsing stages. When such edges are located, we prune them by removing them from the input to further parsing stages. Currently, we prune before the phrasal and full parsing stages.

For example, after the string "Show flight D L three one two" is lexically analysed, edges for "D" and "L" as individual characters are pruned because another edge, derived from a lexical entry for "D L" as a known airline code (for Delta Airlines), is deemed far more plausible. Similarly, edges for "one" as a determiner and as a noun are pruned because, when adjacent to another number, "one" is far more likely to function as a number.

Phrasal parsing then creates a number of new edges, including one for "flight D L three one two" as a noun phrase. This edge is deemed far more likely to serve as the basis for a correct full parse than any of the edges spanning substrings of this phrase; those edges, too, are therefore pruned. As a result, full parsing is very quick, and only one analysis (the correct one) is produced for the sentence. In the absence of pruning, processing takes more than five times as long and produces thirty seven analyses in total.

4.2.1   Discriminants for Pruning

Our pruning algorithm uses discriminants to estimate the probability of correctness of each edge at a given stage of parsing: that is, the probability that the edge will contribute directly (as an immediate daughter of a correct edge to be built later in parsing) to a correct full analysis of the sentence, given certain lexical and/or syntactic information about it. The pruning algorithm can be viewed as a variant of the analysis choice algorithm given in Section 4.1, the main differences being:

- Rather than operating on complete analyses, we are operating on chart edges, each of which may eventually form part of many possible analyses.
- Rather than identifying the edges most likely to contribute to a single correct full interpretation, we have a less ambitious aim, consonant with the reduced information available at this earlier stage: to identify and remove those edges we can be reasonably sure are useless.
- As a consequence, only negative discriminants, not positive ones, are applied.

We will describe in Section 4.2.3 the way in which the probability estimates for different discriminants are calculated, taking into account data sparseness and the influence of acoustic scores. For the moment, we will take these estimates as given.

The discriminants currently used in pruning, each associated with an edge in the chart, are as follows:

- the edge's *right bigram(s)*. A right bigram is a sequence consisting of the current edge followed by an edge immediately to its right, considering only the following data about each of the two edges:
  - its *class*. For a lexical edge, the class is the *semantic word class* predefined for the word in question: words with similar distributions, such as city names, are grouped into classes to overcome data sparseness. If no explicit class is defined for the word, the word itself is used. For a nonlexical edge, the name of the final (topmost) grammar rule that was used to create it is used as the class.
  - its *tag*: usually its major category symbol, although a few categories correspond to several tags to allow additional distinctions derived from feature values to be represented.
- the *left bigram(s)* for the edge: as above, but considering the current edge and one of its left neighbours.
- The *treegram* for the tree of grammar rules, with words at the leaves, that gave rise to the edge in question. The treegram for a tree is a triple consisting of the class and tag (see above) of the leftmost terminal node, the mother (root) node of the tree, and the rightmost terminal node. For example, the treegram for a noun-phrase analysis of "the first Delta flight" would be

```
(the/detn, np_det_nbar/np, flight/nbar)
```

Here, the leftmost and rightmost daughters "the" and "flight" are their own classes; the tags are the major category symbols, except that the tag detn stands for a det (determiner) which cannot function on its own as a noun phrase (contrast "which"). np_det_nbar is the grammar rule used to analyse this phrase as an NP.

Other discriminants, such as trigrams, finer grained tags, and alternative definitions of treegrams, are obviously possible, and could be applied straightforwardly within the framework described here. The system, in fact, allows trigrams to be applied, but on ATIS data, their use seems unnecessary.[1]

---

[1] When a test was run on 100 unseen test English N-best lists, and trigram-based pruning was applied after treegram- and bigram-based, only 5 percent more constituents were pruned out. However, there were nearly three times as many trigram-based pruning rules (i.e., trigram discriminants with sufficiently low probability estimates) as treegram and bigram ones put together, and using trigrams more than doubled the time required for the first pruning stage.

Our discriminant algorithm again assumes maximal statistical dependence between factors. The score (probability estimate) for an edge is therefore defined as the minimum of several component scores. In this case, there are three: its treegram score, its maximum left-bigram score over all the possible choices of left neighbour, and its maximum right-bigram score over all the possible choices of right neighbour.

We take the maximum over possible neighbours because a correct edge participates in only one left bigram and one right bigram (at a given level) in the winning parse tree. Thus, for example, "to" can function either as preposition ("p") or as an infinitive marker (encoded as a verb, "v", in the CLE grammar of English). In the sentence "Show me flights to that airport", the bigram (to/v, that/detn) scores very badly, but this should not lead to the determiner edge for "that" being penalised, because the bigram (to/p, that/detn) has a much better score, and it is, in fact, this bigram that characterises the correct parse. If we did penalise the determiner edge for "that" because of the first bigram, we would run the risk of reducing its scores to near those of the other (noun phrase and complementiser) edges for "that" and therefore failing to prune those two edges.

As already explained, taking the overall minimum of the component scores involves making an assumption of maximal statistical dependence. Such an assumption makes sense here because there is likely to be a fair amount of dependence between discriminants that all reflect local syntactic information.

We consider only negative discriminants when calculating edge scores because, on the basis of the local information that is all that we have available at this early stage in analysis, it is not usually possible to predict with confidence that a particular edge is highly *likely* to contribute to the correct analysis, since global factors will also be important. However, it is often possible to spot highly *unlikely* edges using one or more of the discriminants available. Extracting a discriminant from an edge involves taking a particular view of that edge by abstracting out a small (but, we hope, relevant) part of the information about it that is present in the chart. The resulting score reflects the number of times edges that, on the view represented by the discriminant, are equivalent to the current one, have been judged right or wrong in training. If we can find a view of (i.e., a discriminant for) an edge that identifies it with a set of training edges that are virtually always wrong, then we are justified in pruning it, regardless of the views of the edge represented by other discriminants. Also, taking minima means there is no need to include in the runtime system any discriminant scores that are not sufficiently low to trigger pruning; this much reduces the amount of data required at run time.

A further advantage of taking minima, relevant to point D3, is that if we do so, the estimate of the joint probability depends much less strongly on the number of events compared, and so estimates for alternative joint events can be directly compared without any possibly tricky normalisation, even if they are composed of different numbers of atomic events. This property is desirable: it means that further discriminants could be introduced that are only defined for some kinds of edge.

4.2.2   Deciding Which Edges to Prune

At each pruning stage (before phrasal parsing, before full parsing, etc.), discriminants, with their accompanying probability estimates, are calculated for each edge in the chart. Currently, an estimate of $\frac{1}{200}$ or lower is taken as sufficient grounds for pruning an edge. Pruning is carried out on edges with successively higher estimates until either this threshold is reached, or (more rarely) pruning the next edge out would destroy the connectivity of the chart, that is, would remove all the remaining complete paths through it and therewith the hope of a full parse.

For efficiency, the implemented system involves a small change to the algorithm so far described. We first calculate treegram scores, then prune out any edges judged sufficiently unlikely on treegram grounds alone (bearing in mind that because the overall probability estimate is defined as the minimum of the treegram and bigram scores, if the treegram estimate is below the threshold then the overall estimate will be also). For noninitial pruning stages, this often results in quite a lot of edges being pruned, which greatly reduces the number of bigrams to be examined, speeding up pruning considerably.

Left and right bigram scores are then calculated together, and those bigrams whose scores fall below the threshold are marked with their scores. All edges whose left bigrams are all marked, and/or whose right bigrams are all marked, are also then marked, as are any still-unmarked bigrams in which they participate. Scores are propagated in this way until no further change occurs, and then marked edges are pruned in order of increasing score.

4.2.3   Probability Estimates for Discriminants

The probability estimate for an edge (or N-gram of edges) according to a certain criterion (discriminant) is a function of the numbers of occasions in training that edges with the same description according to that discriminant did and did not, at the parsing level in question, contribute directly to correct parses. (Equivalently, for analysis choice, we would count the number of times each discriminant was true of a correct analysis, and the number of times it was false.) Suppose, for example, that a given bigram discriminant was correct ("good") on G occasions and incorrect ("bad") on B. Then we would want an estimate for that discriminant of around $G/(G + B)$.

However, this fairly simple picture is complicated in three ways. First, as always with tasks of this kind, smoothing is needed for low values of G and/or B. Second, and relatedly, for either pruning or analysis choice to be as effective as possible we need to look at *generalized* discriminants. In pruning, the specific bigram $(C_1/T_1, C_2/T_2)$ may have $G = 0$ and $B = 2$, which on its own hardly inspires enough confidence to justify a pruning decision; but it may be that the more general set of bigrams satisfying $(C_1/T_1, */T_2)$, where $*$ is any value of C_2, has $G = 0$ and $B = 300$, which presents a rather different picture. Third, the pruner must somehow take account of the acoustic scores for different word candidates contributed by the recogniser – and, by implication, for edges constructed from them during parsing. We discuss each of these complications in turn.

4.2.3.1 Complication 1: Smoothing

Given G good (correct) occurrences of a datum such as a treegram or bigram, and B bad ones, the maximum likelihood estimate of a subsequent occurrence being good is $G/(G + B)$. However, such an estimate is not a good basis for pruning; in particular, if $G = 0$, it evaluates to zero for any positive B, however small or large. One way to smooth the estimate is to assume some prior underlying distribution for the events (*prior* in the sense of it being our best guess prior to seeing any occurrences), and take as our estimate the expected value of the posterior distribution given that prior and our observations of G and B.

Assuming a uniform prior – that is, that a discriminant picked at random is as likely to have any score as any other – gives us a smoothed estimate of

$$\frac{G+1}{G+B+2} \tag{4.1}$$

Although this is, as desired, monotonically increasing in G and decreasing in B, and tends to the maximum likelihood estimate for large G and B, it turns out not to have good behaviour when we compare discriminants with widely differing total counts (i.e., a rarer but consistent discriminant, having $G = 0$, $B = 8$ say, with a more common but less consistent one, having $G = 9$, $B = 89$). Closer examination reveals that our assumption of a uniform prior is unrealistic: discriminants with high G and low B, or vice versa, are much more common than those with balanced G and B. This suggests we would do better to take the posterior distribution based on a uniform prior, and make that our prior distribution instead, because over the discriminant set as a whole it has far more probability mass at the ends of the range than in the middle, as desired. If we do so, we get a formula of

$$\frac{G(G+B+3)+1}{(G+B)(G+B+3)+2} \tag{4.2}$$

which has rather better characteristics. The full mathematical details are given in Appendix A.

Our justification for formula (4.2) is only informal and it is possible that other formulae might give slightly better results. However, our past experience with this kind of problem suggests that what is important is to find a formula that *qualitatively* reflects the nature of the data being processed; once this has been achieved, quantitative optimisations tend to be relatively unproductive. In fact, we have observed *no* failures in pruning (or preference calculations, where this formula is also used; see later sections in this chapter) caused by the formula yielding intuitively wrong values given the (G, B) values it is provided with. This was not the case for the earlier formula (4.1) based on the uniform prior.

4.2.3.2 Complication 2: Generalised Discriminants

Suppose the pruner comes across an edge for "you" as an NP followed by one for "M" as a character. In the ATIS domain, this seems fairly unlikely to be good (and may well result from a recogniser error, such as "A M" being misrecognised as "you M"). This particular bigram is in fact always bad when it occurs in the ATIS training data used for English; the problem is that it only occurs there twice, and *a priori*, counts of $G = 0$, $B = 2$ (giving a probability estimate of $\frac{1}{12}$ from Equation 4.2) do not justify pruning. However, bigrams in which "you" as an NP is followed by *any* character occur a total of 22 times in training, with all the occurrences being bad ones; and bigrams for any NP followed by "M" as a character occur 471 times, again all bad. Either of these counts does justify pruning: the estimates from Equation (4.2) are $\frac{1}{552}$ and $\frac{1}{223\,256}$, which are both under our threshold of $\frac{1}{200}$.

On the other hand, there are also cases where a maximally specific bigram (with all four fields specified) has counts that do (correctly) trigger pruning, but its more general counterpart does not, because the behaviour of other lexemes with the same tag is rather different (some of these others giving rise to good occurrences, which make G nonzero and push the estimate above the threshold). How, therefore, should we decide how general a set of bigrams to consider when returning G and B counts for a datum encountered at run time?

We solve this problem by effectively considering the possible views of a datum implied by each of a range of different abstractions. For bigrams (C_1, T_1, C_2, T_2), we generalise over the left-hand and/or right-hand classes, to give the three patterns $(*, T_1, C_2, T_2), (C_1, T_1, *, T_2)$, and $(*, T_1, *, T_2)$.[2] For treegrams themselves, which have six places, we generalise in thirteen of the sixty three (i.e., $2^6 - 1$) conceivable different ways, those again being the ones that seem likely to yield useful patterns.

At run time, instead of calculating an edge probability by minimising over only three types of discriminant (left bigram, right bigram, and right bigram), we effectively minimise over the three original, specific, types, and the nineteen $(3 + 3 + 13)$ created by generalisation as well. In fact, it is possible to precompile most of this minimisation by only storing event counts that can contribute minimum values for some data that may occur at run time. Thus, for the "you M" example, the bigram $(*, np, M, character)$, for any NP, not just "you", followed by the

---

[2] We do not generalise over tags because there is no particular reason why edges for the same word but different syntactic categories should behave similarly (as would be implied by a pattern like $(C_1, *, C_2, T_2)$), and because generalising over both class and tag in the same position (e.g., $(*, *, C_2, T_2)$) would be equivalent to reducing to (generalised) treegrams, which are themselves a detailed kind of unigram.

character "M", is the one with the most informative score, and this is the only matching one whose score is retained. We also include "inhibitory" records in the data used for pruning, for cases where the counts for more specific data include enough good occurrences, and few enough bad ones, to override the decision to prune that would be implied by more general types.

The data used for pruning at run time in the English ATIS system consists of about 3 000 records at the first (postlexical) level, and 7 000 at the second (post–phrasal-parsing), which with suitable indexing allows reasonably efficient pruning. At each level, about 75 percent of the records are generalised ones, and around 10 percent are inhibitory. This relatively small set of records is derived from around 50 000 different treegrams and bigrams extracted during training *before* generalisation. The reduction in numbers is due partly to the fact that many of these items have counts that in fact do not justify pruning, and so there is no reason to keep them; and partly to the fact that when a generalisation is found that has counts that would trigger pruning, this usually allows most or all of the specific records contributing to it to be discarded.

4.2.3.3 Complication 3: Acoustic Scores

When recogniser output in the form of N-best lists is being processed, it is desirable to allow the pruning decision to be swayed by the acoustic score of the edge(s) involved. In order to do this, when we calculate probability estimates using formula (4.2), we pretend that the sample of G good occurrences on which the estimate is based came not from an overall sample of $G + B$ occurrences but of $(G + B)/\alpha$, where α is an estimate, derived from training on N-best lists, of the probability that a datum covering the given number of adjacent words with a given (maximal) acoustic score shortfall is in fact part of the correct word sequence (as defined by the reference version provided with all ATIS utterances).[3] When the word(s) involved are part of the top hypothesis in the N-best list, with a shortfall of zero, α will be close to 1, reflecting the fact that words in the top hypothesis are usually correct; for larger shortfalls, and to a lesser extent for larger numbers of words forming a sequence, α will be smaller. Some example values are given in Table 4.1.

Penalising acoustically poor edges by multiplying linguistic (treegram and bigram based) and acoustic scores together, rather than taking their minimum, corresponds, as pointed out in Section 4.2.1, to assuming statistical independence between these sources of information. This seems reasonable, because there is no obvious reason why particular *syntactic* patterns should be more characteristic of some positions in the N-best list than others. It is also practically appropriate: if we take minima, we run the risk of finding ourselves in a situation where two edges of the same class and tag (say, two city names) but different acoustic quality both

---

[3] We do not take the more obvious step of multiplying G by α instead of dividing $G + B$ by it, because G may be zero.

Table 4.1. *α values for various shortfalls
and word counts*

Shortfall	α (1 word)	α (3 words)	α (6 words)
0	0.92	0.85	0.75
20	0.27	0.26	0.23
100	0.16	0.14	0.11

get a linguistic score that is worse than either of their acoustic scores and justifies pruning, and hence get the same overall minimum score. However, we suppose, both edges cannot be pruned because to do so would destroy the connectivity of the chart. Clearly, in this case, we want to prune the acoustically poorer edge; but that can only happen if we multiply, rather than take minima.

A similar adjustment should in principle be made during training; if a given datum only ever occurs in acoustically poor hypotheses, it may fail ever to be correct simply because it involves words that were not uttered, rather than because it is linguistically implausible. We do not make any such adjustment, partly because it would complicate the generalisation procedure and other parts of the training process, but also because if, as already argued, syntactic and acoustic scores are likely to be largely independent, then the required adjustment would not in any case make very much difference.

4.2.4 Relation to Other Pruning Methods

As the example presented at the beginning of Section 4.2 and the experiments to be described in Chapter 20 suggest, judicious pruning of the chart at appropriate points can greatly restrict the search space and speed up processing. Our method has points of similarity with some recent work in Constraint Grammar[4] and is an alternative to several other, related schemes.

First, as remarked earlier, it generalises *tagging*. It not only adjudicates between possible labels for the same word, but can also use the existence of a constituent over one span of the chart as justification for pruning another constituent over another span, normally a subsumed one, as in the "D L" example. This is especially true in the second stage of pruning, when many constituents of different lengths have been created. Furthermore, our method applies equally well to lattices, rather than strings, of words, and can take account of acoustic plausibility as well as syntactic considerations.

Second, our method is related to *beam search* (Woods 1985). In beam search, incomplete parses of an utterance are pruned or discarded when, on some criterion,

---

[4] Christer Samuelsson, personal communication; see Karlsson et al. (1995) for background.

they are significantly less plausible than other, competing parses. This kind of pruning is fully interleaved with the parsing process. In contrast, our pruning takes place only at certain points: currently before parsing begins, and between the phrasal and full parsing stages. Potentially, as with any generate-and-test algorithm, this can mean efficiency is reduced: some paths will be explored that could in principle be pruned earlier. However, as the results in Chapter 20 will show, this is not in practice a serious problem, because the second pruning phase greatly reduces the search space in preparation for the potentially inefficient full parsing phase. Our method also has the advantage, compared to beam search, of no need for any particular search order to be followed; when pruning takes place, all constituents that could have been found at the stage in question are guaranteed already to exist.

Third, our method is a generalisation of the strategy employed by McCord (1993). McCord interleaved parsing with pruning in the same way we do, but only compared constituents over the same span and with the same major category. Our comparisons are more wide ranging and, therefore, can result in more effective pruning.

4.3   Choosing among QLF Analyses

The supervised training process to be described in Chapter 5 results in a database of discriminant occurrences. For each discriminant we have a count of its good and bad occurrences. We have already seen (Section 4.2) how these counts are used to provide probability estimates to drive the pruning process, and have been presented with a general version of the algorithm that chooses among complete analyses. This section goes into more detail on the latter and presents examples of it in action.

4.3.1   Analysis Choice: An Example

The utterance "List all flights leaving Denver between eight P M and nine P M" (assuming perfect speech recognition, for simplicity) receives five QLF analyses.
One of the triple-based discriminants for this has the pattern

```
(list/show) + -between + ... and ...
```

This characterises analyses in which certain senses of "list" or "show" (treated as equivalent here) have attached to them (non-low, as indicated by the "-" before "between"), by a prepositional phrase with preposition "between", a noun phrase conjoined by "and". Such a discriminant was judged bad on fifty occasions during training and was never judged good (i.e., $G = 0$, $B = 50$, for which Equation (4.2) gave an estimate of $\frac{1}{2652}$). This makes it the strongest discriminant (the one whose probability estimate is closest to zero or one; in this case, it is close to zero), so it is applied first, and we discard the two analyses it applies to. A further strongly negative discriminant, corresponding to the construction "(list/show) + while + VP-ing", which applies to interpretations that can be paraphrased "List all flights while you're leaving Denver . . .", was the next strongest, having $G = 0$, $B = 23$, and an estimate of $\frac{1}{600}$. One further analysis was removed when this was applied. Next, a triple for "flight(s) + -between + (time) and (time)" has $G = 0$, $B = 12$, and an estimate of $\frac{1}{182}$. Applying this rules out one more analysis, leaving the correct one as the only survivor. In this example, all the discriminants used were negative ones, that is, they had probabilities close to zero; this is fairly typical.

4.3.2   Further Advantages of a Discriminant Scheme

Although this way of applying training data at run time is not necessarily more accurate than other schemes for a given corpus and set of judgments, it has, as we saw Section 4.1, some important practical advantages over more complex schemes such as that of the SLT-1 system (Agnäs et al. 1994; Alshawi and Carter 1994). One advantage is that no optimisation is required here; the most sophisticated mathematics involved is in calculating the probability estimates from the good and bad counts, and the results are not even very sensitive to the exact formula, (4.2), used for that purpose. Furthermore, some of the individual functions required rather a lot of computing time, and a discriminant-based scheme allows most of them to be discarded.

More importantly, however, using discriminants directly makes it easy to detect and repair training errors. When the weighted sum making up the score of an incorrect analysis exceeds that for the correct one in the SLT-1 scheme, it is hard to tell what specific thing, if any, has gone wrong in training. Usually the error can at best be tracked to one particular preference function, and then one can only observe that if the weights had been different, another choice would have been made. In our scheme, however, the discriminants applying to the selected and the correct analyses can be compared. There will be a particular point at which the correct analysis is discarded and the incorrect one kept, and here we can diagnose the problem as follows.

Occasionally, an error is due to the necessary discriminants not having been extracted from the analyses during training. When this occurs, we extend the code that extracts discriminants and redo the automatic part of the training (using the TreeBanker to merge the old discriminant values with the new sets of discriminants, as indicated in Section 5.4.2). An example of this is that initially, we did not distinguish triples resulting from PPs attaching low from other attachments;

when we began to do so, the discriminants for such triples became much more reliable.

More frequently, though, all the required discriminants are present, but one or more of those involved in the choice has an unlikely-looking score. In that case it is straightforward to find which training sentences have contributed to these scores, and to determine whether (rarely) there is a problem in the code that extracts the scores from the judged data, or whether the user has misjudged some of the training sentences. In the latter case, the TreeBanker can be used to extract all sentences involving possible misjudgments of the problematic discriminant(s), present them for rejudging, and integrate them back into the database.

Thus, over time, this iterative process results in increasingly high-quality discriminants, judgments, and extraction code; the errors the system makes direct developers' attention to problem areas much more easily and specifically than do more mathematically sophisticated schemes, and the TreeBanker merging option minimises the rejudging that is required.

4.3.3   Numerical Metrics

Although the functionality of most of the preference functions from the SLT-1 system (Agnäs et al. 1994; Alshawi and Carter 1994) has been taken over by the wider range of discriminants applied directly in the current version, a few of the functions are retained. In the English SLT system, we use four functions. Three of them penalise particular linguistic phenomena; these are, respectively, bare singular noun phrases, subject-predicate disagreements with copular "be", and high attachments of modifiers to VPs. The fourth returns the acoustic cost of the analysis, defined as the maximum acoustic cost (i.e., shortfall from the score of the acoustically top sentence hypothesis provided by DECIPHER^{TM}) of any word in the lattice used to make it up.

One is then faced with the problem of integrating their results into the overall scheme: how can a score returned by a function be compared with the probability estimate provided by a single discriminant?

Our basic technique is to treat the return of a particular value by a particular function as a discriminant like any other. Thus, for example, if the copula-disagreement function returns a count of one on thirty occasions, and this acts as a good discriminant once and a bad one twenty nine times, then the event of that function returning that value will receive a discriminant score (i.e., a correctness probability estimate calculated with Equation (4.2), quite distinct from the value of the function) of $\frac{34}{992}$, which is close to $\frac{1}{30}$, just as any other discriminant would for the same counts.

Two modifications are applied to this basic idea to increase the power of function-based discriminants. Both are based on the fact that for all the functions we use, larger counts should score worse, since the objects counted are signs that the QLF concerned should be dispreferred.

Table 4.2. *Discriminant counts for*
a numerical preference function

N	G	B
0	110	1
1	1	106
2	0	3
3	0	1

4.3.3.1 Sparseness

One problem is that of sparseness: for example, a copula-disagreement count of three or more is very rare, leading to a fairly weak probability estimate, simply because a sentence with as many as three copular verbs will seldom be encountered in training. For a given function F and value N, then, instead of using the counts for exactly the event $F(q) = N$ to estimate the likelihood of a QLF q with this F value being correct, we use the sums of the counts for $F(.) = M$, $N_1 \leq M \leq N_2 \leq N$, where N_1 and N_2 are chosen to minimise the value of the estimate. Thus, if we had the good and bad counts shown in Table 4.2, then for $N = 3$, setting N_1 to 1 and N_2 to 3 would give a revised $G = 1 + 0 + 0 = 1$, $B = 106 + 3 + 1 = 110$, which minimises the value of formula (4.2) over the allowed N_1 and N_2 values. Essentially we are using an *a fortiori* argument here: since larger counts are worse, the score for a larger count should be no higher than the score derived from any range of smaller counts.

4.3.3.2 Minimality

Sometimes, especially when a recogniser error occurs in all sentences in an N-best list, all QLFs exhibit at least one of the phenomena which a given function is intended to penalise. Intuitively, a QLF q for which $F(q) = 2$, say, is much more likely to be correct if there is no QLF q' for which $F(q') < 2$. If we mix together the good and bad counts for occurrences of $F(q) = 2$ from training sentences where 2 is the minimal value of F with those from sentences where it is not, we are likely to lose important information. This is important for all the linguistic numerical metrics; it does not so much affect the acoustic shortfall metric, for which there is always a word sequence (and usually one or more QLFs) with zero shortfall.

   We therefore separate minimal from nonminimal scores, so that the event of function F returning value N, where N is the minimal value of F over QLFs for the sentence in question, is treated as a completely different discriminant from F returning N where N is not minimal. When this is done, the minimal/nonminimal distinction often contributes more information than the numerical differences themselves; for example, the discriminant score for the copula-disagreement metric returning a nonminimal value of 1 is far closer to the score for it returning a nonminimal value of 2 than to that for it returning a minimal value of 1.

4.4   Choosing among Transferred QLFs

Transfer, like analysis, generally creates many outputs, and it is necessary to choose one as input to the generator. A complication, however, is that suboptimal choices made by transfer preferences can result in the most preferred target-language QLF being one that is not licensed by the target-language grammar. It is surprisingly difficult to avoid this problem, since the complex constraints needed to avoid generation of ungrammatical sentences can occasionally mean that a superficially plausible QLF fails to correspond to any surface string at all. The generator may, in other words, fail on any single QLF offered to it, and it is therefore desirable for the transfer preference process to return a number (say, half a dozen) of results in order, with the generator being applied to each in turn until a string is generated.

With one important caveat, the same algorithm can be used for selecting a transfer output (or ordered sequence thereof) as is used for selecting an analysis. The caveat is that the QLFs output by transfer are packed; the transfer process may produce a dozen or so packed QLFs, which if unpacked would sometimes lead to thousands of alternatives. It would be extremely inefficient to unpack all these alternatives and hand them separately to the preference process.

Fortunately, preferences can be applied to packed structures, with only the small number of winners needing to be unpacked. This is done as follows. Each discriminant is associated with a *choice descriptor*, a structure that indicates which unpackings it applies to. A choice descriptor is a disjunction of *choice expressions*, each of which specifies a choice of a single packed QLF and a way to (partially) unpack it: that is, the selections that must be made for each disjunction (packing) inside the QLF.

For example, the packed QLF created when translating "flights on Monday" into French is, in slightly simplified form,

```
term(/|\[def_plur, indef_plural, bare_plur], X,
    [and,
        [vol1,X],
        [/|\[temporal_np, sur1, pour1, avec1], X,
        term(/|\[def_sing, bare_sing], Y,
            [lundi1,Y])]])
```

(see also Section 1.5). It has three disjunctions within it, one for the choice of determiner on *"vol"* ("flight"), one for the choice of preposition, and one for the determiner on *"lundi"* ("Monday"). Different combinations of choices would lead to translations such as *"vols sur lundi"*, *"des vols avec le lundi"*, and so forth. The triple vol + avec + lundi would apply to all unpackings where the choice of preposition (choice point 2) was *"avec"*, regardless of the choices made at points 1 and 3. Thus, if this packed QLF were number 6, the choice descriptor for the triple would be equivalent[5] to:

```
((PackedQLF= ...) \/ ...
 (PackedQLF=6 /\ Choice1=_
              /\ Choice2=#4 /\ Choice3=_) \/ ...
 (PackedQLF= ...))
```

As discriminants are processed, the preference mechanism maintains not a list of surviving QLFs, but an increasingly specific choice descriptor. When this descriptor identifies a single unpacked QLF (i.e., it specifies a single packed QLF and a single value for each choice within it) the descriptor is returned as a result. As for the analysis case, an ordered list of such descriptors can be created by branching at (some) discriminants rather than following a single path. These fully resolved descriptors can then easily be applied to packed QLFs to extract the winning unpacked ones, to which generation is applied. In our example, the winning descriptor, corresponding to the translation *"les vols le lundi"*, would be equivalent to:

```
((PackedQLF=6 /\ Choice1=#1
              /\ Choice2=#1 /\ Choice3=#1))
```

Finally, it should be noted that this scheme only works efficiently for the strongest-first preference algorithm; it is not at all obvious how a scheme based on adding together discriminant scores could be applied without exhaustive unpacking.

4.5   Choosing Paths in the Chart

The discussion so far has implicitly assumed that the choice to be made, at both the analysis and the transfer preference stages, is among full interpretations. Often, however, what is needed is to choose the optimal path through the chart: that is, the best sequence of analyses (or translations) of fragments of the utterance.

Ideally, we would like to train these choices just as we do the ones for full interpretations. That is, we would like to get a human judge to select sequences of fragments for training sentences. However, it is frequently unclear what is the best sequence of analysis fragments when no complete and correct one exists; and on the target side, it is hard to identify the best multiple-fragment translation (given that it will be imperfect) when, as explained in Section 4.4, there are often far too many possible translations for them all to be inspected.

---

[5] In fact, we use Boolean vectors (Mellish 1988) for the ChoiceN values.

For historical and practical reasons, we use slightly different path choice algorithms on the source and target sides. Both, however, make the following assumption: that when there are several competing fragment sequences, one involving the fewest possible fragments (and therefore, on average, longer fragments) is very likely to be best, because it is closer to a complete analysis. Both seem to work well in practice, although we have not compared them quantitatively with any alternatives.

On the source side, we consider *only* sequences with minimal numbers of fragments. We apply a variant of the usual discriminant algorithm (see Section 4.1) to the competing sequences, taking the discriminant set for a sequence as the union of the discriminants in its component fragments. The variation is that it turns out to be possible to apply the algorithm without expanding out all the sequences explicitly, which could lead to a combinatorial explosion. Instead, we apply negative discriminants to rule out fragments, and positive ones to rule out competitors to fragments, checking on each application that the connectivity of the chart would not be broken by doing so. Eventually, we are left with a single connected path. This algorithm can therefore be viewed as a kind of hybrid between the pruning algorithm (see Section 4.2) and the preference algorithm (see Section 4.3).

On the target side, we use a dynamic programming algorithm to select the path with the minimal *sum* of fragment scores (i.e., this is an instance of a more conventional independence-assumption–based method, in contrast to the source-side algorithm, which makes our customary maximal-dependence assumption). The score of a fragment is defined as a simple function of the transfer phase that created it:

- Word-to-word translation fragments score 1.0.
- Phrasal stage QLF translations score 1.2.
- Full parsing stage QLF translations score 1.1.
- Identity translations (translating a source-language word as itself) score 3.0.

Identity translation is only intended as a last resort to fill holes in word-to-word transfer coverage, and for obvious reasons is heavily dispreferred. If we ignore this, we see that the other three alternatives have similar scores: the intention is that the algorithm first minimises the number of fragments, and then applies secondary preferences among the different transfer phases.

Initially, we assumed that later phases, involving deeper linguistic processing, would generally produce better results, so we gave word-to-word translations a higher (i.e., worse) score than either type of QLF-based translation. However, it soon became clear that when word-to-word and QLF-based translations were competing in paths *of the same length*, the former in fact tended to be better: since the word-to-word rule exactly matches the phrase, it can be chosen to optimise the probability of correctness in the given domain. For example, if a fragment consists of a single noun phrase, its QLF representation will discard any possible case marking; so, general QLF-based translation is equally likely to translate the English "I" into the French "*je*", "*me*", or "*moi*". The word-to-word rule for "I", however, can simply be hand coded to the most likely choice, namely "*je*".

5   The TreeBanker

DAVID CARTER

T HIS CHAPTER DESCRIBES THE TREEBANKER, a graphical tool and database management system for the supervised training involved in domain customisation of the CLE. The TreeBanker presents a user, who need not be a system expert, with a range of properties (discriminants) that distinguish competing analyses for an utterance. These properties are relatively easy for a user to judge. Thus, training on a corpus can be completed in far less time, and with far less expertise, than would be needed if analyses were inspected directly. We also describe how the TreeBanker supports the detection and correction of any wrong judgments that may have led to run-time errors, thus supporting more accurate customisation.

In this chapter, most of the emphasis will be on the training of discriminants for choosing among the QLF outputs of analysis. However, the same methods, and much of the same code, also support transfer choice, fragment path choice, constituent pruning, and grammar specialisation.

5.1   Motivation

As we have seen, in a speech-understanding system such as SLT, where full, linguistically motivated analyses of the speaker's utterances are desired, the linguistic analyser needs to generate possible semantic representations and then choose the one most likely to be correct. Even when the recogniser that provides the analyser with its input is able to deliver a unique string with reasonable confidence, the analyser faces the problems of disambiguation that are familiar from text processing. However, the recogniser usually has to produce multiple possible word sequences because the relatively simple language models (typically N-gram based) that are efficient enough to be included in its search process are not rich enough to encode the syntactic, semantic, and, perhaps, pragmatic constraints needed for full word-sequence identification (Rayner et al. 1994).

Therefore, if an utterance is to be correctly interpreted, the analyser needs to create the correct analysis of the correct word string, and to pick that analysis out from any others that are created along with it (see Section 4.3). Because the word-identity problem means the search space will in general be larger than for the text processing case, it is especially important that, where possible, incorrect search paths should be pruned out (see Chapter 3 and Section 4.2) early on.

In practice, we can only come near to satisfying these requirements if the analyser is trained on a corpus of utterances from the same source (domain, task, and language) as those it is intended to process. Since this needs to be done afresh for each new source, economic considerations mean it is highly desirable to do it as automatically as possible. Furthermore, those aspects that cannot be automated should, as far as possible, not depend on the attention of experts in the system and the representations it uses.

The TreeBanker facilitates supervised training by interacting with a nonexpert user. It collates the results of this training to provide the CLE with data in an appropriate format. As we saw in Chapters 3 and 4, the CLE uses this data to analyse speech-recogniser output efficiently and to choose accurately among the interpretations it creates. We assume here that the coverage problem has been solved to the extent that the system's grammar and lexicon license the correct analyses of utterances often enough for practical usefulness (Rayner, Bouillon, and Carter 1995).

5.2   Representational Issues

The QLFs output by the CLE's analyser are designed to be appropriate for the inference or other processing that follows analysis in whatever application the CLE is being used for. However, they are not easy for humans to work with directly in supervised training and some way is needed to characterise the salient differences between plausible and implausible analyses because, of course, we cannot expect to encounter exactly the same QLFs at run time as during training. Both the CLE's preference mechanism and the TreeBanker therefore treat a QLF as completely characterised by certain of its properties that are easy for humans to work with and/or are likely to be repeatedly encountered at run time. The properties used for analysis choice are described in detail in Section 5.4; we have already seen their constituent pruning counterparts in Section 4.2.1.

The TreeBanker presents instances of many kinds of property to the user during training. However, its functionality in no way depends on the specific nature of QLF, and in fact its first action in the training process is to extract properties from QLFs and their associated parse trees, and then never again to process the QLFs directly. The database of analysed sentences that it maintains contains only these properties and not the analyses themselves. It would therefore be straightforward to adapt the TreeBanker to any system or formalism from which properties could be derived that both distinguished competing analyses and could be presented to a nonexpert user in a comprehensible way. Many mainstream systems and formalisms would satisfy these criteria, including ones such as the University of Pennsylvania

Treebank (Marcus, Santorini, and Marcinkiewicz 1993), which are purely syntactic (though of course, only syntactic properties could then be extracted). Thus, although we will ground this discussion of the TreeBanker in its use in adapting the CLE system to the ATIS domain, the work described is of much more general application.

5.3   Overview of the TreeBanker

The TreeBanker is a program for the kind of supervised training that is required to allow the CLE to distinguish correct from incorrect analyses and, as far as possible, to prune out paths likely to be incorrect. The examples we give here are all for English, but the TreeBanker has also successfully been used for the Swedish and French versions of the CLE. The TreeBanker takes as input the following information for each of the (typically) several thousand utterances in a corpus:

- the *reference* version of the utterance: the word string transcribed from the input speech by a human listener
- the *recogniser output* for the utterance: the lattice or (in our case) N-best list produced by the recogniser
- the *properties* applying to the sets of QLFs produced by the analyser both for the reference version of the utterance and for the recogniser output

The TreeBanker carries out three functions. First, as we will see in Section 5.4, it interacts with a user to determine the correct analysis (if any) of each sentence. The user should be familiar with the language and domain to which the system is being adapted and with simple linguistic concepts, but need not be a system expert. Second, the TreeBanker derives from the user's judgments information about the characteristics of correct and incorrect analyses, and packages it in a form that the analyser can use to select correct analyses and, when possible, prune out paths leading to incorrect ones; this process was described in Section 4.3. Third, as described in Chapter 3, it creates a library of verified analyses which are used to train the specialised grammar needed for fast parsing. We conclude with a discussion of the TreeBanker's use in the SLT system, and the degree to which our goals have been achieved.

5.4   The Supervised Training Process

Even for an expert, inspecting all the analyses produced for a sentence is a tedious and time-consuming task. There may be dozens of analyses that are variations on a small number of largely independent themes: choices of word sense, modifier attachment, conjunction scope, and so on. Further, if the representation language is designed with semantic and computational considerations in mind, there is no reason why it should be easy to read even for someone who fully understands it. And in fact, as already argued, it is preferable that selection of the correct analysis not require the involvement of an expert at all. (In practice, at the current state of development, some decisions needed by the TreeBanker are tricky enough that they have to be left for an expert to make them, but these occur in only a very small minority of sentences.)

5.4.1 Properties and Discriminants in Training

We therefore have taken the approach of defining a number of different types of properties that, in most cases, can be presented to nonexpert users in a form they can easily understand. In Section 4.2.1 we defined those properties that hold for some analyses of a particular utterance but not for others as *discriminants*. Discriminants that fairly consistently hold for correct but not (some) incorrect analyses, or vice versa, are likely to be useful in distinguishing correct from incorrect analyses at run time. Thus, for training on an utterance to be effective, we need to provide enough user-friendly discriminants to allow the user to select the correct analyses, and as many as possible system-friendly discriminants that, over the corpus as a whole, distinguish reliably between correct and incorrect analyses. Ideally, a discriminant will be both user friendly and system friendly, but this is not essential.

The TreeBanker derives properties directly from the QLFs produced by the CLE and from their associated parse trees. The database of analysed sentences that it maintains contains only these properties and not the analyses themselves. The TreeBanker presents discriminants (and, optionally, other properties) to the user in a convenient graphical form, exemplified in Figure 5.1 for the sentence "Show me the flights to Boston serving a meal". The user may click on any discriminant with the left mouse button to select it as correct, or with the right button to select it as incorrect. The types of property currently extracted, ordered approximately from most to least user friendly, are as follows; examples are taken from the six QLFs for the sentence used in Figure 5.1.

- *Constituents*: ADVP for "serving a meal" (a discriminant, holding only for readings that could be paraphrased "show me the flights to Boston while you're serving a meal"); VP for "serving a meal" (holds for all readings, so not a discriminant, and not displayed in the figure).
- *Semantic triples*: relations between word senses mediated usually by an argument position, preposition, or conjunction (see Section 2.3.4). Examples here (abstracting from senses to root word forms, which is how they are presented to the user) are "flight to Boston" and "show -to Boston" (the "-" indicates that the attachment is not a low one, i.e., that it is not

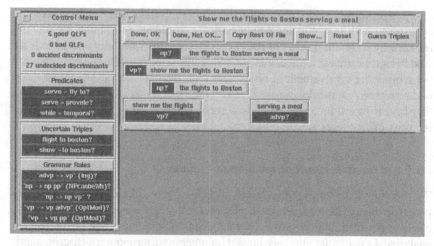

Figure 5.1. Initial TreeBanker display for "Show me the flights to Boston serving a meal".

attached to the closest possible head; this significantly affects the likelihood of such discriminants being correct). Argument-position relations are less user friendly and so are not displayed.

- *Predicates* or word senses: "serve" in the sense of "fly to" ("does United serve Dallas?") or "provide" ("does that flight serve meals?").
- *Sentence type*: imperative sentence in this case (other moods are possible; fragmentary sentences are displayed as "elliptical NP", etc.).
- *Grammar rules used*: the rule name is given. This is occasionally useful for experts in the minority of cases where their intervention is required.
- *Numerical metric values*: values of certain metrics applied to the code (see Section 4.3.3). These are not user friendly at all, and are not displayed, but are often reliable enough for run-time use.

Two additional types of discriminant are not shown to the user but are used at run time for pruning rather than for QLF preferences; they are bigrams and treegrams, as described earlier in Section 4.2.1.

In all, twenty seven discriminants are created for our example sentence, of which fifteen are user friendly enough to display, and a further twenty eight nondiscriminant properties may be inspected if desired. This is far more than the three distinct differences between the analyses ("serve" as "fly to" or "provide"; "to Boston" attaching to "show" or "flights"; and, if "to Boston" does attach to "flights", a choice between "serving a meal" as a nominal or an adverbial modifier). The effect of this is that the user can give attention to whatever discriminants he finds it easiest to judge; other, harder ones will typically be resolved automatically by the TreeBanker as it reasons about what combinations of discriminants apply to which analyses. The first rule the TreeBanker uses in this reasoning process to propagate decisions is:

R1 If an analysis (represented as a set of discriminants) has a discriminant that the user has marked as bad, then the analysis must be incorrect.

This rule is true by definition. The other rules used depend on the assumption that there is exactly one correct analysis among those that have been found, which of course is not true for all sentences; see Section 5.4.2 for the ramifications of this.

R2 If a discriminant is marked as good, then only analyses of which it is true can be correct (since there is at most one correct analysis).

R3 If a discriminant is true only of bad analyses, then it is bad (since there is at least one correct analysis).

R4 If a discriminant is true of all the undecided analyses, then it is good (since it must be true of the correct one, whichever it is).

Thus, if the user selects "the flights to Boston serving a meal" as an NP, the TreeBanker uses these four rules to resolve *all* the other discriminants except the two for the sense of "serve"; and only those two remain highlighted in the display, as shown in Figure 5.2 So, for example, there is no need for the user to make the trickier decision about whether or not "serving a meal" is an adverbial phrase.

The TreeBanker's propagation rules often act like this to simplify the judging of sentences whose discriminants combine to produce an otherwise unmanageably large number of QLFs. As an example of this, the sentence "What is the earliest

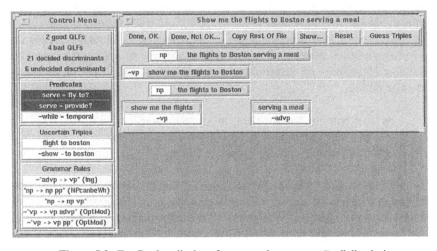

Figure 5.2. TreeBanker display after approving topmost "np" discriminant.

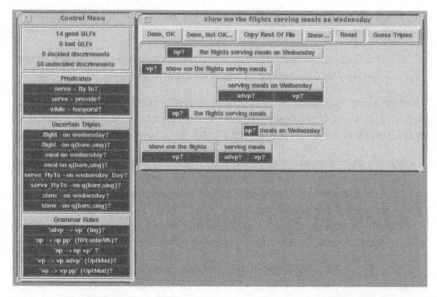

Figure 5.3. Initial TreeBanker display for "Show me the flights serving meals on Wednesday".

flight that has no stops from Washington to San Francisco on Friday?" yields 154 QLFs and 318 discriminants, yet the correct analysis may be obtained with only two selections. Selecting "the earliest flight . . . on Friday" as an NP eliminates all but 20 of the analyses produced, and approving "that has no stops" as a relative clause eliminates 18 of these, leaving 2 analyses which are both correct for the purposes of translation. Thus, 152 incorrect analyses may be dismissed in less than fifteen seconds.

The utterance "Show me the flights serving meals on Wednesday" (see Figure 5.3) further demonstrates the TreeBanker's facility for presenting the user with multiple alternatives for determining correct analyses. The following decisions must be made:

- Does "serving" mean "flying to" or "providing"?
- Does "on Wednesday" modify "show", "flights", "serving", or "meals"?
- Does "serving" modify "show" or "flights"?

but this can be done by approving and rejecting various constituents such as "the flights serving meals" and "meals on Wednesday", or through the selection of triples such as "flight -on Wednesday". Whichever method is utilised, the user can again resolve the fourteen QLFs produced for this sentence within a few seconds.

5.4.2   *Additional Functionality*

Although primarily intended for the disambiguation of corpus sentences that are within coverage, the interactive part of the TreeBanker also supports the diagnosis and categorisation of coverage failures. The user may suspect that *none* of the provided analyses is correct, so that rules R2 through R4 do not hold. This situation often becomes apparent when the TreeBanker insists on automatically assigning incorrect values to some discriminants when the user makes decisions on others; the coverage failure may be confirmed, if the user is relatively accomplished, by inspecting the nondiscriminant constituent properties as well and verifying that the correct parse tree is not among those offered (when all constituent properties are viewed, what is seen is effectively a parse forest). Then the user may mark the analyses of the sentence as "Not OK" and classify it under one of a number of failure types, optionally typing a comment as well. At a later stage, a system expert may ask the TreeBanker to print out all the coverage failures of a given type as an aid to organising work on grammar and lexicon development.

For some long sentences with many different readings, more discriminants may be displayed than will fit onto the screen at one time. In this case, the user may judge some discriminants (scrolling if necessary to find them), and ask the TreeBanker thereafter to display only *undecided* discriminants; these will rapidly reduce in number as decisions are made, and can quite soon all be viewed at once.

If the user changes his or her mind about a discriminant, he or she can click on it again, and the TreeBanker will take later judgments as superceding earlier ones, inferring other changes on that basis. Alternatively, the "Reset" button may be pressed to undo all judgments for the current sentence.

It has proved most convenient to organise the corpus into files that each contain data for a few dozen sentences; this is enough to represent a good-sized corpus in a few hundred files, but not so big that the user is likely to want to finish his or her session in the middle of a file – though even if he or she does so, by selecting "Copy Rest of File", all work on that file will be preserved.

Once part of the corpus has been judged and the information extracted for run-time use (see Chapter 4), the TreeBanker may be told to resolve discriminants automatically when their values can safely be inferred (i.e., when existing judgments give them a sufficiently strong score). In the ATIS domain, "show -to (city)" is a triple that is practically never correct; the user can then be presented with an initial screen in which that choice, and others resulting from it, are already made. This speeds up his or her work, and may in fact mean that some sentences do not need to be presented at all.

In practice, coverage development tends to overlap somewhat with the judging of a corpus. In view of this, the TreeBanker includes a "merge" option which allows existing judgments applying to an old set of analyses of a sentence to be transferred to a new set that reflects a coverage change. Properties tend to be preserved much better than analyses as coverage changes; only properties, and not analyses, are kept in the corpus database, and so the vast bulk of the judgments made by the user can be preserved.

The TreeBanker can also interact directly with the CLE's analysis component to allow a user or developer to type sentences to the system, see what discriminants they produce, and select one analysis for further processing. This configuration can be used in a number of ways. Newcomers can use it to familiarise themselves with the system's grammar. More generally, beginning students of grammar can use it to develop some understanding of what grammatical analysis involves. It is also possible to use this mode during grammar development as an aid to visualising the effect of particular changes to the grammar on particular sentences.

5.5   Training for Transfer Choice

Preference training for the transfer component of SLT is fundamentally similar to training the analysis component, but presents some additional problems.

As for analysis, the goal is to present the user with enough information to allow him or her to select the correct QLF. At first glance, there might seem to be a straightforward solution: just generate a translation from each QLF output by transfer, and ask the user to indicate the best translation. However, this algorithm is inadequate because, as we saw in Section 4.4, there may be several dozen packed QLFs produced by transfer, representing perhaps tens of thousands of unpacked ones. Both user and machine would be overloaded by the need to handle tens of thousands of candidate translations.

On the other hand, it will be necessary to generate some of these translations to guide the user to a sensible choice of QLF; the proof of the pudding is in the eating, in that a selected QLF is correct if and only if it generates an acceptable translation. The TreeBanker therefore adopts the following approach.

It is possible to extract predicates and semantic triples from the QLFs without unpacking them, and the transfer rules used to create the QLFs can also be recorded. These are therefore presented to the user just as triples and grammar rule names are presented during analysis judging. However, the syntactic constituents that play an important rule in analysis judging are not available, as they could only be created by (exhaustive) generation on the unpacked QLFs.

The TreeBanker also runs the preference algorithm described in Section 4.4 to select a small number (currently five) of unpacked QLFs that seem best on the basis of any existing preference data. A limited amount of such data may have been hand coded, or may have resulted from earlier training runs; if no such data exists the choice will be arbitrary. The generator is applied to these winning QLFs, and any results produced are presented to the user as discriminants.

In the simplest case, the user selects one of these translations as correct; this will identify a single QLF as correct,[1] and all discriminants will be resolved. However, more often, it will be apparent that all the translations offered make some wrong choice(s). In this case, the user should be able to mark some triple or predicate not involved in any of these translations as in fact correct. A "Generate" button is provided which will cause the system to select an unpacked QLF from among those still licensed by the choices made so far and to generate from it. Although the resulting translation may not be completely right, it will at least involve the triple or predicate the user has selected, and in that sense will be a step in the right direction. In this way it is possible to iterate towards a translation of the best QLF available.

For example, at one point in development, the only English translation initially offered for the Swedish sentence

> *Visa avgångar med United Airlines*
> (Show departures on United Airlines)

was "Show departures with United"; the preposition "with" is at best rather unnatural. However, the triple `"departure on united_airlines"` was among those offered. When this was approved, the alternative triple `"departure with united_airlines"` was ruled out. Hitting the "Generate" button at this point resulted in the rather better translation "Show departures on United."

If the best translation achievable by iterating between judgment and generation in this way is acceptable, the user marks it as such, and all discriminants are resolved, just as if the translation had been present when the sentence was first presented. However, it may be unacceptable in a way that is clear to the user; for example, no adequate translation may be offered of one of the source words, because a lexical transfer rule is missing. An example of this is:

> *Vid vilken tid mellanlandar flight tre fyrtiotre i Denver?*
> (What time does flight three forty three stop in Denver?)

The translations offered were:

> By which time does flight three forty three stop in Denver?
> At which time does flight three forty three stop in Denver?

The user was able to determine that the second translation was the best available through iteration. However, "which" ought to be replaced by "what"; and "at", while certainly better than "by", is perhaps too formal and should be dropped altogether.

---

[1] If the same translation was produced from several QLFs, some uncertainty will remain; but by definition, the remaining choices involved are unimportant, since they cannot affect the translation.

In such cases, the user can select the relevant problem type(s) from a menu, extending the menu if this problem has not been encountered before, and approve the translation subject to this rider. The translation will then be used in the calculation of preference scores – it is, after all, the best that can be done with the current rule set.

After a few hundred sentences have been judged, a set of problems, each with one or more associated sentences, will have been collected, and system developers may then go to work in writing additional transfer rules (and, sometimes, target-language grammar rules). If the TreeBanker then redoes the transfer step, a wider range of transfer outputs, which we hope includes a correct one, will be produced. For our "which time" example, a rule translating between "vilken" and "what", which existed, but had incorrectly been made to apply only in the English-to-Swedish direction, was made bidirectional, so that QLFs supporting translations involving "what time" were also produced.

The system offers a facility to merge the extended QLF set with the old judgments: QLFs identified as wrong when first judged will have that status preserved, but if one or more problems were flagged for a sentence, the system will remain agnostic on the relative merits of new QLFs and the one originally judged optimal. The upshot of this is that if another judgment run is carried out, the user will see the same sentence again with most of the discriminants already decided, but some, corresponding to the new material and the earlier winner, still uncertain. In our example, the user had to mark a translation involving "what time" as preferable to any involving "which time", but the system retained the negative judgment on the use of "by". Thus, earlier work is preserved through the change of rule set, while still allowing the selection of the best translation to be altered as new options become available.

5.6   Evaluation and Conclusions

Using the TreeBanker it is possible for a linguistically aware nonexpert to judge around 40 sentences per hour after a few days of practice. When the user becomes more practised, as will be the case if he or she judges a corpus of thousands of sentences, this figure rises to around 170 sentences per hour in the case of our most experienced user. Thus, it is reasonable to expect a corpus of 20 000 sentences to be judged in three or four person-weeks. A much smaller amount of time needs to be spent by experts in making judgments the user felt unable to make (perhaps for 1 percent of sentences once the user is familiar with the system) and in checking his or her work. (The TreeBanker includes a facility for picking out sentences where errors are mostly likely to have been made, by searching for discriminants with unusual values.) From these figures it would seem that the TreeBanker provides a much quicker and less skill-intensive way to arrive at a disambiguated set of analyses for a corpus than the manual annotation scheme involved in creating the University of Pennsylvania Treebank; however, the TreeBanker method depends on the prior existence of a grammar for the domain in question, which is of course a nontrivial requirement.

Engelson and Dagan (1996) present a supervised training scheme for selecting corpus sentences whose judging is likely to provide useful new information, rather than those that merely repeat old patterns. The TreeBanker offers a related facility whereby judgments on one sentence may be propagated to others having the same sequence of parts of speech. This can be combined with the use of *representative corpora* in the CLE (see Section 8.6) to allow only one representative of a particular pattern, out of perhaps dozens in the corpus as a whole, to be inspected. This, together with the preresolution of strong discriminants alluded to above, already significantly reduces the number of sentences needing to be judged and hence the time required, and we expect further reductions as Engelson and Dagan's ideas are applied at a finer level.

6   Acquisition of Lexical Entries

IAN LEWIN

O NE important aspect of porting the CLE to a new domain is to ensure that the lexical coverage is adequate: that words likely to be used are included in the system's lexicon, and that the right senses of those words are specified. We approach this lexical acquisition task by working with a corpus: determining which words need to be added to the existing lexicon to achieve reasonable coverage of it, and then providing, in a machine-understandable format, descriptions of the surface forms, morphology, syntax, and semantics of those words.

Unaided, this can be a highly time-consuming and error-prone task. It can be time consuming simply on account of the sheer volume of work. The task involves examining the corpus occurrences of many words, and then coding complex machine-understandable lexical entries to represent them. This can also require the use of linguistic and system-specific expertise; although such expertise may be exercised only infrequently, as most words to be added to a lexicon will be new instances of commonly occurring known word types.

In order to help automate and de-skill this task we have developed a set of procedures for lexical acquisition, which are tailorable both for different languages and for different levels of linguistic expertise.

6.1   The Lexical Acquisition Tool, LexMake

The lexical acquisition tool, LexMake, is strongly corpus based, although interactive parts can be used without a corpus. Lexical development can be spread over several sessions and carried out by several different users; we refer to these users as *trainers* to distinguish their role from that of end users of the SLT system.

First, a new corpus is searched for occurrences of words not currently in the lexicon. The search uses a simple string equality test and attempts no morphological analysis. Unknown words, ordered by frequency of occurrence, are automatically extracted and a file of dummy lexical entries in CLE format is generated. In this file, each dummy entry is associated with the corpus sentences in which it occurs, up to some predefined limit.

The dummy entries must then be converted into real entries. A graphical user interface is provided for this task. For each entry, the trainer sees the word he or she is currently defining, its occurrences in the corpus, and a structured menu of the different choices that he or she is required to make. The choices themselves are presented in a linguistically motivated format and abstract away from the details of any underlying data structures. Apart from linguistically categorising the entry, the trainer may also annotate it in various ways. Entries can be marked as "Save for Later" and "Alert Expert" to encourage trainers not to spend too much of their time worrying over cases that might require extra thought or advice. There is a search menu for lexical entries that includes options to allow a trainer (e.g., an expert reviewer) to find any such specially marked entries easily. Arbitrary notes can also be added to lexical entries. LexMake can be run quite independently of development and run-time images of the translation software but it is also possible to allow it to communicate with a development image, if one is available. In this case, trainers can also submit their proposed lexical entries to the development image which will generate back all the possible inflections for the word, given its categorisation. Also, arbitrary text can be submitted for parsing by the development image. In particular, it is thereby easy to test whether the current corpus examples shown for a word can be parsed or not given the current lexical definition.

Figure 6.1 illustrates what the trainer sees during the definition of the lexical entry for the Swedish word *"hotell"* ("hotel"). At the very top of the screen are generic process and file manipulation commands, giving the ability to quit, save a file, step forwards and backwards through a file, delete an entry, and so on. Below that are data associated with *"hotellet"* ("the hotel"). First, five examples from the corpus in which *"hotellet"* appears are shown in a scrollable window. Second, the middle of the screen shows the word's main properties: its stem is currently shown as *"hotellet"* and its category and sense are both currently unknown. (An unknown sense is marked as XXX). Since the category is unknown, no category-dependent features (declension, conjugation, etc.) are displayed. The trainer's task is to fill in the information required.

First, the trainer must define the correct word stem – in this case *"hotell"*. (The stems of Swedish nouns are their singular indefinite form, this information being made available in the help menu, whose contents are also parameterisable for different languages and trainers.) By clicking on the current category "unknown", a tree-structured menu of alternative choices such as "count:noun" and "reflexive transitive verb" is posted and can be selected from. On selecting "count:noun", default modifiable values for the features declension, gender, and infix are enabled. This is illustrated in Figure 6.2.

These features are the only ones valid for the count:noun category. Again, clicking on the currently displayed value will bring up a menu of alternatives.

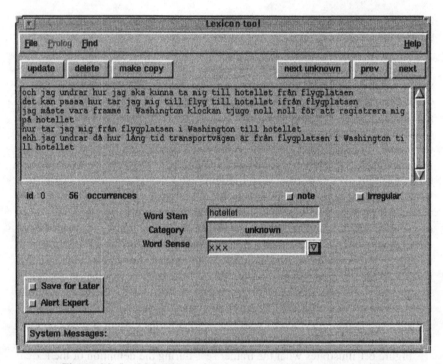

Figure 6.1. LexMake display for *"hotellet"* before any trainer modifications are made.

In this instance, the trainer needs to alter the default declension value (which is "-or (blomma)") to "-ø (hus)"[1] and the default gender ("common") to "neuter". Finally the trainer needs to add a sense or predicate name for (this meaning of) *"hotell"*. In the CLE, a predicate name is conventionally the word itself followed by an underscore and then a paraphrase. The trainer may either add a paraphrase of his or her own, such as *"Härbärge"* ("place one can stay"), or select from a predetermined list of semantic class names (the very same ones used for preference functions and pruning; see Section 4.2.1). This list can be posted by clicking on the small arrowhead shown to the right of "Word Sense". The trainer may also add a note, that is, some arbitrary comment, by clicking on the "note" flag, enter a dialogue for adding entries for irregular forms by clicking on the "irregular" flag, or mark the entry as "Save for Later" or "Alert Expert". Once the trainer is happy with his or her entry, he or she may move onto the next word in the lexicon file by selecting "next" from the top of the screen.

---

[1] This information specifies the relevant plural ending: the plural form of *"hotell"* is the same as the singular (like *"hus"*), as opposed, for example, to ending in *"-or"*, like *"blomma"*.

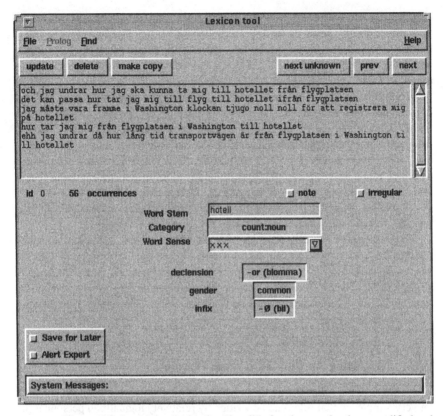

Figure 6.2. LexMake display for *"hotell"* after the stem has been modified and the correct category selected.

The graphical interface is not intended to be used for all lexical entries. Only those describable in terms of *paradigms* – commonly occurring patterns of categories, features, and values representing word classes such as count nouns and transitive verbs – are suitable (see Carter 1987 for the original motivation). Such words form the vast majority of cases in adaptation to a new corpus. The set of available paradigms constitutes one parameter to the graphical interface.

The same interface is usable and reconfigurable for lexica in different languages or for trainers with different levels of expertise in formal linguistics. In either case, the same processing is used – all that differs is the language description that is processed. We have found that it is useful to tailor the tool for trainers with different levels of linguistic expertise. Users may be confident in their ability to handle simple count nouns and proper nouns, for example, but lack confidence in their ability to identify the complex subcategorisation properties of certain kinds of verbs. Rather than have them attempt an unreliable categorisation, it is more efficient if such entries are marked "Alert Expert" and left uncategorised. It has also proved useful simply to be able to modify the prompt messages for the entry fields for particular trainers so that they can easily remind themselves, in terms they understand, what a particular choice means or what distinction they are being asked to make.

Definition of the language description is an expert task because it requires knowledge of the structure of the lexicon for the language in question and in how the CLE encodes that structure. The description includes a hierarchy of lexical category names (and associated help strings describing them), a list of associated category features and their possible values (plus descriptive help strings) including a default value, a list of special characters allowed in lexical entries, and a list of commonly occurring patterns of irregularity.[2] When an irregular form is required, the trainer is prompted for it in a form that he can readily understand and the internal format (often some kind of stem) is derived automatically.

For example, in Swedish there are irregular adjectives that add an umlaut when forming the comparative and superlative forms. When such a word is entered into the lexicon, the trainer is prompted with the string "Enter the new comparative string (in the form: *"lägre"*)".[3] This encourages him or her to type something familiar, namely, the comparative form of the adjective. The comparative and superlative stems are derived automatically, in this case by deleting the terminal *"re"*.

6.2   Acquiring Word-to-Word Transfer Rules

The word-to-word transfer rule formalism (see Section 2.2) has been designed to be very simple, so that rules can be written by relatively unqualified personnel. In practice, it turns out that the process of coding the rules can be systematised to a high degree and turned into a mechanical form-filling task. In order to facilitate this, we take a similar approach to that applied for lexical acquisition. We tag a suitable domain corpus up to the lexical level, and collect a set of corpus examples for each word-tag pair. Then we generate a dummy or fill-in-the-blanks set of word-to-word rules, one for each word. Each rule has the left-hand-side pattern filled in with the word in question and the right-hand-side pattern empty. The transfer-rule writer then only needs to examine the corpus examples, decide on a translation of the current word appropriate for the given examples, and fill in the

---

[2] Of course, strictly speaking, irregularities by definition do not follow a pattern. By "irregularities" here, we mean forms that do not conform to the spelling rules (see Chapter 7) for the current language description. In this sense, a Swedish noun such as *"stad"* ("city") has an irregular plural form *"städer"*, and a verb such as *"springa"* ("run") has an irregular supine form *"sprungit"*, although in both cases there are other words in the language that follow similar patterns. In English, similar examples might be "mouse/mice" and "louse/lice".

[3] *"lägre"* ("lower") is the irregular comparative of *"låg"* ("low").

right-hand side. If more than one translation is feasible, multiple copies of the rule may be created, or distinguishing context added to the left-hand side. Again, rules may be marked as "Alert Expert" or "Save for Later" in order to help discourage rule writers from spending too much time on difficult cases.

Our experiences show that people with minimal knowledge of linguistics and no previous experience with the system are capable of writing word-to-word rules at the rate of many hundreds per day; for system experts, the figure can be in excess of 1 500 rules per day.

6.3   Evaluation and Conclusions

The LexMake tool enables a trainer to add new lexical entries to the system quickly through a friendly graphical interface. The interface is also designed for corpus-based development by showing corpus examples for each word to be added and naturally ordering the words to be added by their frequency of occurrence in the corpus. The tool reflects the general SLT philosophy of separating linguistic descriptions from computational processing. After an initial English version had been constructed and tested at SRI, a Swedish version was quickly and easily generated by SRI and Telia staff and successfully used for lexicon development at Telia.

Use of the graphical tool has also led us to reconsider some of our existing linguistic descriptions (e.g., verbs, as described in the preceding section). The previous use of a purely text-based feature-value declaration style had enabled some less linguistically natural descriptions to be developed. Representation in a graphical tool immediately highlighted the less intuitive features of the description.

A graphical tool for updating word-to-word translation rules also enables fast corpus-based development of a simple transfer component.

7   Spelling and Morphology

DAVID CARTER AND PIERRETTE BOUILLON

I N THIS CHAPTER, we describe the CLE's compiler and development environment for feature-augmented two-level morphology rules. This part of the CLE is used in the SLT system but the work involved was done for other projects; therefore, we consider here issues that arise in text processing. (From the point of view of morphological processing, speech processing is rather simpler, since the recogniser will be loaded with a vocabulary that is known in advance, so that we can precompute all morphological analyses that may be required; this is done in SLT for the more common words.)

The morphology compiler is optimised for a class of languages including many or most European ones, and for rapid development and debugging of descriptions of new languages. In contrast to the best-known compiler of this type (Karttunen, Kaplan, and Zaenen 1992), the key design decision is to compose morphophonological and morphosyntactic information, but not the lexicon, when compiling the description. This results in typical compilation times of about a minute, and has allowed a reasonably full, feature-based description of French inflectional morphology to be developed in about a month by a linguist new to the system.

7.1   Introduction

The paradigm of two-level morphology (Koskenniemi 1983) has become popular for handling word formation phenomena in a variety of languages. The original formulation has been extended to allow morphotactic constraints to be expressed by feature specification (Alshawi et al. 1991; Trost 1990) rather than by Koskenniemi's less perspicuous device of continuation classes. Methods for the automatic compilation of rules from a notation convenient for the rule writer into finite-state automata have also been developed, allowing the efficient analysis and synthesis of word forms. The automata may be derived from the rules alone (Trost 1990), or may involve composition with the lexicon (Karttunen et al. 1992).

However, there is often a tradeoff between run-time efficiency and factors important for rapid and accurate system development, such as perspicuity of notation, ease of debugging, speed of compilation and the size of its output, and independence of the morphological and lexical components. In compilation, one may compose any or all of

    (a) the two-level rule set,
    (b) the set of affixes and their allowed combinations, and
    (c) the lexicon.

(See Kaplan and Kay 1994 for an exposition of the mathematical basis.) The type of compilation appropriate for rapid development and acceptable run-time performance depends on, at least, the nature of the language being described and the number of base forms in the lexicon; that is, on the position in the three-dimensional space defined by (a), (b) and (c).

For example, English inflectional morphology is relatively simple; dimensions (a) and (b) are fairly small, so if (c), the lexicon, is known in advance and is of manageable size, then the entire task of morphological analysis can be carried out at compile time, producing a list of analysed word forms that need only be looked up at run time, or a network that can be traversed very simply. Alternatively, there may be no need to provide as powerful a mechanism as two-level morphology at all; a simpler device such as affix stripping (Alshawi 1992, 119ff.) or merely listing all inflected forms explicitly may be preferable.

For agglutinative languages such as Finnish, Korean, and Turkish (Koskenniemi 1983; Kwon and Karttunen 1994; Oflazer 1993), dimension (b) is very large, so creating an exhaustive word list is out of the question unless the lexicon is trivial. Compilation to a network may still make sense, however, and because these languages tend to exhibit few nonconcatenative morphophonological phenomena other than vowel harmony, the continuation class mechanism may suffice to describe the allowed affix sequences at the surface level.

Many European languages are of the inflecting type, and occupy still another region of the space of difficulty. They are too complex morphologically to yield easily to the simpler techniques that can work for English. The phonological or orthographic changes involved in affixation may be quite complex, so dimension (a) can be large, and a feature mechanism may be needed to handle such varied but interrelated morphosyntactic phenomena as umlaut (Trost 1991), case, number, gender, and different morphological paradigms. On the other hand, while there may be many different affixes, their possibilities for combination within a word are fairly limited, so dimension (b) is quite manageable.

This chapter describes a representation and associated compiler intended for two-level morphological descriptions of the written forms of inflecting languages. The CLE supports both a built-in lexicon and access to large external lexical databases, and in that context, highly efficient word analysis and generation at run time are less important than ensuring that the morphology mechanism is expressive, is easy to debug, and allows relatively quick compilation. Morphology also needs to be well integrated with other processing levels. In particular, it should be possible to specify relations among morphosyntactic and morphophonological rules and lexical entries; for the convenience of developers, this is done by means of feature equations. Further, it cannot be assumed that the lexicon has been fully specified when the morphology rules are compiled. Developers may wish to add and test further lexical entries without frequently recompiling the rules, and in text processing applications it may also be necessary to deal with unknown words at run time, for example, by querying a large external lexical database or attempting spelling correction (Alshawi 1992, 124–127). Also, both analysis and generation of word forms are required. Run-time speed need only be enough to make the time spent on morphology small compared to other processing phases.

These parameters – languages with a complex morphology/syntax interface but a limited number of affix combinations, tasks where the lexicon is not necessarily known at compile time, bidirectional processing, and the need to ease development rather than optimise run-time efficiency – dictate the design of the morphology compiler described in this chapter, in which spelling rules and possible affix combinations (items (a) and (b)), but not the lexicon (item (c)), are composed in the compilation phase. Descriptions of English, French, Swedish, Danish, Spanish, and (parts of) Polish and Korean inflectional morphology have been developed for the compiler, and we show how various aspects of the mechanism allow phenomena in some of these languages to be handled.

7.2   The Description Language

7.2.1   Morphophonology

The formalism for *spelling rules* (dimension (a)) is a syntactic variant of that of Ruessink (1989) and Pulman and Hepple (1993). A rule is of the form

> spell (*Name, Surface Op Lexical, Classes, Features*).

Rules may be optional (*Op* is "⇒") or obligatory (*Op* is "⇔"). *Surface* and *Lexical* are both strings of the form

> "*LContext | Target | RContext*"

meaning that the surface and lexical targets may correspond if the left and right contexts and the *Features* specification are satisfied. The vertical bars simply separate the parts of the string and do not themselves match letters. The correspondence

```
spell(change_e_è1, "|è|" ⇔ "|e|1+e",
      [1/tr1], [cdouble=n]).
spell(default, "|1|" ⇒ "|1|", [1/letter], []).
spell(boundary, "||" ⇒ "|1|", [1/bmarker],[]).
```

Figure 7.1. Three spelling rules.

Surface:	c	h	è	r		e	
Lexical:	c	h	e	r	+	e	+
Rule:	*def.*	*def.*	*c.e_è1*	*def.*	*bdy.*	*def.*	*bdy.*

Figure 7.2. Partitioning of *"chère"* as cher+e+.

between surface and lexical strings for an entire word is licensed if there is a partitioning of both so that each partition (pair of corresponding surface and lexical targets) is licensed by a rule, and no partition breaks an obligatory rule. A partition breaks an obligatory rule if the surface target does not match but everything else, including the feature specification, does.[1]

The *Features* in a rule is a list of *Feature* = *Value* equations. The allowed (finite) set of values of each feature must be prespecified. *Value* may be atomic or it may be a Boolean expression.

Members of the surface and lexical strings may be characters or classes of single characters. The latter are represented by a single digit N in the string and an item $N/ClassName$ in the *Classes* list; multiple occurrences of the same N in a single rule must all match the same character in a given application.

Spelling rules of the same format are also used in the CLE to handle interword effects, as will be described in Section 7.3.4.

As an example of the use of the formalism, Figure 7.1 shows three of the French spelling rules developed for this system. The change_e_è1 rule (simplified slightly here) makes it obligatory for a lexical "e" to be realised as a surface *"è"* when followed by t, r, or l (the 1 class), then a morpheme boundary (+), then e, as long as the feature cdouble has an appropriate value. The default rule that copies characters between surface and lexical levels and the boundary rule that deletes boundary markers are both optional. Together these rules permit the following realisation of *"cher"* ("expensive") followed by "e" (feminine gender suffix) as *"chère"*, as shown in Figure 7.2. An alternative realisation *"chere"*,

---

[1] The default rule, mapping a lexical character into the same surface character, and the boundary rule, mapping a morpheme boundary symbol into the empty string at surface level, are both optional rules. Other optional rules, which tend to be few in number, describe genuine free variation in spelling. For example, the "y" in French verbs such as *"payer"* can remain the same or change to "i" before silent "e": "pay+e" → either *"paye"* or *"paie"*.

involving the use of the default rule in third position, is ruled out because of the obligatory nature of change_e_èl, and the fact that the orthographic feature restriction on the root *"cher"*, [cdouble=n], is consistent with the one on that rule.[2]

Unlike many other flavours of two-level morphology, the *Target* parts of a rule need not consist of a single character (or class occurrence); they can contain more than one, and the surface target may be empty. This obviates the need for "null" characters at the surface. However, although surface targets of any length can usefully be specified, it is in practice a good strategy always to make lexical targets exactly one character long, because, by definition, an obligatory rule cannot block the application of another rule if their lexical targets are of different lengths. The example in Section 7.4.1 will clarify this point.

7.2.2   Word Formation and Interfacing to Syntax

As explained in Sections 2.4.2 and 2.4.3, the allowed sequences of morphemes, and the syntactic and semantic properties of morphemes and of the words derived by combining them, are specified by morphosyntactic production rules known as *morphology rules* (dimension (b)) and lexical entries both for affixes (dimension (b)) and for roots (dimension (c)). Affixes may appear explicitly in morphology rules or, like roots, they may be assigned complex feature-value categories. Information, including the creation of logical forms, is passed between constituents in a rule by the sharing of variables. These feature-augmented morphology rules are just the same device as those used in the CLE's syntacticosemantic descriptions, and are a much more natural way to express morphotactic information than finite-state devices such as continuation classes (see Trost and Matiasek 1994 for a related approach).

Irregular forms, either complete words or affixable stems, are specified by listing the morphology rules and terminal morphemes from which the appropriate analyses may be constructed, for example:

```
irreg(dit,[dire,'PRESENT_3s'],[v_v_affix]).
```

Here, PRESENT_3s is a pseudoaffix which has the same syntactic and semantic information attached to it as (one sense of) the affix "t", which is used to form some regular third person singulars. However, the spelling rules make no reference to PRESENT_3s; it is simply a device allowing categories and logical forms for irregular words to be built up using the same morphology rules as for regular words.

---

[2] The cdouble feature is in fact used to specify the spelling changes when "e" is added to various stems: cher+e=*"chère"*, achet+e=*"achète"*, but jet+e=*"jette"*.

7.3   Compilation

All rules and lexical entries in the CLE are compiled to a form that allows normal Prolog unification to be used for category matching at run time. The same compiled forms are used for analysis and generation, but are indexed differently. Each feature for a major category is assigned a unique position in the compiled Prolog term, and features for which finite value sets have been specified are compiled into vectors in a form that allows Boolean expressions, involving negation as well as conjunction and disjunction, to be conjoined by unification (see Mellish 1988; Alshawi 1992, 46–48).

The compilation of morphological information is motivated by the nature of the task and of the languages to be handled. As discussed in Section 7.1, we expect the number of affix combinations to be limited, but the lexicon is not necessarily known in advance. Morphophonological interactions may be quite complex, and the purpose of morphological processing is to derive syntactic and semantic analyses from words and vice versa for the purpose of full natural-language processing. Reasonably quick compilation is required, and run-time speed need only be moderate.

7.3.1   Compiling Spelling Patterns

Compilation of individual `spell` rules is straightforward; feature specifications are compiled to positional/Boolean format, characters and occurrences of character classes are also converted to Boolean vectors, and left contexts are reversed (cf. Abramson 1992) for efficiency. However, although it would be possible to analyse words directly with individually compiled rules (see Section 7.5), it can take an unacceptably long time to do so, largely because of the wide range of rule choices available at each point and the need to check at each stage that obligatory rules have not been broken. We therefore take the following approach.

First, all legal sequences of morphemes are produced by top-down nondeterministic application of the morphology rules (see Section 7.2.2), selecting affixes but keeping the root morpheme unspecified because, as explained earlier, the lexicon is undetermined at this stage. For example, for English, the sequences `*+ed+ly` and `un+*+ing` are among those produced, the asterisk representing the unspecified root.

Then, each sequence, together with any associated restrictions on orthographic features, undergoes analysis by the compiled spelling rules (see Section 7.2.1), with the surface sequence and the root part of the lexical sequence initially uninstantiated. Rules are applied recursively and nondeterministically, somewhat in the style of Abramson (1992), taking advantage of Prolog's unification mechanism to instantiate the part of the surface string corresponding to affixes and to place some spelling constraints on the start and/or end of the surface and/or lexical forms of the root.

This process results in a set of *spelling patterns*, one for each distinct application of the spelling rules to each affix sequence suggested by the morphology rules. A spelling pattern consists of partially specified surface and lexical root character sequences, fully specified surface and lexical affix sequences, orthographic feature constraints associated with the spelling rules and affixes used, and a pair of syntactic category specifications derived from the morphology rules used. One category is for the root form, and one for the inflected form.

Spelling patterns are indexed according to the surface (for analysis) and lexical (for generation) affix characters they involve. At run time, an inflected word is analysed nondeterministically in several stages, each of which may succeed any number of times including zero:

- stripping off possible (surface) affix characters in the word and locating a spelling pattern that they index;
- matching the remaining characters in the word against the surface part of the spelling pattern, thereby, through shared variables, instantiating the characters for the lexical part to provide a possible root spelling;
- checking any orthographic feature constraints on that root;
- finding a lexical entry for the root, by any of a range of mechanisms including lookup in the system's own lexicon, querying an external lexical database, or attempting to guess an entry for an undefined word; and
- unifying the root lexical entry with the root category in the spelling pattern, thereby, through variable sharing with the other category in the pattern, creating a fully specified category for the inflected form that can be used in parsing.

In generation, the process works in reverse, starting from indexes on the lexical affix characters.

7.3.2   *Representing Lexical Roots*

Complications arise in spelling-rule application from the fact that, at compile time, neither the lexical nor the surface form of the root, nor even its length, is known. It would be possible to hypothesise all sensible lengths and compile separate spelling patterns for each. However, this would lead to many more patterns being produced than are really necessary.

Lexical (and, after instantiation, surface) strings for the unspecified roots are therefore represented in a more complex but less redundant way: as a structure

$$L_1 \ldots L_m \text{ v} (L, R) \; R_1 \ldots R_n.$$

Here the L_is are variables later instantiated to single characters at the beginning of the root, and L is a variable, which is later instantiated to a list of characters,

Compile	Rule:	*def.**	*c.e_èl*	*def.*	*bdy.*	*def.*	*bdy.*
time:	Variable:	v(*L*, *R*)	R_1	R_2		...	
Run	Surface:	c	h	è	r		e	
time:	Lexical:	c	h	e	r	+	e	+

Figure 7.3. Spelling pattern application to the analysis of *"chère"*.

for its continuation. Similarly, the R_is represent the end of the root, and R is the continuation (this time reversed) leftwards into the root from R_1. The v(*L*, *R*) structure is always matched specially with a Kleene star of the default spelling rule. For full generality and minimal redundancy, L_m and R_1 are constrained not to match the default rule, but the other L_is and R_is may. The values of n required are those for which, for some spelling rule, there are k characters in the target lexical string and $n - k$ from the beginning of the right context up to (but not including) a boundary symbol. The lexical string of that rule may then match $R_1, \ldots, R_k$, and its right context match $R_{k+1}, \ldots, R_n, +, \ldots$. The required values of m may be calculated similarly with reference to the left contexts of rules.[3]

During rule compilation, the spelling pattern that leads to the run-time analysis of *"chère"* given in Section 7.2.1 is derived from $m = 0$ and $n = 2$ and the specified rule sequence, with the variables R_1 R_2 matching as in Figure 7.3.

7.3.3   Applying Obligatory Rules

In the absence of a lexical string for the root, the correct treatment of obligatory rules is another problem for compilation. If an obligatory rule specifies that lexical X must be realised as surface Y when certain contextual and feature conditions hold, then a partitioning where X is realised as something other than Y is only allowed if one or more of those conditions are unsatisfied. Because of the use of Boolean vectors for both features and characters, it is quite possible to constrain

---

[3] Alternations in the middle of a root, such as umlaut, could be handled by altering the root/affix pattern from $L_1 \ldots L_m$ v(*L*, *R*) $R_1 \ldots R_n$ to $L_1 \ldots L_m$ v(*L*, *R*) M v(*L'*, *R'*) $R_1 \ldots R_n$, with M forbidden to be the default rule. The implementation of this change would not be expected to lead to any great decrease in run-time performance, because the nondeterminism it induces in the lookup process is no different in kind from that arising from alternations at root-affix boundaries. However, it has not been found necessary for the CLE descriptions of Swedish and Danish, where umlaut does occur, because the existing mechanism allows similar umlaut rules to be specified separately for each of the small number of word-final patterns (VC, VCC and VCCC) for which umlaut can occur.

The current implementation has another limitation which, however, has no effect for any of the languages currently processed. It is that spelling changes resulting from prefixation are not handled. Such changes do not occur in the inflectional morphology of the languages we handle, at least in the ATIS domain.

each partitioning by unifying it with the complement of one of the conditions of each applicable obligatory rule, thereby preventing that rule from applying. For English, with its relatively simple inflectional spelling changes, this works well. However, for other languages, including French, it leads to excessive numbers of spelling patterns, because there are many obligatory rules with nontrivial contexts and feature specifications.

For this reason, complement unification is not actually carried out at compile time. Instead, the spelling patterns are augmented with the fact that certain conditions on certain obligatory rules need to be checked on certain parts of the partitioning when it is fully instantiated. This slows down run-time performance a little but, as we will see later, the speed is still quite acceptable.

7.3.4   *Interword Rules*

Interword rules, to handle phenomena such as the English "a/an" alternation and the French *"de le"* → *"du"*, are specified in the CLE in just the same way as intraword rules, except that no feature specifications are allowed. However, because the interactions among these rules tend to be relatively simple, and because whole sentences rather than individual words are being processed, the algorithms used to apply them are rather different. In analysis, the system applies the rules directly (rather than in compiled spelling-pattern form) to form possible "lexical"-level character sequences,[4] some of which it then rules out by considering obligatory rules. In generation, because only one solution is typically required, a simple depth-first search is made for a full mapping from the lexical character sequence to the surface, with obligatory rules being applied before optional ones. In practise, this always completes in a negligible time.

7.3.5   *Timings*

The compilation process for the entire rule set takes under half a minute for a fairly thorough description of French inflectional morphology, running on a 450MHz Pentium II processor. Run-time speeds are quite adequate for full NLP, and reflect the fact that the system is implemented in Prolog rather than (say) C and that full syntacticosemantic analyses of sentences, rather than just morpheme sequences or acceptability judgments, are produced.

Analysis of French words using this rule set and only an in-core lexicon averages around 40 words per second, with a mean of 11 spelling analyses per word leading to a mean of 1.6 morphological analyses (the reduction being because many of the roots suggested by spelling analysis do not exist or cannot combine

---

[4] The "lexical" level for interword rules is the surface level for intraword rules, since the two rule sets are applied in sequence.

with the affixes produced). If results are cached, subsequent attempts to analyse the same word are much faster. Generation is slightly faster than analysis because only one spelling, rather than all possible analyses, is sought from each call. Because of the separation between lexical and morphological representations, these timings are essentially unaffected by in-core lexicon size, as full advantage is taken of Prolog's built-in indexing.

Development times are at least as important as computation times. A rule set embodying a quite comprehensive treatment of French inflectional morphology was developed in about one person-month. The English spelling rule set was adapted from Ritchie et al. (1992) in only a day or two. Rule sets for Swedish, Danish, Spanish, Korean, and (for nouns only) Polish have also been developed.

7.4 Some Examples

To clarify further the use of the formalism and the operation of the mechanisms, we now examine several further examples.

7.4.1 Multiple-Letter Spelling Changes

Some obligatory spelling changes in French involve more than one letter. For example, masculine adjectives and nouns ending in *"eau"* have feminine counterparts ending in *"elle"*: *"beau"* ("nice") becomes *"belle"*, *"chameau"* ("camel") becomes *"chamelle"*. The final *"e"* is a feminizing affix and can be seen as inducing the obligatory spelling change $au \rightarrow ll$. However, although the obvious spelling rule

```
spell(change_au_ll, "|ll|" ⇔ "|au|+e")
```

allows this change, it does not rule out the incorrect realisation of beau+e as *"*beaue"*, shown in Figure 7.4, because it only affects partitionings where the au at the lexical level forms a single partition, rather than one for a and one for u. Instead, the following pair of rules, in which the lexical targets have only one character each, achieve the desired effect:

```
spell(change_au_ll1, "|l|" ⇔ "|a|u+e")
spell(change_au_ll2, "|l|" ⇔ "a|u|+e")
```

Surface:	b	e	a	u		e	
Lexical:	b	e	a	u	+	e	+
Rule:	*def.*	*def.*	*def.*	*def.*	*bdy.*	*def.*	*bdy.*

Figure 7.4. Incorrect partitioning for beau+e+.

Here, change_au_111 rules out the a : a partition in Figure 7.4, and change_au_112 rules out the u : u one.

In contrast, it is not necessary for the surface target to contain exactly one character for the blocking effect to apply, because the semantics of obligatoriness is that the lexical target and all contexts, taken together, make the specified surface target (of whatever length) obligatory for that partition. The reverse constraint, on the lexical target, does not apply.

7.4.2   *Using Features to Control Rule Application*

Features can be used to control the application of rules to particular lexical items where the applicability cannot be deduced from spelling alone. For example, Swedish adjectives finishing with *"el"*, *"en"* or *"er"* drop the *"e"* when the comparative ending *"are"* is added unless the final syllable is stressed. Thus, for example:

> säker+are → *säkrare* ("more certain"), but
> sen+are → *senare* ("later")

because only *"säker"* has an unstressed final syllable.

Such phenomena can be handled by providing an obligatory rule for the case where the change occurs, but constraining the applicability of the rule with a feature and making the feature clash with that for roots where the change does not occur. For our example:

```
spell(comp_LRNare_eLRN, inf,
      "||", <=>, "|e|1+are+",
      [1/"lrn"], [stresslast=n]).

orth(sen,[stresslast=y]).
orth(säker,[stresslast=n]).
```

This spelling rule cannot apply to "sen+are" because of the feature clash, but can (and therefore must, because it is obligatory) apply to "säker+are" because the features agree.

Rather complex problems arise from the fact that spelling changes in French generally cannot be predicted from the surface form of the word alone. This means the application of these rules, too, must be controlled; we again do so by specifying feature constraints, which must match between the rule and all morphemes to which it applies. The following extended example describes our treatment of one of the most challenging cases.

Nouns, adjectives, and verbs ending in *"-et"* or *"-el"* can either double the *"t"* or *"l"* before a silent *"e"* or change the prefinal *"e"* to *"è"*: "cadet+e" → *"cadette"*, but "complet+e" → *"complète"*. The application of the spelling rules is therefore controlled by means of a feature spelling_type, with value double in the first case and change_e_è in the second.

This situation is further complicated by the fact that the *"e"* that begins future and conditional endings sometimes affects preceding letters as if it were silent, and sometimes as if it were not. For example, "appel+erai" → *"appellerai"*, doubling the *"l"* just as in "appel+e" → *"appelle"*, where the final *"e"* actually is silent. However, "céd+erai" → *"céderai"*, not *"*cèderai"* as would be expected from the silent-e behaviour "céd+e" → *"cède"*. To make this distinction, we use a feature muet ("silent") for specifying if the *"e"* in the suffix is silent (muet=y for *"e"*), not silent (muet=n for *"ez"*) or the *"e"* of the future or conditional tenses (muet=fut_cond_e for *"erai(s)"*). Then, we restrict the rule for doubling the consonant with the features

```
spelling_type = double, muet = y ∨ fut_cond_e
```

and the one for *"é"* → *"è"* with the features

```
spelling_type = change_é_è, muet = y.
```

7.4.3   *Interword Spelling Changes*

In English, interword spelling changes occur only in the alternation between "a" and "an" before consonant and vowel sounds respectively. In French, such changes are far more widespread and can be complex. However, they can be handled by judiciously specifying contexts in two-level rules and, in a few cases, by postulating nonobvious underlying lexical items. Some important cases are:

- The *"e"* in the function words *"de"*, *"je"*, *"le"*, *"me"*, *"ne"*, *"que"*, *"se"*, and *"te"* is elided before (most) words starting in a vowel sound, except when the function word follows a hyphen: "le+homme" → *"l'homme"*, "je+ai" → *"j'ai"*, but "puis-je+avoir" does not elide, so the elision rule specifies that the hyphen be absent from the context. *"Ce"* also elides when used as a pronoun ("ce+est" → *"c'est"*), but when used as a determiner it takes the form *"cet"* before a vowel: *"cet homme"*. We therefore take the underlying form of the determiner to be "cet", which loses its *"t"* when followed by a consonant-initial word ("cet+soir" → *"ce soir"*). The elision rule is as follows:

  ```
  spell(iw_e_muet0, inter, "|'|", <=>, "3+1|e|+2",
  [1/"djlmnst", 2/iwv, 3/not("-")]).
  ```

  Numerals do not allow elision either: "le+onze" does not become *"*l'onze"*. We therefore treat the lexical form as being "#onze", where "#" acts as an underlying consonant but is realised as a null. (Syntax plays a role here too: "le+un" → *"l'un"* when "un" is a determiner, but not when it is a numeral. Thus lexically we have "un" as determiner and "#un" as numeral.)

- The very common preposition/article combinations *"de"/"à"* and *"le"/"les"*: "de+le" → *"du"*, "à+les" → *"aux"*, and so on. These contractions need to be treated as spelling effects, not as lexical items proper, first because they span constituent boundaries (we view *"du vol"* as being syntactically [PP de [NP le vol]]) and second because vowel elision takes precedence: "de+le+homme" → *"de l'homme"*, not *"*du homme"*.

- Hyphens between verbs and clitic pronouns are treated as lexical items in our grammar. They are realised as *"-t-"* when preceded by *"a"* or *"e"* and followed by *"e"*, *"i"* or *"o"*: "va+-+il" → *"va-t-il"*, but "vont+-+ils" → *"vont-ils"*. Hyphens joining nouns or names are treated as different lexical items not subject to this change: *"les vols Atlanta-Indianapolis"* does not involve introduction of *"t"*.

7.5   Debugging the Rules

The debugging tools help in checking the operation of the spelling rules, either (1) in conjunction with other constraints or (2) on their own.

For case (1), the user may ask to see all inflections of a root licensed by the spelling rules, morphology rules, and lexicon; for *"cher"*, the output is as shown in Figure 7.5, meaning that when *"cher"* is an adjp (adjective) it may combine with the suffixes listed to produce the inflected forms shown. This is useful in checking over and undergeneration. It is also possible to view the spelling patterns and morphology rule tree used to produce a form; for *"chère"*, the trace (slightly simplified here) is as in Figure 7.6. The spelling pattern 194 referred to here is the one depicted in a different form in Figure 7.3. The notation {clmnprstv=A} denotes a set of possible consonants represented by the variable A, which also occurs on the right-hand side of the rule, indicating that the same selection must be made for both occurrences. Production rule tree 17 is that for a single application of the rule adjp_adjp_fem, which describes the feminine form of an adjective, where the root is taken to be the masculine form. The Root and Infl lines show the features that differ between the root and inflected forms, while the Both line shows those that they share. Tree 18, which is not shown here but which is also pointed to by the spelling pattern, describes the feminine forms of nouns analogously.

```
[cher,e]: adjp -> chère
[cher,e,s]: adjp -> chères
[cher,s]: adjp -> chers
```

Figure 7.5. Forms of *"cher"* licensed by the French spelling rules.

```
"chère" has root "cher" with pattern 194 and
tree 17.

Pattern 194:
    "___è{clmnprstv=A}e" <-> "___e{clmnprstv=A}+e+"
    => tree 17 and 18 if [doublec=n]
    Uses: default* change_e_èl default boundary
            default boundary
Tree 17:
    Both = adjp:[dmodified=n,headfinal=y,mhdfl=y,
                synmorpha=1,wh=n]
    Root = adjp:[agr=agr:[gender=m]]
    Infl = adjp:[agr=agr:[gender=f]]
    Tree = adjp_adjp_fem=>[*,e]
```

Figure 7.6. Debugger trace of derivation of *"chère"*.

For case (2), the spelling rules may be applied directly, just as in rule compilation, to a specified surface or lexical character sequence, as if no lexical or
morphotactic constraints existed. Feature constraints, and cases where the rules
will not apply if those constraints are broken, are shown. For the lexical sequence
cher+e+, for example, the output is as in Figure 7.7. This indicates to the user

```
Surface: "chère" <->
Lexical: "cher". Suffix: "e"
c :: c <- default
h :: h <- default
è :: e <- change_e_èl
r :: r <- default
  :: + <- boundary
Category: orth:[cdouble=n]
e :: e <- default
  :: + <- boundary

Surface: "chere" <->
Lexical: "cher". Suffix: "e"
c :: c <- default
h :: h <- default
e :: e <- default (breaks "change_e_èl")
r :: r <- default
  :: + <- boundary
e :: e <- default
  :: + <- boundary
```

Figure 7.7. Debugger trace for cher+e+.

that if *"cher"* is given a lexical entry consistent with the constraint cdouble=n, then only the first analysis will be valid; otherwise, only the second will be.

7.6   Conclusions and Further Work

The rule formalism and compiler described here work well for European languages with reasonably complex orthographic changes but a limited range of possible affix combinations. Development, compilation, and run-time efficiency are quite acceptable, and the use of rules containing complex feature-augmented categories allows morphotactic behaviours and nonsegmental spelling constraints to be specified in a way that is perspicuous to linguists, leading to rapid development of descriptions adequate for full NLP.

The kinds of nonlinear effects common in Semitic languages, where vowel and consonant patterns are interpolated in words (Kay 1987; Kiraz 1994) could be treated efficiently by the mechanisms described here if it proved possible to define a representation that allowed the parts of an inflected word corresponding to the root to be separated fairly cleanly from the parts expressing the inflection. The latter could then be used by a modified version of the current system as the basis for efficient lookup of spelling patterns which, as in the current system, would allow possible lexical roots to be calculated.

Agglutinative languages can be handled efficiently by the current mechanism if specifications are provided for the affix combinations that are likely to occur at all often in real texts and/or if the rules are written only to allow such combinations; this approach is the one adopted for the CLE's treatment of Korean (Park 1998).

The interaction of morphological analysis with spelling correction (Bowden 1995; Carter 1992; Oflazer 1994) is another possibly fruitful area of work. Once the root spelling patterns and the affix combinations pointing to them have been created, analysis essentially reduces to an instance of affix stripping, which is amenable to the technique outlined in Carter 1992. As in that work, a discrimination net of root forms is required; however, this can be augmented independently of spelling-pattern creation, so that the flexibility resulting from not composing the lexicon with the spelling rules is not lost. The CLE corrects spellings in this way when required, achieving essentially the same results as the Carter version.

8   Corpora and Data Collection

IVAN BRETAN, ROBERT EKLUND, JAAN KAJA,
CATRIONA MacDERMID, MANNY RAYNER
AND DAVID CARTER

IN ORDER TO FUNCTION WELL IN A PARTICULAR DOMAIN, many different parts of the SLT system must be trained on data derived from domain corpora. This chapter is concerned with the process of creating such corpora. In the SLT project, we have used the original ATIS data (Hemphill et al. 1990) for English, and French corpora have been derived only by translating this; we therefore focus on our efforts for Swedish. Section 8.1 begins by discussing general issues relating to corpus collection, following which Sections 8.2 through 8.5 describe how the Swedish data was collected using a variety of methods. Section 8.6 concludes by sketching our methodology for developing hand-coded rule sets, which is largely driven by representative corpora derived from the original corpus data.

8.1   Rationale and Requirements

In a corpus-oriented development framework, the quality of the system depends crucially on the quality of the corpora used. Thus, in SLT, significant efforts have been devoted to obtaining high-quality linguistic data. A question that must be answered before embarking on such an undertaking is, "What are the measures of quality?".

Perhaps the most obvious source of data is genuine human–human conversations; other speech translation projects (Bub et al. 1997; Waibel et al. 1996) have used such material. However, the linguistic behaviour of users engaging in dialogue with a machine varies with the behaviour of the system (Bretan et al. 1995). Because of this, we are faced with a chicken-and-egg problem. We want to tune the system to the kinds of things people will say to it, and its performance will depend on how successful this tuning is; but, conversely, what people will say will in turn depend on the performance of the system. As far as possible, then, we need to imagine the best system we can build assuming the availability of suitable training data, and then somehow go about acquiring the kind of material that such a system, if it existed, would elicit from users. There are dangers both of undershooting and of overshooting here. We may be overcautious, and imagine a system of only limited capabilities, which will prompt a correspondingly limited set of user utterances that provides no incentive to extend the system's coverage beyond them; or we may be too ambitious, and end up with corpus data that, even with the best system we can build, we cannot hope to deal with. There is also a risk of shooting wide, and creating a corpus that is suitably challenging but that does not reflect the kinds of things native speakers would really say to any system. This is a particular risk if we create a corpus by translation from another natural language, because translations have a tendency to retain idiosyncrasies of the source language.

Thus, the data obtained from human–human dialogues do not transfer straightforwardly into the design of human–machine dialogues;[1] even with perfect tuning, present-day systems cannot hope to mimic a human conversational partner. We therefore need to turn to data collection methods that are geared more towards human–machine dialogues.

There are two principal such methods: Wizard-of-Oz (WOZ) simulations, and what we call "bootstrapping". WOZ simulations (see Section 8.2.1) are carried out by setting up a scenario where the user interacts with an alleged speech-understanding system partly or fully simulated by a human, exhibiting the type of capabilities that the system to be constructed ideally should possess.

Bootstrapping, in this context, is the procedure of constructing a rudimentary version of a speech-understanding system with a minimal vocabulary (which may be collected through a very limited WOZ study or other less costly sources and complemented by means of manual inspection), and putting it straight into use. This system will obviously not have the intended coverage, but will still elicit many user utterances and words that were previously not recorded. These additional data can be used to improve the system's recognition and understanding capabilities, whereupon new user sessions can be initiated to collect even more data, and so on. It is not clear how useful the linguistic material thus obtained really is, especially in comparison with a WOZ simulation; its usefulness is also highly dependent on the quality of the bootstrapped system. One problematic issue in this context is the fact that users adapt to the quality and language of a system over time, which could mean that subsequent versions of the bootstrapped system are more unsophisticated than is necessary. This is probably particularly true for systems where complete dialogues need to be recorded in order to obtain the required data, as opposed to one- or two-shot interactions. Life and Salter (1996) claim that bootstrapping and WOZ are both needed, since they are complementary. The WOZ studies give input indispensable for dialogue and interface design, whereas bootstrapping methods are more useful in generating large amounts of data for training acoustic and lower-level language models.

---

[1] There is also the ethical issue of "bugging" people's conversations, which is most critical if the speakers can be identified and if the dialogue contains sensitive or personal information. Ideally, informed consent should then be obtained.

WOZ simulations do have drawbacks – most notably they are laborious, time-consuming, and costly. An informal figure quoted in the work on collecting ATIS data estimates the cost of collecting 10 000 sentences at around one million dollars, that is, one hundred dollars per sentence! Although the WOZ simulations we have conducted ourselves for Swedish indicate much lower costs, it is clear that this way of collecting data is expensive. As a cheap substitute approach, we in fact started by experimenting with "piggybacking" on the existing American English data through text-to-text translation by native Swedish speakers. The resulting data was used to train the initial language model for the Swedish version of SLT (see Section 8.3). One assumption underlying such a project is that spoken utterances can systematically be translated textually on a large scale, preserving the idiomatic traits of spoken language. This assumption proved wrong, but the effort still turned out to be worthwhile, partly for reasons similar to the ones that Life and Salter quote. Since text-to-text translation did not provide good enough data, a WOZ study was conducted; this is described in the next section.

8.2 Simulation Methodology

8.2.1 *Wizard-of-Oz Simulations*

In order to collect more realistic training data for a spoken dialogue system, experimental subjects can be recorded as they conduct task-oriented dialogues with a simulated dialogue system. The subjects are most often led to believe that their dialogue partner is a prototype system, when in fact an accomplice (the *wizard*) is simulating an operational system by performing some or all of the system's functions. Typically, the wizard interprets the subjects' utterances, simulating speech recognition and often language understanding. Other functions, such as dialogue management and speech synthesis, can be handled by a computerised tool operated by the accomplice (Amalberti, Carbonell, and Falzon 1993). Usually, the subjects have no real task they wish to complete, and are given scenarios describing a hypothetical task. Written scenarios are most common, although these can act as a script, strongly influencing the subject's vocabulary and syntactical structures, at least in their opening utterance within the dialogue. To overcome these limitations, the scenario can be presented in tabular or graphical form, such that the subjects have to interpret the scenario using their own words. In this case, the illustrations must be unambiguous for the subjects. In yet another method, subjects are given scenarios in picture form (MacDermid and Goldstein 1996). We will say more about this in Section 8.5.

8.2.2 *American ATIS Simulations*

One example of a WOZ simulation (but with text instead of spoken output from the simulated system) is MADCOW (Hemphill, Godfrey, and Doddington 1990).

A large number of subjects (2 724) were given written scenarios and spoke to what they believed to be a working system, when in fact human wizards were interpreting the subjects' questions, querying the database by hand, and displaying the results on the subjects' screens. After several months, once enough data was acquired in this way to train the system, the system became fully operational, and the wizards were no longer needed. The expectation was that, because the users believed that they were speaking to a real system, the wizard data and real data were equivalent.

8.2.3   Swedish ATIS Simulations

In order to obtain high-quality Swedish data, a spoken language translation system in the ATIS domain was simulated at Telia Research. This was done without the use of any computerised simulation tool. Subjects believed that the "system" translated their Swedish inquiries for English-, French-, or German-speaking travel agents in order to book flights. In fact, no translation occurred in these dialogues. A subject's utterance was conveyed – usually verbatim – by a wizard (W1), a professional actor representing the subject's translation system, to a second wizard (W2) representing the travel agent's translation system. Two wizards were used so as to avoid cognitively overloading a single agent.

Certain simplifications were made to complex utterances; utterances that were not understood or that were longer than twenty words were rejected by W1, who asked the subject to repeat or reformulate the utterance. The utterance was then conveyed by W2 over the telephone to a Swedish accomplice (taking the role of the travel agent), who asked for additional parameters where necessary to complete the booking. W2 then conveyed the travel agent's replies to the subject via W1 according to the same constraints. The two wizards sat in the same room and when they spoke to each other to convey utterances or clarify internal misunderstandings, W1 suspended the microphone contact with the subject. Similarly, W2 used the secrecy button on the telephone. The wizards listened to the respective dialogue partners through headsets.

The actor was trained to speak to the subject with the unnatural prosody characteristic of composite digitised speech and had no script apart from the requests to reformulate or repeat. The "travel agent" used certain standard phrases based on an interview with a real travel agent and had access to a paper database constructed with data from an ATIS-type database used in the travel agency. Otherwise, his speech was spontaneous in response to the subject's queries, which were based on a combination of written and graphical scenarios. The dialogue between the subject and the actor was recorded as sound files on a UNIX workstation and all four input channels were recorded on a DAT recorder for later transcription. The setup is shown in Figure 8.1.

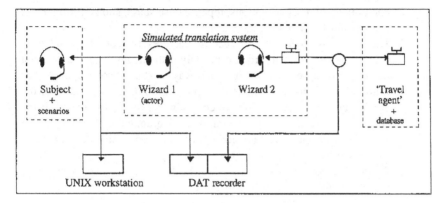

Figure 8.1. Experimental set-up for Swedish ATIS simulation.

8.3   Translations of American WOZ Material

One way to obtain data without having to design WOZ simulations is to translate existing WOZ data collected in another language. This section describes how, during the SLT project, translations of the American WOZ data described in Section 8.2.3 were used for training and language modelling purposes.

8.3.1   Translations: A First Step

During the first stage of the SLT project, 4 021 American WOZ sentences were translated into Swedish by two Swedish native speakers.[2] This corpus, which will be referred to as C1, was taken as the basis for training the first Swedish-language model. In a second step, two members of the Swedish SLT team translated a further 3 264 and 1 888 sentences, respectively, and the minority contributor of the original pair of translators added a further 220 sentences. So as to obtain more idiomatic data, these new translators were instructed to attempt freer translations. In this way, a corpus of 5 372 translated sentences was obtained. This corpus will be referred to as C2.

Analysis of C1 and C2 revealed several general problems associated with the idea of creating corpora by translation.

1. It is very hard for translators to avoid linguistic bias caused by the wordings in the source language, and translations are almost certain to be influenced by expressions idiomatic in the source language but not in the target language.

[2] In fact, more than 80 percent of the sentences were translated by one of these people.

2. Phenomena such as hesitations, repairs, false starts, and so forth are not readily translated in a natural way.
3. Translation is likely to miss certain features typical of spontaneous speech, like agreement errors, especially if the target language does not make use of agreement in the same way as the source language. For example, English-to-French translation would not produce many of the gender agreement errors that are common in French. In general, if the target language has different grammatical granularity than the source language, translators will not add grammatical errors that do not exist in the source-language utterances.
4. A small number of translators – four in this case – are not likely to be able to provide sufficient linguistic variability.

These observations motivated the next phase of data collection.

8.3.2   Email Corpus

Since a WOZ simulation at that point was still out of reach, it was decided to continue in the same vein and spread the translation task between as many translators as possible, with distinct instructions to do *free* translations. To this end, lists of email addresses of Telia employees were obtained. These lists were used for distributing the translation task. The addressees were each sent two emails. The first email contained background information about the task and an explanation as to what the second email was for, and provided the addressee with instructions as to how to approach the task. These instructions are briefly outlined in the following paragraphs.

8.3.2.1   Instructions

In the first email, the addressees were told to avoid literal translations. Instead, they were instructed to consider the meaning of the English sentences and then write down what they would have said themselves in Swedish if they were to require the same information in real life. They were also told to imagine themselves communicating with a computerised system rather than a human partner, and so, for example, to avoid use of overcolloquial language.

The risk of translating too literally was once again pointed out by referring to certain expressions and specific wordings. The example given was the English phrase "ground transportation". This could easily be translated literally as *"marktransport"*, which is also the professional term used in Swedish; however, most nonprofessional Swedes would probably say things along the lines of *"förbindelser"* ("connections") or *"flygbussar"* ("shuttle buses"). The addressees were also told to neglect sentences they found totally incomprehensible or absurd in one way or another.

The format of the second email, containing the sentences, was explained via an example. The addressees were informed that the subsequent email would contain pairs of sentences such as the following:

```
<e5233> Please list all flights between Atlanta and Boston.
<s5233>
<e3665> Is booking necessary?
<s3665>
```

The addressees were asked to fill in the empty, Swedish, lines with free translations, following the guidelines given in the letter. The example given was:

```
<e5233> Please list all flights between Atlanta and Boston.
<s5233> Lista alla flygningar mellan Atlanta och Boston,
        tack
<e3665> Is booking necessary?
<s3665> Måste man reservera?
```

Upon finishing the task, the addressees were told to send the email back by using the "Reply" button in their email client. A contact (address and telephone number) was also given, in case the addressees needed further information in connection with the task.

8.3.2.2   Results

The procedure described above was executed twice. In the first batch, 11 232 sentences from the American ATIS material were divided into files of 18 sentences each and emailed to 624 Telia employees. 1 115 sentences, about 10 percent, were returned. Since it was judged that 18 sentences were perhaps a few too many to look attractive, a second batch of 7 533 sentences was divided into files of only 3 sentences each and emailed to 2 511 Telia employees. The response that time was 1 080 sentences, or about 14.5 percent.

Finally, an additional 500 sentences each were translated by five translators, SLT team members and graduate students of linguistics. In this way, a corpus of 4 595 sentences, translated by approximately 427 persons, was compiled.

8.4   A Comparison of the Corpora

The different corpora thus collected varied according to several parameters, such as lexical size, grammatical coverage, and *idiomaticity*, that is, the use of idiomatic expressions specific to the domain and language. In all the comparisons, C1 and C2 were merged into one corpus, *TC*, created by four translators. TC contains $4\,021 + 5\,372 = 9\,393$ sentences. The email corpus is referred to as *EC*, (about 427 translators). A small Wizard-of-Oz pilot of 127 sentences is called *WOZp* (10 subjects); we refer to the WOZ simulation described in Section 8.2.1 as *WOZ* (52 subjects). Statistics for these corpora are summarised in Table 8.1.

Table 8.1. *Overview of quantitative data for different corpora*

	WOZp	WOZ	TC	EC
# sentences	127	3 578	9 393	4 595
# subjects/translators	10	52	4	~427
# lexical entries (types)	174	977	1 581	1 789
Percentage lexical entries with only one token	(–)	~10	~10	~17

One issue to be examined here is lexical representation. TC contains 1 581 lexical entries (types). Here, inflected forms of the same word are counted as different types. EC contains 1 789 entries, WOZ contains 977 entries, and WOZp contains 174 entries. Figure 8.2 shows growth of lexicon size as a function of the number of collected sentences. As can be seen, the lexicon grows most rapidly in EC, whereas the growth rate is more or less the same for TC and WOZ. This suggests that a quick way to obtain good lexical coverage is to involve many

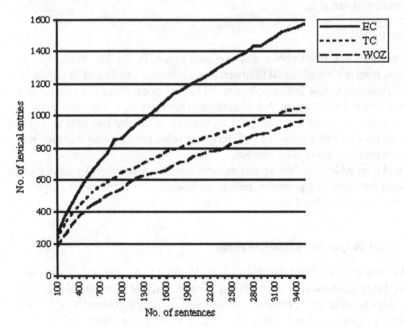

Figure 8.2. Lexicon growth as a function of number of sentences. To avoid sequential effects the data were collected several times in different orders and later averaged.

people in the gathering of data for the target language. Another consequence of using multiple translators is reflected in the proportion of words in the lexicon that occur only once in the corpus. In TC and WOZ, around 10 percent of the lexical entries are singletons, whereas the corresponding figure for EC is 17 percent.

It does not follow from the fact that EC has a larger number of lexical entries than WOZ that EC is the most representative of Swedish usage, because of the previously mentioned problems of colouring effects and the lack of speech-specific phenomena associated with textual translation. In fact, the two lexica vary in several respects.

First, there are words and constructions that exist in both lexica, but whose frequency is quite different. As an example, the Swedish word *"okay"* exists in both lexica, but is far more common in the WOZ material. It exists in 3.8 percent of the sentences in WOZ and 2.5 percent in WOZp, but only in 0.2 percent of the sentences in EC. The opposite is true for other words. The word *"vänlig"* (approximately "kind", as in "would you be kind enough. . .") is far more common in EC (4.8 percent) than in WOZ (0.2 percent). Most of these occurrences seem to be the result of trying to translate "please", a word lacking a good counterpart in Swedish. What Swedes say spontaneously, however, is *"tack"* ("thank you") in sentence-final position. Thus, *"tack"* occurs in 20 percent of the sentences in WOZ but only in 2 percent in EC. The corresponding figure for WOZp is 11.5 percent. Since these words have different syntagmatic properties, they also influence grammatical structure.

Second, some words and constructions common in WOZ do not exist at all in EC. A striking example is that 7 percent of the sentences in WOZ begin with the words *"då"* or *"ja, då"* (fillers that roughly translate as "well"), but none do in EC. The corresponding figure for WOZp is 0.6 percent. The idiomatic expression *"det går bra"* (literally, "it goes well" = "that's fine") occurs in both WOZ and WOZp (about 0.7 percent) but not in EC. Similar examples of skewed material abound, most of which can be accounted for in terms of linguistic bias associated with the translation process. However, it must be borne in mind that the different set-ups for the American ATIS simulations and the Swedish WOZ simulations almost certainly influenced the linguistic material obtained.

8.5   Concluding Remarks on Corpus Collection

One problem with the email approach is that disfluent or strange sentences are less likely to be translated than normal sentences, since the former require more effort from the translator. This means that the method might act as a filter where marginal sentences become underrepresented in the translation process. The costs of the method are hard to judge, since the work is very much hidden. More than 420 persons worked approximately ten to thirty minutes each, on a voluntary basis, at no cost to the project. The bulk of the work consisted of editing the returned files, many of which did not arrive in the desired format.

Although the email approach produced useful data and translators were instructed to respect source-language disfluencies and spoken language style, the results differed from the data obtained in the Swedish WOZ simulation in that certain features of natural speech were notable by their absence in the former corpus. These differences can be attributed partly to a loss of naturalness in the translation process, but more importantly to the fact that typical spoken language phenomena (Fromkin 1980; Linell 1981; Tannen 1982) are very specific to language and modality and cannot be obtained through literal translation of text. One way to circumvent this problem is to record oral translations from sources other than text. A method in which this is used is the *storyboard*. In this method, subjects are given picture, or storyboard, scenarios and asked to formulate an equivalent utterance (MacDermid and Goldstein 1996). In this way, linguistic bias from written scenarios is avoided. The data is gathered as speech rather than in written form, adding realism, though subjects are not in a live dialogue. Consequently, the method is best suited to collecting an initial set of utterances and is a good way to tap possible variations in use of syntax and vocabulary.

In conclusion, a general recommendation is to use WOZ simulations to obtain natural-speech data, complemented by the email approach (or a similar method) where the task is distributed among a large number of people proficient in both languages to obtain wide lexical coverage. WOZ simulations not only provided proper dialogue data, but also idiomatic spoken language. The textually translated utterances gave no information concerning dialogues (since they were translated one by one), and clearly deviated from normal spoken Swedish. On the positive side, the translated corpus contained a much richer variation in vocabulary than the WOZ data: the vocabulary grew more quickly. Thus, in addition to the observation that the growth rate of vocabularies varies from domain to domain (Hetherington and Zue 1993), we note that growth rates vary even among vocabularies collected within the same domain. This difference is mainly attributable to the difference in number of speakers, and to a lesser extent, task formulation and modality.

Achieving lexical completeness in data collection is, of course, decisive when it comes to tuning a speech-understanding system to optimal performance within a given domain. Missing words can lead to system behaviour that slows down, confuses or even misleads a user. Hetherington and Zue also point out that vocabulary completeness is not best achieved by tapping huge generic corpora: 100 000 words from the Wall Street Journal (WSJ) corpus are needed to obtain the same coverage of ATIS as a vocabulary of 300 words derived from 2 000 ATIS training sentences! Oversized vocabularies are, of course, also sources of performance degradation. Collecting utterances representative to the domain is therefore of utmost importance to the lexical competence of the system.

8.6   Representative Corpora and Rational Development

So far in this chapter, we have discussed what could reasonably be called "natural" corpora. In this last section, we switch our focus to consider artificial corpora. We start by explaining our motivation for creating such corpora, and how they are used in the process of system development.

The rule-based components of the SLT system – the lexica, morphological descriptions, sets of grammar and transfer rules, and so on – have all been developed using the same methodology. The basic idea is the usual one: take a set of example utterances (the *development set*), run the system on it, evaluate the results, and carry on iterating the edit-debug-test cycle until performance is high enough. The question we will focus on here is that of how to construct the development set. In the preceding sections, we described how we went about collecting a large sample of more or less realistic domain utterances (the *main domain corpus*). Really, we are interested in improving performance on the main domain corpus; getting better results on the development set is just a means to this end. These remarks motivate the following requirements, some of which represent tradeoffs or tensions:

1. The development set should be small enough that it is practically feasible to run tests on it frequently, and interpret the results easily. For this reason, it is not generally possible to use the main domain corpus as the development set.
2. The development set should be large enough, and balanced enough, that it contains examples of all the important (i.e., frequent) problems in the full corpus.
3. The relative importance of two given sentences from the development set should be clear. Thus, if sentence A contains only instances of common words and constructions, while sentence B contains at least some unusual elements, then failure on sentence A should be more serious than failure on sentence B.
4. It should be as easy as possible to extract the development set from the main domain corpus.

In summary, we want some fairly easy way to derive a smallish set of utterances from the main domain corpus, and be confident that if we do well on the small set then we will do at least reasonably well on the original one. We will call a set of this kind a *representative corpus*. The rest of this chapter will provide a full description of the method we have used to contruct representative corpora; we will illustrate with examples taken from the Swedish WOZ corpus described in Section 8.2.1. Since the representative corpus is an integral part of the development process, we will discuss it in that context.

The basic idea is to extract from the main domain corpus groups of syntactically similar utterances; one example is chosen to represent each group, and assigned a weight determined by the size of the group. The key advantage offered by the representative corpus idea is that it simplifies the task of locating problems that have a large impact on coverage; experience shows that if a particular sentence fails to process correctly, there is a substantial probability that all or at least most of the other sentences conforming to its syntactic pattern will fail in the same way. Thus, the size of the syntactic class represented by each representative corpus sentence provides a natural way of prioritising problems.

The system translates utterances as sequences of independent fragments; so the first step in the process of constructing the representative corpus is manually to split up the utterances in the main domain corpus into suitable segments, each of which can feasibly be translated as an independent unit. We refer to the result as the *split corpus*. The vertical bars in the following example utterances from the Swedish WOZ corpus show how they are segmented in the split corpus:

```
resa stockholm berlin | okej | den andra i sjätte
(trip stockholm berlin | okay | june second)

ehh | vad kostar den biljetten | är det den
billigaste biljetten
(uh | what does that ticket cost | is it the
cheapest ticket)

sexton och femtio den andra juni | hur dags
är jag framme i berlin
(sixteen fifty on june second | when do I
arrive in berlin)
```

The next step is to extend the lexicon to achieve reasonable basic coverage of the domain at the lexical level. We do this using the LexMake lexicon acquisition tool (see Chapter 6). We then extend the grammar to achieve some level of nontrivial grammatical coverage on the split corpus. Coverage does not need to be terribly good for the subsequent steps to work; our experience suggests that being able to get analyses for about half the utterances is enough. Once the initial lexicon and grammar are in place, we create and judge a treebank (Chapter 5), and derive a first set of pruning data (Section 4.2).

We can now use the initial phases of linguistic analysis as a part-of-speech tagger, by analysing up to and including the lexical pruning phase and then extracting (see Section 4.5) the best sequence of lexical edges. Tags consist of the major category symbol only, for example, "noun" and "verb"; more fine-grained distinctions are discarded. We perform this type of tagging on the split corpus, and call the result the *tagged corpus*.[3] We then group utterances from the tagged

---

[3] It would have been equally feasible to perform this step using a standard part-of-speech tagger instead, but we found our solution simpler and more accurate.

corpus into equivalence classes under the relationship of having the same tag sequence.

The equivalence classes produced by the previous step are generally quite useful as they stand, but we have found it worthwhile to spend some time manually cleaning them up. In some cases, this involves reclassifying utterances that were incorrectly tagged; in others, a group may be split into two or three smaller groups, if the relevant utterances are intuitively dissimilar enough. For instance, the following two utterances receive the same tag sequence, since `flyger` ("fly") and `finns` ("there are") are both tagged as v.

```
vilka bolag flyger från dallas till denver
(which companies fly from dallas to denver)

vilka turer finns från boston till oakland
(which flights are there from boston to oakland)
```

However, the difference between an intransitive and an existential verb is great enough that it seems reasonable to assign the utterances to different groups.

The regrouping step can be performed by nonexperts at the rate of several thousand sentences a day, using a text editor, once the corpus has been formatted to facilitate this. For each of the new classes, we also manually designate an element that intuitively is most typical of the class. This step can also be performed quickly by nonexperts using an editor.

Finally, we construct the representative corpus by selecting the designated element from each class, and order the results by the size of the classes represented. Since short utterance classes otherwise tend to receive disproportionate weight, we have found it most meaningful to define the size of a class as the total number of words represented, as opposed to counting utterances.

We conclude the chapter by presenting an initial segment of the representative corpus derived from the Swedish WOZ corpus. The actual corpus file lists for each representative utterance the full set of utterances that it represents; here, we have suppressed this extra information in the interests of brevity. The format of each record in the file is

```
rep_sent(<N>,<Utterance>).
```

where <Utterance> is the representative sentence, and <N> is the total number of words in the group of similar utterances that it represents.

```
rep_sent(423,'tack så mycket').
(thank you very much)
rep_sent(284,'urban kalle trea femma').
(u k three five)
```

```
rep_sent(279,tack).
```
(thank you)
```
rep_sent(209,ja).
```
(yes)
```
rep_sent(177,'den sjätte maj').
```
(may seventh)
```
rep_sent(161,och).
```
(and)
```
rep_sent(157,'jag vill boka en resa från washington
till chicago den sextonde maj').
```
*(i want to book a flight from washington to chicago
on may sixteenth)*
```
rep_sent(151,'går planet direkt till new york').
```
(does the plane fly direct to new york)
```
rep_sent(130,'jag skulle vilja boka en resa från
washington till chicago den sextonde maj').
```
*(i would like to book a flight from washington to
chicago on may sixteenth)*
```
rep_sent(126,'då bokar jag den resan').
```
(then i'll book that flight)
```
rep_sent(125,'jag skulle vilja boka en resa från
chicago till stockholm').
```
*(i would like to book a flight from chicago
to stockholm)*

(...)

PART II

Linguistic Coverage

9　English Coverage

MANNY RAYNER

9.1　Overview of English Linguistic Coverage

This chapter describes the coverage of the English grammar and lexicon on the ATIS domain corpus. Historically, the English grammar was developed first, as part of the original CLE project (Alshawi 1992); the Swedish and French grammars described in Chapters 10 and 11 were adapted from it. Our presentation of the material will reflect this. The present chapter provides a detailed description of the English grammar, including all the rules. The later chapters avoid recapitulating this material in the case of rules that have been carried over to the other languages with minimal or no changes; instead, they concentrate on the portions of these grammars that exhibit interesting differences compared with the English one. All three grammars are with some very minor exceptions completely domain independent. The domain adaptation required to achieve practically useful performance is carried out using the methods described in Chapter 3 and Section 4.2.

Our presentation in this chapter will divide up analyses of types of construction into pretheoretically meaningful chunks: lexical items, noun phrases, verb phrases, preposition phrases, numbers, clauses, and whole utterances. Section 9.2 briefly describes the lexicon, after which Section 9.3 provides a detailed description of the grammar. We give examples and approximate frequencies for the different types of constituents, and describe how each type of phrase is defined by the grammar. Since the features used are by the nature of things somewhat arbitrary, we will not specify them in detail. Instead, we describe what the effect of the feature settings is intended to be, in terms of licensing some desired derivations while blocking other undesired ones. We consequently present the rules in a highly schematic form.

The concrete presentation of the grammar occupies the main body of the chapter: in the final two sections, we briefly consider sentences currently outside coverage, examining them to discover the extent to which they represent problems for the present framework, and summarise the respects in which the English grammar differs from its French and Swedish counterparts.

9.2   Lexical Items

Before looking at the grammar proper, we briefly review the lexical entries; the main point we will focus on is the extent to which the lexicon is domain dependent. First, however, we summarise some overall frequency statistics to provide a background for the following results. The portion of the development corpus that is currently within coverage (about 85.5 percent of a set of 21 116 A-, D-, and X-class sentences of fifteen words or less) included examples of 1 367 distinct lexical entries, counting different inflections of the same entry as distinct. Of these, 590 occurred more than ten times; 801 occurred between three and ten times, inclusively; 131 occurred twice; and 342 occurred only once. If we conflate different inflections, we have 1 068 different root entries, with 501 occurring more than ten times, 232 occurring three to ten times, 102 occurring twice, and 233 once.

Deciding which entries are domain dependent is unfortunately not clear cut. Many entries are for words and phrases that are particularly common within the ATIS domain. If, however, it seems clear that they occur with reasonable frequency, used in the same way, in other contexts, then we will count them as domain independent on the grounds that a sufficiently large general lexicon for English would include them. It is unclear how to count the large number of entries for proper nouns, particularly names of cities and airports, and the common-noun entries for types of aircraft. If we exclude them, there are only a handful of entries that can reasonably be called domain dependent. These are singular and plural forms of the following common-noun phrases (in most cases only one form occurs): "class of service", "seating capacity", "round trip", "rental car", "car rental", "a m flight", "p m flight", "coach economy class", and "international airport". All of them in theory could have been derived compositionally from their components, but there was, in each case, some reason that suggested that they would be better treated as lexicalised constituents. For example, the phrase "class of service code" occurs frequently in the corpus, and it is not generally desirable to allow an NP as complex as "class of service" (read compositionally) to act as an NBAR premodifier. The argument is that the phrase is permissible precisely because "class of service" is lexicalised in the context of the ATIS domain; similar considerations apply to the other phrases listed.

9.3   The English Grammar

9.3.1   Noun Phrases

We will now begin our walk through the grammar proper by looking at NPs, partly because these are by a considerable margin the most common type of phrase. Our analysis of NPs is slightly nonstandard in two respects. First, we assign a constituent structure to postmodified NPs that includes a core, or inner, NP, the postmodifiers attaching to this core NP rather than to a possible NBAR. For example, the top-level constituent structure of "All flights to Boston" would in most grammars be

$[_{NP}[_{DET}$ *all* $][_{NBAR}$ *flights to Boston*$]]]$.

The CLE grammar, however, assigns this phrase the structure

$[_{NP} [_{NP}$ *all flights*$] [_{PP}$ *to Boston*$]]$.

The PP "to Boston" is, in other words, modifying the inner NP "all flights" rather than the NBAR "flights": similar analyses obtain for NPs with VP, relative clause (REL) or ADJP postmodification.

This treatment of NP postmodification can be backed up by a fair amount of linguistic evidence. Most clearly, there are cases of postmodification in NPs that lack a clear NBAR, for instance, "those leaving before one p m", "something after lunch", or "are there [any on Tuesday]". On a standard account, NPs like these will need several extra rules. There are also cases where extraction of the inner NP appears to take place, for example, "What flights do you have with first class". The simplest way of dealing with these must be to have "with first class" modify the NP gap associated with "what flights". Our treatment of NPs makes this type of example easy to handle.

Second, superlative adjectives and ordinals are treated in an unusual way. Unlike other adjectives, superlatives are classed as a type of ordinal expression like "first" or "next"; then NPs containing an ordinal are given a constituent structure that makes the ordinal part of the determiner (DET). So, for example, the top-level constituent structure of "the cheapest flight" is

$[_{NP}[_{DET}$ *the cheapest*$][_{NBAR}$ *flight*$]]$

The main advantages resulting from adoption of this analysis are semantic, and are relevant to CLE processing stages not used in the SLT project. It is however worth noting some linguistic data that are at least not inconsistent with the "ordinal determiner" analysis. A noun phrase can consist of a determiner+superlative adjective combination (e.g., "the largest", "the least expensive"), which is predicted by the hypothesis that these expressions are determiners. Also, superlative adjectives cannot premodify bare plurals (e.g., "*Cheapest flights") while others can, another fact that falls out of our treatment.

Because of the way in which NP postmodification is handled by the grammar, it makes sense to split the treatment of NPs into recursive NPs and nonrecursive NPs. We define an NP to be *recursive* if at least one of its constituents is an NP; the remaining NPs are either lexical or *nonrecursive*.

9.3.2   Nonrecursive NPs

We divide our treatment of nonrecursive NPs under the following headings:

Basic nonrecursive NPs We will refer to NPs built up from recursive application of a core set of rules for NPs, NBARs, ADJPs, DETs, and

ORDINALs as basic NPs: these account for about 75 percent of the nonrecursive NPs in the corpus. Examples are "fares", "all flights", "breakfast", "Sunday night", "the fare codes", "the cheapest one way flights", "the San Francisco limousine service".

Time-and-date NPs Nonrecursive NPs formed using constructions specifically associated with dates and times account for about 10 percent of the nonrecursive NPs. Examples are "eight o'clock", "September fifteenth", "seven fifty five a m", "three", "five forty", "next Wednesday", "Tuesday October first".

Code NPs Nonrecursive NP constructions using code expressions, and often one or more of the core nonrecursive NP rules as well, represent about 10 percent of the nonrecursive NPs. Examples are "American flight four eight seven", "D L seven four six", "flight U A one thirty", "flight four seven six", "fare code F N", "flight number seventeen sixty five", "Delta flight number seven oh nine".

Bare-determiner NPs NPs consisting of a bare determiner constitute about 2 percent of the nonrecursive NPs. Examples are "any", "which", "one", "the same", "some", "how many", "the latest", "the least expensive".

"kind of" NPs NPs using the "kind/sort/type of" construction account for about 2 percent of the nonrecursive NPs. Examples are "what type of plane", "what kind of aircraft", "what types of ground transportation", "what sort of ground transportation", "types of planes".

9.3.2.1 Basic Nonrecursive NPs

The greater part of the nonrecursive NPs in the corpus are built up by recursive application of a core set of thirteen rules: two for NPs, four for NBARs, six for DETs, and one each for ADJPs and ORDINALs. At the top level, we have the two core NP rules,

```
NP -> DET NBAR
NP -> NBAR
```

These, respectively, construct an NP out of a determiner+NBAR combination ("[the] [flight]", "[all] [morning flights]", "[just the] [one way flights]"), and an NP out of a bare singular or plural NBAR ("[information]", "[Wednesday]", "[travel arrangements]", "[Delta flights]"). In earlier versions of the grammar, the second rule was split into two subcases. The first of these was for bare plural NPs; the second, which was specifically for bare singular NPs, was constrained only to allow mass+ NPs. However, empirical analysis of the corpus data convinced us that there were many bare singular NPs (e.g., "arrival time", "one way fare") which are in no way clearly mass+. It was consequently possible to merge the bare singular and bare plural versions into a single bare NP rule.

We now turn to the six basic NBAR rules,

```
NBAR -> ADJP NBAR
NBAR -> NBAR NBAR
NBAR -> NP:[name=y] NBAR
NBAR -> NBAR CONJ NBAR
```

The first rule licenses prenominal modification of an NBAR by a nonsuperlative adjective (e.g., "[direct] [flights]", "[early] [weekday flights]"); the second allows combination of two NBARS to form a compound NBAR (e.g., "[afternoon] [flights]" or "[limousine] [service]").

The third basic NBAR rule permits compound nominals formed by combining a name+ NP and an NBAR. The use of the name feature is unfortunately not as clear cut as one would wish. It is indeed the case that in most instances of application of the rule the NP is an obvious proper name, for instance, "[Delta] [flights]", "[Boston] [ground transportation]". However, there are also a fairly large number of cases like "the [[five forty five] [flight]]" or "the [[A P fifty seven] [restriction]]" that the rule is also intended to cover; for this to be possible, time of day NPs like "five forty five" and code NPs like "A P fifty seven" consequently need to be name+.

The fourth rule, which constructs conjoined NBARs (e.g., "all [flights and fares]", is much less frequent than the others and is unproblematic.

The fifth and sixth rules both have to do with DETs, which in the CLE grammar include ordinals and superlative adjectives (cf. the discussion at the beginning of this section). There is a rule for forming superlative adjective phrases, and another for making a superlative ADJ into an ORDINAL.

```
ADJP -> most/least ADJ
ORDINAL -> ADJP:[form=superlative]
```

Finally, we look at the six rules for complex DET expressions:

```
DET -> the ORDINAL
DET -> ORDINAL
DET -> PREDET DET
DET -> NUMBER
DET -> less/more than NUMBER
DET -> POSSESSIVE
```

The first rule, which is by far the most common of the six, combines an occurrence of "the" with an ORDINAL to form an "ordinal DET", for example, "[the] [first]", "[the] [longest]", "[the] [least expensive]". The second rule is a variant, common in spoken language, that omits the article, for example, "[greatest fare]", "[latest flight]".

The third rule combines a PREDET (e.g., "all", "only", or "just") with a DET to form a DET; the daughter DET is in practice always "the". The remaining rules are straightforward.

9.3.2.2   Time-and-Date NPs

The rules for time-and-date expressions are fairly simple, and give nearly complete coverage of the examples found in the corpus. By adding a feature to the NUMBER category to distinguish among different types of number expressions, it was possible to code the rules (in particular, those for time expressions) fairly compactly: one slightly unobvious trick that we found useful was to allow expressions like "oh five" to count as a special type of number.

Examples of the types of time-and-date expressions covered, listed in descending order of frequency of occurrence, are the following: "eight o'clock", "September fifteenth", "seven fifty five a m", "three", "five forty", "next Wednesday", "Tuesday October first", "July eighteen", "July twenty fifth nineteen ninety one", "Monday November eleventh nineteen ninety one", "July the fourth", "the tenth of November", "sixteen hundred hours", "fifteen July", "Wednesday the twenty first".

The rules actually permit more types of expression, though several were not observed to occur in the corpus.

9.3.2.3   Code NPs

NPs involving spelt-out alphanumerical codes are also common in the corpus; the grammar deals with them as follows. There are two domain-independent rules for code NPs, and one domain-independent rule for CODE,

```
NP -> CODE
NP -> NBAR CODE
CODE -> NUMBER
```

These are supplemented by a set of seven domain-specific rules for CODE, which define the sequences of letters, numbers, and names commonly occurring as codes in the corpus. The rules permit codes to be any of the following: sequences of one, two, or three spelt-out letters; sequences of one or two spelt-out letters or a name, followed by a number; or any of the above preceded by the word "number". For the purposes of these rules, the word "slash" is treated as a letter. Examples of types of phrases covered by these rules, bracketed to show phrase structure, follow.

[$_{NP}$ [$_{NBAR}$ *American flight*][$_{CODE}$ *four eight seven*]]

[$_{NP}$ [$_{CODE}$ *D L seven four six*]]

[$_{NP}$ [$_{NBAR}$ *flight*] [$_{CODE}$ [$_{NAME}$ *Delta*] *one thirty*]]

[$_{NP}$ [$_{NBAR}$ *flight*] [$_{CODE}$ *four seven six*]]

[$_{NP}$ [$_{CODE}$ *E A*]]

[$_{NP}$ [$_{NBAR}$ *fare code*] [$_{CODE}$ *F N*]]

[$_{NP}$ [$_{NBAR}$ *restriction*] [$_{CODE}$ *A P slash five five*]]

[$_{NP}$ [$_{NBAR}$ *flight*] [$_{CODE}$ *number seventeen sixty five*]]

[$_{NP}$ [$_{NBAR}$ *airline*] [$_{CODE}$ *U S*]]

[$_{NP}$ [$_{NBAR}$ *Delta flight*] [$_{CODE}$ *number seven oh nine*]]

[$_{NP}$ [$_{CODE}$ *two oh four five*]]

9.3.2.4 Bare-Determiner NPs

NPs consisting of a bare determiner are formed using the rule

```
NP -> DET
```

A feature limits the range of DETs that can appear on the right-hand side. The DET is most commonly lexical, for instance, "any", "which", "one", "both", "either", "the same", "some", "how many", or "all". It can also be an ordinal determiner, for instance, "the cheapest", "the latest", or "the least expensive".

9.3.2.5 "Kind of" NPs

The corpus contains numerous NPs formed using the "kind/sort/type of" construction; typical examples are "what kind of plane", "what sort of ground transportation", and "the type of aircraft". The words in question all have lexical entries subcategorising for "of" and an NBAR, and the construction can thus be analysed using the general rule:

```
NBAR:[subcat=[]] -> NBAR:[subcat=[COMP]]
                    COMP
```

which combines an NBAR with its lexically subcategorised complements (COMP) to form a larger NBAR. The mechanism is the same as that used to handle the much more common case of verb subcategorisation, as described in Section 9.3.6.1.

9.3.3 Recursive NPs

The structure of the recursive NPs in the domain is on the whole fairly simple. As with the nonrecursive NPs, we begin by breaking them down into types, giving examples of each type together with its approximate frequency of occurrence.

Basic recursive NPs About 85 percent of the recursive NPs consist of a nonrecursive NP which has been postmodified by a PP, a VP, a relative clause (REL), an ADJP, or some combination of these. Examples are "the flights from Dallas to Boston", "United flights between Boston and Denver departing at nine a m", "a flight that leaves Atlanta before noon", "the fares available for Eastern flight two oh five".

Conjoined NPs About 10 percent of the recursive NPs are formed using a conjunction rule. The majority occur in the "between A and B" construction.

Sentential NPs About 2 percent of the recursive NPs are sentential NPs, in practice either embedded questions or "to"-infinitive VPs. Examples are "to fly from Boston to Baltimore on a Saturday", "to get from Denver to Oakland", "what city they stop in", "if Delta flight two ninety six serves breakfast".

Quote-apposition NPs About 1 percent of the recursive NPs are constructions of the type we dub, for want of a standard term, "quote appositions": a typical example would be "the designation Y N" or "the fare code F". The relatively common occurrence of the construction is clearly due to the frequent occurrence of code expressions in the domain.

9.3.3.1 Basic Recursive NPs

Most of the recursive NPs in the corpus are constructed from a nonrecursive NP postmodified by a PP, a REL, a VP, an ADJP, or some combination of these. The following six rules and one schema capture these constructions:[1]

```
NP -> NP PP
NP -> NP REL
NP -> NP VP:[vform=(ing\/passive)]
NP -> NP ADJP
REL -> S:[type=rel,gapsin=[],gapsout=[]]
REL -> S:[type=normal,gapsin=[np:_],gapsout=[]]
ADJP -> ADJ:[subcat=COMPS]
        COMPS
```

The first two rules are self-explanatory. Features are used on the third rule to restrict the VP to ones whose main verb is either progressive or passive; the second case covers reduced relatives like "[a meal] [served on a plane]" or "[the type of aircraft] [used]". The fourth rule uses a feature to restrict the ADJPs that can occur as postnominal modifiers. This feature is set on complex ADJP expressions in which the adjectival head does not occur in final position (e.g., "cheaper than two hundred dollars" or "available for Eastern flight two oh five"), and also on a few lexical ADJPs like "first class", "one way", and "round trip".

The fifth and sixth rules cover relative clauses. The fifth is for relatives introduced by a relative pronoun, such as, "flights [that serve breakfast]", or "flights

---

[1] Rule schemas are described in Appendix B.2.

[where the round trip fare is under one thousand dollars]". Setting the feature `type` to `rel` ensures that the S is introduced by an element that can serve as a relative pronoun (see Section 9.3.7.1). The sixth rule is for relatives without a relative pronoun, for example, "the cheapest fare [I can get] from Dallas to Denver". The `gaps in` and `gapsout` features (cf. also Section 9.3.6.1) capture the difference between the explicit relative pronoun required by the fifth rule and the implicit relative pronoun required by the sixth.

The final rule schema is for adjectives that take a complement: the only common case in the corpus is "available", which is treated as subcategorising for a PP.[2]

9.3.3.2 Conjoined NPs

Two rules are used to handle conjoined NPs:

```
NP -> NP CONJ NP
NP -> NP NP
```

The first rule handles normal conjunction of two NPs, for example, "Boston and Atlanta". The second rule is used in combination with the first to analyse constructions like "Boston Atlanta and Denver". It creates a conjoined NP, marked with a feature that only allows it to be used to appear as the leftmost daughter in an application of the first rule.

9.3.3.3 Sentential NPs

The grammar covers two types of sentential NPs: "to"-infinitive VPs like "to get from Atlanta airport into the city of Atlanta", and embedded questions like "what city they stop in" and "if these flights serve meals". Three rules are used,

```
S:[type=norm] -> VP:[vform=inf]
NP -> S:[type=q, inv=n, whmoved=_]
NP -> COMPLEMENTISER S:[type=norm]
```

The first rule makes a "to"-infinitive VP into an S, so that it can then be used by the other rules. The second rule covers sentential NPs which are either "to"-infinitive VPs or embedded WH questions; the third rule is for embedded Y-N questions. The features used are explained in Section 9.3.7.1.

9.3.3.4 Quote-Apposition NPs

About 1 percent of all recursive NPs are *quote appositions*, NPs consisting of a nonrecursive definite NP followed by a code expression. Examples are "the fare code Q W" and "the abbreviation U S". These expressions differ both syntactically

---

[2] Rule schemas are described in Appendix B.2.

and semantically from the code expressions described earlier. For example, "flight U A one oh four" means "the flight whose code is U A one oh four", while "the code U A one oh four" means "the code which is equal to U A one oh four". There is a simple rule to deal with these, of the form.

```
NP -> NP CODE.
```

9.3.4   Prepositional Phrases

The grammar deviates somewhat from standard practice with regard to its handling of PP sequences. Contrary to most traditional grammars, which would assign a VP like "travel from Atlanta to Boston" the constituent structure

$$[_{VP} [_{VP} [_{VP} \, travel] [_{PP} \, from \, Atlanta]] [_{PP} \, to \, Boston]]$$

we give it the flatter structure

$$[_{VP} [_{VP} \, travel] [_{PP} \, from \, Atlanta \, to \, Boston]]$$

The idea is realized by a rule of the form

```
PP -> PP PP
```

which combines a sequence of two PPs into a single *big PP*. The left-hand daughter may itself be a big PP, allowing arbitrarily long sequences of PPs to be PP constituents.

There are five types of basic PP, all of which can either occur on their own or in PP sequences:

> **Normal PPs** Normal PPs, consisting of a preposition followed by an NP, make up more than 90 percent of all single PPs. Examples are "from Dallas", "to downtown Pittsburgh", "on a flight from Boston to Denver".
>
> **Temporal NPs** *Temporal* NPs (i.e., NPs whose `temporal` feature has the value y) can also act as PPs, and make up about 5 percent of all PPs. Examples are "what time", "that afternoon", "Thursday", "July twenty third".
>
> **A-to-B PPs** Expressions of the form "A to B", with A- and -B names, account for a further 1.5 percent of all PPs. Examples are "Baltimore to Philadelphia", "Atlanta to Pittsburgh".
>
> **Stranded prepositions** About 0.5 percent of all PPs are stranded prepositions, that is, PPs from which the NP has been removed by a movement rule, leaving a lone preposition.
>
> **Conjoined PPs** There are a small number of examples of conjoined PPs, for example, "in Boston and in Baltimore", "after five p m and before eight a m".

The above constructions are handled by the following rules, none of which are problematic:

```
PP -> P NP
PP -> NP:[temporal=y]
PP -> NP:[name=y] to NP:[name=y]
PP -> PP CONJ PP
```

9.3.5   Numbers

Numbers occur frequently in the corpus: they can be cardinals ("[one thousand one hundred] dollars"), ordinals ("September [twenty first]") or codes ("D L [seven six four]"). The rules for numbers are simple but fairly numerous; they seem to give a coverage of the domain which is virtually complete.

Examples of some types of numbers covered are the following: "five eight nine", "four fifty nine", "twenty first", "fifty five", "ten twenty eight", "one seven nine three", "eight thirteen", "four hundred", "one thousand", "three three", "fourteen nineteen", "thirty seven forty nine", "three hundred and thirty six".

9.3.6   Verb Phrases

The rules for verb phrases are certainly the most complex part of the grammar, mirroring the wide variety found in verb-phrase constructions; the proportion of VPs in the corpus that are outside grammatical coverage, at about 1 percent, is not, however, higher than for most constituents.

We will divide up the material along three dimensions: first, by the type of main verb (transitive, intransitive, modal, etc.); second, by the types of modification and transformation of the verb phrase (WH moved, passivised, PP modified, etc.); and, finally, by context of occurrence of the verb phrase (predicate in clause, imperative, postnominal modifier, etc.).

Perhaps the main justification for adopting a principled linguistic approach to grammar coverage is that different possibilities along each of these three dimensions can combine freely, giving rise to the large observed range of surface constructions.

9.3.6.1   Types of Verbs

Classifying first by main verb, thirteen types of verbs occur with reasonable frequency:

> **"Be" as main verb** The most common type of verb in the corpus, accounting for about 25 percent of all verb occurrences. The forms "'s", "am", "are", "be", and "is" all occur.

Transitives About equally as common as "be" verbs; make up another 25 percent of all verb occurrences. Common examples are "have", "like", and "leave".

Ditransitives About 15 percent of all verb occurrences; the only commonly occurring ones are "show", "tell", "give", and "find".

Intransitives About 15 percent of all verb occurrences: common examples are "fly", "arrive", "leave", and "go".

Modal auxiliaries About 5 percent of all verb occurrences. The commonly occurring modals in the corpus are "would", "could", "can", "may", and "will".

Auxiliary "do" and "does" About 5 percent of all verb occurrences.

Verbs taking "to" infinitives About 5 percent of all verb occurrences. The commonly occurring examples are "like", "need", and "want".

Auxiliary "be" About 2 percent of all verb occurrences. The forms "am", "are", "be", and "is" occur, with both passive and "-ing" VP complements.

Particle verbs About 0.5 percent of all verb occurrences. The most common are "stand for", "get off", and "stop over".

Verbs taking extraposed sentential complements About 0.5 percent of all verb occurrences. The only examples are "cost" and "take", for example, "How much does it cost to fly on American from Dallas to Baltimore".

Ditransitive verb with embedded question About 0.25 percent of all verb occurrences are examples of "show" or "tell", used as in "Can you tell me what city they stop in?" or "Can you show me what's available?".

Ditransitive verb taking PP complement About 0.25 percent of all verb occurrences are examples of "tell about", as in "tell me about limousine services".

Transitive verb with embedded question There are a small number of occurrences of "know" used as a question-embedding verb, as in "I need to know what flights leave Atlanta on Sunday evening and arrive in Baltimore".

The basic verb phrase consists of the main verb together with its complements (if any) and is formed, irrespective of verb type, using the central rule-schema:[3]

```
VP -> V:[subcat=COMPS]
      COMPS
```

---

[3] Rule schemas are described in Appendix B.2. For a detailed discussion of the CLE grammar's treatment of subcategorisation, the interested reader is referred to Alshawi 1992, 62–68.

The only type of verb appearing in the corpus whose complement requires special grammar rules is "be" as a main verb, for which three rules exist; "be" subcategorises for a constituent called a COMP, which can be an NP, ADJP or PP. The rules are

```
COMP:[subjform=normal] -> NP
COMP:[subjform=normal] -> ADJP
COMP:[subjform=normal] -> PP
```

The use of the COMP category is motivated by technical reasons explained later in Section 9.3.7.1.

9.3.6.2 Transformations and Modifications of Verb Phrases

We next consider the different ways in which the basic verb phrase can be transformed or modified.

PP postmodifier About 15 percent of all VPs have a PP modifier following the basic verb phrase, for example, "go from Denver to Atlanta", "is used on U A five five one", "leaving Atlanta in the afternoon".

Movement About 10 percent of all VPs have their word order changed by some kind of movement phenomenon, normally occurring in the context of a question or relative clause. Typical examples are the VPs (bracketed) in "what cities [does Continental service]", "the earliest flight you [have on Wednesday September fourth]".

Modal or higher verb About 10 percent of all VPs contain a modal or higher verb, for example, "would like to go at ten a m", "want to see the cheapest flight from Denver to Pittsburgh", "will be served on U A ninety one".

ADVP premodifier About 5 percent of all VPs have an ADVP preceding the basic VP. This is most commonly "please" or "also", for example, "please repeat your answer", "also give me a list of flights between Oakland and Boston".

Passivisation About 2.5 percent of all VPs are passivised, for example, "is served on flight one six nine", "offered on this flight", "is being used on flight number ninety eight".

Conjoined VP About 1 percent of all VPs involve a conjunction, for example, "departing San Francisco and arriving in Oakland", "want to leave Philadelphia and arrive in Atlanta on a Thursday".

ADVP postmodifier About 1 percent of all VPs have an ADVP modifier following the basic VP, for example, "would like to see the flights from Baltimore to Philadelphia again", "want to fly from Baltimore to Dallas round trip".

"-ing" VP post-modifier About 0.5 percent of all VPs have an "-ing" VP used as a modifier after the basic VP, for example, "go from Denver to Dallas leaving after three p m", "depart from San Francisco heading towards Boston after noon".

"to" VP postmodifier   A small number of VPs have a "to" VP used as an adverbial postmodifier, for example, "leaving on Tuesdays from Denver [to go to Boston]".

Negation   A small number of VPs are negated, for example, "do not go through Oakland".

The structured nature of the grammar allows all these possibilities to be captured compactly. Seven rules cover basic VP structure:

```
VP -> VP PP
VP -> VP ADVP
VP -> ADVP VP
ADVP -> VP:[vform=ing]
ADVP -> VP:[vform=to]
VP -> VP CONJ VP
VP -> not VP
```

Of these, the first three permit VPs to be postmodified by PPs and ADVPs and premodified by ADVPs; the fourth and fifth make "-ing" and "to" VPs into ADVPs, thus allowing them to act as VP modifiers via the second and third rules. The sixth and seventh allow VP conjunction and VP negation.

The last four rules handle the empty productions associated with WH movement of NPs, PPs, ADJPs and ADVPs:[4]

```
NP:[gapsin=[np:_|Rest],gapsout=Rest] -> []
PP:[gapsin=[pp:_|Rest],gapsout=Rest] -> []
ADJP:[gapsin=[adjp:_|Rest],gapsout=Rest] -> []
ADVP:[gapsin=[advp:_|Rest],gapsout=Rest] -> []
```

In these rules, the pair of features (`gapsin`, `gapsout`) functions as a *gaps list* (Pereira 1981). A detailed discussion of the way in which this mechanism is used in the CLE grammar can be found in Alshawi (1992, 70–74) (see also Section 9.3.7.1).

9.3.6.3 Verb-Phrase Contexts

Finally, we consider the possible contexts in which a VP can occur. Apart from combining with an NP to form a clause (the most common case), the following

---

[4] The NP-gap rule is also used to handle passivisation (cf. Pulman 1987); the basic idea is to treat the subcategorised semantic object as a *passive gap*, linked to the surface subject through the gap-threading mechanism.

possibilities exist:

Imperatives About 30 percent of all VPs occur free as imperatives, for example, "Show me the flights from Dallas to Boston".

"-ing" VP modifiers About 5 percent of all VPs are "-ing" VP modifiers to NPs, for example, "flights going to San Francisco".

Reduced relatives About 0.5 percent of all VPs are reduced relatives, for example, "a meal served on a plane".

"to"-infinitive VP as NP About 0.5 percent of all VPs are "to"-infinitive VPs functioning as sentential NPs, for example, "to travel from Oakland airport to downtown".

The rules needed to realise these possibilities are described in other sections.

9.3.7 Clauses and Top-Level Utterances

Having discussed the other constituents, we finally consider the structure of clauses and top-level utterances. (We will use the terms "utterance" and "top-level utterance" interchangeably to designate the start symbol of the grammar; remember also that many utterances are not clauses.) The following types of utterance exist:

Unmoved WH questions WH questions not exhibiting movement are the most common type of utterance in the corpus, accounting for about 30 percent of the utterances. Examples are "what is the cheapest flight from Boston to San Francisco", "what flights go from Pittsburgh to Baltimore after eight o'clock next Wednesday", "what type of aircraft is used on the five forty flight from Philadelphia to Dallas".

Imperatives Imperatives are about equally as common, accounting for another 30 percent of the utterances. Examples are "list all flights on United from San Francisco to Boston", "show me ground transportation in Dallas please", "now show me the flights from Denver to Philadelphia on a Saturday".

Y-N questions About 10 percent of the utterances are Y-N questions, for example, "is U S Air flight four seventy six a nonstop flight", "all right do you have a flight from Atlanta to Boston", "okay can you tell me the flight cost between Denver and Atlanta", "could you repeat that please".

Declarative sentences About 10 percent of the utterances are declarative sentences, though naturally most of these have the force of requests, commands, or questions. Typical examples are "I need to know what flights leave Atlanta on Sunday evening and arrive in Baltimore", "I need information on a flight from Boston to Denver", "yes I want to go to San Francisco late that afternoon".

Moved WH questions WH questions with movement are much less frequent than ones without, accounting for only about 5 percent of the utterances. Despite this, moved WH questions exhibit considerably more variety than unmoved ones. Examples are "what cities does Continental service", "what ground transportation is there from Denver", "how much does it cost to fly on American from Dallas to Baltimore", "how do I get from Pittsburgh airport to downtown Pittsburgh", "how long is the flight from Oakland to Washington D C", "what time are the flights leaving from Denver to Pittsburgh on July seventh".

Elliptical NPs Elliptical utterances are common: more than half of them are NPs, possibly introduced by an interjection or a phrase like "how about" or "what about", or followed by "please". These account for another 5 percent of the corpus. Typical examples are "the most expensive flight between Boston and Philadelphia", "six fifty three a m", "flights from Atlanta please", "how about twelve thirty p m", "what about a flight from Boston to San Francisco stopping in Denver".

Elliptical PPs and ADVPs A further 5 percent of the corpus consists of elliptical PPs and ADVPs, with PPs accounting for about two-thirds of these. As with elliptical NPs, they can be accompanied by interjections and phrases like "please" or "how about". Examples: "from Pittsburgh", "how about on Sunday night", "and for Lufthansa", "one way", "round trip please".

9.3.7.1 Clauses

It is clear from the percentage figures shown in the preceding list that clauses (which include WH questions, Y-N questions, imperatives, and declarative sentences) are the most common type of utterance, and we will consequently consider the rules used for forming them. We begin with the five rules that do not have to do with WH movement or subject-verb inversion:

```
S:[type=T] -> NP:[type=T] VP
S:[type=imp] -> VP:[vform=inf]
S -> ADVP:[advtype=sentential] S
S -> S ADVP:[advtype=sentential]
S -> S CONJ S
```

The type feature on S can have values q (question), imp (imperative), r (relative) or norm (normal, the default). q or r values are passed up from the subject, when the clause does not exhibit movement, and otherwise from the fronted element as explained below.

The first of the rules just presented is the basic one which combines subject NP and VP to form a clause; the second forms an imperative clause from a VP with infinitive main verb.[5] The third and fourth allow pre and postmodification of clauses by sentential adverbs, and the fifth forms conjoined clauses. All of these are straightforward. We now consider the six rules used for dealing with inversion and WH movement, which are more complex in structure:

```
S:[inv=y] -> V:[subcat=List]
              NP
              VP:[svi=movedv:[subcat=List])]
V:[subcat=[vp:VP],svi=movedv:[subcat=[vp:VP]]] -> []
V:[subcat=[comp:COMP],svi=movedv:[subcat=[comp:COMP]]]
    -> []
S:[whmoved=y,type=T,inv=I] ->
    NP:[type=T] S:[inv=I,gapsin=[np:_],gapsout=[]]
S:[whmoved=y,type=T,inv=I] ->
    PP:[type=T] S:[inv=I,gapsin=[pp:_],gapsout=[]]
S:[whmoved=y,type=q,inv=I] ->
    ADJP:[wh=y] S:[inv=I,gapsin=[adjp:_],gapsout=[]]
```

The first three rules cover subject-auxiliary inversion; two new features play important roles. The `inv` feature distinguishes clauses with inverted word order from normal ones; the `svi` (subject-verb inversion) feature is used to pass information about the fronted verb to the place in the VP where it would have occurred in an uninverted clause.

The first rule defines the basic structure of a clause with subject-auxiliary inversion, as a sequence of auxiliary verb, subject, and inverted-verb phrase. The `svi` feature propagates the fronted verb down through the verb phrase to reach the main verb: there it can be picked up by either the second or third rule.

The second covers all the verbs that can be fronted except copula or predicate "be"; all other such verbs subcategorise for a VP. The third rule handles the specific case of fronted "be": the need to include the complement of "be" as the value of the `subcat` feature is the reason for including the COMP category described earlier in Section 9.3.6.1.

The fourth, fifth, and sixth rules cover movement and make essential use of the `whmoved` feature. The fourth and fifth are for fronted NPs and PPs. These rules can be used for WH questions occurring as main clauses, embedded WH questions, or relatives, the type of clause being determined by the `inv`, `type`, and `whmoved` features. Thus, for example, embedded WH questions are whmoved=y, inv=n, and type=q, while relative clauses are whmoved=y, inv=y, and type=r. The `type` feature is passed up from the fronted constituent; so, for example, "that" has an NP entry with type=r, allowing it to introduce relative clauses but not

---

[5] In English, the imperative and infinitive forms of the verb coincide.

inverted WH questions. In contrast, the NP entry for "what" has `type=q`, giving it the opposite distribution.

The sixth rule is for fronted ADJPs: these can only introduce questions, for example, "How expensive is the San Francisco limousine service".

9.3.7.2 Utterances

We distinguish two main types of top-level utterances: clauses and elliptical phrases. We consider the rules for elliptical phrases first:

```
PHRASE    -> PP
PHRASE    -> ADVP
PHRASE    -> NP
UTTERANCE -> PHRASE
UTTERANCE -> CONJ PHRASE
UTTERANCE -> how/what about PHRASE
```

The first three rules allow PPs, ADVPs, and NPs to stand alone as elliptical phrases. The remaining rules specify utterances that consist of elliptical phrases possibly preceded by a conjunction or an expression of the form "how/what about", for instance, "and from Dallas to Atlanta", "and United", "how about for Eastern Airlines", "what about a seven three four".

The five remaining rules are for clausal utterances:

```
UTTERANCE -> S:[type=imp]
UTTERANCE -> S:[type=q,inv=y,whmoved=y]
UTTERANCE -> S:[type=q,inv=n,whmoved=n]
UTTERANCE -> S:[type=norm,inv=y,whmoved=n]
UTTERANCE -> S:[type=norm,inv=n,whmoved=n]
```

These cover, in order, imperative clauses, WH-word questions with WH movement, WH questions without WH movement, Y-N questions, and simple declarative clauses. The features used were explained in Section 9.3.7.1.

9.4   Coverage Failures

In the previous sections, we have described the constructions currently covered by the grammar. We will now consider the corpus utterances that are still outside coverage. We give a top-level classification of common coverage failures, with examples, discussing each class briefly. The list we present is based on analysis of a random sample of 200 corpus utterances that were judged as being outside current grammar coverage. Most of them received no analyses at all; in a few cases, the system was able to find one or more analyses, but they were all judged incorrect. Some utterances fail analysis for more than one reason, so the numbers total a little more than 200.

We start with the more or less obviously spurious problems, and work towards those that are genuinely grammatical in nature.

Data collection problems Thirty-six utterances (18 percent) are clear instances of data collection problems resulting in bad corpus utterances. The majority (twenty eight) appear to be the result of subjects incorrectly using the "push to talk" button, yielding examples like "show me flights from denver to" or "what stopover cities does" or, in a few cases, simply the empty utterance. There are also a few examples of transcription errors ("could you please give me the type of aircraft that flys from boston to denver after five p m"), and inclusion of noncorpus utterances ("begin scenario c m u dash forty one").

Meta-utterances Six utterances (3 percent) are correctly recorded and transcribed, but represent meta-utterances not even peripherally part of the domain. ("Show me oh wrong question"; "cheapest round trip fare from boston to I don't believe I keep doing that one").

System-internal problems A further eleven failures (5.5 percent) are caused by system-internal problems unrelated to the grammar. Most of them are caused by incorrect pruning decisions.

Multi-unit utterances Twenty six examples (13 percent) were judged to be *multi-unit utterances*, in the sense that they are most naturally regarded as a sequence of two or more complete utterance fragments produced as a single utterance; the parser analyses these as a list of top-level constituents (see Section 2.7.1), so no extension to the grammar is required.

Repairs A further thirty one examples (15.5 percent) were judged to be repairs or other types of disfluencies. These are also regarded as extra-grammatical in nature, but are not currently handled in the SLT system.

Lexicon holes Forty seven examples (23.5 percent) include one or more holes in lexical coverage. The most frequent problems (twelve examples and thirteen examples, respectively) were missing variants of names for airports and other geographical locations, and missing senses of verbs. For instance, the lexicon contains an entry for "mean" taking an NP complement ("what does that code mean"), but lacks one for "mean" taking a sentential complement ("does this mean american airlines has a hub in boston"). There were nine cases of missing entries for common nouns, six for adjectives, and a total of six for other parts of speech.

Grammar holes Thirty seven examples (18.5 percent) represent clear holes in grammatical coverage. The most frequent problems (twelve examples) concern expressions for codes and numbers ("the code B

DEN", "flight number five three nine dash six oh six oh nine six oh five", "four hundred fifty dollars or less", "the least number of stops"). There are four examples each of problems involving conjunction ("on december twenty seventh and twenty eighth", "i need to know the price and whether a meal is served") and superlatives ("the soonest", "cheapest fares possible"), and a total of seventeen examples of other grammatical problems.

Overtly ungrammatical utterances Ten examples (5 percent) are ungrammatical in the strong sense of actively breaking established grammatical rules, rather than merely representing constructions not in the grammar. For example, there are several examples of sentences that break subject-verb agreement rules, for instance, "does the seventy three S model has a good safety record"; it is possible that the requirement on subject-verb agreement could be relaxed to cover them, but this is a step we have been reluctant to take. Other utterances are simply incorrect in more or less haphazard ways ("how much of the flights that leave after seven cost", "what are the fares for flights from san francisco to either boston or to philadelphia or baltimore"). It is hard to see how to capture sentences like these in an explicitly grammatical framework like the one we have here, but their low frequency is reassuring.

In summary, the system is currently able to assign a grammatical analysis to approximately 85.5 percent of the utterances in the corpus. Of the remainder, about 2.8 percent appear to be the result of faulty data collection procedures, 5.7 percent are performance-related problems (repairs, meta-utterances, multisentence utterances and incorrect user grammar), and 0.8 percent are due to system-related issues, generally incorrect pruning decisions. The final 6.5 percent represent true coverage problems, breaking down into 3.6 percent lexicon and 2.8 percent grammar.

9.5   Comparison with French and Swedish Grammars

To a striking degree, the English grammar turns out to be properly included in the union of the grammars for Swedish and French. (The history of the English language makes it easy to hypothesise explanations for this fact.) To conclude this chapter, we will summarise the very small number of features unique to the English version.

Least interestingly, there are obvious surface divergences in the phrasal rules for number, time, and date expressions. For instance, English commonly uses the word order for dates exemplified by "the third of January", which lacks an exact counterpart in the other two languages.[6] In all cases, however, the differences are

---

[6] The closest Swedish can get is *"den tredje januari"*, omitting the "of"; in French, *"le trois janvier"* uses a cardinal rather than an ordinal.

restricted to surface syntax: at the level of semantic representation, the rules are identical.

There are a number of English grammar rules relating to compound nominals that lack any close correlate in French. In a narrow sense, it is also correct to say that there are no similar grammar rules in Swedish either. This, however, is due to the fact that Swedish generally realises noun compounds at the level of morphology rather than syntax, with an extremely close correspondence between English syntax rules and Swedish morphology rules. For example, the main structural difference between the English "ground transportation" and the Swedish *"marktransport"* is that Swedish omits the space between the two nouns. These ideas are explored in more detail in Section 19.2.

The most significant examples of purely English-specific rules occur in connection with clausal structure: in particular, the phenomena of subject-verb inversion, WH movement, negation, and adverbial modification. In all of these cases, the point is essentially that the possibilities for English are much more restrictive than for either of the other two languages, allowing a simpler and more efficient treatment. Thus, English only permits inversion with auxiliaries and the verbs "be" and "have", allowing the treatment described in Section 9.3.7.1; in contrast, the French and Swedish grammars are forced to use a more general rule that potentially allows any verb to invert. Similarly, the English negation construction can be specified very simply by including a single rule that allows the word "not" to occur before a VP, together with a few lexical entries for negated auxiliaries like "isn't" and "don't". A corresponding treatment is not available in the other two languages.

In the following two chapters, we describe in detail the unique features of the French and Swedish grammars.

10   French Coverage

MANNY RAYNER AND PIERRETTE BOUILLON

10.1   Introduction

This chapter describes the French version of the CLE, which, like the Swedish one covered in the next chapter, was created by intelligent manual adaptation of the original English version. The general style of exposition will also be similar to that adopted in the chapter on Swedish coverage; rather than recapitulate the many similarities between the French grammar and the English one from which it was derived, we will concentrate on the differences. We attempt throughout to highlight the general nature of the adaptation process, and argue that it constitutes a general recipe that could be applied to other unification-based systems.

The French grammar covers nearly all the basic constructions of the language, including the following: declarative, interrogative, and imperative clauses; formation of Y-N and WH questions using inversion, complex inversion, and *"est-ce que"*; clitic pronouns; adverbial modification; negation; nominal and verbal PPs; complements to *"être"* and *"il y a"*; relative clauses, including those with *"dont"*; partitives, including use of *"en"*; passives; pre- and postnominal adjectival modification, including comparative and superlative; code expressions; sentential complements and embedded questions; complex determiners; numerical expressions; date and time expressions; conjunction of most major constituents; and a wide variety of verb types, including modals and reflexives. There is a good treatment of inflectional morphology that includes all major paradigms.

We will describe the adaptation process in detail. The only components that required manual alteration were "rule" modules: hand-coded, unification-based descriptions of the grammar, lexicon, morphology, and so on. As noted in Alshawi (1992), Section 14.2.2, the effort involved in adapting a set of rule modules to a new language depends on how directly they refer to surface form; unsurprisingly, modules defining surface phenomena are the ones that require most work. During the process of adapting the system to French, problems arose almost exclusively in connection with morphology and syntax rules.

When comparing the French and English grammars, there are two types of objects of immediate interest: syntax rules and features. Looking first at the rules themselves, about 80 percent of the French syntax rules are either identical with or very similar to the English counterparts from which they have been adapted. Of the remainder, some rules (e.g., those for date, time, and number expressions) are different, but essentially too trivial to be worth describing in detail. Similar considerations apply to features.

Examining the grammar, we find that there are three large groups of rules and features interesting from this point of view, describing three separate complexes of linguistic phenomena: question formation, clitic pronouns, and agreement. As we have argued previously in Section 1.5, all of these are rigid and well-defined types of construction that occur in all genres of written and spoken French. It is thus both desirable and reasonable to attempt to encode them in terms of feature-based rules, rather than (for instance) expecting to derive them as statistical regularities in large corpora. In Sections 10.2, 10.3, and 10.4, we describe how we handle these key problems.

10.2   Question Formation

10.2.1   Constraints on Question Formation

We start this section by briefly reviewing the way in which question formation is handled in the English CLE grammar (cf. Section 9.3.7.1). There are two main dimensions of classification: English questions can be either WH or Y-N; and they can use either the inverted or the uninverted word order. Y-N questions must use the inverted word order, but both word orders are permissible for WH questions. The phrase-structure rules analyse an inverted WH question as constituting a fronted WH+ element followed by an inverted clause containing a gap element. The feature inv distinguishes inverted from uninverted clauses. The following examples illustrate the top-level structure of Y-N, unmoved WH, and moved WH questions, respectively.

[Does he love Mary]$_{S:[inv=y]}$

[Who loves Mary]$_{S:[inv=n]}$

[[Whom]$_{NP}$ [does he love []$_{NP}$]$_{S:[inv=y]}$]

The French rules for question formation are structurally fairly similar to the English ones. However, there are several crucial differences that mean that the constructions in the two languages often differ widely at the level of surface form. Two phenomena in particular stand out. First, English only permits subject-verb inversion when the verb is an auxiliary, or a form of "have" or "be"; in contrast,

French potentially allows subject-verb inversion with any verb. For this reason, English question formation using auxiliary "do" lacks a corresponding construction in French.

Second, French permits two other common question formation constructions in addition to subject-verb inversion: prefacing the declarative version of the clause with the question particles *"est-ce que"* or *"est-ce qui"*, and *complex inversion*, that is, fronting the subject and inserting a dummy pronoun after the inverted verb. Particularly in spoken French, it is also possible to form a nonsubject WH question out of a fronted WH+ phrase followed by an uninverted clause containing an appropriate gap. We refer to this last possibility as "pseudoinversion". A subject pronoun following an inverted verb needs to be linked to it by a hyphen, which can be realised as a *"-t-"* (cf. Section 7.4.3). Figure 10.1 presents examples illustrating the main French question constructions.

The nontrivial problem is formalising the highly complex constraints that determine which question-formation constructions are available in a given context. The following properties of the sentence may potentially affect the decision: our initial analysis was based on the data in Grevisse (1993), Chapter 5, Section 2, and refined using the specially constructed test suite described later in Section 10.2.3.

Type of question Either Y-N or WH.

Type of subject The choice is between personal pronouns (*"je"*, *"tu"*, *"il"*, and so on), demonstrative pronouns (*"ça"* or *"cela"*), and other NPs.

Presence of complements and/or adjuncts to main verb There appear to be at least five distinct cases to consider and that can overlap: (i) No complements or adjuncts; (ii) A "complement essentiel" (Grevisse 1993, sec. 388), which can be a nongap direct object, an infinitive VP complement, or a predicative complement to a verb like *"être"* or *"devenir"*; (iii) A fronted occurrence of *"qui"* or *"quel"*, used as a complement to a verb like *"être"* or *"devenir"*; (iv) A fronted occurrence of *"que"*, used as a direct object; (v) A fronted occurrence of *"pourquoi"*.

A complete specification of the implemented constraints on question formation follows. We present the rules in the order of least specific to most specific:

1. The noninverted word order is always acceptable, though possibly only in spoken French:

Le vol part?
(The flight leaves?)

Y-N, inversion:
Aime-t-il Marie?
(Loves he Marie?)

Y-N, *"est-ce que"*:
Est-ce que Jean aime Marie?
(*Est-ce que* Jean loves Marie?)

Y-N, complex inversion:
Jean aime-t-il Marie?
(Jean loves he Marie?)

Y-N, pseudoinversion:
Jean aime Marie?
(Jean loves Marie?)

WH, subject question, no inversion:
Quel homme aime Marie?
(Which man loves Marie?)

WH, inversion:
Quelle femme aime-t-il?
(Which woman loves he?)

WH, *"est-ce que"*:
Quelle femme est-ce que Jean aime?
(Which woman *est-ce que* Jean loves?)

WH, complex inversion:
Quelle femme Jean aime-t-il?
(Which woman Jean loves he?)

WH, pseudoinversion:
Quelle femme Jean aime?
(Which woman Jean loves?)

Figure 10.1. Main French question constructions.

Combien ça coûte?
(How much that costs?)

Pourquoi il part?
(Why he leaves?)

2. The word order with *"est-ce que"* or *"est-ce qui"* is always acceptable, unless there is a fronted occurrence of *"quel"* or *"qui"* used as a predicative complement:

Est-ce que le vol part?
(*Est-ce que* the flight leaves?)

Combien est-ce que le vol coûte?
(How much *est-ce que* the flight costs?)

Quand est-ce qu'il part?
(When *est-ce que* it leaves?)

*Quel est-ce que le vol le plus cher est?
(*What *est-ce que* the most expensive flight is?)

*Qui est-ce qui cet homme est?
(*Who *est-ce qui* that man is?)

3. With a pronominal subject, normal inversion is always correct and complex inversion is always incorrect:

Part-il?
(Leaves he?)

Pourquoi part-il?
(Why leaves he?)

*Combien il coûte-t-il?
(*How much it costs it?)

*Pourquoi il part-il?
(*Why he leaves he?)

4. In a Y-N question with a nonpronominal subject, real inversion is blocked:

Le vol part-il?
(The flight leaves it?)

Est-ce que le vol part?
(*Est-ce que* the flight leaves?)

*Part le vol?
(*Leaves the flight?)

The rules just presented are relatively straightforward, and cover the cases of Y-N questions, WH questions with pronominal subject, and WH questions using the *"est-ce que"* and pseudoinverted word orders.

The difficult rules are the ones that determine when inversion and complex inversion are permitted in a WH question with a nonpronominal subject. By default, both are possible, with the following exceptions:

5 In a WH question, presence of a fronted *"quel"* or *"que"* blocks complex inversion:

Quel est le premier vol?
(What is the first flight?)

*Quel le premier vol est-il?
(*What the first flight is it?)

Que veut l'homme?
(What wants the man?)

*Que l'homme veut-il?
(*What the man wants he?)

6 In a WH question with nonpronominal subject, a nongap complement essentiel or nongap verbal PP modifier blocks normal inversion:

*Quand sera cet homme sage? (predicative complement)
(*When will be this man sensible?)

Quand cet homme sera-t-il sage?
(When this man will be he sensible?)

*Quand sert ce vol un repas? (direct object)
(*When serves this flight a meal?)

Quand ce vol sert-il un repas?
(When this flight serves it a meal?)

Où l'homme veut-il partir? (infinitival complement)
(Where the man wants he to leave?)

*Où veut l'homme partir?
(*Where wants the man to leave?)

Quand le vol va-t-il à Baltimore? (nongap PP modifier)
(When the flight goes it to Baltimore?)

*Quand va le vol à Baltimore?
(*When goes the flight to Baltimore?)

*Quand est un repas servi? (*être* as passive auxiliary)
(*When is a meal served?)

Quand un repas est-il servi?
(When a meal is it served?)

7 Fronted *"pourquoi"* (but not any other fronted WH+ PP) blocks normal inversion with a nonpronominal subject:

Pourquoi le vol part-il?
(Why the flight leaves it?)

*Pourquoi part le vol?
(*Why leaves the flight?)

8 *"Ça"* (or *"cela"*) as subject blocks normal inversion:

*Combien coûte ça?
(*How much costs that?)

10.2.2 Implementation of the Rules for Question Formation

Modification of the English syntax rules to capture the data described in the preceding section was in fact surprisingly simple; the greater part of the English question-formation rules are retained more or less unchanged. Most importantly, the English semantic rules can still be used, and produce QLF representations of similar form. The rest of the section describes the concrete changes that have been made.

In the French grammar, we added three extra rules to cover the *"est-ce que"*, complex-inversion, and pseudoinversion constructions: the second of these rules combines the complex-inverted verb with the following dummy pronoun to form a verb, in essence treating the dummy pronoun as a kind of verbal affix. A further rule deals with the hyphen linking an inverted verb with a following subject.

With regard to the feature set, the critical changes involve the `inv` feature. In English, as we saw, this feature had two possible values, `y` and `n`. In French, the corresponding feature has five values: `inverted`, `uninverted`, `est-ce-que`, `complex`, and `pseudo`, distinguishing clauses formed using the different question-formation constructions. (It is important to note, though, that the semantic representation of the clause is the same, irrespective of its inversion type.)

In order to capture the complex constraints 3 through 8 above, two more features are required. First, a clausal feature `subjpron` distinguishes pronominal from nonpronominal subjects. Second, a feature `invsubjpron` is added to VP, V, PP, and NP categories. Examination of constraints 5 through 8 shows that the correctness of combining inverted word order and a nonpronominal subject is essentially determined by the complements and adjuncts of the VP; so the `invsubjpron` is threaded through the complement and adjunct rules until it can be unified with the `subjpron` feature in the main clause.

We illustrate with an example involving constraint 7 (fronted *"pourquoi"*), which is probably the hardest case. If the (incorrect) sentence **Pourquoi part le* *vol* were valid, it would have the constituent structure

$$[[Pourquoi]_{PP} [part [le vol]_{NP} [[]_V []_{PP}]_{VP}]_S]_S$$

in which the final PP gap is linked to the fronted *"pourquoi"*. The invsubjpron feature on the lexical entry for *"pourquoi"* is set to uninverted: this value is threaded through the PP gap rule and the VP PP modification until it reaches the top-level clausal inversion rule and blocks the derivation. The cases with direct objects and predicative complements are similar but slightly simpler.

It would almost be true to claim that the above constituted our entire treatment of French question formation. In practice, we have found it desirable to add a few more features to the grammar in order to block infelicitous combinations of the inversion rules with certain commonly occurring lexical items. It is possible that the effect of these features could be achieved equally well by statistical modelling or other means, but we describe them here for completeness:

> **Fronting of heavy NPs** Most languages prefer not to front heavy NPs, and this dispreference is particularly strong in French. We have consequently added an NP feature called heavy, which has the value y on NPs containing PP and VP postmodifiers. Thus for example generation of
>
> **Quels vols en partance de Dallas y a-t-il?*
> (*What flights from Dallas *y a-t-il*?)
>
> is blocked, but the preferable
>
> *Quels vols y a-t-il en partance de Dallas?*
> (What flights *y a-t-il* from Dallas?)
>
> is permitted.
>
> **Inverted-subject NPs** Occurrence of some pronouns (in particular, *"cela"* and *"ça"*) is strongly dispreferred in inverted-subject position. A binary feature enforces this as a rule, for example blocking
>
> **Combien coûte ça pour aller à Boston?*
> (*How much costs that to go to Boston?)
>
> but instead permitting
>
> *Combien ça coûte pour aller à Boston?*
> (How much that costs to go to Boston?)

10.2.3 Empirical Evaluation Using a Multidimensional Test Suite

The rules for question formation were tested with the aid of a multidimensional test suite specially constructed for the purpose. The following dimensions were taken into consideration:

- Semantic question type (six possibilities): Y-N, WH-subject NP, WH-object NP, WH-fronted PP (not *"pourquoi"*), WH-fronted *"pourquoi"* or WH in predicative position (*"quel"*, etc.).
- Subcategorisation properties of main verb (five possibilities): predicative (i.e., *"être"*, *"devenir"*), intransitive, transitive with a direct object, transitive with an infinitive complement, or bitransitive.
- Form of subject (two possibilities): personal pronoun or nonpronominal subject.
- Inversion type (five possibilities): real inversion, complex inversion, *"Est-ce que"*, *"Est-ce qui"*, no inversion.
- VP modification (two possibilities): no modifier or PP modifier.

Multiplying out, this yielded 600 theoretically possible combinations, of which 356 were meaningful. Of these meaningful combinations, 263 were judged grammatical, and the remaining 93 ungrammatical.

Somewhat to our surprise, the implemented rules resulted in a perfect fit on the test suite; all 263 grammatical sentences were within coverage, and all 93 ungrammatical ones were outside.

10.3   Clitics

The most difficult technical problems in adapting an English grammar to a Romance language are undoubtedly caused by clitic pronouns. In contrast to English, certain proform complements of verbs do not appear in their normal positions; instead, they occur adjacent to the main verb, and possibly are joined to it by a hyphen. The position of the clitics in relation to the verb (pre- or postverbal) is determined by the mood of the verb, and whether or not the verb is negated. If two or more clitics are affixed to the verb, their internal order is determined by their surface forms. Several attempts to account for the above and other data have previously been described in the literature (e.g., Bès and Gardent 1989; Estival 1990; Grimshaw 1982; Miller and Sag 1995); we have particularly been influenced by the last of these.

Although the underlying framework is very different from the HPSG (Head-driven Phrase Structure Grammar) formalism used by Miller and Sag (1995), our basic idea is the same: to treat clitic movement by a mechanism similar to the one used to handle WH movement. More specifically, we introduce two sets of new rules. The first set handles the surface clitics. They define the structure of the verb/clitic complex, which we, like Estival, regard as a constituent of category V composed of a main verb and a clitic list. A second set of gap rules defines empty constituents of category NP or PP, occurring at the notional "deep" positions occupied by the clitics. Thus, for example, on our account the constituent structure of *Est-ce que vous le voulez?* will be

[*Est-ce que [vous$_{NP}$ [le voulez]$_V$ []$_{NP}$]$_S$]$_S$

where the gap NP category represents the notional direct object of *"voulez"*, realised at surface level by the preverbal clitic *"le"*.

To make this work, we add an extra feature, clitics, to all categories that can participate in clitic movement: in our grammar, these are V, VP, S, NP, and PP. The clitics feature is used to link the cliticised V constituent and its associated clitic gap or gaps. We have found it convenient to define the value of the clitics feature to be a bundle of five separate subfeatures, one for each of the five possible clitic positions in French. Thus, for instance, the second-position clitics *"le"*, *"la"*, and *"les"* are related to object-position clitic gaps through the second subfeature of clitics; the fourth-position *"y"* clitic is related to its matching PP gap through the fourth subfeature; and so on. The linking relation between a clitic gap and its associated clitic is formally exactly the same as that obtaining between a WH gap and its associated antecedent, and can, if desired, be conceptualised as a type of coindexing.

The clitics feature bundle is threaded through the grammar rule that defines the structure of the list of clitics associated with a cliticised verb, and enforces the constraints on ordering of surface clitics. These constraints are encoded in the lexical entry for each clitic.

This basic framework is fairly straightforward, though a number of additional features need to be added in order to capture the syntactic facts. We summarise the main points:

Position of surface clitics Clitics occur postverbally in positive imperative clauses, otherwise preverbally. The clitic-list constituent consequently needs to share suitable features with the verb it combines with.

Surface form of clitics The first- and second-person singular clitics are realised differently depending on whether they occur pre- or postverbally: for example *"Vous me réservez un vol"* ("You book me a flight") versus *"Réservez-moi un vol"* ("Book me a flight"). Moreover, *"me"* and *"te"* are first-position clitics (e.g., *"Vous me les donnez"* ["You me them give"]), while *"moi"* and *"toi"* are third-position (*"Donnez-les-moi"* ["Give me them"]). This alternation is achieved simply by having separate lexical entries for each form. The entries have different syntactic features, but a common semantic representation.

Special problems with the *"en"* clitic The most abstruse problems occur in connection with the *"en"* clitic, and are motivated by sentences like

Combien en avez-vous?
(How many *en* have you?)

Here, our framework seems to dictate a constituent structure including three gaps, namely,

[Combien [[en avez]$_V$ [vous$_{NP}$ [[]$_V$ [[]$_{NP}$ []$_{PP}$]$_{NP}$]]$_S$]$_S$]$_S$

in which the V gap links to *"avez"*, the NP gap to *"combien"*, and the PP gap to *"en"*. The specific difficulty here is that the *"en"* PP gap ends up as an NP modifier (it modifies the NP gap). Normally, however, PP modifiers of NPs cannot be gaps, and the above type of construction is the only exception we have found.

Rather than relax the very common NP → NP PP rule to permit a gap PP daughter, we introduce a second rule of this type which specifically combines certain NPs, including suitable gaps resulting from WH movement, and an *"en"* clitic gap. A feature, takespartitive, picks out the NPs that can participate as left daughters in this rule.

10.4   Agreement

Although grammatical agreement is a linguistic phenomenon that plays a considerably larger role in French than in English, the adjustments needed to the lexicon and syntax rules are usually obvious. For instance, a feature has to be added to both daughters of the rule for prenominal adjectival modification to enforce agreement in number and gender. In nearly all cases, this same procedure is used. A feature called agr, whose value is a bundle representing the category's person, number, and gender, is added to the relevant categories. The agr feature is shared between the categories that are required to agree.

There are, however, some instances where agreement is less trivial. For example, the subject and nominal predicate complement of *"être"* may occasionally fail to agree in gender, for example,

> *La gare est le plus grand bâtiment de la ville*
> (The station-FEM is the biggest building-MASC in the city)

However, if the predicate complement is a pronoun (*"lequel"*, *"celui-ci"*, *"quel"*...)[1] agreement in both gender and number is obligatory: thus, for instance

> *Quel/*quelle/*quels est le premier vol?*
> (Which is the first flight?)

It would be most unpleasant to duplicate the syntax rules, with separate versions for the pronominal and nonpronominal cases. Instead, we add to the NP category a

---

[1] Most French grammars regard *"quel"* as an adjective, but for semantic reasons we have found it more convenient to treat it as a pronoun in this type of construction and as a determiner in expressions like *"quel vol"*.

second agreement feature (compagr) that is constrained to have the same value as agr on pronominal NPs; subject-predicate agreement can then use the compagr feature on the predicate, getting the desired behaviour.

Similar considerations apply to the rule allowing modification of an NP by a "*de*" PP. In general, there is no requirement on agreement between the head NP and the NP daughter of the PP. However, for certain pronominal NP (*"lequel"*, *"l'un"*, *"chacun"*) gender agreement is obligatory, for example,

> *lequel/*laquelle de ces vols*
> (Which of these flights)
>
> *laquelle/*lequel de ces dates*
> (Which of these dates)

This is dealt with correspondingly, by addition of a new agreement feature specific to the NP → NP PP rule.

10.5 Conclusions

The preceding sections describe in essence all the changes we needed to make in order to adapt a substantial English-language processing system to French. We have perhaps presented some of the details in a more compressed form than we would ideally have wished, but nothing important has been omitted. Creation of a good initial French version required about five person-months of effort. We do not believe that we were greatly aided by any special features of the Core Language Engine, other than the fact that it is a well-engineered piece of software based on sound linguistic ideas. Our overall conclusion is that an English-language system conforming to these basic design principles should, in general, be fairly easy to port to Romance languages.

11 Swedish Coverage

MANNY RAYNER, MATS WIRÉN,
AND ROBERT EKLUND

11.1 Introduction

Like the French grammar described in the preceding chapter, the Swedish grammar was originally adapted from its English counterpart, exploiting the large overlap between the structures of the two languages; the general remarks about the adaptation process made in Section 10.1 apply equally well here.[1] The Swedish grammar also covers all the main constructions of the language, including the following: declarative, interrogative, and imperative clauses; formation of Y-N and WH questions; topicalisation; adverbial modification, including constraints on word order in subordinate clauses; negation; nominal and verbal PPs; complements to *"vara"* and *"finnas"*; relative clauses; passives; adjectival modification, including comparative and superlative; agreement rules for number, gender, and definiteness; compound nominals; code expressions; sentential complements and embedded questions; complex determiners; numerical expressions; date and time expressions; conjunction of most major constituents; and a wide variety of verb types, including modal, particle, impersonal, deponent, and reflexive.

Adopting the treatment in the French chapter, we focus on the interesting ways in which the Swedish and English grammatical descriptions differ. This time, we divide our presentation into the following three parts: clausal constructions, particularly those relating to inverted word order and adverbial modification (Section 11.2); verbs and verbal constructions (Section 11.3); and NP constructions (Section 11.4).

---

[1] Pre-SLT versions of the grammar are described in Alshawi et al. (1991) and Gambäck and Rayner (1992). The state of the grammar after the first project phase is described in the SLT-1 report (Agnäs et al. 1994). An independent description of what roughly corresponds to the SLT-1 version is furthermore provided by Gambäck (1997).

11.2   Clausal Constructions

11.2.1   *Inverted Word Order and Verb-Second Phenomena*

The unmarked declarative clause in both Swedish and English has Subject-Verb-Object (SVO) order.[2] However, in Swedish, as in the other Scandinavian languages, there is an alternative X-Verb-Subject-Object (XVSO) order, where X can be almost any type of constituent. The following examples illustrate fronting of noun phrases, prepositional phrases, and sentential adverbs, respectively.

> *Det flyget kan jag ta*
> That flight can I take
> (That flight, I can take)

> *Före klockan tio finns det bara ett flyg*
> Before ten o'clock is there only one flight
> (Before ten o'clock, there is only one flight)

> *Då vill jag flyga med Delta*
> Then want I fly with Delta
> (Then I want to fly with Delta)

A characteristic property of the main clause in Swedish is, thus, that the finite verb always appears in second position, causing the clause to be inverted when it is introduced by a fronted X constituent. In contrast to English, which only allows inversion of auxiliaries, any Swedish verb can be inverted. The English grammar makes use of two verb features which, respectively, distinguish verbs that can invert and verbs that appear as main verbs in a clause; in Swedish, these features are consequently not needed.

For these reasons, Swedish rules relating to inversion and extraposition are more uniform than those for English. In particular, the English grammar includes several rules specifically for topicalised clauses, in which no inversion takes place, operating in parallel with the rules for WH fronting and inversion. The Swedish grammar conflates these two sets of rules to a single set that can be used for either purpose. Thus, for example, the same clausal rule is used for both *"Böcker läser han"* ("Books, he reads") and *"Vad läser han?"* ("What does he read?").

The strongly verb-second nature of Swedish has prompted many linguists to write grammars in which this idea is made the central theme; the main line of development stems from the work of Diderichsen (1946). In contrast to our treatment, which describes inverted word order in terms of verb movement, descriptions based

---

[2] We would like to thank Elisabet Engdahl and Lars Ahrenberg for several helpful discussions concerning the material in this section.

on the Diderichsen sentence schema posit a sentential structure consisting of three main components called fields.[3] The first field contains a preverbal introductory phrase, corresponding to the X constituent mentioned above. The second field is divided into subfields containing, among others, the finite verb and (possibly) the sentential adverb. The third field, which is again divided into subfields, contains the main verb as well as postverbal complements and adjuncts. The sentence schema thus consists of a fixed sequence of (sub)fields, each of which are filled or empty for a given clause. In particular, the structure is the same, irrespective of whether the clause uses inverted or uninverted word order.

It is certainly tempting to argue that this offers a simpler description of the linguistic facts. While we do not want to deny the possible independent advantages of descriptions based on sentence schemas, we think we can offer a fairly convincing counterargument in favour of our verb-movement treatment.

The verb-movement and sentence-schema accounts can both deal comfortably with simple clauses; the crucial cases arise when VP conjunction is involved. In English, strong evidence in favour of the verb-movement account is provided by contrasting pairs of examples like the following:

Has John paid his bill and left?
*Has John paid his bill and will leave?

One can explain the clear ungrammaticality of the second sentence by saying that the phrase structure would have to be:

Has John [[[]$_V$ paid his bill]$_{VP}$ and [will leave]$_{VP}$]$_{VP}$

This is impossible because of the widely applicable Coordinate Structure Constraint (Ross 1967; Williams 1977): a conjunction either has no gap in either conjunct, or else matching gaps in both conjuncts. The constraint is realised concretely by ensuring that the English VP conjunction rule is schematically of the form

```
VP:[svi=MovedV] ->
    VP:[svi=MovedV] CONJ VP:[svi=MovedV]
```

where, as explained in Section 9.3.7.1, the `svi` (subject-verb inversion) feature holds the value of the moved verb, if there is one, and is otherwise set to n.

However, the situation in Swedish is different. Examples analogous to the one above are quite acceptable:

Har han betalat och ska åka?
(Has he paid and will leave?)

---

[3] For an approach that combines a phrase-structure–based unification grammar and a sentence-schema component, see Ahrenberg (1990).

though in practise it is much more common for the inversion to be with a main rather than an auxiliary verb:

> *Helst åker jag med Delta och mellanlandar i Boston*
> (Preferably fly I with Delta and stop in Boston)

Our first impression was that examples like these provided evidence in favour of the sentence-schema approach; on a verb-movement account we have, as already noted, a case where the Coordinate Structure Constraint is violated.

Further consideration convinced us that the contrary was true. It is in fact not at all obvious how to extend sentence-schema rules to deal cleanly with conjoined VP examples, while the verb-movement account requires no more than a trivial change. Specifically, the conjoined VP rule differs from English in that it extracts the V not from both conjuncts, but rather only from the first one. The constraint is implemented by simply modifying the English VP conjunction rule so that the svi feature is passed down to the first conjunct but *not* the second,

```
VP:[svi=MovedV] ->
    VP:[svi=MovedV] CONJ VP:[svi=n]
```

This gives the following phrase structure for our example:

> *Helst åker jag* [[[]$_V$ *med Delta*]$_{VP}$ *och* [*mellanlandar i Boston*]$_{VP}$]$_{VP}$

Although the idea may seem counterintuitive, we have been unable to find any clear reasons to doubt its correctness.[4] Our overall conclusion is that the implemented verb-movement account of Swedish inverted word order is at least as good as a nonmovement account based on sentence schemas.

11.2.2   Adverbs and Negation

Another important difference between English and Swedish word order concerns adverbs and negation. The Swedish negation particles (*"inte"*, *"ej"*, and *"icke"*) behave syntactically and semantically like sentential adverbs, so it makes sense to discuss them under the same heading.

In modern English, it is reasonable to claim that a clause-level adverb is only able to modify VP or S constituents (cf. Sections 9.3.6.2 and 9.3.7.1). There is, in contrast, abundant evidence that Swedish adverbs can modify V constituents as well. In the Swedish grammar, we allow adverbs to occur in five different

---

[4] Note that we only break the Coordinate Structure Constraint with regard to extraction of V constituents; unbalanced extraction of NP or PP constituents is just as incorrect in Swedish as in English, and the VP conjunction rule enforces this.

positions:

Initial Both sentential and verbal adverbs can introduce a clause. This is similar to English, except that in most cases it requires the inverted word order (*"Då tar jag det"*; "**Then** take I that"). A few adverbs also permit use of the uninverted word order (*"**Kanske** jag tar det"*; "**Maybe** I take it").

Final As in English, a verbal adverb can appear finally in a VP (*"Jag tar flyget **hem** "*; "I take the flight **home**"), and a sentential adverb finally in a clause (*"Jag tar flyget **förresten** "*; "I take the flight **for that matter**").

Postverbal Both sentential and verbal adverbs can appear directly after a verb (*"Jag vill **helst** åka med Delta"*; "I want **preferably** to travel with Delta"). This is sometimes also possible if the verb is fronted (*"Vill **inte** du ta det?"*; "Want **not** you take it?" = "Don't you want to take it?").

Preverbal Both sentential and verbal adverbs can also appear directly before a verb. For most adverbs, this possibility only exists in subordinate clauses (*"Han sade att han **inte** ville flyga"*; "He said that he **not** wanted to fly").

V gap With inverted word order, an adverb can occur in the notional position of the V gap (*"Tar du **inte** det flyget?"*; "Take you **not** that flight?").

In general, only some of the above possibilities are available in any given context. The choice is determined partly lexically (different adverbs behave differently), and partly depending on whether the adverb appears in a main or subordinate clause. In particular, there is a large class of adverbs that, when juxtaposed with the verb, must occur postverbally in main clauses but preverbally in subordinate clauses. Many common sentential adverbs, including the negation particles, exhibit this behaviour.

The constraints on adverb placement sketched above are implemented as follows in the grammar. Three features, `mainorsub`, `advpos`, and `invinitial` are used to codify the syntactic context in which the adverb appears. The binary feature `mainorsub` is passed down from the clause, and distinguishes main and subordinate clauses. The feature `advpos` is set by the ADVP rule in question, and classifies the adverb's position as one of the five possibilities listed above. Finally, `invinitial` is used to capture the special case of an adjective appearing clause initially, and if so encodes whether the clause uses the inverted word order or not.

The grammar rules for initial and final adverbial modification are analogous to the English ones, except that they have been extended to handle the new features appropriately. For example, the rule for clause-initial sentential adverbial modification is of the form

```
S:[inv=I, mainorsub=MS] ->
    ADVP:[invinitial=I, mainorsub=MS, advpos=init],
    S:[inv=I, mainorsub=MS]
```

There are also three Swedish-specific rules[5] that handle preverbal, postverbal and V-gap modification, as follows:

```
V:[mainorsub=MS, gap=n] ->
   ADVP:[mainorsub=MS, advpos=preverbal],
   V:[mainorsub=MS, gap=n]

V:[mainorsub=MS, gap=n] ->
   V:[mainorsub=MS, gap=n],
   ADVP:[mainorsub=MS, advpos=postverbal]

V:[mainorsub=MS, gap=y] ->
   V:[mainorsub=MS, gap=y],
   ADVP:[mainorsub=MS, advpos=vgap]
```

Lexical entries for adverbs must consequently specify the permitted combinations of values for `mainorsub`, `advpos`, and `invinitial`. By making sensible use of macros (cf. Section 2.5), it is possible to write these entries succinctly. We started by identifying a base set of adverbs to serve as paradigms, and defined one macro for each paradigm word; entries for other adverbs were then defined with reference to the paradigms. For example, the following lexical entry

```
@'advp:sentential'(då,då1,like_förresten).
```

makes use of two macros (`advp:sentential` and `like_förresten`) to specify that *"då"* ("then") is a sentential adverb with associated QLF constant då1, which has the same syntactic distribution as *"förresten"*.

11.2.3 Other Clausal Constructions

The Swedish grammar also contains two important clausal constructions lacking English counterparts, both of which are fairly common. First, there is the *"vad ... för"* construction (similar to German *"was ... für"*), illustrated in the following examples:

> *Vad har Delta för turer till Boston?*
> What has Delta for flights to Boston?
> (What flights does Delta have to Boston?)

---

[5] For uninteresting technical reasons concerning the QLF representation of verbal and sentential adverbs, these are actually broken up into a number of subcases.

What finns det för turer idag?
What are there for flights today?
(What flights are there today?)

This is handled by a gapping rule (cf. Section 2.4.4) of the form

```
NP:[gapsin=[NP:[lex=vad]], gapsout=[]] ->
för
NP:[det=null]
```

Semantically, the QLF for the mother NP is formed by replacing the conceptual bare singular or plural quantifier in the daughter NP with a special WH+ quantifier.

The second construction is concerned with embedded subject questions, which in Swedish are required to take a dummy relative pronoun between the subject and the VP, for example:

Jag vill veta vilka turer som går till Pittsburgh
I want to know which flights that go to Pittsburgh
(I want to know which flights go to Pittsburgh)

This is handled by a special version of the S → NP VP rule, schematically of the following form:

```
S:[somclause=y] -> NP som VP
```

The feature `somclause` restricts use of the special type of clause generated by this rule to the single context where it is permitted.

11.3   Verbs and Verbal Constructions

This section considers divergences relating specifically to verbal constructions.[6] First, Swedish, like French, Spanish, and many other languages – but unlike English – has reflexive verbs; that is to say, verbs that subcategorise for a semantically null reflexive pronoun agreeing with the subject in person and number, as in the following example:

Hur tar jag mig fram i Boston?
How get I myself around in Boston?
(How do I get about in Boston?)
*Hur tar jag sig fram i Boston?
How get I himself/herself around in Boston?

---

[6] We would like to thank Eva Lindström for several helpful discussions concerning the material in this section.

Another difference concerns separable verbs, that is, verbs that occur both compounded with a particle (an adverb or preposition) attached before the word and separated with the particle following the verb, for example, *bortföra – föra bort* ("carry away"). As in German, these verbs always form the past participle with the particle attached before the verb: *bortförd*. This requires a morphology rule of the form:

```
V:[vform=past_part] ->
  P:[lex=L]
  V:[vform=impera, subcat=[P:[lex=L], NP]]
```

These two cases are easy to deal with; more interesting problems arise in connection with passive verb forms. Swedish permits formation of a periphrastic passive, using the auxiliary verbs *"vara"* and *"bliva"*, for example, *"var sedd"* ("was seen") or *"blev mördad"* ("was killed"). This is close to the English passive. As in the other Scandinavian languages, most verbs can also be made passive by addition of the suffix *"-s"*. For example, *"köpa"* ("to buy") becomes *"köpas"* ("be bought"), *"sålde"* ("sold") becomes *"såldes"* ("was sold"), and so on.

The passivising *"s"* form in Swedish can be used in a manner similar to the English passive, for example:

> *Middag serveras på flyget*
> Dinner serve-PASSIVE on the flight
> (Dinner is served on the flight)

There are, however, other possibilities. A common construction is the impersonal passive construction, in which the subject is replaced by the dummy subject *"det"* ("it" or "there"), for example:

> *Serveras det någon middag på flyget?*
> Serve-PASSIVE it any dinner on the flight?
> (Is there any dinner served on the flight?)

As a general rule, only transitive verbs can be passivised. Intransitive verbs with the *"s"* form do not indicate passivisation, but rather different aspectual phenomena, for example, *"Det pratas mycket här"* ("A lot of talking is going on here"). Our grammar currently does not cover these cases.

Some verbs lack *"s"* forms, for example, *"regna"* ("rain") and *"åska"* ("thunder"), which take neither subject nor object. Also, as a general rule, reflexive verbs do not have *"s"* forms, for example, *"ändra sig"* ("to change [oneself]") but not *"det ändras sig"*.

There are also verbs that are classed as deponent; that is, they are passive with respect to form, but their meaning is active. The most common of these is the important verb *"finnas"* ("to exist"):

> *Finns det några flighter till San Francisco på fredag?*
> Exist it any flights to San Francisco on Friday?
> (Are there any flights to San Francisco on Friday?)

Deponency is specified for each verb as a binary lexical feature deponent in the Swedish grammar. In a few cases, the same stem may have two lexical entries, one of which is deponent, the other not:

> *Olle retas med flickorna*
> Olle tease-DEPONENT with the girls
> (Olle is teasing the girls)

> *Olle retas av flickorna*
> Olle tease-PASSIVE by the girls
> (Olle is being teased by the girls)

In the first example, the base verb is the intransitive and deponent verb *"retas"* ("to tease"), and *"Olle"* is both the subject and the agent of the sentence. The prepositional phrase *"med flickorna"* constitutes the oblique object. In the second example, the verb is the transitive *"reta"* ("to tease") in its passivised form, which makes *"Olle"* the subject of the sentence and patient argument of the verb. The prepositional phrase here constitutes the agent. Such verbs consequently need two lexical definitions: in the above examples, we would have deponent=y in the first case and deponent=n in the second.

The *"s"* forms of Swedish verbs also have several other functions currently not covered by our grammar. One example would be where the *"s"* signals reciprocal activity:

> *Brita och Gunnar pussas*
> Brita and Gunnar kiss
> (Brita and Gunnar are kissing [each other])

Here, the base verb is *"pussa"* ("to kiss"), and the effect of the suffixed *"s"* is that the verb binds both nominals in the conjoined NP.

11.4   NP Constructions

We now describe divergences among parts of the Swedish and English grammars that cover NP constructions. Most obviously, there is the fact that Swedish marks nouns and adjectives for definiteness; for example, "a red car" is *"en röd bil"*, but "the red car" is *"den röda bilen"*. Definite NBARs, if not pre-modified, may stand on their own as definite NPs. A rule of the following form is used to express this:

```
NP:[def=y] -> NBAR:[def=y, premod=n]
```

A second obvious divergence concerns the possessive construction. In English, this is realised by affixation of a possessive element ('s) to the NP; Swedish, however, forms the possessive by putting the head N of the NP into the genitive, for example:

> *Deltas turer idag*
> Delta-GEN flights today
> (Delta's flights today)

There are four Swedish-specific rules used to handle possessive relations. Two morphology rules derive the genitive forms of NBARs and names from their base forms, and a third rule derives a possessive DET from a genitive NP. A fourth rule is used to capture the special case (common in the ATIS domain) of an NP simultaneously premodified by a genitive and postmodified by a code expression, for example:

> *Deltas flygning tvåhundrafem*
> Delta-GEN flight two hundred fifty five
> (Delta flight two hundred fifty five)

It follows that the Swedish noun has, in general, eight distinct inflectional forms corresponding to the product of three two-way choices along the orthogonal dimensions of singular/plural, definite/indefinite, and genitive/nongenitive.

A third topic is adjectives, which in Swedish may be used productively as nouns, for example:

> *Jag måste ha rökfritt*
> I must have nonsmoking-NEUTER
> (I must have (a) nonsmoking (one))

> *Jag tar den tidiga*
> I take the early-DEF
> (I'll take the early (one))

The relevant rule is of the form

```
NBAR:[adjnbar=y] -> ADJP
```

The feature `adjnbar` blocks use of nominalised adjectives in some contexts, most importantly when forming compound nominals. This brings us to the final topic of the section.

11.4.1   Compound Nominals

One of the most obvious and important differences between Swedish and English noun phrases concerns the subject of compound nominals (see also Section 19.2). English nominal compounds normally consist of units separated by intervening spaces, for example:

> Flight information
> Delta flights
> Boston ground transportation

Hence English compounding rules are formally grammar rules.

In contrast, Swedish as a rule forms nominal compounds without intervening spaces. It follows that Swedish compounding rules are formally morphology rules. Swedish nominal compounds may be formed by premodifying a common noun with a proper noun, an adjective, or another common noun, for example:

> *Deltaflygningar*
> Delta flights
>
> *enkelflygningar*
> one way flights
>
> *morgonflygningar*
> morning flights

Normally, only some adjectives may be used in compounds; this is captured in a special feature. Furthermore, in some cases the meaning of an adjective depends on whether it combines with its head noun by compounding or by normal premodification, for example:

> *en enkelflygning*
> a one way flight
>
> *en enkel flygning*
> a simple flight

These two examples are distinguished prosodically, much as English makes a prosodic difference between "a black bird" (adjective + noun) and "a blackbird" (compound noun).

The compounding construction may be applied recursively to produce compounds containing three or more elements, for example:

> *marktransportinformation*
> ground transportation information

enkelbiljettpris
one way ticket cost

If the first element of the compound is a noun, it may require addition of a joining segment (typically *"s"*) or a hyphen:

förhandsbokning
advance (s) booking

tur och retur-flygning
return (hyphen) flight

In certain cases, the segments *"o"*, *"e"*, *"a"*, and *"u"* are also used, for example:

resebokning
travel (e) booking

kvinnosakskvinna
woman (o) movement (s) woman
(feminist)

Swedish compounds are nontrivial; in particular, the question of selecting the correct segment when generating compounds is well known to be difficult, and we have as yet no very satisfactory solution. We regard this as an important topic for future work.

12   Transfer Coverage

MANNY RAYNER, PIERRETTE BOUILLON,
AND IVAN BRETAN

12.1   Introduction

The three previous chapters have discussed the coverage of the monolingual rule sets (grammars and lexica) for English, Swedish, and French, respectively. The present chapter will now go on to consider the coverage of the bilingual (transfer) rules used for QLF-based translation. We present a fairly complete description of the three hand-coded transfer rule sets to which we have devoted serious attention (English → French, English → Swedish, and Swedish → English). Since we expect our readers on the whole to have greater familiarity with French than Swedish we will draw most of our examples from English → French, but most of the points we make are applicable to all three language pairs.

When using QLF as a transfer formalism (see Chapter 2), the ideal is that source- and target-language QLFs have identical structures; QLF transfer would then just consist of suitably substituting target-language QLF constants for source-language QLF constants. The reality falls short of this ideal for three main reasons:

- **True linguistic differences** Sometimes, two languages simply express the same idea in different ways; it is natural that QLF, which is a grammatical representation formalism, will register corresponding differences. For example, the English expression "I need X" is most naturally realised in French as *"il me faut X"* ("it me needs X"). In cases like this, we naturally expect that transfer rules will define correspondences between complex source- and target-language structures.
- **Inadequacies in the QLF formalism** In other cases, one intuitively feels that the grammatical structure is essentially similar in both languages, but for some reason is represented differently at QLF level. This may be due to intrinsic shortcomings of the QLF formalism, or simply to more or less arbitrary divergences in the way the two grammars are written.

- **Inadequacies in the transfer formalism** Finally, it may be the case that QLF adequately captures the similarities in the grammatical structures of the two languages, but that the transfer formalism permits no clean way to express this similarity.

The rest of the chapter presents a detailed description of the three sets of transfer rules. Section 12.2 gives a statistical breakdown of the transfer rules by type. Section 12.3 describes the rules themselves, focussing on those which cover cases of linguistically motivated structural differences; finally, Section 12.4 discusses the cases in which either the QLF formalism or the transfer-rule formalism proves inadequate.

12.2   Statistical Breakdown of Rule Types

Transfer rules can be divided into classes in different ways. The primary distinction we will employ here is the degree of structural complexity. Thus, rules will be divided into the following top-level groups:

- **Identity** rules whose left- and right-hand sides are identical atomic expressions
- **Atomic** rules whose left- and right-hand sides are distinct atomic expressions, normally corresponding to specific lexical items
- **Nonatomic fixed** rules whose left- and right-hand sides are distinct fixed expressions, at least one of which is nonatomic
- **Recursive** rules whose left- and right-hand sides are distinct nonatomic expressions, and that involve recursive translation of subexpressions

This division will be used in the overview of the transfer rules in Section 12.3. Figure 12.1 shows the type distribution of the transfer rules for the three transfer pairs under consideration. Since the majority of the nonatomic fixed rules in the English → French pair are related to numbers (cf. Section 12.3.3), we have counted

Rule type	Eng → Swe		Swe → Eng		Eng → Fre	
Identity	168	14.4%	168	14.6%	164	14.2%
Atomic	872	74.7%	861	75.0%	579	50.0%
Nonatomic fixed (numbers)	2	0.2%	1	0.1%	187	16.2%
Nonatomic fixed (others)	70	6.0%	70	6.1%	114	9.9%
Recursive	55	4.7%	48	4.2%	113	9.8%
Total	1167	100%	1148	100%	1157	100%

Figure 12.1. Transfer rules broken down by rule types.

Rule type	E == S	E >= S	E =< S
Identity	168	0	0
Atomic	760	112	101
Nonatomic fixed	54	18	17
Recursive	33	22	15
Total	1015	152	133
Percentage	78.0%	11.7%	10.2%

Figure 12.2. Reversibility of English ↔ Swedish transfer rules.

these separately in order to facilitate comparison with the other transfer pairs. Transfer rules are counted before macroexpansion (transfer macros are described in Section 2.6); bidirectional rules are counted twice, once in each direction.

For English and Swedish, where we have made a serious effort to achieve transfer coverage in both directions, it makes sense to consider the extent to which the rules are bidirectional. As can be seen from Figure 12.2, bidirectional rules (those indicated by the == operator) comprise the majority of the set.

12.3   Overview of the Rules

In this section, we will present a more detailed breakdown of the English ↔ Swedish and English → French transfer rules for the ATIS domain. In Sections 12.3.1 through 12.3.3, we start by disposing of the simple cases that account for the bulk of the data: rules that map QLF constants to themselves, rules that map QLF constants to other QLF constants, and rules that map fixed QLF structures to fixed QLF structures. The rest of the section deals with the more interesting problems that arise due to nontrivial mismatches among source and target QLFs, and that require more complex transfer rules.

12.3.1   Identity Rules

There are 168 identity rules for English/Swedish and 164 for English/French, all of the format atom == atom. An example rule, which holds for both transfer pairs, is

```
trule(ynq == ynq).
```

This rule expresses the fact that the ynq (Y-N question) marker means the same thing in English QLFs as in French and Swedish ones. Identity rules are not expected to vary from domain to domain.

Part of speech	Eng → Swe	Swe → Eng	Eng → Fre
Proper names	330	327	323
Nouns	277	250	84
Verbs	129	116	81
Prepositions	69	65	40
Adjectives	45	39	23
Determiners	5	7	3
Adverbs	7	5	6
Interjections	18	34	6
Other	8	11	13

Figure 12.3. Distribution of lexical transfer rules translating atoms into atoms, broken down by relevant part of speech.

12.3.2 Lexical Rules Translating Atoms into Atoms

As one would hope, the largest group of rules consists of those that map atomic lexical constants to atomic lexical constants. Rules of this kind apply to constants denoting proper names, nouns, adjectives, verbs, prepositions, and adverbials. Figure 12.3 presents a breakdown of atomic-atomic lexical rules, classified by the part of speech to which they relate.

Two points are worth noting explicitly. First, a transfer rule that maps an atomic QLF constant to an atomic QLF constant can at surface level affect phrases containing several words. The most obvious examples are provided by verbs subcategorising for particles or reflexives. For example, the Swedish particle verb *"ta om"* (literally, "take again") translates to the English intransitive verb "repeat": this is represented by the atom-to-atom rule

```
trule(repeat1 =< ta_om1).
```

Second, it is often the case that several atom-to-atom rules can apply to the same QLF constant; in this case, the choice between the different alternatives will be made by transfer preferences, as illustrated in more detail in Sections 1.5 and 4.4. For example, the English preposition "for" can be translated to any of the French prepositions *"pour"*, *"de"*, and *"à"*, or become an (empty) temporal NP marker. The relevant rules are simply

```
trule(on1 >= pour1).
trule(on1 >= de1).
trule(on1 >= à1).
trule(on1 >= temporal_np).
```

12.3.3   Lexical Rules Translating Nonatomic Fixed Structures

Most transfer rules involving nonatomic structures are intended to capture various types of structural divergences between source and target QLFs. The simplest cases are those in which the rule is nonrecursive (i.e., contains no transfer variables: cf. Section 2.6), and the source and target expressions are consequently both fixed QLF fragments.

One of the simplest examples concerns translation of numbers in English → French. English two-digit numbers are represented compositionally; however, the highly idiosyncratic nature of the French number system persuaded us to include separate lexical entries for all numbers up to 100. It is consequently necessary to include rules such as the following, which map the compositional representations of English "seventy four" and "ninety seven",

```
'SF'('N'('70')+'N'('4'))
'SF'('N'('90')+'N'('7'))
```

into the atomic representations of French *"soixante-quatorze"* (literally: "sixty-fourteen") and *"quatre-vingt-dix-sept"* (literally: "four-twenties-seventeen"), which are simply

```
'N'('74')
'N'('97')
```

The rules need do no more than state the correspondences between these different representations:

```
trule('SF'('N'('70')+'N'('4')) == 'N'('74')).
trule('SF'('N'('90')+'N'('7')) == 'N'('97')).
```

It is interesting to note that the problem could not have been solved by recoding the English lexicon so that number entries were represented in the same way as in the French one, since the same issues arise in translating code expressions. For instance, "flight seven seven four" cannot be translated compositionally as *"le vol sept sept quatre"*, but must be rendered as *"le vol sept cent soixante-quatorze"* ("flight seven hundred and seventy four").

Most of the remaining rules in this group relate to determiners and pronouns. As we have previously seen in Chapter 2, determiners are represented by expressions of one of the forms ref(_,_,_) (referential determiners) or q(_,_) (nonreferential determiners). Thus, rules that translate determiners typically have expressions of one of these types on each side. For example, the following rule translates the English bare plural determiner ("fares") into the French definite plural (*"les billets"*):

```
trule(q(bare,plur) == ref(def,le,plur)).
```

The examples of pronouns presented in the grammar fragments from Chapter 2 show that their QLF representations are typically of the form

```
term(<Det>, X, [<Pred>, X])
```

where `<Det>` is a determiner representation and `<Pred>` is either `entity` or `personal`. Many rules for translating pronouns are thus either included in the rules for determiners, or else in simple extensions of them. For example, the following rule translates English "it" into French *"il"*:

```
trule(term(ref(pro,it,sing),X,[impersonal,Y])
    ==
    term(ref(pro,il,sing,),X,[entity,Y])).
```

12.3.4 Date, Time, and Code Expressions

For obvious reasons, date, time, and code expressions are important in the ATIS domain, and we have devoted a fair amount of effort to getting them right. Although the constraints are not complex, it is worth describing the rules required to capture them adequately.

Calendar dates are easy to translate, as they can be mapped straightforwardly into a uniform QLF representation. More interesting problems arise in English → French when translating day-of-week expressions. The problem is that, when used together with weekdays, several common determiners have conventional meanings that cannot be predicted from their normal meanings and do not necessarily correspond across the two languages. For this reason, we cannot always translate compositionally and rely on transfer preferences, but must also supply a number of special rules. Specifically, we have the following:

1. Current day: in both English and French, this is expressed as a bare singular ("Monday"; *"lundi"*). Note that English bare singular is usually best translated as French definite singular ("dinner" → *"le déjeuner"*) or partitive singular ("wine" → *"du vin"*). Translating a bare singular to a bare singular is not particularly common.
2. Next day: in both English and French, this is expressed as a bare singular combined with an adjective ("next Monday"; *"lundi prochain"*). Here, the problem is that in other contexts "next" is more likely to be translated as prenominal *"le prochain"*, for example, "next flight" → *"le prochain vol"*.

3. Generic day: in English this can be either an indefinite singular or a bare plural ("a Monday", "Mondays"), but in French it is a definite singular (*"le lundi"*). There is one rule for each case.
4. Part of weekday: English uses a compound nominal ("Monday morning"). French employs the same word order (*"lundi matin"*). Once again, the problem is this is not predictable from the normal rules for translating English compounds (see Section 12.3.5).

The basic problem concerning time-of-day expressions is that the English clock by default has twelve hours, while the Swedish and French ones have twenty-four; so English "three p m" becomes French *"quinze heures"* and Swedish *"klockan femton"*. In addition, French strongly prefers to use the words *"midi"* and *"minuit"* to express time in the hours including twelve noon and twelve midnight, respectively. Though hardly very complicated, these requirements in fact necessitate a couple of dozen rules for each transfer pair.

Finally, we consider code expressions; these can be translated compositionally in English ↔ Swedish, but involve two problems in English ↔ French. First, English permits omission of the determiner with a code expression ("flight three one two"), while French demands introduction of a definite article (*"le vol trois cent douze"*). More interestingly, English code expressions may stand on their own as NPs ("U S one five three"), while in French a noun must be supplied (*"le vol U S cent cinquante-trois"*). In general, finding an appropriate noun could require nontrivial reasoning. In the ATIS domain, however, the choice is always clear from the syntactic form of the code, and the rules are simple to formulate.

12.3.5   Nominals

Having disposed of the more or less trivial cases, we now proceed to those in which there are genuine divergences in deep grammatical structure between source and target language. We start with nominal expressions.

In the English ↔ Swedish rule set, there are twenty nonatomic rules (thirteen bidirectional) that deal with the translation of specific nominals. Eighteen of these deal with translating between compounds and noncompounds or vice versa, as in the following rule that translates "fare" into *"biljettpris"* (literally, "ticket price"):

```
trule([fare1,X]
    >=
       @nn_simple_compound(biljett1, pris1, X))
```

Here, nn_simple_compound is a macro that encodes the structure of the QLF compound nominal representation (see Section 2.6).

There are also three English ↔ Swedish structural rules triggered by adjectives. The most interesting of them translate nouns modified by adjectives into adjective-noun compounds, which in Swedish differ from ordinary prenominal adjectival modification with respect to orthography, prosody, and semantics. For instance, "one way flight" translates into *"enkelflygning"* rather than *"enkel flygning"* ("simple flight"). The rule is currently restricted to a small class of adjectives that trigger this compound formation.

In English → French, the fact that French lacks most kinds of productive nominal compounds complicates the problem. The currently implemented rules permit English compounds to be translated in the following ways:

1. Phrase of the form "noun + PP" ("rental car" → *"voiture de location"*; "flight information" → *"renseignement sur les vols"*; "Denver airport" → *"aéroport de Denver"*). This possibility is encoded in two general structural rules, for common nouns and proper names respectively, which can potentially apply to any English compound of the appropriate type. The choice of French preposition is determined by transfer preferences.
2. Phrase of the form "noun + proper name" ("Delta flight" → *"vol Delta"*). Any French proper name can potentially be used as a postnominal modifier, so this is also encoded as a general rule for translating English compound nominals whose first element is a proper name. The choice between this rule and the preceding one is again made by transfer preferences.
3. Phrase of the form "noun + adjective" or "adjective + noun" ("economy fare" → *"tarif économique"*; "return flight" → *"vol aller-retour"*). Some English nouns, when appearing as the first element of a compound, can productively be translated into French adjectives. This possibility is captured in a single transfer rule, parameterised by a nondeterministic transfer macro that expands out to the relevant pairs of English noun and French adjective (cf. Section 2.6).
4. Lexically determined cases. There are many cases where compounds must be translated idiosyncratically, with a specific transfer rule required for each case. Examples from the ATIS domain include "fare code" → *"code-tarif"*, "ground transportation" → *"transports publics"*, and "downtown X" → *"centre de X"*. The rule set currently contains twenty nine rules of this kind.

12.3.6 Verbs

The problems that turn up in translating verb constructions are similar to those for nominals, though a greater range of possibilities exists. There are forty rules of this kind in English → French, and forty five in English → Swedish.

The majority of the rules are lexically determined. A simple example is provided by the English → French rules used for "depart" and "leave", which, when used with a direct object, ("leave Boston"), need to be translated into a VP with postmodifying PP, (*"partir de Boston"*). The rule is as follows:

```
trule([[leave1,E,tr(subj),tr(place)]]
    >=
        [[de1,E,tr(place)],
        [partir1,E,tr(subj)]]
```

Another common case is that of an intransitive verb translating into a transitive verb with a fixed NP complement: for instance, the English verb "stop" ("Does the flight stop in Denver?") is most naturally translated into French as *"faire escale"* (*"Est-ce que le vol fait escale à Denver?"*). This time, the rule is:

```
trule([stop1,E,tr(subj)]
    ==
        [faire1,E,tr(subj),
        @bare_sing_term(X,escale1)]).
```

A third example illustrates translation of an impersonal construction: English "it costs X to VP" becomes French *"cela coûte X pour VP"* ("that costs X for to VP"). Note that in this case the English VP is notionally the deep subject of "costs", while the French VP is the object of the preposition *"pour"*. The transfer rule is however uncomplicated:

```
trule([[cost1,E,tr(vp),tr(price)]]
    ==
        [[pour1,E,tr(vp)],
        [coûter1,E,@cela,tr(price)]]).
```

In order to convey some idea of the wide variety of problems that occur when translating verbal constructions we quickly list some other cases, giving English → French or English ↔ Swedish examples but omitting the actual rules:

1. Rules involving copula. "How much is X" → *"Combien coûte X"* ("How much costs X"); "How long is X" → *"Combien de temps dure X"* ("How long lasts X").
2. Extra noun and transitive verb. "need X" → *"avoir besoin de X"* ("have need of X").
3. Politeness constructions. English "I want to VP" sounds too abrupt if literally translated into French, so a rule is needed to soften it to *"Je voudrais VP"* ("I would like to VP"). Similar rules are needed for several other verbs of requesting.
4. Introduction of extra verb. English "I want X" cannot be rendered literally into Swedish, but has to be turned into *"Jag vill ha X"* ("I want to have X").

5. Sequences of modal verbs. Swedish sometimes uses two modals where English would only use one. For example, *"skulle kunna"* (*"Skulle jag kunna se biljetterna?"*; "Would I be able to see the tickets?") becomes simply "could" ("Could I see the tickets?").

All five of these examples involve rules similar in form to those in the first three. In general, there are no problems involved in writing rules that can be formulated in terms of some combination of transposition of arguments to verbs, introduction of extra arguments, and restrictions on the syntactic form of arguments to specific items.

12.3.7   Adjectives

There are only a handful of nontrivial transfer rules that deal with adjectives. In English → Swedish, the literal translation of "least expensive" is somewhat strained, and it is worth introducing a rule to produce the nonperiphrastic *"bil-ligaste"* ("cheapest"). Conversely, a literal translation of "cheapest" into French (*"plus bon marché"*) is not good, and a rule is needed to produce *"moins cher"* ("least expensive") instead. There are also two rules in English → French that turn adjectives into PPs: these translate "early" into *"de bonne heure"*, and "first class" into *"en première classe"*, respectively.

12.3.8   Prepositional Phrases

English → French contains several rules for translating PPs. The most important of these concern the constructions "from . . . to" and "to . . . from", which for obvious reasons are frequent in ATIS. When used nominally, French prefers to realise "from . . . to" as a simple hyphen, for instance, "flights from Boston to Denver" → *"les vols Boston-Denver"*. As a verbal modifier, however, the hyphen is not possible, and the expression is most correctly translated as *"de . . . à"*, for instance, "I want to fly from Boston to Denver" → *"Je voudrais aller de Boston à Denver"*. "To . . . from" is rendered as *"à . . . en partance de"* irrespective of whether it occurs as a nominal or verbal modifier, for example, "flights to Denver from Boston" → *"les vols à Denver en partance de Boston"*. Three rules cover these examples.

Another important group of rules concerns possessive, genitive, and related constructions. The English preposition "of" and the French preposition *"de"* are both represented specially at QLF level. English → French thus requires rules for translating "of" into *"de"* ("the cost of that flight" → *"le prix de ce vol"*), other prepositions into *"de"* ("the airport in Denver" → *"l'aéroport de Denver"*) and possessive into *"de"* ("Delta's flights" → *"les vols de Delta"*. Similar considerations apply to English ↔ Swedish, where it is possible to translate English "of" into either Swedish genitive ("the number of the flight" → *"flygningens nummer"*) or a normal preposition ("the cost of the ticket" → *"priset på biljetten"* [literally, "the price on the ticket"]).

Four more English → French rules deal with numerical comparison PPs of the form "under/over NP" ("fares under two hundred dollars"). The most obvious French translation will be of the form *"à moins/plus de ... "* (*"des billets à moins de deux cents dollars"*). The problem is not entirely trivial, since "under" and "over" are being treated as prepositions in English, while *"à moins/plus de"* form part of a determiner expression in French. Two structural transfer rules are consequently required.

Finally, French lacks a clear equivalent to the common English PP expressions "what about NP" and "how about NP", which we have chosen to render using the verbal expression *"qu'en est-il de NP"*. Two more rules are used to implement this.

12.3.9   Tense, Aspect, Mood, and Voice

Translation of tense and aspect is notoriously difficult: the real problems are often pragmatic in nature, and cannot be solved in a surface-semantics framework like the one we have here. In the context of a simple domain like ATIS, it is, however, feasible to address most of the immediate issues.

Most importantly, neither Swedish nor French has anything that directly corresponds to English progressive aspect. Consequently, a rule is needed to suppress the progressive marker in finite verb-phrase representations; for example "I am flying to Boston" becomes *"Jag flyger till Boston"* in Swedish or *"Je vais à Boston en avion"* in French, both meaning essentially "I fly to Boston". A more complex structural rule maps between progressive-tense VPs and relative clauses; so "flights going to Boston" becomes *"flygningar som går till Boston"* in Swedish and *"les vols qui vont à Boston"* in French (literally, "flights that go to Boston"). The relevant rule, which is common to both language pairs, is as follows:

```
trule(
  @form(verb(no,no,yes,no,yes),X,tr(body))
  ==
  [relative_clause,
    @form(verb(pres,no,no,no,yes),X,tr(body))]).
```

The verb form on the left-hand (English) side describes an untensed, progressive VP; that on the right-hand (Swedish/French) side, describes a relative clause with a simple present tense (cf. Section 2.3.2).

Although the English and French future tenses are expressed quite differently (English uses the auxiliary "will"; French uses a verb inflection), the semantics of the two tenses agree well, and the representations at QLF level are similar (cf. Figure 2.7). The rule needed to translate one to the other is consequently unproblematic:

```
trule(verb(no,no,no,will1,yes)
    ==
    verb(fut,no,no,no,yes)).
```

(The meaning of the QLF `verb` construct, which holds tense, aspect, and voice information, is explained in Section 2.3.2.) In contrast, Swedish, like English, expresses the future using an auxiliary. However, there are two auxiliary constructions available, *"ska"* and *"komma att"*: the first expresses simple future, while the second implies some kind of commitment. Swedish also makes frequent use of the present tense to express future action, and choosing among these various possibilities is not at all straightforward, despite the apparent syntactic similarities between the two languages. In practice, we have chosen only to allow the English present to translate into the Swedish present; however, the Swedish present may translate into either the English present or the English future, with the present as the default choice. Domain-specific collocational preferences can override the default; thus *"Jag tar det"* is translated as "I'll take it" rather than "I take it", on the grounds that "take" in the ATIS scenario is typically a future action. This is a good example of a case where more sophisticated translation methods than QLF transfer are needed to solve the problem properly.

Similar considerations apply to the problem of translating the English passive voice, but with the languages reversed. English expresses passive using the auxiliary verb "be" ("What meal is served on this flight?"), while Swedish prefers to use a verb inflection (*"Vilken måltid serveras på det här flyget?"*; *"serveras"* is the passive present form of *"servera"*). However, there is close enough correspondence between English and Swedish passives to permit literal translation, and one simple transfer rule is all that is required. In French, even though the syntactic representation of passive is similar to the English one, a literal translation often sounds odd, and a more complex treatment is required. To translate the previous example into French, we turn passive into active, and render the implicit passive subject as the impersonal subject *"on"*; thus the result is *"Quel repas sert-on à bord de ce vol?"* ("What meal do they serve on this flight?").

12.3.10 Determiners and Pronouns

Most of the rules needed to translate determiners and pronouns have already been covered in Section 12.3.3. There are, however, some nontrivial problems left in English → French, which we will describe here. We start with one of the most interesting and common cases, the expression "how many".

In English, "how many" can uncontroversially be classified as a determiner, ("How many flights are there?"), which, like many determiners, can also occur as a bare NP ("How many do you have?"). The normal French translation of "how many Xs" is *"combien de Xs"*. Unfortunately, the evidence suggests that *"combien de"* cannot reasonably be thought of as a determiner. To start with, it can be split off from the noun and fronted, for instance, *"Combien avez-vous de vols?"* ("How many have you of flights?"). Also, "how many" as a bare NP becomes *"combien"* together with the clitic *"en"* ("How many do you have?" → *"Combien en avez-vous?"*). Examples like these, rather, indicate that the natural analysis is to treat *"combien de Xs"* as an NP+PP construction. We thus have the following rule:

```
trule(term(q(how_many,plur),X,tr(restr))
    ==
    term(q(combien,plur),
         X,
         [and, [entity,X],
               @de_pp(X, term(q(bare,plur),Y,
                                   tr(restr)))]])).
```

where the restriction of the English "how many" NP becomes the restriction of the French NP that forms the complement to the preposition *"de"*. We also need a second rule to cover the special case of "how many" as a bare NP:

```
trule([eng,fre],semi_lex(how_many-combien_en),
      term(ell(q(how_many,plur)),X,[entity,X])
    ==
    term(q(_,combien,plur),
         X,
         [and, [entity,X],
               @de_pp(X, @clitic_en)]])).
```

Another typical case involves the English proforms "one" and "ones" ("Which one serves breakfast?"; "the ones that leave in the morning"). French has no word directly corresponding to "one", and combinations of determiner + "one(s)" need to be mapped into appropriate pronouns. Thus "which one" becomes *"lequel"*, while "the ones" becomes *"ceux"*. Each combination needs a separate rule. For example, the rule translating "which one(s)" into some form of *"lequel"* is as follows:

```
trule(term(q(wh(which),Num),X,@proform_one_body(X))
    ==
    term(q(wh(lequel),Num),X,[entity,X])).
```

Even this degree of complexity would be bad enough; but in fact, the situation is worse, since yet more rules are needed to cover the cases where "one" appears modified. For example, the following covers the case where "the ones" take a nominal modifier:

```
trule(term(ref(def,the,plur),X,
            [and, @pronoun_one_body(X),
                  tr(mod)])
    ==
         term(ref(pro,ceux,plur),X,
              [and, [entity,X],
                    tr(mod)]))).
```

This complex of rules is quite the most unsatisfactory part of the English → French set; we will discuss the problem further in Section 12.4.

12.3.11 Conjunction

In most cases, translation of conjunction is unproblematic, but an interesting exception is that of NBAR conjunction in English → French. English freely permits conjunction of NBARs ("the flights and fares"; "an afternoon or evening flight"). French, however, strongly prefers to realise these constructions as conjunctions of NPs (*"les vols et les billets"*; *"un vol l'aprés-midi ou le soir"*). In each case, it is essentially necessary to duplicate the translation of the article.

Just as in the examples discussed in the previous section, we cannot cover the phenomenon with a single rule. The following is adequate for the case of an unmodified conjunction of NBARs:

```
trule(
 term(tr(det), X,
      @nbar_conj(tr(conj), [tr(nbar1),
                            tr(nbar2)]))
     ==
 term(@np_conj_det(tr(conj)), X,
      @np_conj(tr(conj),
                 [term(tr(det),_,tr(nbar1)),
                  term(tr(det),_,tr(nbar2))])))).
```

However, extra rules must again be added if we are to deal with cases where the conjoined NBAR appears modified. The following deals with the case of a single modifier, for example, a PP:

```
trule(
 term(tr(det), X,
      [and, @nbar_conj(tr(conj), [tr(nbar1),
                                     tr(nbar2)]),
            tr(mod)])
     ==
 term(@np_conj_det(tr(conj)), X,
      [and, @np_conj(tr(conj),
                      [term(tr(det),_,tr(nbar1)),
                       term(tr(det),_,tr(nbar2))]),
            tr(mod)])).
```

In this section, we have presented the transfer rules that constitute the whole of the three transfer sets under consideration. In the rest of this chapter, we will consider what they say about the adequacy, or otherwise, of our transfer formalism.

12.4   Adequacy of the Transfer Formalism

Let us briefly review QLF transfer again. The first step is to carry out a pretransfer operation on the source QLF. It is then passed to the transfer phase proper, which nondeterministically produces a set of possible transferred QLFs. Each of these is subjected to post-transfer, and finally the transfer preferences select the best target-language QLF.

The heart of the QLF transfer process is the combination of transfer rules and transfer preferences. If we are to talk about the adequacy of the transfer-rule formalism in isolation, there are two ways in which it can fail to do its job:

> **Expressiveness** The formalism may be insufficiently expressive to write the transfer rules intuitively required. In some cases, it may be possible to solve the problems that arise by means of further manipulation of the target QLFs during the post-transfer phase, but this is not generally desirable.
>
> **Formal properties** The formalism may have bad formal properties. In particular, it may be difficult to extend the set of transfer rules if new rules interact with previously existing ones in a way that is hard to predict.

We will discuss these issues separately.

12.4.1 *Expressiveness of the Rule Formalism*

There is one common case where the transfer-rule formalism fails to be sufficiently expressive, arising from the big-PP construction currently used in all the SLT grammars. This is a normalised QLF representation of a sequence of PPs that function as joint modifiers of a phrase (cf. Section 9.3.4); the PP representations are grouped together in the QLF as a list. For instance, the QLF for the English phrase "a flight from Boston to Denver" is schematically

```
term(q(a,sing),X
     [and, [flight1,X],
           form(pp_sequence, _,
                [[from1, <''boston''>],
                 [to1, <''denver''>]])])
```

Representing a sequence of PPs as a constituent has both positive and negative aspects for transfer. On the plus side, it is often necessary to reorder a sequence of target-side PPs; this is much easier to do if the sequence is represented as a list. It is also useful when writing transfer rules not to have to distinguish between single and multiple PP modifiers. The price we pay is that it sometimes becomes harder to write compositional transfer rules: the resulting problems need to be sorted out in the post-transfer phase.

An example illustrating both sides of the coin is provided by the English → French rule from Section 12.3.7, which translates the English adjective "first class" ("a first class ticket") into the French PP *"en première classe"* (*"un billet en première classe"*). Now suppose that the English noun modified by "first class" is already modified by a PP ("a first class ticket to Boston"). The normal result will be a transferred French QLF with the structure

```
term(q(un,sing),X
     [and, [and, [billet1,X],
                 [en1, <''première classe''>]],
           [pour1, <''boston''>]])
```

However, there are two things wrong here. First, the QLF is not well formed, since it fails to respect our treatment of PP sequences: we want the representations of the PPs *"en première classe"* and *"pour Boston"* to occur at the same level, as part of the representation of a big PP. Second, French has an ordering constraint that requires that locative PPs precede nonlocative ones; so the result we really want is not *"un billet en première classe pour Boston"*, but rather *"un billet pour Boston en première classe"*.

Our solution is to move part of the task to the post-transfer phase. We perform transfer compositionally, yielding the QLF structure shown immediately above.

Post-transfer first regularises the PPs into a single big PP:

```
term(q(un,sing),X
     [and, [billet1,X],
           form(pp_sequence, _,
                [[en1, <''première classe''>],
                 [pour1, <''boston''>]])])
```

and then reorders the PPs:

```
term(q(un,sing),X
     [and, [billet1,X],
           form(pp_sequence, _,
                [[pour1, <''boston''>],
                 [en1, <''première classe''>]])])
```

In the small ATIS domain this approach has proved adequate, but it is unclear how well it scales up. To give an example of the kind of problem we have in mind, application of the "first class" → *"en première classe"* rule in the reverse direction will create new complications: if we apply it to a French QLF in which *"en première classe"* occurs as part of a PP sequence, we will produce a malformed English QLF in which an adjective representation occurs as part of a big PP. It is possible to add a new post-transfer rule that suitably reformulates the QLF; the question is how many such rules are going to be needed in the long run. The simple nature of the QLF formalism gives reason to hope that a fairly small rule set may in fact be enough, but we are not at present able to back this up with any very solid argument.

The second reasonably common case where the transfer-rule formalism fails to be sufficiently expressive is related to the phenomenon of *head switching*. The standard examples of head switching in the literature involve translation mismatches where a sentential adverb in one language corresponds to a verb taking a VP complement in the other. In English → French, a natural example is the French verb *"falloir"* (*"J'ai failli rater l'avion"*), which is easiest to translate as the English adverb "nearly" ("I **nearly** missed the plane"). Note that the heads of the two phrases fail to correspond; the head of the French sentence is *"falloir"*, while that of the English one is "miss".

If we line up a few simple examples of English and French sentences involving the "nearly"/*"falloir"* mismatch, it becomes clear that there is no easy way to formulate a general QLF transfer rule. The QLF for the English sentence "I nearly left" is:

```
[dcl,
 form(adv(nearly1),_,
      form(verb(past,no,no,no,yes),E,
           [[leave1,E,
             term(ref(pro,i,sing),X,[personal,X])]])))]
```

while the QLF for the corresponding French sentence *"J'ai failli partir"* is:

```
[dcl,
 form(verb(pres,yes,no,no,yes),E,
     [[falloir1,E,
        term(ref(pro,je,sing),X,[personal,X])
        form(verb(inf,no,no,inf,yes),E1,
           [[partir1,E1,X]])]])]
```

Note that since *"falloir"* is now the main verb, the subject of the sentence (*"je"*) is one of its arguments, while the subject of *"partir"* ("leave") is the control variable X. A transfer rule thus needs to match the subjects of the three verbs involved in the correct way. Something like the following is appropriate:

```
trule(
 form(adv(nearly1),_,
     form(verb(past,no,no,no,yes),E,
          [[tr(v),E,tr(subj)|tr(args)]]))
==
 form(verb(pres,yes,no,no,yes),E,
      [[falloir1,E,tr(subj,term(_,X,_)),
        form(verb(inf,no,no,inf,yes),E1,
           [[tr(v),E1,X|tr(args)]])]]))
```

Now suppose that we change the sentence by adding a PP modifier. The English sentence becomes "I nearly left from Boston", with QLF

```
[dcl,
 form(adv(nearly1),_,
     form(verb(past,no,no,no,yes),E,
          [[from1,E,
            term(proper_name,Y,[name_of,Y,boston1])]],
           [leave1,E,
            term(ref(pro,i,sing),X,[personal,X])]])))]
```

while the French one is *"J'ai failli partir de Boston"*, with QLF

```
[dcl,
 form(verb(pres,yes,no,no,yes),E,
     [[falloir1,E,
        term(ref(pro,je,sing),X,[personal,X])
        form(verb(inf,no,no,inf,yes),E1,
           [[de1,E1,term(proper_name,Y,
                          [name_of,Y,boston1])],
            [partir1,E1,X]])]])]
```

Unfortunately, the transfer rule we have just presented no longer works; we need to add a variant that matches the PP modification pattern, as follows:

```
trule(
 form(adv(nearly1),_,
      form(verb(past,no,no,no,yes),E,
           [tr(mod), [tr(v),E,tr(subj)|tr(args)]]))
 ==
 form(verb(pres,yes,no,no,yes),E,
      [[falloir1,E,tr(subj,term(_,X,_)),
          form(verb(inf,no,no,inf,yes),E1,
               [tr(mod), [tr(v),E1,X|tr(args)]])]]))
```

In general, each distinct QLF modification pattern will require a new variant of the transfer rule.

Verb/adverb head switching examples like this in fact occur rarely if at all in ATIS; the significant cases are those like the "which ones"/"*lequel*" and conjoined NBAR examples discussed earlier in Sections 12.3.10 and 12.3.11, but the issues are essentially similar. The real problem is that simple unification is not sufficient to describe the relevant patterns, which involve two or more QLF elements that can be separated by arbitrary intermediate modifiers. Thus, there is no way to write a single transfer rule that generalises over the different modification possibilities.

12.4.2   Formal Properties

Finally, we consider the issue of whether the transfer rule formalism has any undesirable formal properties; in practice, the interesting one is monotonicity. This is clearly an important question, since the task of debugging a growing set of transfer rules becomes much more complex if addition of new rules can invalidate old translations.

The QLF transfer mechanism is nearly, but not quite monotonic; the exception is that compositional transfer of a QLF expression is, by default, not attempted if a complex transfer rule matches the expression. The reason for enforcing this restriction is a concern for efficiency: without it, every complex transfer-rule application results in an ambiguity, which typically increases the number of transferred QLFs by one to two orders of magnitude. It is possible to override the default behaviour by explicitly declaring that a specific complex transfer rule should not block compositional translation. In practice, we have found that we wished to do this with at most a half-dozen complex rules in each rule set; these represent the few cases where the translations blocked by addition of a new complex rule were in fact desirable. Once again, the problem is real, but uncommon.

12.5   Summary

We have presented a detailed description of the transfer rule sets for English ↔ Swedish and English → French, and considered what they say about the adequacy of our transfer-rule formalism. There are some problems with rules that involve substantial divergences in form at the level of QLF representation, of which the worst are those arising from head switching and related phenomena; there are also some slight problems resulting from the fact that the framework is not completely monotonic. It is important to note, however, that the rules affected represent less than 2 percent of the total rule set: in the main, we think it reasonable to say that the transfer framework is performing well. The evaluation in Section 20.4 further supports this claim.

13   Rational Reuse of Linguistic Data

MANNY RAYNER, DAVID CARTER, IVAN BRETAN,
MATS WIRÉN, ROBERT EKLUND,
SABINE KIRCHMEIER-ANDERSEN,
AND CHRISTINA PHILP

13.1   Introduction

The basic idea explored in this chapter is simple and uncontroversial. All natural languages are in some sense similar (some are obviously very similar), so software written to process one language to some extent ought to be applicable to other languages. If the languages L_1 and L_2 are similar enough, then it should be easier to recycle software applicable to L_1 than to rewrite it from scratch for L_2.

We will describe two related approaches in this general direction, which have been successfully applied within the SLT project. The first is the most obvious: we start with a functioning grammar and lexicon for L_1, and port it to the similar language L_2. This is not, of course, a novel idea, but we think that we have refined it in a number of ways. In particular, we show that it is practically feasible in the case of sufficiently close languages to generalise an existing grammar for L_1 to cover both L_1 *and* L_2 (i.e., produce a single grammar, which, through the setting of a single parameter, becomes valid for either language). We also describe a method that makes it possible to port the language-dependent lexicon for L_1 so as to maximise sharing of data between the systems for the two languages.

The second idea is specifically related to translation. Suppose we have already developed sets of transfer rules for the two language pairs $L_1 \rightarrow L_2$ and $L_2 \rightarrow L_3$. We describe a method that allows us to compose the two sets of rules off-line to create a new set for the pair $L_1 \rightarrow L_3$.

Both methods might be said to operate according to the principle memorably described by Mary Poppins as "Well begun is half done". They do not solve either problem completely, but automatically take care of most of the drudgery before any human has to become involved. In each case, the initial result is a machine-written set of linguistic data (lexicon entries and transfer rules) that is not quite adequate as it stands; a system expert can, however, clean it up into satisfactory shape in a small fraction of the time that would have been required to write the relevant rules and lexicon entries from scratch.

The practical experiments we describe have been carried out using versions of the SLT system involving the languages English, French, Swedish, and Danish. Initial results are promising. In particular, we were able to combine both methods to create fairly credible Swedish-to-French and English-to-Danish spoken language translation systems[1] using only a few person-weeks of expert effort.

The rest of the chapter is structured as follows. Section 13.2 describes the methods we have developed for porting linguistic descriptions between closely related languages. Section 13.3 summarises the transfer-composition method. Section 13.4 describes preliminary experiments, Section 13.5 presents an empirical evaluation, and Section 13.6 concludes.

13.2   Porting Grammars and Lexica among Closely Related Languages

The original version of the CLE had a single language description for English, written by hand from scratch. Subsequently, language descriptions have been developed for Swedish (Chapter 11) and French (Chapter 10). In each of these cases, the new language description was created by manually editing the relevant English-language grammar and lexicon files. There are, however, some serious drawbacks to this approach. First, it requires a considerable quantity of expert effort; second, there is no mechanism for keeping the resulting language descriptions in step with each other. Changes are often made to one language description and not percolated to the others until concrete problems show up in test suites or demos. The net result is that the various grammars tend to drift steadily apart.

When we decided to create a language description for Danish, we thought it would be interesting to experiment with a more principled methodology, which explicitly attempts to address the problems mentioned above. The conditions appeared ideal: we were porting from Swedish, Swedish and Danish being an extremely closely related language pair. The basic principles we attempted to observe were the following:

- Whenever feasible, we have tried to arrange things so that the linguistic descriptions for the two languages consist of shared files. In particular, the grammar-rule files for the two languages are shared. When required, rules or parts of rules specific to one language are placed inside macros whose expansion depends on the identity of the current language, so that the rule expands when loaded to an appropriate language-specific version.
- When files cannot easily be shared (in particular, for the content-word lexica), we define the file for the new language in terms of declarations

---

[1] In fact, we do not currently use a Danish speech synthesiser, but it would be straightforward to incorporate one.

listing the explicit differences against the corresponding file for the old language. We have attempted to make the structure of these declarations as simple as possible, so that they can be written by linguists who lack prior familiarity with the system and its notation.

Although we are uncertain how much generality to claim for the results (Swedish and Danish, as already noted, are exceptionally close), we found them encouraging. Only 4 of the 175 existing Swedish grammar rules turned out to be inapplicable to Danish, and 2 others had to be replaced by corresponding Danish rules. Five more rules had to be parameterised by language-specific macros. Some of the morphology rules needed to be rewritten, but this only required about two days of effort from a system specialist working together with a Danish linguist. The most significant piece of work, which we will now describe in more detail, concerned the lexicon.

Our original intuition here was that the function-word lexicon and the paradigm macros (cf. Section 2.5) would be essentially the same between the two languages, except that the surface forms of function words would vary. To put it slightly differently, we anticipated that it would make sense as a first approximation to say that there was a one-to-one correspondence between Swedish and Danish function words, and that their QLF representations could be left identical. This assumption indeed does appear to be borne out by the facts. The only complication we have come across so far concerns definite determiners: the feature-value assignments between the two languages need to differ slightly in order to handle the different rules in Swedish and Danish for determiner-noun agreement. This was implemented, as with the grammar rules, by introduction of a suitable call to a language-specific macro.

With regard to content words, the situation is somewhat different. Since word choice in translation is frequently determined both by collocational and by semantic considerations, it does not make as much sense to insist on one-to-one correspondences and identical semantic representations. We consequently decided that content words would have a language-dependent QLF representation, so as to make it possible to use our normal strategy of letting the Swedish-to-Danish translation rules, in general, be many-to-many, with collocational preferences filtering the space of possible transfers.

The remarks above motivate the concrete lexicon-porting strategy that we now sketch. All work was carried out by Danish linguists who had a good knowledge of computational linguistics and Swedish, but no previous exposure to the system. The starting point was to write a set of word-to-word translation rules (cf. Section 2.2), which for each Swedish surface lexical item defined a set of possible Danish translations. The left-hand side of each word-to-word rule specified a Swedish surface word form and an associated grammatical category (verb, noun, etc.), and the right-hand side, a possible Danish translation. An initial blank version of the rules was created automatically by machine analysis of a corpus; the left-hand side of the rule was filled in correctly, and a set of examples taken from the corpus was listed above. The linguist only needed to fill in the right-hand side appropriately with reference to the examples supplied. Examples of Swedish → Danish word-to-word rules are shown in Figure 13.1.

The next step was to use the word-to-word rules to induce a Danish lexicon. As a first approximation, we assumed that the possible grammatical (syntactic/semantic) categories of the word on the right-hand side of a word-to-word rule would be the same as those of the word on its left-hand side. (Note that, in general, a word will have more than one lexical entry.) Thus, lexicon entries could be copied across from Swedish to Danish with appropriate modifications. In the case of function words, the entry is copied across with only the surface form changed. For content words, the porting routines query the linguist for the additional information needed to transform each specific item as follows.

If the left-hand (Swedish) word belongs to a lexical category subject to morphological inflection, the linguist is asked for the root form of the right-hand (Danish) word and its inflectional pattern. If the inflectional pattern is marked as wholly or partly irregular (e.g., with strong verbs), the linguist is also queried for the relevant irregular inflections. All requests for lexical information are output in a single file at the end of the run. This mode of interaction makes it possible for the linguist to process large numbers of information requests quickly and efficiently using a text editor, and to feed the revised declarations back into the porting process in an iterative fashion.

One particularly attractive aspect of the scheme is that transfer rules are automatically generated as a by-product of the porting process. Grammar rules and function words are regarded as interlingual; thus, for each QLF constant C involved in the definition of a grammar rule or a function-word definition, the system adds a transfer rule that maps C into itself. Senses of content words are not interlingual. However, since each target lexical entry L is created from a source counterpart L', it is trivial to create simultaneously a transfer rule that maps the source-QLF constant associated with L' into the target-QLF constant associated with L.

We will present an empirical evaluation of the Swedish-to-Danish porting work later, in Section 13.4.2. Before doing so, we describe a second method for recycling linguistic rule sets: transfer composition.

```
trule_ww([och/conj] >= [og]).         % "and"
trule_ww([det/np] >= [det]).          % "it"
trule_ww([jag/np] >= [jeg]).          % "I"
trule_ww([noll/number] >= [nul]).     % "zero"
trule_ww([resa/nbar] >= [rejse]).     % "trip"
trule_ww([kostar/v] >= [koster]).     % "cost"
trule_ww([flyg/nbar] >= [fly]).       % "flight"
```

Figure 13.1. Sample Swedish → Danish word-to-word rules.

13.3   Transfer Composition

13.3.1   Introduction

There is a well-known argument in the machine-translation literature that goes something like this. Suppose that we want to build a multilingual MT system, that is, a system that covers several languages, and that can translate from any one of them into any other. If our MT framework is transfer based, and we have N languages, we will need to implement $N(N - 1)$ sets of unidirectional transfer rules. Considering how much work is involved in implementing even one set of transfer rules, N need not be very large for a serious problem to arise. Even $N = 3$ will be enough to make one look for a way to simplify the task.

At this point in the story, the idea of an interlingua is often introduced. If we can translate from each language into the interlingua, and from the interlingua into each language, then we will only need to implement $2N$ sets of rules. As soon as N exceeds 3, we are winning. Unfortunately, and despite various claims to the contrary, we are still a long way from knowing how to build robust interlingua-based systems; indeed, there are reasonable philosophical arguments for believing that such things may be impossible in principle. Right now, at any rate, transfer is our main option if we want to build even moderately large systems that perform useful tasks. So we are back where we started.

Rather than describe yet another angle on the interlingua approach, in this section we will explore a less common attempt to get around the obstacle. Suppose we have three languages, L_1, L_2, and L_3, and that we have implemented sets of transfer rules for the pairs $L_1 \rightarrow L_2$ and $L_2 \rightarrow L_3$. Then we already have a possible way of translating from L_1 to L_3: we translate into L_2 using the first set of rules, and then apply the second set to the result to get an output in L_3. Of course, this has also been tried before. The problem is that today's MT systems are so far from perfect that even one translation step gives output of dubious quality; the result of two or more successive steps is generally too poor to be useful.

It is here that we think we have something new to offer. In contrast to most of the nontrivial MT systems reported in the literature, the SLT transfer component has been designed to consist almost exclusively of declaratively specified information. More specifically, a version of the system for a given transfer pair and domain contains two types of knowledge: unification-based transfer rules and numerical preference information. As explained in detail in Chapter 2, transfer proceeds in two phases. The rules define a set of possible transfer candidates, and the preferences then select the most plausible of them as the output translation.

Since the information in our system's transfer components consists of declaratively expressed rules, it is possible to compose off-line the sets of transfer rules for the $L_1 \rightarrow L_2$ and $L_2 \rightarrow L_3$ language pairs, and produce a set of rules for the $L_1 \rightarrow L_3$ pair. In practice, this automatically composed set of rules will be of considerably lower quality than either of the two original sets. However, our experiments to date indicate that it is possible to use the automatically composed rule set as the initial point in a standard test-and-debug cycle, which can quickly improve it to a useful level of performance; the effort involved is very much less than that which would have been required to construct a good $L_1 \rightarrow L_3$ rule set from scratch. Transfer-rule composition thus can also be viewed as a kind of software reusability technique.

13.3.2   *Transfer Composition as a Program Transformation*

This section explains the theoretical basis of the transfer composition idea. Since our transfer-rule formalism has clean, declarative, semantics, it is possible, using techniques borrowed from logic programming, automatically to compose rules from the sets $L_1 \rightarrow L_2$ and $L_2 \rightarrow L_3$ to produce a set of rules for $L_1 \rightarrow L_3$. We will begin with a series of increasingly less trivial examples, showing in abstract terms how transfer rules can be composed. These examples provide the background needed to motivate the algorithm currently used to perform transfer rule composition; the algorithm itself is described in Section 13.3.3. In the remainder of this section, we will use 11, 12, 13 to denote the source, intermediate, and target languages in our prototypical instances of transfer rule composition.

As described in Section 2.7.2, transfer rules compile into Horn clauses. We will use the notation defined there, writing

```
trule([11,12], LHS >= RHS).
```

for the transfer rule in the 11-to-12 language pair, whose left-hand (source) side is LHS and whose right-hand (target) side is RHS. We write a compiled transfer rule in the form

```
transfer([11,12], LHS1, RHS1) <- Body.
```

for some (possibly trivial) formula Body; this is interpreted as meaning that the QLF LHS1 in language 11 can be transferred to the QLF RHS1 in language 12 if Body holds.

We can now write the basic composition principle as the formula (C):

```
(C)  transfer([11,13],Q1,Q3) <-
        transfer([11,12],Q1,Q2),
        transfer([12,13],Q2,Q3).
```

which says that Q1 in 11 can be transferred to Q3 in 13 if it can be transferred through the intermediate expression Q2 in 12. For technical reasons, we will also find it convenient to assume the converse composition principle C′:

```
(C')  transfer([11,13],Q1,Q3) ->
        transfer([11,12],Q1,Q2),
        transfer([12,13],Q2,Q3).
```

which says that transfer from 11 to 13 can *only* be accomplished in this way.[2]

Our first example is chosen to be as simple as possible. We are given the transfer rules (1) and (2), compiling to (1a) and (2a):

```
(1)   trule([11,12], a >= b).
(1a)  transfer([11,12], a, b).

(2)   trule([12,13], b >= c).
(2a)  transfer([12,13], b, c).
```

Now successively resolving (1a) and (2a) with (C), we get (3a)

```
(3a)  transfer([11,13], a, c).
```

a compiled form of (3):

```
(3)  trule([11,13], a >= c).
```

Thus, we have formally proved that if it is possible to transfer the QLF expression a in language 11 to b in language 12 and b in language 12 to c in language 13, it is also possible to transfer a in language 11 to c in language 13.

Our second example is slightly more complex, and illustrates composition of recursive transfer rules. We start with transfer rules (4) compiling to (4a) and (5) compiling to (5a):

```
(4)   trule([11,12],
            p(tr(v1)) >= q(tr(v1))).
(4a)  transfer([11,12],p(X),q(X1)) <-
            transfer([11,12],X,X1).

(5)   trule([12,13],
            q(tr(v1)) >= r(tr(v1))).
(5a)  transfer([12,13],q(Y),r(Y1)) <-
            transfer([12,13],Y,Y1).
```

---

[2] We are, of course, aware that the converse composition principle is at best an approximation to linguistic truth.

Resolving C with (4a), we obtain

```
transfer([l1,L3],p(X),Q3) <-
    transfer([l1,l2],X,X1),
    transfer([l2,L3],q(X1),Q3).
```

and then resolving again with (5a) we get

```
transfer([l1,l3],p(X),r(Y1)) <-
    transfer([l1,l2],X,X1),
    transfer([l2,l3],X1,Y1).
```

We can now use the converse composition principle C′ to replace the body of this last expression, obtaining

```
transfer([l1,l3],p(X),r(Y1)) <-
    transfer([l1,l3],X,Y1).
```

which, as can be seen, is a compiled form of

```
trule([l1,l3], p(tr(v1)) >= r(tr(v1))).
```

The two examples so far were both of the same form: schematically, we composed an l1-to-l2 rule and an l2-to-l3 rule, such that the right-hand side of the first rule was identical to the left-hand side of the second rule. It is unsurprising that such rules can be combined. What is less obvious is that sometimes rules also can be composed when the match in the intermediate (l2) language is not exact. The following is a minimal example.

We start with the l1-to-l2 rule (6) compiling to (6a) and the l2-to-l3 rule (7) compiling to (7a). We will attempt to compose (6) with (7); for reasons that shortly will become apparent, we will need at least one more rule for this to be possible. We consequently assume a second l1-to-l2 rule, (8), with compiled version (8a):

```
(6)    trule([l1,l2],
           p(tr(v1)) >= q(tr(v1))).
(6a)   transfer([l1,l2], p(X), q(Y)) <-
           transfer([l1,l2], X, Y).

(7)    trule([l2,l3], q(b) >= r).
(7a)   transfer([l2,l3], q(b), r).

(8)    trule([l1,l2], a >= b).
(8a)   transfer([l1,l2], a, b).
```

We start by resolving the composition rule, C, with (6a), to get

```
transfer([l1,l3], p(X), Q3) <-
    transfer([l1,l2], X, Y),
    transfer([L2,L3], q(Y), Q3).
```

Then resolving again with (7a), the result is

```
transfer([l1,l3], p(X), r) <-
    transfer([l1,l2], X, b).
```

Intuitively, what we have done so far is to translate the right-hand side of (6), that is, q(tr(v1)), using (7), to get r. The condition left in the body shows that this is only possible if tr(v1) translates into the constant b.

The current result is not a well-formed l1-to-l3 transfer rule, since it makes reference to transfer between l1 and l2. The condition, however, can be removed by a further resolution with (8a), producing the final result

```
transfer([l1,l3], p(a), r).
```

which is the compiled form of the l1-to-l3 rule

```
trule([l1,l3], p(a) >= r).
```

In effect, the final resolution step uses (8) to perform a backward (l2-to-l1) translation of b. Viewed in terms of transfer rules, we previously had the condition on the composed rule that tr(v1) translated into the l2 constant b. The backward translation step showed that one way to satisfy this condition was to restrict the left-hand side (l1) occurrence of tr(v1) by forcing it to be specifically a.

13.3.3   *Procedural Realisation of Transfer-rule Composition*

We will now describe our concrete algorithm for composition of transfer rules. We stress that this algorithm is not complete; there are many (in general, an infinite number) of valid l1-to-l3 transfer rules that it will not discover. This appears to be inevitable, however, since the problem of generating a complete set of composed transfer rules is in the worst case highly intractable.[3] Our experimental findings, described in more detail in the next section, suggest, though, that the algorithm has considerable practical utility. By creating a manageably small set of composed rules, which contains all the intuitively straightforward compositions, it greatly diminishes the effort involved in creating a new set of l1-to-l3 rules.

---

[3] We strongly suspect that it is undecidable.

As usual, we refer to our three languages as 11, 12, and 13, and compose in the order 11 → 12 → 13. The basic idea is to follow the procedure sketched in the examples from the previous subsection. We start with two language pairs; for each language pair, we take each rule in turn from that language pair and successively attempt to compose it with all the rules from the other language pair. Thus, schematically, there are two cases, which we refer to as "forward" and "backward" composition. In the forward case, we take an 11-to-12 rule

```
trule([11,12], LHS >= RHS).
```

and attempt to use 12-to-13 rules to translate RHS into the 13 expression RHS'; this may involve adding restrictions to LHS to produce LHS'. The final rule will be

```
trule([11,13], LHS' >= RHS').
```

The backward case is similar; we start with an 12-to-13 rule

```
trule([12,13], LHS >= RHS).
```

and use 11-to-12 rules (in reverse) to translate LHS into the 11 expression LHS'; this may involve adding restrictions to RHS to produce RHS'. The final rule is again

```
trule([11,13], LHS' >= RHS').
```

Since the two cases are symmetrical, we can restrict ourselves to the forward one without loss of generality. In more detail, we go through the following steps for each 11-to-12 rule[4]

```
trule([11,12], LHS >= RHS).
```

1. Translate RHS into 13 using 12-to-13 rules, giving the result RHS'.
2. Transfer is carried out in such a way that a transfer variable tr(Id,Pat) may be unified with the term T if and only if Pat unifies with T. Call the list of all Id/T pairs produced in this way the "unification-pair list".
3. For each Id/T pair in the unification-pair list, translate the 12 expression T into an 11 expression T', using the 11-to-12 rules in the inverse direction. Perform this step nondeterministically, to create a set of possible "inverse unification-pair lists", each of which associates all the Id with their respective values of T'.
4. Use each inverse unification-pair list to restrict the transfer variables in LHS. Thus, if tr(Id,Pat) is a transfer variable in LHS, Id/T' is

---

[4] Note that we use the *uncompiled* version of the rule, that is, the one in which transfer variables are left unchanged.

an entry in the inverse unification-pair list, and `Pat` unifies with `T'`, replace `tr(Id,Pat)` with `tr(Id,T')`. The result of performing all these replacements is `LHS'`.

5. The final composed transrule is

```
trule([l1,l3], LHS' >= RHS').
```

13.3.4   Composing Transfer Preferences

As explained in Section 2.7.2, the transfer-preference model contains two components: a channel component, expressing the *a priori* plausibility of the rules used to perform a transfer, and a target-language component expressing the *a priori* plausibility of the result.

Our initial approach to composition of transfer preferences is very simple. Let us assume, as usual, that we are composing `l1-to-l2` and `l2-to-l3` to create `l1-to-l3`. The target-language component for the composed rule set is simply the target-language component from the `l2-to-l3` transfer set. The intuition is that since the target-language component estimates the intrinsic plausibility of the resulting `l3` QLF, it should make no difference whether this result was produced by transfer from `l1` rather than `l2`. The channel-model score assigned to each composed rule is also calculated straightforwardly as the sum of the channel-model scores for all of the rules used by the algorithm in the previous section to form the composition.

Although the transfer-preference–composition method as currently defined is clearly no more than a coarse approximation, it does appear to be good enough to function as a reasonable starting point, and in practise preserves most of the strong preferences induced from the original transfer pairs. Problems pertaining to composed transfer preferences are discussed at greater length in Section 13.4.1.2.

13.3.5   Improving Automatically Composed Rule Sets

Our basic system-development methodology makes use of rationally constructed, balanced, domain corpora to focus the effort on frequently occurring problems (cf. Section 8.6). The development cycle for improving a set of automatically composed transfer rules is the same as for other phases of the system. After the latest round of improvements has been added, the representative corpus is run, and the results evaluated by a bilingual judge. The priority order implicit in the corpus determines the next set of problems to be attacked, and the cycle repeats.

In the context of automatic transfer composition, three specific problems may arise: overgeneration of composed rules, problems with composed preferences, and undergeneration of composed rules due to lack of coverage in the hand-coded rules. The rest of this section briefly describes these generic problems at an abstract level. In the next section, we present practical examples taken from our experiences in the Swedish → English → French language triple.

13.3.5.1 Overgeneration of Composed Rules

Although the transfer-composition algorithm cannot, in a sense, find $L_1 \to L_3$ rules that are actually invalid, it can certainly create ones that are irrelevant. In practise, the main consequence of overgeneration in transfer-rule composition is increased processing time due to spurious nondeterminism.

If the composed $L_1 \to L_3$ rule set is found to contain undesirable rules, we allow the developer to supply declarations blocking the combinations that gave rise to them. (Each rule is tagged with an identifier, which makes this a simple operation.) The format of the declarations allows blocking of classes of rule combinations, for example, inhibiting composition of a given rule from $L_1 \to L_2$ with all but one of a set of potentially composable rules from $L_2 \to L_3$.

13.3.5.2 Composed Preferences

As described in Section 13.3.4, the initial set of composed preferences is only a rough approximation, and requires considerable adjustment to achieve high performance. The issues involved are described in more detail in Section 13.4.1. More generally, if L_1 and L_3 have a lexical granularity in common, which is not matched by that of L_2, we risk ending up with overly general lexical transfer rules as the result of rule composition.

13.3.5.3 Lack of Coverage in Hand-Coded Rules

Holes in the $L_1 \to L_3$ set result either from blocked compositions (as described above) or from cases not covered by the $L_1 \to L_2$ or $L_2 \to L_3$ transfer rules. When such holes are found, the developer can plug them by writing his or her own rules, adding them to the automatically composed set. The hand-written and automatically composed portions of the new rule set are kept in separate files, so that the composed portion can be recompiled without affecting the hand-coded additions.

13.4   Experiments

We conclude this chapter by describing how we applied the methods described to rapidly construct translation systems for two new language pairs. All of the translation modules involved operate within the same domain as other versions of SLT, and have been integrated into the main SLT system to produce versions that can perform credible translation of spoken Swedish into French and spoken English into Danish, respectively. Results of an empirical evaluation of the resulting systems appear in Section 13.5.

13.4.1 *Swedish → English → French*

This section describes our experiences in constructing a Swedish-to-French transfer module using the methods of Section 13.3. We invested a total of about three
person-weeks of expert effort in successively improving the performance of the
QLF-based translation component on a Swedish corpus of 654 sentences, representing between them a total of 13 990 words. In the end, approximately 87 percent
(frequency weighted) of this corpus produced some translation, and 72 percent a
translation deemed adequate by a bilingual judge. We now explore in detail the
concrete problems that arose, using the classification of Section 13.3.5.

13.4.1.1 Dealing with Overgeneration

In the version of the system used for these experiments,[5] the Swedish-to-English
transfer rule set contained 1 454 rules and the English-to-French rule set 1 281 rules
(both sets counted after macro expansion). The automatically composed Swedish-
to-French transfer rule set contained 4 525 rules. As can be seen, it is considerably
larger than either of the two hand-coded rule sets.

This disparity in size appears to be the main reason for the appreciably slower
processing times delivered by the composed Swedish-to-French rule set, compared,
for example, with the hand-coded English-to-French rules. Using the relevant version of the system and the English and Swedish representative corpora described
above, the average processing time for the English-to-French transfer and generation phase was 5.3 seconds/utterance, running Quintus 3.2 on a Sun UltraSparc 1;
9.5 percent of the utterances (frequency weighted) took more than 10 seconds. We
ran a corresponding test on the first 140 sentences of the Swedish-to-French representative corpus, representing 7 780 words of the original corpus. This produced
fourteen time-outs, using a time-out threshold of 90 seconds; over the remaining
sentences, we recorded an average processing time for the transfer and generation phase of 16.2 seconds/utterance, with 40.0 percent of the utterances (again,
frequency weighted) taking more than 10 seconds.

Examination of the composed rule set revealed that a substantial portion of the
rules was created by forward or backward composition (cf. Section 13.3.3) with
a small set of "problem" rules. A typical offender is the Swedish-to-English rule
that results in English day-of-week/time-of-day expressions like "Monday morning". These phrases are a specific type of compound nominal; English compound

---

[5] The experiments were carried out in the first half of 1997; unfortunately, time constraints
made it impossible to repeat them using the version of the system employed for the tests in
Chapter 20. For present purposes, the most important difference between the two system
versions is that the new one has a rather better treatment of transfer preferences. When
we performed the composition experiments, transfer preferences were coded by hand; we
would now train them using the methods described in Section 4.4.

nominals can be translated into French in many ways, most often as noun+PP combinations. Consequently, forward composition from the Swedish-to-English rule results in a large set of Swedish-to-French rules. However, the only acceptable way to translate these particular compound nominals is as French compound nominals ("Monday morning" → "lundi matin", etc.; cf. Section 12.3.4). The forward composition with the appropriate English-to-French rule is correct, and all the other compositions are irrelevant.

The above example illustrates how addition of a small set of blocking declarations (cf. Section 13.3.5.1) makes it possible to effect a substantial reduction in the size of the composed rule set. In the current version of the system, 53 declarations between them block creation of 2 126 out of the 4 525 composed Swedish-to-French rules. Suitable declarations were found by inspecting utterances for which transfer was clearly slow; the total time required to write them was on the order of two to three days. Rule filtering using the blocking declarations reduced the average frequency-weighted processing time for transfer and generation from 16.2 seconds/utterance to 4.6 seconds/utterance, with the portion taking more than 10 seconds falling from 40 percent to 8 percent. The new figures are comparable to those for English-to-French quoted above.

13.4.1.2 Dealing with Preference Problems

The automatically composed transfer-rule preferences are sometimes insufficient to select the correct lexical target constant. The problems that arise most often concern incorrect lexical choice when translating prepositions, articles, and compound nominals. This section describes a typical case in detail.

Consider the translation of the Swedish preposition *"på"*. In the Swedish → English transfer rule set there are two lexical transfer rules: *"på"* → "on", and *"på"* → temporal-NP marker. The first of these is rather more common, and consequently gets a positive channel score.

The English → French set contains several lexical transfer rules translating "on" into various prepositions, but in the ATIS domain, there is no strong default translation of "on". Thus, for instance, "on Delta" becomes *"avec Delta"*, "on that flight" becomes *"à bord de ce vol"*, and so on. The channel scores for all these rules are close to zero. Consequently, the Swedish → French transfer rules *"på"* → *"avec"* and *"på"* → *"à bord de"* receive positive channel scores.

Both *"på"* → "on" and "on" → *"avec"* are very reasonable transfer rules, and it is correct to assign a positive score to the first and an approximately zero score to the second. However, the composition *"på"* → *"avec"* is unlikely, especially in this domain. The problem is that the English-to-French rule "on" → *"avec"* is mainly appropriate in contexts where the object of "on" is an airline, which will frequently be the case in ATIS. However, the object of the Swedish preposition *"på"* is hardly ever an object of this type, and so the two transfer rules in practise rarely are capable of combination. A positive score for the composed rule is thus incorrect.

This example shows that straightforward summing of preferences may sometimes lead to awkward results; a number of similar cases of badly composed transfer preferences were corrected by hand.

13.4.1.3 Dealing with Lack of Coverage in Hand-Coded Rules

When no translation at all is generated, this is normally due to the incompleteness of the two underlying transfer rule sets. This is especially apparent for $L_2 \rightarrow L_3$, in this case English to French. This transfer rule set performs relatively well on the standard collected English corpus data used for testing, but much worse on the type of English generated by the Swedish-to-English translation module. The degradation in transfer quality is only to be expected, since English generated spontaneously and English generated by translating Swedish differ in many important respects. This is at least true in a transfer framework, where generation of target-language utterances is not independent of the syntactic realisation of the source-language utterance (as perhaps could be the case in an interlingua-based system).

For similar reasons, rule composition also can lead to translations that are strained or unnatural. Consider, for example, the Swedish construction *"Vad kostar X?"*, having a literal English counterpart in "What does X cost?", which occurs seldom in the English training corpus used. Because of this, in the original composed set of Swedish-to-French rules, no correct rule existed for translating "What does X cost?" into *"Combien coûte X?"*. This in turn led to the common construction *"Vad kostar X?"* being compositionally translated into *"Que coûte X?"*, which, although formally correct, is extremely uncommon in spoken French. Problems of this kind were corrected by adding extra hand-coded rules.

13.4.2   English → Swedish → Danish

This section briefly describes a second series of experiments, in which we converted an English → Swedish system into an English → Danish system using the methods described earlier. The total investment of system-expert effort was around two person-weeks.

About half the effort was used to port the Swedish language description to Danish, employing the methods of Section 13.2. We then used a Swedish representative corpus containing 331 sentences representing an original corpus of 9 385 words, to carry out two rounds of testing and bug fixing on Swedish → Danish QLF-based translation. These tests uncovered a number of new problems resulting from previously unnoted divergences between the Swedish and Danish grammars. About half the problems disappeared after the addition of twenty or so small hand-coded adjustments to the morphology, function-word lexicon, transfer rules, and transfer preferences.

After the second round of bug fixing, 95 percent of the Swedish representative corpus (frequency weighted) received a Danish translation, and 79 percent a fully acceptable translation. Most of the translation errors that did occur were minor ones. Finally, we composed the English → Swedish and Swedish → Danish rules to create an English → Danish rule set. An empirical evaluation of the resulting system is described in the next section.

13.5   Evaluation

We used the Danish grammar and lexicon and the Swedish → French, Swedish → Danish, and English → Danish rule sets described in the preceding sections to contruct versions of the full SLT system for the three language pairs in question; among other things, this involved adding sets of word-to-word transfer rules. The Swedish → Danish set was produced as part of the lexicon-porting process described in Section 13.2, and the Swedish → French set was also written by hand.[6] Finally, we produced the English → Danish set by composition of the English → Swedish and Swedish → Danish sets using a simple algorithm not described here.

The resulting systems were evaluated, using the methodology described in Section 20.1, on two held-out sets of 200 recorded speech utterances each (one for English and one for Swedish). Judging was done by subjects who had not participated in system development, were native speakers of the target language, and were fluent in the source language. Table 13.1 presents the results. These

Table 13.1. *Evaluations of three versions of SLT built using rational methods for reusing linguistic data*

Source Language	Swedish	Swedish	English
Target Language	French	Danish	Danish
Fully acceptable	19.0%	36.5%	27.0%
Unnatural style	15.0%	0.0%	0.0%
Minor syntactic errors	13.0%	37.5%	28.0%
Clearly useful	**47.0%**	**74.0%**	**55.0%**
Major syntactic errors	13.0%	0.0%	0.0%
Partial translation	17.5%	1.5%	1.5%
Borderline	**30.5%**	**1.5%**	**1.5%**
Nonsense	18.0%	13.0%	30.5%
Mistranslation	3.5%	9.0%	10.5%
No translation	1.0%	2.5%	2.5%
Clearly useless	**22.5%**	**24.5%**	**43.5%**

---

[6] This work was performed by Eleonora Beshai at Telia Research, as part of her bachelor's thesis.

are admittedly inferior to those given later in Section 20.4 for hand-coded rule sets; but taking into account the modest investment of effort, we feel that they are nonetheless quite a good advertisement for the ideas we have described here.

13.6   Conclusions

We have demonstrated that it is practically feasible in the case of sufficiently close languages to generalise an existing grammar for one language to produce a grammar that, through the setting of a single parameter, becomes valid for either language. As well as providing major efficiency gains over writing a grammar for the second language from scratch, this technique means that subsequent enhancements to the grammar, in those areas where the characteristics of the two languages are equivalent, will apply automatically to both of them.

We have also described an algorithm for composition of transfer rules. We have demonstrated that it can be used to automatically compose nontrivial sets of transfer rules containing on the order of thousands of rules, and have shown that by small adjustments the performance can be improved to a level only slightly inferior to that of a corresponding set of hand-coded rules. Our experience is that the amount of work involved in using these methods is only a fraction of that needed to develop similar rules from scratch.

PART III

Speech Processing

14 Speech Recognition

VASSILIS DIGALAKIS AND HORACIO FRANCO

E ARLY versions of the speech recognition module used in SLT were based on DECIPHER^{TM}, and later ones on its descendant, the Nuance speech recognition system. Both these systems are speaker-independent recognisers capable of handling large-vocabulary continuous speech, and both are based on statistical methods and, specifically, on hidden Markov models (HMMs), a methodology that has been very popular among speech researchers. For completeness, we give in this chapter a brief introduction to HMMs and statistical approaches to continuous speech recognition in general. Our decision to include this material is also partly due to the fact that use of HMMs is still not common in the natural language processing (NL) community, even though they are applicable to many problems in language understanding and language modelling. The class-based model, for example, that we discuss in Chapter 16, can be seen as an instance of an HMM.

14.1   Speech Recognition Based on Statistical Methods

Today's state-of-the-art speech recognisers are based on statistical techniques, with hidden Markov models being the dominant approach (Young 1996). The main components of a speech-recognition system are the front-end processor, the decoder, the acoustic models, and the language models. The remainder of this section briefly reviews these four components and the relationships among them.

The *front-end processor* compresses the speech signal into a sequence of parameters that will be used to recognise spoken words. The front end typically operates on short *frames* (windows) of the speech signal, performing frequency analysis and extracting a sequence of observation vectors of frequency parameters (or *acoustic* vectors) $\mathcal{X} = [X_1, X_2, \ldots, X_T]$, one for each frame. Many choices exist for the acoustic vectors, but Mel-frequency–warped cepstral coefficients (MFCCs) have exhibited the best performance to date (Davis and Mermelstein 1980).

The sequence of continuous-valued acoustic vectors X_t can be modeled directly using a *continuous HMM*. Alternatively, acoustic vectors can first be fed into a *vector quantiser* (VQ), which maps a vector of continuous parameters to an index corresponding to a centroid, that is, a prototype vector in the multidimensional space. The sequence of acoustic vectors then becomes a sequence of discrete indices that can be modeled using a *discrete HMM*.

The central component of the recogniser is the *decoder*, which is based on a communication-theory view of the recognition problem; it tries to extract the most likely sequence of words $W = [W_1, W_2, \ldots, W_N]$ given the set of acoustic vectors $\mathcal{X}$. This can be done using Bayes' rule:

$$\hat{W} = \underset{W}{\text{argmax}} \frac{P(W)p(\mathcal{X} \mid W)}{p(\mathcal{X})}. \tag{14.1}$$

The discrete probability $P(W)$ of the word sequence W is obtained from the *language model*, whereas the acoustic model determines the likelihood of the acoustic vectors for a given word sequence $p(\mathcal{X} \mid W)$.

Speech can be viewed as a discrete message source with a hierarchical structure: phonemes are joined to form syllables, then words, phrases, and finally continuous discourse. In modern speech-recognition systems, stochastic models are postulated for certain units of speech, such as words or phonemes. The basic acoustic models are then combined to form models for larger units with the aid of dictionaries, and/or probabilistic grammars.

In designing a speech recogniser, an important decision to be made concerns the set of events that will be modeled. The question "what is a good unit of speech for recognition?", can be translated under the hierarchic structure perspective into the question "what level – or levels – of the hierarchy should we model?". If unlimited amounts of training data[1] were available, we would benefit by using models for words, or even groups of words; by modelling larger speech units, it is possible to eliminate the variability due to context. However, given practical limitations, we are forced to use units from lower levels of the hierarchy (e.g., phonemes) that are easier to train. The phoneme is a natural and popular choice as the basic modelling unit, and the approach that we present in the following section, namely hidden Markov models, uses the phoneme as the basic building block.

14.2   Hidden Markov Models

14.2.1   Definition

Hidden Markov models (Bahl, Jelinek, and Mercer 1983; Baker 1975; Jelinek 1976) are currently the most popular approach to statistical speech recognition. In HMM-based recognisers, the probability of an observation sequence for a given

---

[1] The set of speech utterances that will be used for the estimation of the models' parameters.

word is obtained using a finite-state model that is constructed by concatenating models of the elementary speech sounds or phonemes. To model *coarticulation*, the influence of neighboring phonemes on the pronunciation of a phoneme due to the inertia of the vocal tract, different HMMs are used for a particular phoneme based on the context in which it appears. This results in a large number of context-dependent phone models. A *phone* is the acoustic realisation of a specific phoneme in a particular context. Each of these models consists of a number of states (typically three to five) that correspond to the beginning, middle, and end of the phone.

A main characteristic of the various speech units and the phone is their variable duration. In acoustic modelling, variable duration is captured by modelling the state sequence $S = [s_1, s_2, \ldots, s_T]$ as a Markov chain, whose probability can be expressed as the product of the *state-transition probabilities* $a_{ij} = P(s_j \mid s_i)$. The state sequence is not observed, and at each state s_t and time t, an acoustic vector is observed based on the distribution $b_{s_t}(X_t) = p(X_t \mid s_t)$, which is called the *output distribution*. Hence, the two basic components of a hidden Markov model are its state-transition probabilities, which model duration variability, and its output distributions, which model spectral variability in the acoustic realisations of the phonemes.

If the front end performs vector quantisation on the acoustic vectors, the output distributions take the form of discrete probability distributions. If the acoustic vector generated by the front end is passed directly to the acoustic model, then continuous-density output distributions are used. Multivariate-mixture Gaussians are the most common choice, according to the formula

$$b_s(X_t) = \sum_{q=1}^{K} P(q \mid s) \mathcal{N}(X_t; \mu_{sq}, \Sigma_{sq}), \tag{14.2}$$

where $P(q \mid s)$ is the weight of the qth mixture component in state s, and $\mathcal{N}(X; \mu, \Sigma)$ is the multivariate Gaussian with mean μ and covariance Σ. The mixture weights are nonnegative and must sum to one. The advantage of mixture distributions is that they can approximate any distribution with arbitrary shape by using an appropriate number of mixture Gaussians. Continuous-density HMMs (CDHMMs) are used in most state-of-the-art large-vocabulary continuous-speech recognition systems, including the DECIPHER^{TM} system (Digalakis et al. 1996). The main disadvantage of CDHMMs is their computational complexity, and we shall present techniques that speed up this computation in Chapter 15.

In the next three sections, we briefly review the three fundamental problems that have to be solved in a computationally efficient way if HMMs are to be practically useful for the task of performing speech recognition. In order, these are (1) computation of the observation-sequence probability (Section 14.2.2), (2) estimation of the hidden-state sequence (Section 14.2.3), and (3) estimation of the model parameters (Section 14.2.4).

14.2.2   Observation-Probability Computation

Given that the model corresponding to a word or a word sequence $\mathcal{W}$ is $P(\mathcal{X} \mid \mathcal{W})$, the probability of a sequence of observations $\mathcal{X} = [X_1, X_2, \ldots, X_T]$ can be expressed as the sum over all the possible state sequences of the joint probability $P(\mathcal{X}, \mathcal{S} \mid \mathcal{W})$

$$P(\mathcal{X} \mid \mathcal{W}) = \sum_{\mathcal{S}} P(\mathcal{X}, \mathcal{S} \mid \mathcal{W}) = \sum_{\mathcal{S}} P(\mathcal{X} \mid \mathcal{S}, \mathcal{W}) P(\mathcal{S} \mid \mathcal{W}). \tag{14.3}$$

Because the observation vectors are assumed to be conditionally independent given the state sequence, the first factor can be expanded as

$$P(\mathcal{X} \mid \mathcal{S}, \mathcal{W}) = b_{s_1}(X_1) b_{s_2}(X_2) \cdots b_{s_T}(X_T). \tag{14.4}$$

The second factor in (14.3) corresponds to the probability of the hidden-state sequence $P(\mathcal{S} \mid \mathcal{W}) = P(s_1, s_2, \ldots, s_T \mid \mathcal{W})$ conditioned on the model parameters. Since we have assumed that the state sequence is a Markov chain, its probability can be expressed as the product of the state-transition probabilities $a_{ij} = P(s_j \mid s_i)$ for the model $\mathcal{W}$, that is,

$$P(\mathcal{S} \mid \mathcal{W}) = \pi(s_1) a_{s_1 s_2} \cdots a_{s_{T-1} s_T}, \tag{14.5}$$

where $\pi(s_1)$ represents the initial-state probability.

Substituting back into (14.3), we obtain the desired probability in terms of the model parameters

$$P(\mathcal{X} \mid \mathcal{W}) = \sum_{\mathcal{S}} \pi(s_1) b_{s_1}(X_1) a_{s_1 s_2} b_{s_2}(X_2) \cdots a_{s_{T-1} s_T} b_{s_T}(X_T), \tag{14.6}$$

where the sum is over all possible state sequences of length T in the model $\mathcal{W}$. The expression (14.6) has the following intuitive interpretation. For an arbitrary state sequence, the model is in the state s_1 at time $t = 1$ with probability π_1, and in that state generates the observation X_1 with probability $b_{s_1}(X_1)$; then for $t = 2$ the model makes a transition to state s_2 with probability $a_{s_1 s_2}$ and generates the observation X_2 with probability $b_{s_2}(X_2)$; and this process continues until the end of the sequence at time T.

The direct computation of (14.6) for all possible state sequences is computationally intractable. However, a recursive procedure – the *Forward-Backward method* introduced by Baum and colleagues (1970) – permits efficient computation of (14.6). Let us introduce the probability $\alpha_t(j) = p(X_1, X_2, \ldots, X_t, s_t = j \mid \mathcal{W})$ of the partial observation sequence $(X_1, X_2, \ldots, X_t)$ from the beginning of the sequence up to an arbitrary time t, jointly with the event corresponding to the model being in the state $s_t = j$. Using an argument similar to that used for obtaining (14.6), we can write

$$\alpha_t(j) = \sum_{\text{all } s_1, s_2, \ldots, s_{t-1}} \pi(s_1)b_{s_1}(X_1)a_{s_1 s_2}b_{s_2}(X_2)\cdots a_{s_{t-1}j}b_j(X_t). \tag{14.7}$$

Summing separately over the predecessors of the state j in (14.7), we can express $\alpha_t(j)$ recursively as

$$\alpha_t(j) = \sum_{i=1}^{N} \alpha_{t-1}(i)a_{ij}b_j(X_t), \tag{14.8}$$

where N is the number of states in the model $\mathcal{W}$. By definition $\alpha_1(j) = \pi_1 b_j(X_1)$. Starting with $\alpha_1(j)$ and using (14.8), we can compute $\alpha_t(j)$ for all t and j; then, from its definition we can obtain the desired probability of observing the complete sequence as

$$P(\mathcal{X} \mid \mathcal{W}) = \sum_{j=1}^{N} \alpha_T(j). \tag{14.9}$$

The number of operations needed to compute (14.9) is proportional to $N^2 T$, that is, linear in the duration of the sequence. If the connectivity between states in the HMM is sparse, typically the case in speech models, the number of operations is also approximately linear with respect to the number of states.

Similarly, we can define the probability $\beta_t(i) = p(X_{t+1}, X_{t+2}, \ldots, X_T \mid s_t = i, \mathcal{W})$ of the partial observation sequence $X_{t+1}, X_{t+2}, \ldots, X_T$ from the arbitrary time $t + 1$ up to the end of the sequence T given the event corresponding to the model being in the state $s_t = i$ at time t. The following recursion formula for $\beta_t(i)$ can also be derived

$$\beta_t(i) = \sum_{j=1}^{N} a_{ij}b_j(X_{t+1})\beta_{t+1}(j). \tag{14.10}$$

The recursion can be arbitrarily initialised with $\beta_T(i) = 1$ for the set of possible final states. The previous recursion formulae also allow us to compute certain probabilities useful for solving the parameter estimation problem; for instance, based on the definitions of α and β, it is easy to show that $p(\mathcal{X}, s_t = j)$, the joint probability of observing the whole state sequence and the event of being at the state j at time t, can be computed as

$$p(\mathcal{X}, s_t = j) = \alpha_t(j)\beta_t(j). \tag{14.11}$$

14.2.3   Estimation of the Hidden-State Sequence

In HMMs the state sequence is not observable, and we can only estimate the best state sequence based on a given criterion. This is the second basic problem in HMMs. The Viterbi algorithm allows us to obtain the optimal state sequence $\hat{S} = [\hat{s}_1, \hat{s}_2, \ldots, \hat{s}_T]$ that maximises the posterior probability $P(S \mid \mathcal{X})$ of the state sequence S given the sequence of observations $\mathcal{X}$, that is,

$$\hat{S} = \operatorname*{argmax}_{S} P(S \mid \mathcal{X}). \tag{14.12}$$

The argument that maximises $P(S \mid \mathcal{X})$ is the same one that maximises $P(S, \mathcal{X})$, and therefore

$$\hat{S} = \hat{s}_1, \hat{s}_2, \ldots, \hat{s}_T = \operatorname*{argmax}_{\text{all } s_1, s_2, \ldots, s_T} P(s_1, s_2, \ldots, s_T, X_1, X_2, \ldots, X_T). \tag{14.13}$$

This expression is similar to (14.3) except that the sum over all state sequences is replaced by a maximisation over them. The Viterbi algorithm is a Dynamic Programming technique, which maximises the previous expression efficiently using the function $\phi_t(j)$ defined as the maximum joint probability of the partial observation sequence $X_1, X_2, \ldots, X_t$ and the partial state sequence $s_1, s_2, \ldots, s_{t-1}, (s_t = j)$ constrained to end in the state j at time t. The maximisation occurs over all the partial state sequences that finish at state j at time t, that is,

$$\phi_t(j) = \max_{\text{all } s_1, s_2, \ldots, s_{t-1}} p(s_1, s_2, \ldots, s_{t-1}, (s_t = j), X_1, X_2, \ldots, X_T). \tag{14.14}$$

Similarly to (14.7), it can be expressed in terms of the model parameters,

$$\phi_t(j) = \max_{\text{all } s_1, s_2, \ldots, s_{t-1}} \left[\pi(s_1) b_{s_1}(X_1) a_{s_1 s_2} b_{s_2}(X_2) \cdots a_{s_{t-1} j} b_j(X_t) \right]. \tag{14.15}$$

Separating the maximisation over the predecessors of the state j, (14.15) can be written recursively as

$$\phi_t(j) = \max_i [\phi_{t-1}(i) a_{ij}] b_j(X_t). \tag{14.16}$$

The recursion can be initialised with $\phi_1(j) = \pi_j b_j(X_1)$.

According to the definition of $\phi_t(j)$, it is clear that the optimal joint probability of the complete observation sequence and the corresponding optimal state sequence is given by

$$\max_{S} p(S, \mathcal{X}) = \max_j \phi_T(j). \tag{14.17}$$

Recovery of the optimal state sequence is based on the formula for $\phi_t(j)$ given by (14.16). For each state j at each time t we can obtain the predecessor state over the optimal path that ended in the state $s_t = j$ by finding the argument that maximises (14.16),

$$\psi_t(j) = \underset{i}{\text{argmax}}\,[\phi_{t-1}(i)a_{ij}] \quad \text{for} \quad 2 \geq t \geq T. \tag{14.18}$$

The final state over the optimal state sequence is the argument that maximises (14.17),

$$\hat{s}_T = \underset{j}{\text{argmax}}\,\phi_T(j). \tag{14.19}$$

Then, we can recover iteratively the predecessor states over the optimal state sequence going backwards from the optimal final state $\hat{s}_T$,

$$\hat{s}_{t-1} = \psi_t(\hat{s}_t) \quad \text{for} \quad T \geq t \geq 2. \tag{14.20}$$

The Viterbi algorithm is used by HMM-based speech recognisers to search for the most likely word sequence $\mathcal{W}$. This is often approximated by finding the most likely state sequence in a finite-state network that is built by connecting the basic phone HMMs according to a set of grammar rules. An important technique that further reduces the computational load is a variation of the Viterbi algorithm, the *Viterbi beam search*. Time-synchronous beam search is a suboptimal version of the Viterbi algorithm, in which only the most likely states survive (are *active*) at each time. The set of states that are active at each time constitutes the *search space*. Decoding time can be adjusted by controlling the beam width, that is, the maximum distance (on a logarithmic scale) that a particular theory can have from the current best in order to survive. Reducing the beam width speeds up decoding, but can also introduce search errors, as we shall see in Chapter 15, where we compare a number of different techniques, including beam search, in an effort to speed up a continuous HMM recogniser.

14.2.4   Estimation of Model Parameters

The problem of obtaining the parameters of an HMM is posed as an optimisation problem; that is, an optimality criterion is chosen, usually maximum likelihood (ML), and the parameters are chosen to maximise that criterion on the training data. This is a very difficult problem and there is no known method to solve for the maximum likelihood parameters analytically. However, there is an iterative procedure, known as the Baum-Welch training method (Baum et al. 1970), that, starting from a given initial value of the parameters, allows us iteratively to reach a local maximum of the likelihood. The derivation of the estimation procedure is beyond the scope of this book, but we review the iterative method that provides us with an intuitive interpretation of how the parameters are estimated.

We define $\gamma_t(j) = P(s_t = j \mid \mathcal{X})$, the posterior probability of being in state j at time t, given the sequence of observations, which can be computed in terms of the recursions derived in the first problem as

$$\gamma_t(j) = \frac{p(s_t = j, \mathcal{X})}{p(\mathcal{X})} = \frac{\alpha_t(j)\beta_t(j)}{\sum_{i=1}^{N} \alpha_t(i)\beta_t(i)}. \tag{14.21}$$

Similarly we define, $\varepsilon_t(j) = P(s_t = i, s_{t+1} = j \mid \mathcal{X})$, the posterior probability of being in state i at time t and at state j at time $t + 1$, given the sequence of observations; it can be computed as

$$\varepsilon_t(i, j) = \frac{p(s_t = i, s_{t+1} = j, \mathcal{X})}{p(\mathcal{X})} = \frac{\alpha_t(i)a_{ij}b_j(X_{t+1})\beta_{t+1}(j)}{\sum_{i=1}^{N} \alpha_t(i)\beta_t(i)}. \tag{14.22}$$

The sum of $\gamma_t(j)$ over time can be interpreted as the expected number of times that state j is visited, and the sum over time of $\varepsilon_t(i, j)$ can be interpreted as the expected number of times that a transition from state i to state j is observed. The ratio of these two quantities can be used as an estimate of the conditional probability of making a transition to state j given that the current state is i, that is, $P(s_j \mid s_i)$; this estimate actually corresponds to the Baum-Welch reestimation formula for the transition probability

$$\bar{a}_{ij} = \frac{\sum_{t=1}^{T-1} \varepsilon_t(i, j)}{\sum_{t=1}^{T-1} \gamma_t(i)}. \tag{14.23}$$

Note that through the definition of α and β, the new estimate of the transition probability, $\bar{a}_{ij}$, is a function of the previous (or initial) value of the transition probability a_{ij} as well as of the other previous model parameters and the training data $\mathcal{X}$.

The reestimation formulae for the observation-distribution parameters depend on the type of output distribution used (discrete, Gaussian, Gaussian mixture, etc.). As an example, the reestimation formula for the mean vector μ_j of a Gaussian output distribution for state j is

$$\bar{\mu}_j = \frac{\sum_{t=1}^{T-1} \gamma_t(j)X_t}{\sum_{t=1}^{T-1} \gamma_t(j)}, \tag{14.24}$$

where again there is a simple intuitive interpretation of the reestimation formula: the reestimated mean vector for state j is the weighted average of the observation vectors, where the weight is the posterior probability of being in state j at each time.

The new parameter estimates are guaranteed to increase the likelihood of the data $\mathcal{X}$ unless they correspond to a critical point of the likelihood function. Thus, we can iterate the procedure using the new parameters in the place of the previous ones until a local maximum of the likelihood is reached. The final values of this iterative procedure are the estimated parameters for the HMM.

The Baum-Welch algorithm, a corpus of utterances and their associated word transcriptions, and a phonetic pronunciation dictionary (or lexicon) are required to train the acoustic model of a speech recogniser. A network of states is built for each utterance in the training corpus using the transcription and the lexicon. The Forward-Backward algorithm is then run separately on each utterance, and the statistics required by equations (14.23) and (14.24) are collected over all utterances. Finally, the HMM parameters are reestimated using the Baum-Welch reestimation formulae.

14.3   The Speech Part of the Book

There are many design issues that must be determined in using HMMs for speech recognition. One can use continuous- or discrete-density HMMs, tie parameters at different levels, cluster states, and so on. In Chapter 15 we discuss the specific form of acoustic models used in DECIPHER^{TM} and the Nuance speech-recognition system. We also present some of the acoustic modelling research we performed in the SLT-2 and SLT-3 parts of the project. The language model, the second component of a speech recogniser, is covered in Chapter 16, where we discuss the language modelling issues that came up in SLT where we had to build models from very small amounts of data. Practical issues arising in porting a recogniser to a new language and in handling multiple languages and dialects can be found in Chapters 17 and 18, respectively. Finally, we present the speech/language interface in Chapter 19.

We believe that, after reading these chapters, the NL reader will at least have an idea of what is happening at the other half of the system and what issues his or her speech colleagues are likely to be working on. And, perhaps, there will be a few ideas and suggestions that will come up by looking at things from a different perspective.

15 Acoustic Modelling

VASSILIS DIGALAKIS AND LEONARDO NEUMEYER

15.1 Introduction: Discrete or Continuous? That's the Question

When we started the SLT project in mid-1992, one of our major challenges was to build an accurate real-time[1] ATIS speech-recognition system using general-purpose computer hardware. Many real-time recognisers at that time were using dedicated hardware components for acoustic processing of the sampled speech signal. We decided to implement the whole speech recogniser in software using the standard digital audio input available on high-end computer workstations such as the Sun Sparc2 and Sparc10. Our first SLT prototype recogniser was a version of the DECIPHER^{TM} speaker-independent speech recognition system (Cohen et al. 1990). The system used context-dependent phonetic-based HMMs with discrete observation distributions for four features: cepstrum and energy, and their corresponding time derivatives. Each of the four feature streams were quantised using 8-bit codebooks. Limiting the size of the codebook was the key to achieving real-time performance.

Even though more accurate recognition was possible at the time of the first SLT prototype using continuous-density HMMs (CDHMMs), their computational complexity was too high for a real-time application. In the second phase of the project, we switched to a CDHMM system with very good speed-performance characteristics (Digalakis, Monaco, and Murveit 1993, 1996) and incorporated many techniques for speeding up the likelihood computation and hypothesis search. Together, these allowed us to achieve real-time performance on a Sun UltraSparc machine. In Section 15.2 we describe the genonic CDHMM system used in the final version of the SLT-2 system, and in Section 15.3 we show how the system was tuned to perform accurately at real time.

In the third phase of the SLT project, however, after six years of optimising the continuous system, we discovered that still-better accuracy/speed tradeoffs

---

[1] A recogniser is said to perform at real time if it takes as much time to decode speech as the duration of the signal.

were possible using discrete HMMs (Digalakis, Tsakalidis, and Neumeyer 1999; Tsakalidis, Digalakis, and Neumeyer 1999). It is interesting to mention that our finding was not motivated by speed; we were actually searching for a data-compression technique to send the speech features over narrow-band channels. We not only found efficient compression techniques that did not degrade recognition performance, but also discovered a new HMM technique based on a mixture of discrete distributions. We refer to this technique as discrete-mixture HMMs (DMHMMs), and will describe it in more detail in Section 15.4.

15.2   Continuous-Density HMMs and Genones

Continuous-density HMMs model the acoustic vector X_t obtained by the front-end processing at frame t directly. The feature X_t is generally a vector of real parameters; as we saw in Chapter 14, the distribution of the vector X_t for a given HMM state s takes the form of a multivariate probability density function. The most common approach is to use a Gaussian-mixture distribution of the form

$$b_s(X_t) = p(X_t \mid s) = \sum_{q \in Q(s)} P(q \mid s)\mathcal{N}(X_t; \mu_{sq}, \Sigma_{sq}), \tag{15.1}$$

where $Q(s)$ is the set of mixture Gaussians $\mathcal{N}(X_t; \mu_{sq}, \Sigma_{sq})$ used by state s. We shall use the term *codebook* to denote the set $Q(s)$. HMMs with this form of observation distribution appear in the literature as continuous HMMs (Rabiner et al. 1985). The probabilities $P(q \mid s)$ are known as *mixture weights* and define a discrete distribution $[P(q \mid s), q \in Q(s)]$ for each HMM state s.

The set $Q(s)$ may be state specific, or tied across different states. When tying is not used, the sets of component Gaussians are disjointed for different HMM states; that is, $Q(s) \cap Q(s') = \emptyset$ if $s \neq s'$. We shall refer to HMMs that use no sharing of mixture Gaussians as *fully continuous* HMMs. Fully continuous HMMs provide a detailed representation of the acoustic space at the expense of increased computational complexity and lack of robustness: each HMM state has associated with it a different set of mixture Gaussians that are expensive to evaluate and cannot be estimated robustly when the number of observations per state in the training data is small. To overcome the robustness issue, continuous HMM systems use various schemes, like maximum *a posteriori* (MAP) estimation (Guavain et al. 1994) and state clustering (Woodland et al. 1994).

To overcome the robustness and computation issues, the other extreme has also appeared in the literature: all HMM states share the same set of mixture Gaussians; that is, $Q(s) = Q$ is independent of the state s. HMMs with this degree of sharing were proposed in Bellegarda and Nahamoo (1990) and in Huang and Jack (1990) under the names *tied-mixture* and *semicontinuous* HMMs, respectively. Tied-mixture (TM) HMMs achieve robust estimation and efficient computation of the density likelihoods. However, the typical mixture size used in TM systems is small and does not accurately represent the acoustic space. Increasing the number of the mixture Gaussians is not a feasible solution, since the mixture-weight distributions become too sparse. In large-vocabulary problems, where a large number of basic HMMs are used and each has only a few observations in the training data, sparse mixture-weight distributions cannot be estimated robustly and are expensive to store.

Intermediate degrees of tying have also been examined. In phone-based tying, described in Paul 1989, only HMM states that belong to allophones of the same phone share the same mixture components – that is, $Q(s) = Q(s')$ if s and s' are states of context-dependent HMMs with the same centre phone. We will use the term *phonetically tied* to describe this kind of tying. The choice of phonetically-tied mixtures (PTMs), although linguistically motivated, is somewhat arbitrary and may not achieve the optimum tradeoff between resolution and trainability. Digalakis and colleagues (1993, 1996) introduced an automatic procedure to identify subsets of HMM states that will share mixtures. This particular form of HMM is known as a *genonic* HMM, or state-clustered tied mixture, and is used in the CDHMM models of the final version of the SLT system, as well as by the Nuance speech-recognition engine. The same algorithm was later adopted by others, including BBN laboratories.

Genonic HMMs are constructed following a bootstrap approach from a system that has a higher degree of tying (i.e., a TM or a PTM system), and mixtures are progressively untied using three steps: clustering, splitting, and reestimation.The HMM states of all allophones of a phone are clustered following an agglomerative hierarchical clustering procedure (Duda and Hart 1973). States clustered together based on the similarity of their mixture-weight distributions share the same Gaussians in their output distributions. The term *genone* is used to refer to a Gaussian codebook, that is, to the set of Gaussians shared by a cluster of states.

Any measure of dissimilarity between two discrete probability distributions can be used as the distortion measure during clustering. One possibility is to use the increase in the weighted-by-counts entropy of the mixture-weight distributions that is caused by the merging of the two states. Let $H(s)$ denote the entropy of the discrete distribution $[P(q \mid s), q \in Q(s)]$,

$$H(s) = -\sum_{q \in Q(s)} P(q \mid s) \log P(q \mid s). \tag{15.2}$$

Then, the distortion that occurs when two states s_1 and s_2 with $Q(s_1) = Q(s_2)$ are clustered together into the clustered state s is defined as

$$d(s_1, s_2) = (n_1 + n_2)H(s) - n_1 H(s_1) - n_2 H(s_2), \tag{15.3}$$

where n_1, n_2 represent the number of observations used to estimate the mixture-weight distributions of the states s_1, s_2, respectively. The mixture-weight distribution of the clustered state s is

$$P(q \mid s) = \frac{n_1}{n_1 + n_2} P(q \mid s_1) + \frac{n_2}{n_1 + n_2} P(q \mid s_2), \tag{15.4}$$

and the clustered state uses the same set of mixture components as the original states, $Q(s) = Q(s_1) = Q(s_2)$. This distortion measure can be easily shown to be nonnegative, and, in addition, $d(s, s) = 0$.

The clustering procedure partitions the set of HMM states S into disjoint sets of states

$$S = S_1 \cup S_2 \cup \cdots \cup S_n, \tag{15.5}$$

where n, the number of clusters, is determined empirically. The result of the clustering is the definition of a mapping from HMM state to cluster index

$$g = \gamma(s), \tag{15.6}$$

and the set of mixture components that will be used by each state is $Q(s) = Q(g)$.

The same genone is used for all HMM states belonging to a particular cluster S_i. Each state in the cluster, however, retains its own set of mixture weights. The output distribution of genonic HMMs then takes the form

$$b_s(X_t) = \sum_{q=1}^{K} P(q \mid s) \mathcal{N}(X_t; \mu_{gq}, \Sigma_{gq}), \tag{15.7}$$

where K is the number of Gaussians in the genone $Q(g)$ corresponding to state s. The clustering is based on the mixture weights of a system with a higher degree of tying. Once the state clusters are identified, the final genonic system is constructed by bootstrapping from the first system through the steps described in Digalakis and colleagues (1996). The reestimation of the HMM parameters is based on the Baum-Welch algorithm, and the exact reestimation formulae for genonic HMMs can be found in the same proceedings.

Genonic HMMs achieve an optimum tradeoff between acoustic resolution and robustness through a generalisation of the tying of mixture components. The appropriate degree of tying for a particular task depends on the difficulty of the task, the amount of available training data, and the available computational resources for recognition, since systems with a smaller degree of tying have higher computational demands during recognition. Optimising the degree of tying was very important in the SLT project: this made it possible for us to achieve high performance for recognisers that had to be trained for multiple languages and dialects using small amounts of training data, and also to succeed in attaining an excellent speed-performance tradeoff for a demonstration system that had to operate at or near real time.

15.3   Efficiency Issues

The goals of the second phase of the project were to provide maximum accuracy at real-time performance on the available UltraSparc computer platform, and to build a first version of a Swedish ATIS recogniser. The latter will be presented in Chapter 17. To achieve our speed and accuracy goals, we decided to use as our starting point the Nuance speech-recognition engine, a productised version of the DECIPHER^{TM} engine based on genonic CDHMMs.

15.3.1   Baseline Experiments

We first ran some baseline experiments to compare the various speech-recognition systems without optimising for speed. We compared the old discrete system used in the SLT-1 project with various genonic and PTM systems. We used the same task as in the SLT-1 project, that is, a ten-city ATIS grammar. Experiments were carried out on a version of DECIPHER^{TM} configured with a six-feature front end that output twelve Mel-frequency–warped cepstral coefficients (MFCCs), cepstral energy, and their first- and second-order differences. To train the models we used 21 000 ATIS sentences. A summary of these experiments is shown in Table 15.1.

We trained various genonic systems, each of them with a different number of genones. We used 32 and 16 Gaussian components for the genonic systems and 100 for the PTM system. The total number of Gaussians is the product of the number of genones by the number of Gaussians per genone. The remaining columns in the table indicate the recognition accuracy measured in word-error rate (WER), together with speed expressed as a multiple of real time (RT). The results show a reduction of 40 percent in WER from 11.0 percent to 6.8 percent for the best genonic system compared to the SLT-1 discrete system. We also observe a significant increase in computational complexity (CPU time for discrete system is 5.5 times RT compared to 18.2 for the best genonic system). Our goal for the SLT-2

Table 15.1. *Discrete, PTM, and genonic word-error rates on a ten-city English ATIS task*

HMM Type	Number of Genones	Number of Gaussians per Genone	Total Number of Gaussians	WER (%)	x cpuRT (Sparc20)
Genonic	600	32	19 K	6.8	18.2
Genonic	1 100	32	35 K	7.0	26.4
Genonic	390	32	12 K	7.4	14.3
PTM	38	100	4 K	7.7	9.9
Genonic	600	16	10 K	8.3	12.9
Discrete	–	–	–	11.0	5.5

project was to maintain the increased accuracy provided by the continuous-density HMM, while increasing the speed so as to achieve real-time performance. We considered using a PTM on the grounds that it was significantly more accurate than the discrete system, but much faster than the genonic ones. In the end, however, the large performance differential between the PTM and genonic systems was decisive, and a genonic system was used for the final version of the SLT-2 Swedish recogniser (see Chapter 17). The real-time requirement was achieved through faster hardware and through a series of speed-up techniques that we present in the next section.

15.3.2   Speed Optimisation

The main bottleneck when decoding with a CDHMM is evaluation of the thousands of multivariate Gaussians at each frame. To achieve real-time performance, various speed-optimisation techniques were investigated:

> **Viterbi beam-search pruning** This technique is used in the standard Viterbi beam-search algorithm. During the Viterbi search, all active hypotheses with cumulative probability scores that are within a certain distance in the log domain (called *beam width*) from the best scoring hypothesis are retained, whereas all others are pruned. The pruning is implemented at the phone level: all three HMM states for a given allophone are either pruned or kept.
>
> **Gaussian pruning** This technique aborts Gaussian computation if the probability, up to a given dimension in the vector, is below a given threshold.
>
> **Skip Observation Frames (SkipObsFrames)** Depending on the value of the SkipObsFrame parameter, certain hypotheses in the search will be approximated by repeating Gaussian values from the previous frame. When the SkipObsFrames parameter is zero, all hypotheses use the approximation. As the value increases there is less approximation. This technique is based on the assumption that the acoustic vectors of neighbouring frames are highly correlated.
>
> **Shortlists** This technique significantly reduces the amount of Gaussian computation. Gaussian shortlists are lists that specify the subset of the Gaussian distributions expected to have high likelihood values in a given region of the acoustic space. The shortlists use vector quantisation (VQ) to partition the acoustic space (Digalakis et al. 1996). When an acoustic vector is quantised into a certain region of the space, only the Gaussians that are in the shortlists associated with that region are computed.
>
> **Phonetic pruning (PPR)** This technique is used to prune out hypotheses using phones whose probabilities are below a certain threshold.

Table 15.2. *Optimisation of the English ATIS PTM system*

Baseline run (No optimisation)					
PRUNE	GPRUNE	SHORTL	SOF	WER	x CPU-RT
1 200	75 K	no	no	7.8	11.3

Shortlists (values from 1.0 down to 0.7)					
PRUNE	GPRUNE	SHORTL	SOF	WER	x CPU-RT
1 200	75 K	1.0	no	7.7	7.6
1 200	75 K	0.975	no	7.6	6.9
1 200	75 K	0.950	no	7.8	7.1
1 200	75 K	0.925	no	7.6	7.5
1 200	75 K	0.90	no	7.5	7.3
1 200	75 K	0.85	no	7.3	7.0
1 200	75 K	0.80	no	7.7	7.0
1 200	75 K	0.70	no	7.9	5.9

Viterbi Pruning (values from 1 000 down to 600)					
PRUNE	GPRUNE	SHORTL	SOF	WER	x CPU-RT
1 000	75 K	no	no	7.9	8.5
900	75 K	no	no	8.6	6.9
800	75 K	no	no	9.6	5.8
700	75 K	no	no	11.9	4.8
600	75 K	no	no	16.5	3.7

Gaussian Pruning (values from 50 000 down to 4 000)					
PRUNE	GPRUNE	SHORTL	SOF	WER	x CPU-RT
1 200	50 K	no	no	7.7	10.9
1 200	30 K	no	no	7.6	9.1
1 200	20 K	no	no	7.4	9.0
1 200	10 K	no	no	7.8	8.1
1 200	8 K	no	no	8.0	7.3
1 200	6 K	no	no	7.6	7.3

Skip Obs Frames (values from 1 000 down to 0)					
PRUNE	GPRUNE	SHORTL	SOF	WER	x CPU-RT
1 200	75 K	no	1000	7.8	11.5
1 200	75 K	no	800	7.7	10.1
1 200	75 K	no	600	7.8	10.0
1 200	75 K	no	400	8.0	8.4
1 200	75 K	no	200	7.7	7.5
1 200	75 K	no	0	7.8	7.6

To optimise the system we varied the parameters sequentially to determine the optimum set. A summary of the optimisation runs for the English PTM system is shown in Table 15.2. The PTM system is gender independent (the same models are used for both genders) and uses 56 classes and 100 Gaussians per mixture. The test set consists of 200 waveforms and 2 000 words. All tests were run on a Sparc20

50 Mhz machine. The table shows the results for four techniques: Viterbi pruning (PRUNE), Gaussian pruning (GPRUNE), shortlists (SHORTL), and SkipObsFrames (SOF). We see that aggressive Viterbi pruning can significantly reduce computation but at the cost of high error rates. For example, reducing the CPU time from 11.3 to 5.8 times real time results in an increase in word-error rate from 7.8 percent to 9.6 percent. This occurs because we are pruning correct hypotheses during the search. In general, the Viterbi beam width can be set to 1 000 without sacrificing accuracy.

Based on the first round of optimisation, we selected the values that resulted in maximum speed-up with little degradation in recognition accuracy. The next step consisted of optimising the phonetic pruning parameters. This optimisation further reduced the CPU requirements to 1.5 times real time on the Sparc20 host with an error rate of 8.8 percent. The exact operating point can be easily adjusted based on the CPU cycles available.

15.4   Discrete-Mixture HMMs

Continuous HMMs were introduced in the system during SLT-2 with a substantial improvement in recognition performance. The CDHMMs were further refined in the third and final phase of the project. At the same time, however, our research completed a full circle: we showed that, by introducing better quantisation and modelling techniques, discrete HMMs could perform as well as CDHMMs at significantly faster decoding speeds.

In Digalakis and others (1999) we developed a novel encoding scheme for the transmission of the MFCCs in a client-server architecture for speech-enabled applications over the World Wide Web (WWW) and wireless channels. By using vector quantisation on subvectors of the acoustic vector and a bit-allocation algorithm that was driven by speech-recognition performance, we were able to encode the thirteen MFCCs using as little as twenty bits in noise-free environments, while maintaining the recognition performance of a high-quality CDHMM recogniser. This was a rather surprising result, given that HMM-based state-of-the-art recognition systems today represent the MFCCs using floating-point arithmetic and model their distributions with Gaussian mixtures.

The possibility of representing the MFCCs with a small number of bits, instead of the 416 (=13 coefficients × 32 bits per coefficient) that are traditionally used in CDHMMs, is not only advantageous for transmission and storage, but also has serious implications for acoustic modelling. Using Gaussian mixtures to model a set of coefficients that can be represented with twenty bits is clearly overkill. In Digalakis and others (1999) and Tsakalidis and others (1999) we demonstrated that the high level of recognition performance of CDHMMs can be maintained with a far more efficient type of HMM, the discrete-mixture HMM (DMHMM) with subvector quantisation of the coefficient parameters.

Using subvector quantisation, we first partition the vector of MFCCs into L subvectors, $X_t = [X_{t1}, X_{t2}, \ldots, X_{tL}]$. We then quantise each subvector using a separate vector quantiser, obtaining a vector of discrete indices

$$V_t = [\mathrm{vq}(X_{t1}), \mathrm{vq}(X_{t2}), \ldots, \mathrm{vq}(X_{tL})] = [v_{t1}, v_{t2}, \ldots, v_{tL}],$$

where v_{tj} is the VQ index corresponding to the jth subvector. Then, the Gaussian-mixture output distribution (14.2) in CDHMMs can be replaced with a mixture of discrete probability distributions of the following form:

$$b_s(X_t) \doteq P(V_t) = \sum_{q \in Q(s)} P(q \mid s) \prod_{j=1}^{L} P(v_{tj} \mid q, s), \qquad (15.8)$$

where $P(v_{tj} \mid q, s)$ is the probability of observing the discrete symbol $v_{tj} = \mathrm{vq}(X_{tj})$ for the jth subvector. The output distribution introduced above assumes that the indices of different subvectors are conditionally independent given the state and mixture index. Dependencies among the different subvectors for a given state are modelled through the mixture components.

When compared to conventional CDHMMs, discrete-mixture HMMs replace a multivariate Gaussian density with the product of L discrete distributions, one for each subvector. The amount of computation can be reduced by decreasing L. At the same time, however, the number of bits required to represent each subvector increases, and this corresponds to an exponential increase in the amount of memory required to store the lookup tables of the discrete distributions. In Digalakis and colleagues (1999) and Tsakalidis and colleagues (1999), we found that a good compromise is to use $L = 15$ subvectors, and we showed that a speed-up of a factor of two to three can be achieved using this form of output distribution, while maintaining the level of performance of CDHMMs.

The DMHMM results are summarised in Figure 15.1, where we plot the performance of two systems, a baseline CDHMM and a DMHMM with 15 subvectors, versus the decoding time. We use the English ATIS task, and the decoding time is adjusted by varying the beam width. The DMHMM system performs uniformly better than the baseline CDHMM system. Although the DMHMM is two to three times faster than the CDHMM, the WER increases (search errors are introduced) when the beam width is adjusted so that decoding is performed in less than twice real time, running on a 266 MHz Pentium II processor. We also found, at different operating points, that roughly 90 percent of the decoding time was spent on the phone processor, which performs the Viterbi search within an HMM phone model. 80 percent of this time was spent computing the output probabilities (15.8). In a recent implementation of DMHMMs, we were able to achieve similar recognition performance at a decoding speed of 0.5 times real time on a 450 MHz Pentium II computer.

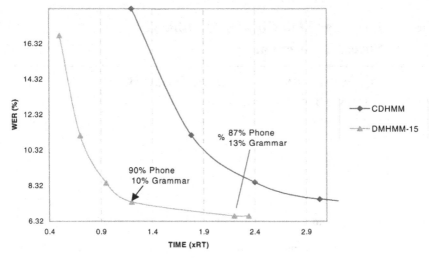

Figure 15.1 A comparison of CDHMM and DMHMM.

15.5   Conclusions

The speech recogniser in the initial SLT system was among the first software-only systems that performed in real time for ATIS-type domains. We started with a discrete HMM system, since this was the most complex system that could run in real time on the hardware platforms that were available at that time. In the subsequent phases of the project, improvements in the acoustic modelling and in hardware allowed us to use better, continuous-density HMMs that reduced the error rate by a factor of almost two over the initial discrete systems. By the end of the third SLT phase, as we shall see in Chapter 17, we had developed continuous HMM systems with thousands of Gaussians that ran faster than real time on the available platforms. At the same time, however, we developed a new form of discrete HMMs that performed at least as well as continuous HMMs at even faster decoding speeds. The extra speed is not really needed for ATIS. We have every reason to believe, though, that suitable use of these new methods will make it possible to achieve similar levels of accuracy for real-time recognition in new domains significantly more challenging in terms of vocabulary size and spontaneity of speech. This opens up exciting new possibilities for building interactive speech-driven systems.

16 Language Modelling for Multilingual Speech Translation

FULIANG WENG, ANDREAS STOLCKE,
AND MICHAEL COHEN

16.1 Introduction

As we saw in Chapter 14, the speech-recognition problem can be formulated as the search for the best hypothesised word sequence given an input feature sequence. The search is based on probabilistic models trained on many utterances:

$$W = \operatorname*{argmax}_{W} P(X \mid W)P(W).$$

In the equation above, $P(X \mid W)$ is called the acoustic model, and $P(W)$ is called the language model (LM).

In this chapter we present several techniques that were used to develop language models for the speech recognisers in the SLT system. The algorithms presented here deal with two main issues: the data-sparseness problem and the development of language models for multilingual recognisers.

As with acoustic modelling, sparse training data is one of the main problems in language-modelling tasks. In both cases, we ideally want to have enough properly matched data to train models for all the necessary conditions. One may think that today's technology, especially the Internet and the World Wide Web, lets us take for granted the availability of any amount of language-modelling training data. Unfortunately, this is not entirely true, for three reasons:

> **Style mismatch** Internet-derived data is usually written text, which does not have the same style as spoken material.
>
> **Language mismatch** The available texts are not uniformly distributed with respect to different languages: there are plenty of data available for English, but not for other languages.
>
> **Domain mismatch** The texts are not specifically organised for any speech-recognition task.

Ignoring these mismatches can cause significant degradation to the performance of speech-recognition systems. On the other hand, fully satisfying them may introduce data-sparseness problems.

For these reasons, we want to investigate various ways that allow us to rapidly collect proper amounts of data for new domains and new languages, and to train compact language models with high performance. Since human beings are the ultimate producers and consumers of human languages, it is also desirable to leverage the strength of symbolic approaches for statistical language modelling.

We have experimented with several approaches aimed at tackling the data-sparseness problem. In the following sections, we will present data-fabrication techniques, data-retrieval techniques, class-based N-gram approaches and class-based N-gram generalisation algorithms. We will also present our methods and experiments for handling multilingual language modelling.

In the interests of making the chapter self-contained, we briefly summarise a couple of key technical ideas. One very common type of LM is the *statistical N-gram language model*; this is an $(n - 1)$th order Markov model, where the probability of one word in the sentence depends on the $n - 1$ previous words. n is most often equal to 2, resulting in the *bigram language model*. In a bigram LM, the probability of one word w_n in the sentence, given the history of all previous words $w_1, w_2, \ldots, w_{n-1}$, depends only on the previous word:

$$p(w_n \mid w_1, w_2, \ldots, w_{n-1}) = p(w_n \mid w_{n-1}).$$

LMs are also frequently constructed by use of interpolation. An interpolated language model computes the probability of a word w, given the history of previous words (or word classes) H, as a linear combination of the probabilities given by two or more language models. In the case of two models, A and B, this probability can be expressed as

$$p(w \mid H) = \lambda \cdot p_A(w \mid H) + (1 - \lambda) \cdot p_B(w \mid H),$$

where $p_A(w \mid H)$, $p_B(w \mid H)$ are the two language models and λ is the interpolation weight between 0 and 1. Notice that λ can also be a function of H.

16.2   Fabricating Domain-Specific Data

The data-sparseness problem for language-model training can be alleviated using grammars written by human language experts. It is well known that it is difficult to write a full-sentence grammar for a general domain, or even for a limited domain. However, our experience has shown that it is quite reasonable to assume that a grammarian can write a phrase grammar for a limited domain within a few weeks. The key advantage of a phrase grammar is that it can capture almost all the necessary information needed for the domain without having to exhaustively consider all the possible phrase combinations. For example, in the ATIS domain, it is quite easy to write down the most frequently used expressions for dates, times,

Table 16.1. *Word-error rate with fabricated LM training data*

System	Training Data	WER (%)
Baseline	220 000 words	5.73
No LM	0	39.10
FabPhrase	1 300 000 words	14.66
FabSentence	1 500 000 words	12.49

costs, locations, transportation, meals, and arrival and departure events. Because phrase subgrammars are modular (Weng and Stolcke 1995), many expressions, such as dates, times, locations, and numbers, can be used across different domains. Therefore, moving into a new domain is even easier after phrase grammars have been written for some initial domains.

There are two potential ways to apply phrase grammars for language modelling. One is to use phrase grammars to generate random phrases and to train statistical language models, that is, to *fabricate* domain-specific data. The other is to embed phrase subgrammars in statistical-language models, in a way similar to class-based language modelling. We will discuss in detail the second approach in Section 16.5.

We conducted a set of initial experiments in 1995, when we first took an English-phrase grammar adapted from SRI's ATIS template matcher system (Jackson et al. 1994). This phrase grammar uses a vocabulary of 1 750 words, and about 200 non-terminals with approximately 3 600 rules. The majority of the rules are simply names (city names, airport names, etc.) with indicative words, such as preposition *from* for departure location and *to* for destination.

The SRI 1994 ATIS speech-recognition benchmark system (Cohen, Rivlin, and Bratt 1995) was adapted for our real-time SLT task. The resulting baseline speech recogniser has 5.73 percent word-error rate with a bigram language model trained on 220 000 words of ATIS domain data.[1] Table 16.1 contrasts performance of this LM with bigram LMs trained on two artificial corpora. The first of these, FabPhrase, consists of 300 000 phrases (1.3 million words) randomly generated using the phrase grammar. The second, FabSentence, has 100 000 fabricated sentences (1.5 million words) with in-vocabulary words randomly inserted among the phrases. For completeness, we also conducted a set of experiments that linearly interpolated the FabSentence model with the models trained on different amounts of real data. The results are presented in Table 16.2.

Without using any real training data, the LM trained on 100 000 fabricated sentences led to an almost usable speech recogniser, which we found quite

---

[1] All the experiments in this section were carried out on the 1994 DARPA benchmark evaluation male test set, which contains 443 sentences and a total of 4 660 words.

Table 16.2. *Word-error rate with interpolated real training data*

Real Data	Interpolated LM		Real Data Only LM
(# Words)	Weight	WER (%)	WER (%)
0	0.0	12.49	39.10
10 000	.9	7.75	9.14
20 000	.97	7.10	7.81
30 000	.97	6.65	7.12
40 000	.97	6.52	7.10
50 000	.95	6.27	6.89
100 000	.92	5.86	6.12
220 000	.97	5.69	5.73

encouraging. A refinement, which we hope to investigate in the future, is to incorporate phrase tags in the tag set of the corpus. This could then be used to create a statistical N-gram tag model which in turn would be used to fabricate sentences. The idea is related to the class N-gram generalisation approach discussed in Section 16.5.

16.3   Better Use of Domain-General Data

Successful statistical language modelling requires large amounts of domain-specific data, which are not always available. As discussed above, direct use of widely available domain-general data often leads to unsatisfactory results, due to vocabulary and style mismatches. One straightforward way to attack the problem (Iyer, Ostendorf, and Rohlicek 1994) is to interpolate an N-gram LM trained on small amounts of available domain-specific data with another N-gram LM trained on large amounts of domain-general data. By adjusting the weight of the domain-specific LM to a high value, one can reduce the effect of the mismatches in training data, but at the same time inherit robustness from the general LM.

By interpolating a domain-specific N-gram LM with a general N-gram LM, we utilise only local properties of the domain-general data, typically counts for bigram LMs. However, many of these local counts are irrelevant both to the domain and to the global constraints of the language. Including them, therefore, serves no useful purpose, and only degrades the quality of the LM. Instead of extracting N-gram counts directly from domain-general data, an alternative approach is to start by attempting to identify a subset of the general data related to the domain we are interested in, and extract counts only from that.

One of the assumptions of this approach is that so-called general data really consist of a mixture of data from many different specific domains. A strand of research in traditional Artificial Intelligence (AI) has for a long time advocated a script-based approach to language understanding (Schank and Abelson 1977), based on the assumption that shared human knowledge is organised in the form of scripts: routine procedures that people perform for different tasks and have an organisation that is well reflected in language. They are possibly related to the concept of domain organisation. Interestingly, our observations have several points of contact with script-based research.

With these ideas in mind, we designed a set of experiments in 1995. We selected some relevant news articles from Usenet news groups and the Switchboard corpus[2] LM data to conduct the experiments. To filter these corpora and retrieve relevant data, a distance measure was required. Adopted from information theory, perplexity is commonly used in language modelling as a measure of the fit between model and data. It is defined as:

$$Perplexity = 2^{-\sum_{x \in V_T} p'(x)*\log p(x)},$$

where $p(x)$ is the probabilistic distribution of the model, $p'(x)$ is the estimated probability from text data T, and V_T is the vocabulary of T. The lower the perplexity number, the better the model fits the data. Here, we use it as a distance measure for selecting sentences that are close to a given seed model.

We first took articles from Usenet rec.travel.* news groups covering May and August of 1995, using the FabPhrase model from Section 16.2 as the seed model. Because many words in the general data were out of domain vocabulary (OOV), we only obtained 1 700 sentence fragments or chunks (as opposed to full sentences) totaling 11 000 words. We also tried using the Switchboard corpus as the domain-general data, hoping that the conversational styles and travel topics captured by that data could be helpful for the ATIS domain. The filtering process on Switchboard data yielded about 85 000 chunks, totaling 288 000 words. Two language models, which we will call *gnus*[3] and *swb*, were built using the two data sets just described.

We performed conventional interpolation of the models as baselines. As we can see in Table 16.3, the interpolated models gnus+FabPhrase and swb+FabPhrase both produce significant improvements over all the three individual models, and in particular over the FabPhrase model. We also combined all three language models (gnus+swb+FabPhrase) obtaining a further small improvement. All the recognition results are listed in Table 16.3.

These results show that using general-domain data can significantly improve an in-domain model. We also experimented with selective usage of general-domain data. A language model was built, that weighted more heavily (0.9) the low perplexity fragments from the general-domain (Switchboard and gnus)

---

[2] The Switchboard corpus is a conversational speech database, collected over the telephone, that includes a variety of conversation topics.

[3] gnus is the name of the software used to access Usenet.

Table 16.3. *Word-error rate with
interpolated real training data*

Model	WER (%)
gnus (40K words)	30.19
swb (1.5M words)	18.88
FabPhrase	14.66
gnus+swb	14.76
swb+FabPhrase	11.57
gnus+FabPhrase	10.79
gnus+swb+FabPhrase	10.41
gnuswb.median+FabPhrase	10.17

data extracted using the FabPhrase model: we called it *gnuswb.median*. This
LM was then interpolated with the fabricated data to yield yet another model,
gnuswb.median+FabPhrase. The gain from selective usage of general-domain data
was smaller than expected, and we attribute this largely to our simplistic use of
perplexity as a distance measure for retrieving relevant sentence fragments. For
example, chunks ending with "the", such as "I was just wondering if the", and
"when checking into the originating flight and the", are quite frequent, and this
distorts the perplexity of relevant phrases in the general data that end with "the".
Hence, some preprocessing is required in order to make this distance measure more
effective. Alternative distance measures also need to be investigated, including
labeling sentences with phrase grammars and preferring ones with high phrase-
label coverage. Another possible reason for this smaller-than-expected gain can be
the fabricated seed model, FabPhrase. As explained before, FabPhrase is trained
on randomly generated phrases from the phrase grammar. Therefore, this model
does not fully reflect the real probabilistic distribution of any real in-domain data,
especially in the case of phrase boundaries. An improvement would be to use the
technique proposed at the end of Section 16.2 to build a seed model.

16.4   Unsupervised Language-Model Adaptation

When there are not enough domain-specific data, a possible solution is to perform
unsupervised adaptation of the language model. In unsupervised adaptation, the
language model is reestimated on in-domain speech data without human transcriptions, using a recogniser to obtain automatic, albeit imperfect, transcriptions.

We thought it would be interesting to attempt to do this using the gnuswb.me-
dian+FabPhrase LM from the previous section; recall that this language model
was trained entirely on non–domain-specific data, with the phrase grammar as its
only domain-specific knowledge. To investigate dependence on the quantity of
adaptation data used, we selected the 1994 DARPA ATIS male development

Table 16.4. *Word-error rate with*
unsupervised adaptation

Unsupervised Adapt. Data	WER (%)
none	10.17
hyp-d1994m	9.08
hyp-e1994m	9.01
hyp-(e1994m+e1993m)	8.78
hyp-(e1994m+e1993m+d1994m)	8.76

(d1994m) and 1993 DARPA ATIS male evaluation test sets (e1993m) as adaptation, in addition to the 1994 DARPA ATIS male evaluation test set (e1994m). A first recognition pass on e1994m, d1994m, and e1993m was performed to obtain automatic transcriptions for the three data sets. After this, the three automatically transcribed data sets, hyp-e1994m, hyp-e1993m, and hyp-d1994m, were incrementally merged to form three adaptation data sets, hyp-e1994m, hyp-(e1994m+e1993m) and hyp-(e1994m+e1993m+d1994m), with 4 654, 9 210, and 13 541 words, respectively. These were then used to build three models for adaptation. All three models were interpolated with the gnuswb.median+FabPhrase model, using a weight of 0.9 for the three models created from adaptation data. Three new recognition systems with the three corresponding unsupervised adapted models were tested on e1994m data.

The results are shown in Table 16.4. The best version, hyp-(e1994m+e1993m+ d1994m), displays a 13.9 percent relative improvement over the baseline system, using 13 541 words of unsupervised adaptation data. With less than 5 000 words of unsupervised adaptation data, whether on the same data set (hyp-e1994m) or another data source (hyp-d1994m), we still obtained more than 10 percent relative improvement. However, additional iterations of unsupervised adaptation did not improve the recognition performance.

Our significant improvements in word-error rates can be explained by two reasons. First, the baseline system incorporates a variety of grammatical instances from the phrase grammar and selected data, and, although the distribution of the fabricated data is distorted, this LM is a satisfactory starting point. Second, this relatively low word-error rate baseline system is used in unsupervised mode to create reliable hypotheses, which are weighted heavily during unsupervised adaptation.

16.5   Class-Based Language Models

There are two extreme sets of approaches in language modelling. The first is to model flat word strings using statistical N-gram, techniques, without considering the internal structure of sentences. This approach has the merit of simplicity: it is easy to implement, and it is easy to train robust models. On the other hand, because it does not take internal structure into consideration, it will either not model long-distance dependencies when n is small, or we will face a data-sparseness problem when n is big. The second approach is to model whole sentence structures. This approach has the merit of precision: it provides detailed information and improves predictability. It does, however, suffer from a severe data-sparseness problem, making it very hard to train such models.

As a compromise approach, class-based N-gram language modelling has been a very successful technique that can be used when the amount of available data is limited (Brown et al. 1992). A more flexible approach, which we will talk about later in this section, is to model important phrases in a sentence. In our SLT work, we implemented a class-based bigram LM and tested it with our English and Swedish ATIS systems.

The class-based bigram LM is defined as:

$$P(w_2 \mid w_1) = \sum_{(C_1,C_2),\text{where } w_2 \in C_2, w_1 \in C_1} P(C_2 \mid C_1) * P(w_2 \mid C_2),$$

where C_1, C_2 are the classes of words w_1, w_2, respectively. Notice that the class-based bigram LM is essentially an HMM (see Chapter 14) with the state-transition probability being the class bigram ($P(C_2 \mid C_1)$) and the output distribution being the class-membership distribution ($P(w_2 \mid C_2)$). In our experiments, the English classes were created manually; they include city names, airlines, airline codes, and so on. The Swedish classes were manually translated from English ones with some minor modifications.

Table 16.5 lists the recognition word-error rates for the English ATIS system with different amounts of language-modelling training data, using word-bigram

Table 16.5. *Word-error rates of word bigrams vs. class bigrams with respect to different amounts of data in English ATIS*

LM	Training (words)	WER (%)
word	220 000	7.02
word	150 000	7.38
word	100 000	7.73
word	50 000	8.26
class	220 000	6.91
class	150 000	7.10
class	100 000	7.40
class	50 000	7.40
word+class	220 000	6.37
word+class	100 000	7.10
word+class	50 000	7.21

Table 16.6. *Perplexities of word-bigram model, class-bigram model, and interpolated models for English, with OOV rate being 0.1%*

	Perplexity
word	33.0
class	25.4
word+class	24.6

(*word*), class-bigram (*class*), and interpolated (*word+class*) language models. The test set was again the 1994 DARPA benchmark evaluation male data.

The results of Table 16.5 show that with larger amounts of training data (220 000 words), pure class-based bigram LMs perform as well as word-bigram LMs, while with small amounts of training data (50 000 to 100 000 words), pure class-based bigram LMs outperform word-bigram LMs significantly. The interpolated word-bigram and class-bigram systems gave further improvement over the pure class-bigram systems. The results also show that the interpolated systems perform as well as the word-bigram systems that are trained with twice as much data. Compared with existing recognisers that have word-bigram LMs trained with large amounts of data, the new English system with class-based bigram LMs mixed with word-bigram LMs reduced the WER from 7.02 percent to 6.37 percent on a test set of 4 660 words, a significant improvement. The perplexity improvements of the class-based and interpolated LMs over the word-bigram LM using the 220 000 words of training data are consistent with the word-error–rate reductions (see Table 16.6).

We repeated a subset of experiments on our Swedish system, and obtained slightly better perplexity reduction, but only slight word-error–rate reduction (see Table 16.7). This difference is probably due to the limited variability of our Swedish test set.

Table 16.7. *Word-error rates and perplexity of word-bigram model, class-bigram model, and interpolated models for Swedish on 444 sentences (3 758 words)*

	WER (%)	Perplexity
Baseline	7.90	40.260
class	8.01	22.208
word+class	7.64	20.715

Class N-gram LMs allow convenient combination of hand-coded linguistic knowledge (in the form of class definitions) with statistical parameters trained from data (the class N-gram probabilities). In structuralist terms, class-based LMs improve generalisation along the *paradigmatic* dimension: substitutions of known words into contexts they haven't been previously observed in. In the remainder of this section we will investigate a way to improve the generalisation of N-gram models along the *syntagmatic* dimension, by inferring N-grams that were not observed in training, but are plausible given the observed ones. While the technique can be applied to word- or class N-grams, it makes most sense in combination with class N-grams, leveraging the generalisation afforded by the word classes.

At the core of our technique for N-gram generalisation is an algorithm that was orignally developed for compressing word lattices generated by speech recognisers (Weng, Stolcke, and Sankar 1998). The idea is to merge nodes in a lattice based on shared left or right contexts. Nodes with identical or largely overlapping contexts are inferred to be instances of the same underlying grammatical context and combined, resulting in a more compact representation. The version of the algorithm that considers right contexts is given below:

Backward lattice reduction algorithm. Let $S_{out}(n)$ be the set of successor nodes of node n. Let $word(n)$ denote the word name of lattice node n.

For each lattice node n in reverse topological order (starting with the final node):

- for each pair of predecessor nodes (i, j) of node n:
  - if $word(i) = word(j)$ and $\frac{\|S_{out}(i) \cap S_{out}(j)\|}{\| \min \{S_{out}(i), S_{out}(j)\} \|} \geq r_{\min}$
    (or, $word(i) = word(j)$ and $\frac{\|S_{out}(i) \cap S_{out}(j)\|}{\| \max \{S_{out}(i), S_{out}(j)\} \|} \geq r_{\max}$),
    then merge nodes i and j.

In the algorithm, $r_{\min}$ and $r_{\max}$ are context overlap ratios to be adjusted empirically. Setting $r_{\min} = 1$ (or, $r_{\max} = 1$) forces the two outgoing node sets to be the same; this variant is called the *exact-reduction algorithm*, and would preserve the set of strings represented by the lattice, i.e., give no generalisation. When $r_{\min} < 1$ or $r_{\max} < 1$, the algorithm generalises the coverage of the lattice by allowing additional transitions. For example, before the reduction process, as shown in Figure 16.1.a, word string *ead* is not in the lattice; after the reduction process (Figure 16.1.b), the word string *ead* is included. The decision to include word string *ead* in the lattice relies on the overlap of the existing word strings. In our example, word strings *...eab...* and *...fab...* overlap after *ab*, and word strings *...fab...* and *...fad...* overlap before *fa*. Therefore, it is reasonable to assume that *...ead...* is a valid string. Intuitively, the reliability of the new word string(s) correlates with the overlap ratios. The higher the proportion of overlap between two

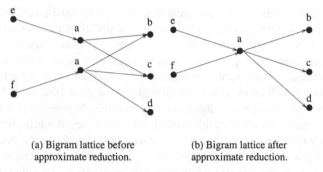

(a) Bigram lattice before   (b) Bigram lattice after
approximate reduction.   approximate reduction.

Figure 16.1. Illustration of the reduction algorithm.

sets of strings, the more confident we can be that the new word string(s) are grammatical.

Instead of testing the overlap ratios of the outgoing node sets, the algorithm can be executed equally well by requiring minimal overlap ratios for two incoming node sets. This gives the forward version of the reduction algorithm. Forward and backward versions can be performed several times in alternation to locate new merging opportunities created by the respective other processing direction.

We can embed the lattice reduction algorithm in a new algorithm that generalises word-class sequences obtained from a training corpus. The generalised lattice representation is used to generate a new set of N-grams (including ones not observed in training), from which a new N-gram LM can be constructed. As a final tuning step, we interpolate the resulting N-gram model with the word N-gram model obtained directly from our original training data. This counteracts possible overgeneralisation and ensures that the overall model is no worse than the standard word-based LM. The complete procedure is as follows:

Class n-gram generalisation algorithm.

1. Automatically tag the training data with a (hand-written) class or phrase grammar. This yields a new training corpus in which defined words and phrases have been replaced with class names. Where multiple tag sequences are possible, select the one that replaces the largest number of words with class/phrase tags.
2. Combine the tagged training sentences in parallel, so as to form a large lattice of disjoint paths, sharing only the same initial and final nodes.
3. Apply the lattice reduction algorithm to the lattice thus constructed.
4. Generate a large sample of word sequences from the reduced lattice, by combining random walks through the lattice with randomly generated word sequences for the class labels encountered.
5. Train a word N-gram LM from the artificial sentence sample.

We tested this algorithm using a small set of training sentences from the English ATIS corpus, comprising about 20 000 words; the test set was, as before, the 1994 DARPA male evaluation data. Classes of words and phrases were predefined by a hand-written finite state grammar consisting of about 144 nonterminals and approximately 4 000 rules. The majority of the rules defined proper name classes, such as city and airport names, with some additional classes for numbers, dates and similar productive phrase types. An important difference to the previous experiments with class-based LMs was the inclusion of the latter types of classes, which generate an infinite set of word sequences.

Both the approximate (generalising) and the exact lattice reduction algorithms were applied to the lattice built from this data. The overlap ratio threshold for generalising (r_{min}) was 0.5, i.e., if lattice nodes shared more than half their predecessors or successors they were considered mergeable. The exact approach gives us a baseline with which to compare the effect of generalisation. Since the set of word and class N-grams is not generalised, the results should be comparable to that of a standard class N-gram LM in this case. To build the generalised N-gram model we generated random sentences from the lattice, totalling about 1 500 000 words. Finally, the generalised N-gram LM was interpolated with a standard word N-gram model trained from the same original 20 000 word corpus.

The interpolation weight was set in a jack-knifing procedure: the data was first split in two halves, the algorithm was executed separately on each half, and the interpolation weights optimised on the respective other half (by minimising perplexity). The algorithm was then run on the full training data, using the average of the two previously optimised interpolation weights.

Table 16.8 shows the results obtained, for both bigram and trigram LMs. For comparison, the performance of various previously discussed LMs trained on the same amount of data are also given: the simple word-based LM, the interpolated class-based LM (as described earlier in this section) and the interpolated LM based on fabricated data (see Section 16.2).

Table 16.8. *Results of generalized n-gram LMs and various baseline models, trained on 20 000 words of ATIS data*

	WER (%)	
Model	Bigram	Trigram
Word n-gram	7.81	7.96
Word+Class n-gram	7.51	7.12
Word+FabSentence	7.10	6.82
Word+Exact lattice	7.38	6.57
Word+Generalized lattice	7.40	6.46

We see that the lattice-based models perform well compared to all the base-line models, especially for the trigram case. The bigram LM using fabricated data performs somewhat better than the other bigram LMs, but it should be noted that model makes crucial use of a hand-written phrase grammar and is thus not directly comparable. Compared to the class-based LM, the model generated from the exact lattice shows some improvement, which can be attributed to the more productive phrase-class definitions. Finally, for the trigram case, we see an additional improvement over the exact-lattice approach, which we attribute to the generalising effect of the approximate lattice reduction.

While the observed improvements remain small, we see the class-based N-gram generalization technique presented here as a promising new tool to improve LMs trained from very little raw training data. Future work will have to address additional research questions and potential improvements. These include the question of how to find optimal parameters to control the generalisation algorithm, and how to best combine the method with the other techniques presented in this chapter.

16.6   Multilingual Language Modelling

In today's world, a significant number of people speak multiple languages, and *code switching* is becoming more pervasive. Code switching is used to refer to situations where people switch languages within sentences. This can be a very frequent phenomenon in multilingual systems like SLT. Despite its growing significance, code switching is not well studied in language modelling and speech recognition. We have carried out some initial investigations of this problem in the context of our Swedish/English bilingual recognition system (Weng et al. 1997). We discuss the acoustic-modelling aspects of multilingual systems in Chapter 18. In this section we present two LM approaches that were tested in the bilingual recogniser.

The first approach pools together the Swedish language model data with the English one. A bigram language model (called *shared LM*) was built on the pooled data. Because there are no code-switching instances in the training data, Swedish words can only be followed by Swedish words and English words can only be followed by English words. Transitions between the words of the two languages in the bigram language model can however still be realised through its *backoff node*: in bigram language models, probabilities for word pairs that have no (or very few) occurences in the training data are approximated by appropriate weighting of the unigram probabilities, and this can be efficiently implemented through a backoff node (Katz 1987).

A second approach uses a *constrained LM* that does not allow any transition between the two languages, except in the initial state (Figure 16.2) When tested on English data, the recognition system with the constrained LM performs almost the same as the one with the shared LM. However, when tested on Swedish data,

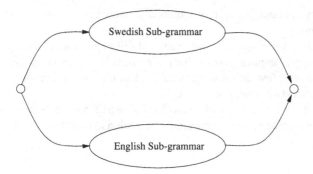

Figure 16.2. Illustration of the constrained LM.

the constrained LM performs significantly better than the shared LM. More details about these experiments, including different types of acoustic models, can be found in Chapter 18.

The above approaches represent two extremes: one allows transitions at any time, and the other allows no transitions at all. Motivated by this study and our work on phrase-based LMs, we plan to pursue approaches that exploit some of the advantages of the extreme positions without inheriting all of their weaknesses. One possibility is to allow proper names to be switchable among different languages. Among others, these proper names would include personal names, location names (cities, airports, etc.), and names of companies and products. A more flexible and generic approach is to allow language switching between phrases, which can be done using the phrase-based language modelling techniques discussed in Section 16.5. Unfortunately though, it is difficult to evaluate these approaches empirically without a multilingual corpus that includes code-switching phenomena. We see collection of such a corpus as an important task for future work.

16.7   Conclusions

In specialised-application domains and in multilingual environments, as in SLT, acquiring a corpus to train the language model is a serious task involving nontrivial design problems, as we saw in Chapter 8. In many practical applications, we are faced with the problem of building a language model using little or no training data. For a multilingual environment, additional issues, such as code switching, need to be properly addressed. These have been the main foci of our language modelling effort in SLT.

We dealt with the first problem in a number of different ways, including: (1) various applications of hand-written phrase grammars, such as fabricating domain-specific data and class-based N-gram generalisation; (2) automatic extraction and selection of relevant phrasal components from readily available data for training; and (3) unsupervised adaptation of the language model. Some of the approaches have led to very encouraging results. Others also show certain promise, or point to new directions.

With regard to multilinguality, we examined different issues in the construction of multilingual language models for our recognition systems, proposed and experimented with a few different approaches, and obtained interesting results, especially for code-switching phenomena.

We hope that our continuing LM research effort in SLT contributes to the maturity of speech technology and its increasing application to multilingual interaction in the world.

17 Porting a Recogniser to a New Language

ROBERT EKLUND, JAAN KAJA,
LEONARDO NEUMEYER, FULIANG WENG,
AND VASSILIS DIGALAKIS

I N THE SECOND PHASE OF THE SLT PROJECT, we developed one of the first continuous speech recognisers for Swedish, a CDHMM system based on the techniques outlined in Chapter 15. This chapter describes the three central issues that must be addressed when porting a recogniser to a new language. First, a speech corpus has to be collected to train and test the statistical acoustic and language models (Section 17.1). Second, the recogniser needs to know how specific words are pronounced in the target language. This can be done through automatic pronunciation tools, or through a lexicon (Section 17.2). Finally, the acoustic and language models of the recogniser are trained using the speech corpus (Section 17.3).

17.1 The Swedish Speech Corpus

The Swedish speech material was collected in three different batches, which will be described in the following paragraphs. The first corpus was based on read material, whereas the second and third were WOZ collections based on mainly iconic instructions.

17.1.1 Read-Text Corpora

When we started building the Swedish recogniser, the first task was to record a Swedish speech corpus. Several issues were considered when compiling the material to be recorded. First, in order to cover all Swedish phonemes and allophones, a set of phonologically and phonetically balanced sentences was created. To provide even more phonetic information, another set was created to cover most of the major formant transitions in CVC sequences (where C defined nine different places of [consonant] articulation and V defined three extreme positions in the vowel space). These two sets served as the acoustic-phonetic baseline. In order to tune the system to the ATIS domain, original ATIS material

(Hemphill et al. 1990) from the Linguistic Data Consortium was obtained and translated, as described in Section 8.3. To obtain wider coverage, texts from the Stockholm-Umeå Corpus (Ejerhed et al. 1992; Källgren 1990, 1991, 1993) were also used.

A problem with the ATIS-domain material arose from non-Swedish sounds encountered in loan words and proper nouns, for example the dental fricatives in the frequently occurring name "Northwest". It has been shown that Swedes, to a large extent, expand their (Swedish) phone inventory when pronouncing words and names of English origin (Eklund and Lindström 1996, 1998; Lindström and Eklund 1999a, 1999b). Consequently, a set of sentences containing such sounds of English origin – so-called *xenophones* – was added to the material.[1] Recordings were made on location all over Sweden to cover the major dialects.[2] The approximately 460 subjects were between 15 and 75 years old, came from 40 different locations throughout Sweden, and were balanced with respect to gender. The recordings were made with the SRI *Generic Recording Tool* (GRT) on a Sun Sparc5, using a standard A/D converter. The subjects used a Sennheiser HMD 410-6 headset with a close-talking microphone. Simultaneous recordings were also made using ten different kinds of telephones. In this way, 160 000 recorded utterances were collected, based on a total of 11 275 text sentences.

During the second phase of the SLT project, only the data from Stockholm-dialect speakers were available for development. The number of utterances that we actually used for training is even smaller, since we excluded the phonetically rich sentences that were common across speakers, so that the triphone inventory of the recogniser would not be biased. The phonetically rich sentences were, however, used in the dialect-adaptation experiments described in Section 18.2.

17.1.2   WOZ Corpora

In order to obtain spontaneous speech-and-language data, two Wizard-of-Oz simulations were conducted. In the first simulation (MacDermid and Eklund 1996), the subjects were given ten tasks each in written form with some additional pictures to illustrate the task. The subjects were told that they were speaking to a live travel agent in another country, but that the communication link included an automatic system that could translate in both directions between Swedish (the subject) and either English, German, or French (the agent). All parts of the system were simulated by "wizards" (professional actors, a behavioral psychologist, and

---

[1] Xenophones are also needed in Swedish synthetic speech, and were consequently recorded for inclusion in the Telia Research concatenative synthesiser (Eklund and Lindström 1998).

[2] For a description of the Swedish dialect areas, compare Bruce and Garding (1978); Elert; Fries; Garding; Meyer (1937, 1954).

a computer scientist). In this way, 52 subjects (29 male/23 female), aged 18 to 55 years, recorded around 360 dialogues, totalling 3 708 utterances.

In a second simulation (MacDermid and Eklund 1997), the tasks were given in pictorial form only, in order to avoid linguistic biassing from the instructions. This time the subjects were told that they were speaking to a fully automatic travel-booking system, and were asked to book business trips within Sweden. This time, 49 subjects (34 male/15 female) recorded 137 dialogues totalling approximately 3 600 utterances. The WOZ-simulation experiments are described in more detail in Section 8.2.3.

17.2 The Swedish Lexicon

The second resource needed to create the recogniser was the recognition lexicon. Our starting point was a lexicon originally designed for a speech synthesis task, the *Svenskt Uttalslexikon* (SUL) (Hedelin, Jonsson, and Lindblad 1987). This synthesis lexicon contained a larger number of phones than was appropriate for a recognition system. The problem is that although synthesis and recognition have obvious points of contact, the amount of data needed for the two tasks differs considerably; very infrequently occurring phones can still be synthesised, but cannot be modeled well for a recognition task due to insufficiency of training data.

17.2.1 Phone Set

Selecting a phone set is a crucial first step in creating a new recognition lexicon. For Swedish, that selection posed two main challenges – phones from loan words, and the retroflex series of phones introduced by phonological rules.

The first problem, that of non-Swedish phones, was solved in the following way. The training corpora (see Section 17.1) contained a few loan words for which the initial lexicon had pronunciations containing non-Swedish phones, such as the voiceless velar fricative from German (/x/) or the voiced palato-alveolar fricative of French (/ʒ/). For the purposes of the ATIS, these words could be classified into two groups: those within the ATIS corpus and those within other training corpora only. For the phones occurring only in non-ATIS words, we simply eliminated from the training set the very small number of utterances containing those words. The phones occurring in ATIS words were mapped to native Swedish phones. These were mainly English diphthongs which were mapped to a sequence of two Swedish vowels or a Swedish vowel+/j/.

The second problem was that of handling the Swedish retroflexes. The problem in dealing with the retroflex series was an instance of the general problem of what level of representation to use for any speech-recognition lexicon, on the spectrum of phonetic to phonological. The retroflex phones in Swedish are not separate phonemes, but rather are allophones derivable from underlying coronal phonemes when preceded by /r/ or other retroflex. Moreover, the retroflection process is recursive, so it may affect more than one consonant. Thus, the underlying phonological form of "child" in Swedish is /barn/, but the /r/ and /n/ merge into [baɳ]. The underlying form of "child's" is /barns/, where the /r/ affects both the /n/ and the /s/, turning them into retroflex phones, and thus producing [baɳʂ]. This process frequently occurs across words, and can even occur across sentences. We considered three ways of representing retroflection in the Swedish lexicon.

First, we considered leaving out the retroflexes completely and representing only the underlying forms of the words in the lexicon. Thus, we would essentially rely on triphones to model sequences such as /r n/ as though there were really one phone /ɳ/.

The other two possibilities involved representing the retroflex phones in the lexicon. When dealing with a word with an underlying noninitial /r n/ sequence, we would represent that with the single phone /ɳ/. There is still a question, however, of how to deal with words beginning with a coronal, since these coronals are susceptible to undergoing the retroflex rule if they follow a word ending in /r/ or other retroflex. Thus, the second representation we considered involved making multiple pronunciations for all coronal-initial words, one starting with the nonretroflex allophone, the other with the retroflex allophone.

The third possible representation involved ignoring the word-initial variations, and representing the retroflex process only as a lexical process (i.e., within words in the lexicon, not across words or sentences).

The first representation was impractical because we could not easily recover the underlying forms from the lexicon with which we were starting. We decided on the second representation over the third in hopes of capturing some of the cross-word changes that would occur. One possible disadvantage of this approach is the risk of overgeneration of pronunciations, since we are not constraining where the retroflex pronunciation may occur (i.e., only after words ending in /r/ or other retroflex). There is also the point that the true rule would not only retroflex the initial coronal, but would delete the previous /r/ as well, a phenomenon we failed to model.

17.2.2 Phonetic Transcription

An issue to consider when compiling a recogniser lexicon is to what extent alternative pronunciations should be catered for. The way people pronounce words not only differs interindividually, but also intraindividually. The same person may use different degrees of reduction, and these may vary from time to time. Moreover, some reductions are more likely to occur than others, and some reductions have a tendency to co-occur. Thus, the issue boils down to deciding exactly how much should be covered explicitly in the lexicon, and how much should be left to the discretion of the training. We opted for the latter method, where most linguistic-phonetic variation was left to the training, that is, we did not include heavy reductions in the lexicon. Thus, we only listed some very common reduced forms, notably grammatical endings, since these are almost invariably reduced in speech.

In order to create such a lexicon, we first created a base lexicon from SUL, in order to provide standard pronunciation, that is, clear standard Swedish. It must be pointed out that this lexicon was not phonological, but rather represented clearly articulated pronunciation. Some typical lexical entries are shown in the following example:

```
egentligen    e j e n t l i g e n
ekipage       e k i p a: rs
emotionell    e m o t sj o n e l
```

Here, the first column is the word in standard orthography, and the second column represents a clear pronunciation. (The phonetic symbols were inherited from previous systems.) Each phone is denoted by one or more characters and is separated by a space. A colon indicates a long vowel, otherwise the vowels are short.

In order to cover alternative, more reduced pronunciations, a set of phonological rules were written that automatically generated alternative surface forms. The rules were conceived as phonological rewrite rules of standard format:

$$\alpha \rightarrow \beta / \Gamma\_\Delta$$

with the interpretation "α becomes β between Γ and Δ". Application of the relevant rules to the entries given above expands them to the following larger set:

```
egentligen    e j e n t l i g e n
egentligen    e j e n t l i j e n
egentligen    e j e n k l i j e n
ekipage       e k i p a: rs
ekipage       e k i p a: sj
emotionell    e m o t sj o n e l
emotionell    e m o sj o n e l
```

The lexicon thus created contained all words from both the phonetically-phonologically balanced material and the supplementary material. For the ATIS domain, special lexica were created that were more strictly pruned than the main lexicon, so that only relevant word senses and pronunciations were left.

Since Swedish morphology is more productive than English, we were initially worried that this would cause problems with data sparseness. We considered adding to the recognition vocabulary other inflections of words found in the training data or splitting words up into morphemes, but in general decided not to do so because of the nontrivial problems it would cause for language modelling. The only exception concerned compounds, which in Swedish include numbers: the issues are described in detail in Section 19.2.

17.2.3   Lexicon Statistics

The final Swedish ATIS lexicon contained 1 265 words. The average number of pronunciations per word was 1.68. In comparison, the previous English lexicon for ATIS contained 1 751 words, with an average of 1.41 pronunciations per word. If we had not included the alternate retroflex pronunciation of all coronal-initial words (see Section 17.2.1), the number of pronunciations per word in the Swedish lexicon would have gone down to 1.22.

17.3   Acoustic Models

The Swedish models were trained by SRI and optimised to provide maximum accuracy at real-time performance using a genonic CDHMM system, as we discussed in Chapter 15. PTM modeling was used in SLT-2, and in the third phase of the project the availability of faster hardware and additional training data allowed us to switch to the better performing genonic models.

17.3.1   SLT-2 Models

Our approach to building a Swedish recogniser was to boot the training process using English models. To do this, we created an approximate mapping from English to Swedish phonemes (see Table 17.1).

We trained Swedish gender-independent PTM models using 23 000 utterances of the read-text corpus, coming from 94 speakers of the Stockholm dialect. In Table 17.2 we show English and Swedish baseline-recognition results before any speed optimisation is carried out on small 200-utterance test sets. We notice that the main differences between the Swedish and English experiments are the number of training speakers and out-of-vocabulary (OOV) rate.[3] A larger number of training speakers makes the recogniser more robust to variation in speaker voices. The larger OOV rate in the Swedish test set is probably responsible for the difference in error rate compared with the English system. Using a conservative estimate of one OOV resulting in one error,[4] we could assume that the adjusted Swedish error

---

[3] The OOV rate is the percentage of words in the test set that are outside of the recogniser grammar's vocabulary.

[4] A more typical estimate for the effect of OOV words on the error rate is 1.6 errors for each OOV word because of the language-model constraints.

Table 17.1. *Mapping phonemes from English to Swedish for initialisation*

SWE	ENG	SWE	ENG
a	ah	o	aa
a:	ah	oe	axr
aa	aa	oe2	axr
aa:	aa	oe2:	axr
ae	ae	oe:	axr
ae2	ae	ow	ow
ae2:	ae	p	p
ae:	ae	r	r
ay	ay	rd	d
b	b	rl	l
d	d	rn	n
e	eh	rs	sh
e:	ey	rt	t
f	f	s	s
g	g	sh	sh
h	hh	sj	sh
i	ih	t	t
i:	iy	th	th
j	y	tj	ch
k	k	u	uh
l	l	u:	uw
m	m	v	v
n	n	w	w
ng	ng	y	y
o:	aa	y:	iy

Table 17.2. *Comparison of English and Swedish baseline-recognition experiments*

Language	Swedish	English
Training speakers	94	408
Training sentences	23K	21K
Test speakers	27	29
Test sentences	200	200
Test words	1 749	2 000
Perplexity	24	20
Out-of-vocab words	2.2	0.1
Insertion errors	1.8	1.6
Deletion errors	1.2	1.7
Substitution errors	6.0	4.6
Word-error rate	9.2	7.8

rate is on the order of 9.2 percent − 2.2 percent = 7.0 percent, that is, similar to the English word-error rate.

17.3.2 SLT-3 Models

In the third phase we had to develop a speech recogniser for an extended domain in the Swedish language, with a much more spontaneous speaking style, using data collected from WOZ simulations, as we saw in Section 17.1. These changes made the domain significantly more difficult in terms of recognition, and better acoustic models had to be developed.

In addition to the 23 000 utterances that were available for training the acoustic models in SLT-2, we used the 3 000 and 2 850 utterances, respectively, that were collected in the two phases of the Wizard-of-Oz data collection (WOZ1 and WOZ2). The training procedure we followed was similar to the one used in Phase 2, where we bootstrapped the Swedish system from an English one. We trained PTM and genonic models using the SLT-2 training data, the SLT-2 data augmented with the WOZ1 (SLT-2+WOZ1) and the SLT-2 data augmented with both WOZ1 and WOZ2 (SLT-2+WOZ1+WOZ2) data. The genonic models had approximately 800 genones with 32 Gaussians per genone (see Chapter 15).

A new language model was built for the extended domain, and the recognition performance of the different combinations of acoustic models and training data is shown in Table 17.3. We see that there is a significant reduction in word-error rate when moving from a PTM system to a genonic one. The additional spontaneous training data from the WOZ1 and WOZ2 data collections improved performance significantly on the spontaneous test set, whereas the performance on the SLT-2 test set remains unchanged. Combined, the additional training data and the improved acoustic models reduced the WER of the SLT-2 acoustic models from

Table 17.3. *Word-error rates (%) for different combinations of acoustic models and training data on the SLT-2 and WOZ1 test sets*

		Test Set	
Training Data	Acoustic Models	SLT-2	WOZ1
SLT-2	PTM	12.9	24.6
	Genones	10.7	23.9
SLT-2+WOZ1	PTM	12.8	20.8
	Genones	10.9	19.0
SLT-2+WOZ1+WOZ2	PTM	13.3	20.5
	Genones	11.1	18.3

12.9 percent to 11.1 percent on the SLT-2 test set and from 24.6 percent to 18.3 percent on the WOZ1 test set.

17.4   Conclusions

In this chapter we discussed the porting of the recogniser to Swedish during SLT-2 and SLT-3. In SLT-2 we implemented real-time PTM English and Swedish speech-recognition systems for the ATIS task. Based on the available test sets, it appears that the speech-recognition performance (after adjusting for errors caused by OOV words) is similar for both languages. In SLT-3 we developed a recogniser for an extended domain with a spontaneous speaking style. Better acoustic modeling and the use of a small amount of spontaneous training data allowed us to reduce the error rate by 25.6 percent from SLT-2 to SLT-3. In all cases, the operating point in the speed-accuracy curve was adjusted using various optimisation techniques, achieving real-time performance on the target platforms.

18   Multiple Dialects and Languages

VASSILIS DIGALAKIS AND LEONARDO NEUMEYER

18.1   Introduction

In this chapter we show how the SLT recogniser can handle multiple dialects and languages. In Chapter 17 we described how the DECIPHER^{TM} recogniser was ported to Swedish. However, even a fairly small country like Sweden has multiple dialects, and it is important to note that the recognition results in the last chapter were obtained by testing on speakers of the Stockholm dialect that matched the training population. Other tests revealed a significant degradation in performance when the system was used by speakers of non-Stockholm dialects, especially the southern Swedish Scanian dialect. In Section 18.2, we show how the speech recogniser can successfully handle different dialects even when little dialect data is available for training.

A multilingual translation system, in addition to being able to handle multiple dialects in a given language, must be able to cope with multiple input languages. The straightforward method of implementing a system that translates in any direction between an arbitrary pair of languages from a given set is to first identify the language and then run the recogniser for the identified language. This approach, however, increases the complexity and the hardware requirements (both memory and speed) of the system. Section 18.3 describes a multilingual recogniser that is capable of recognising speech from any language in a given set. There is no need to identify the language in advance; identification becomes a by-product of the recognition process. In addition, the multilingual recogniser is capable of handling phenomena like code switching.

18.2   Dialect Adaptation

We are interested in developing speech recognisers that are robust to the large dialect variability that exists in spoken languages. However, the recognition accuracy of large-vocabulary speech-recognition systems has proven to be highly related to the correlation between training and test conditions. Performance degrades dramatically in the presence of a mismatch between these conditions, such as different channel, different speaker's voice characteristics, or, in our case, different dialect.

In SLT-2, we considered the dialect issue on a speaker-independent (SI) speech-recognition system. Based on the Swedish-language corpus we presented in Section 17.1, we investigated the development of a Swedish multidialect SI speech-recognition system that would require only a small amount of dialect-dependent data. We first investigated the effect of mismatched conditions in training and testing, and found that the recognition performance of an SI system trained on a large amount of training data from the Stockholm dialect decreased dramatically when tested on speakers of another Swedish dialect, namely, Scanian.

To improve the performance of the SI system for speakers of dialects for which minimal amounts of training data are available, we used *dialect adaptation* techniques. We applied both maximum likelihood (ML) transformation-based approaches (Digalakis, Neumeyer, and Rtischer 1995; Leggetter and Woodland 1995; Neumeyer, Digalakis, and Sankar 1995; Sankar and Lee 1996), as well as combined transformation-Bayesian approaches (Digalakis and Neumeyer 1996), in an effort to minimise the effect of different dialects.

18.2.1 Dialect Adaptation Methods

The SI speech-recognition system for a specific dialect is modeled using genonic HMMs, with the output distributions that we saw in Chapter 15;

$$b_{s,SI}(X_t) = \sum_{q=1}^{K} P(q \mid s) \mathcal{N}(X_t; \mu_{gq}, \Sigma_{gq}). \tag{18.1}$$

These models need large amounts of training data for robust estimation of their parameters. Since the amount of available training data for some dialects of our database was small, the development of dialect-specific SI models was not a robust solution. Alternatively, an initial SI recognition system trained on some seed dialects can be adapted to match a specific target dialect, in which case the adapted system utilises knowledge obtained from the seed dialects. We chose to apply algorithms that we had previously developed and applied to the problem of speaker adaptation, since in our problem there were consistent differences in the pronunciation among the different dialects that we examined.

From the theoretical point of view, adaptation is not different from training. Both training and adaptation start with a seed model and reestimate its parameters using training data (cf. Section 14.2.4). Hence, adaptation is actually a method of model training. What distinguishes adaptation from training is the amount of data that is available to estimate the model. In conventional training, one assumes that there are enough data available to train all the model parameters, whereas in adaptation one must operate under the assumption of limited training data. Hence, in adaptation one must limit the number of parameters that need to be estimated. Instead of reestimating all thousands of Gaussians in the seed genonic system, we constrain the form of the dialect-adapted (DA) models as follows:

$$b_{s,DA}(X_t) = \sum_{q=1}^{K} P(q \mid s) \mathcal{N}\left(X_t; A_g \mu_{gq} + b_g, A_g \Sigma_{gq} A_g^T\right), \qquad (18.2)$$

where A^T denotes the transpose of matrix A, and μ_{gq}, Σ_{gq} are the parameters of the seed system. Hence, to adapt the initial SI recognition system, the parameters $A_g, b_g, g = 1, \ldots, N_g$ must be estimated. N_g denotes the number of transformations for the whole set of genones. By keeping N_g small, we can adapt the genonic system with a small amount of adaptation data. Parameter estimation for this scheme can be performed using the Expectation-Maximisation (EM) algorithm (Dempster, Laird, and Rubin 1977).

In our experiments we considered two variations of the generic transformation. In the first variation (method I), we assume that the matrix A_g is diagonal (Digalakis et al. 1995), and is applied to both the means and covariances of the models, as in equation (18.2). The second method (method II, [Leggetter and Woodland 1995; Neumeyer et al. 1995]) assumes that A_g is a *block diagonal* matrix that transforms only the means of the Gaussian distributions:

$$b_{s,DA}(X_t) = \sum_{q=1}^{K} P(q \mid s) \mathcal{N}(X_t; A_g \mu_{gq} + b_g, \Sigma_{gq}). \qquad (18.3)$$

This adaptation scheme is used on an acoustic vector that consists of three subvectors, namely, the MFCCs and their first- and second-order derivatives. The three blocks of this matrix perform a separate transformation on each subvector. For the speaker-adaptation problem, it was shown in Neumeyer and Colleagues (1995) that method II with a block diagonal matrix significantly outperforms both method II with a full matrix and method I with a diagonal matrix.

An alternative to transformation-based adaptation is to use Bayesian techniques. These techniques have several useful properties, such as asymptotic convergence and text independence. However, they suffer from slow adaptation rates. By combining the Bayesian with the transformation-based approach, we have shown in Digalakis and Neumeyer (1996) that one can achieve faster adaptation as well as better convergence to the dialect-specific models as the number of training sentences increases. To implement the combined approach, we first adapted the SI models to match the new dialect by using a transformation method. Then, these dialect-adapted models served as prior knowledge for the Bayesian adaptation step. Details about how the combination is performed can be found in Digalakis and Neumeyer (1996).

18.2.2 Experimental Results

The adaptation experiments were carried out using the multidialect Swedish (see Section 17.1). The core of the database was recorded in Stockholm by using more than 100 speakers; several other dialects were recorded across Sweden. For our dialect-adaptation experiments, we used seed and target data from the Stockholm and Scanian dialects, respectively. The Scanian dialect was chosen for the initial experiments because it is one of three that are clearly different from the Stockholm dialect. The main differences between the dialects are that the long (tense) vowels become diphthongs in the Scanian dialect, and that the usual supradental /r/ sound becomes uvular. In the Stockholm dialect, a combination of /r/ with one of the dental consonants /n/, /d/, /t/, /s/, or /l/ results in supradentalisation of these consonants and a deletion of the /r/ (cf. Section 17.2.1). In Scanian, since the /r/ sound is different, this does not happen. There are also prosodic differences.

The Scanian speech data was collected in the cities of Malmö, Helsingborg, Trelleborg, and Kristianstad. The dialect varies to a certain degree among these four locations. In our experiments, the training and test sets consist of sentences chosen equally from these varieties to create a generic, subdialect-independent system. A total of forty speakers of the Scanian dialect, both male and female, each recorded more than forty sentences. We selected eight of the speakers (half of them male) to serve as testing data, and the rest composed the adaptation/training data with a total of 3 814 sentences.

The SI continuous HMM system, which served as a seed model for our adaptation scheme, was the Swedish recogniser used in SLT-2 on the Swedish ATIS domain, which, as we saw in Chapter 17, was trained on approximately 23 000 sentences from ninety four speakers of the Stockholm dialect. The system's recognition performance on the Stockholm speakers had improved by the time we performed the dialect adaptation experiments from 9.2 percent word-error rate to 8.9 percent word-error rate using a bigram language model. On the other hand, its performance degraded significantly when tested on the Scanian-dialect test set, reaching a word-error rate of 25.08 percent. The degradation in performance was uniform across the various speakers in the test set (see Table 18.1), suggesting that there were consistent differences across the two dialects.

In the first set of experiments, we adapted the Stockholm-dialect system by using various amounts of adaptation data from the training speakers of the Scanian dialect, and evaluated the performance of the adapted system to a separate set of testing speakers. This gave us a measure of the dialect-adapted, speaker-independent performance, since the adaptation and test sets consisted of different speakers. We also trained from scratch a Scanian-dialect system using standard maximum-likelihood training based on the same adaptation data (ML-trained system), in order to estimate the adaptation benefits.

The results are summarised in Figure 18.1. We see that even with method I, which does not take full advantage of large amounts of training data, we get a

Table 18.1. *Word-recognition performance across Scanian-dialect test speakers using nonadapted and combined-method–adapted Stockholm dialect models*

		WER (%)	
Speaker	Nonadapted	Meth.I + Bayes 198 Sent.	Meth.II + Bayes 3814 Sent.
d09	24.94	8.53	8.31
d0b	27.05	12.32	9.90
d0k	21.92	8.49	5.42
d0j	28.64	9.24	6.70
d0r	29.85	13.93	6.71
d0v	19.72	7.66	5.10
d12	26.29	10.07	6.39
d13	22.88	5.26	2.75
Average	25.08	9.37	6.40

significant improvement in performance. With as few as 198 sentences, we got a 38 percent reduction, and the word-error rate dropped to almost 15 percent. Method II produced even better results, and the error rate for the same amount of training sentences was approximately 13 percent. However, when compared with the ML-trained system, we see that the transformation adaptation methods

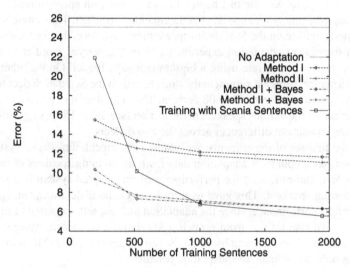

Figure 18.1. Dialect-adaptation results for adaptation methods I and II, and their combination with Bayes and with standard ML training.

outperform the standard ML training only when a very small amount of training data is used (i.e., fewer than 400 sentences). For larger amounts of training data, the ML-trained system performs better, and this is due to the bad asymptotic properties of the transformation adaptation, as well as the relatively small vocabulary of ATIS.

In Figure 18.1, we also present the results of the combination of methods I and II with Bayesian adaptation. The combined schemes were proven to be far more efficient than the simple transformation methods I and II, taking advantage of larger amounts of training sentences. The error rate was reduced by 63 percent, 69 percent, and 75 percent, with 198, 500, and 2 000 adaptation sentences, respectively. Although no direct comparison can be made, using as few as 198 adaptation sentences, the error rate of 9.37 percent approached the Stockholm dialect-dependent performance. For more sentences the error rate dropped even more, to 6.40 percent. In addition, the combined approach significantly outperformed the ML-trained system when less than 1 000 sentences were used, providing a solution that is more robust and easier to train.

Table 18.1 shows that improvement in terms of performance was almost uniform across the speakers when the combined method was used. This result verified the assumption that there is a consistent mismatch across speakers of these two different dialects.

To compare the robustness and trainability of the standard ML training and adaptation algorithms, we performed training and adaptation experiments using fewer speakers, specifically twelve and six speakers, in the training set. We use the term *trainability* to refer to the ease with which a dialect-specific system can be developed. Clearly, the capability of developing a dialect-specific system with as few training speakers as possible is desirable, since it saves both time and money.

The smaller subsets of speakers were selected randomly out of the total number of thirty one speakers available in the initial training set, and were equally divided across the two genders. We tried to select speakers from all four subdialects, so that the resulting system remained subdialect independent. The results are illustrated in Figure 18.2. We see that for standard ML training, the error rate was very large when fewer than 1 000 sentences from thirty one speakers were used. Moreover, the ML-training error rate grew even larger as the number of speakers in the training set decreased. For example, if we used roughly 500 training sentences, the thirtyone-speaker error rate increased by 9 percent and 29 percent when sentences from twelve and six speakers were considered, respectively. On the other hand, for the dialect-adapted system, the error rate using twelve and six speakers in the adaptation data remained as small as when using the full set of thirty one speakers. The small differences are within the range of statistical error.

The reason for the significantly better performance of the adaptation schemes over standard ML training for a few speakers is that speaker variability in the systems developed using adaptation techniques is captured from the prior knowledge, which the systems trained using standard ML techniques lack. In general, when

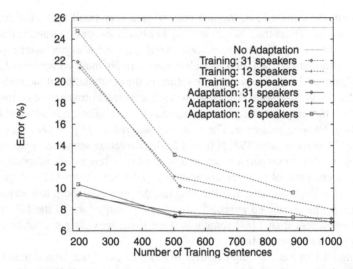

Figure 18.2. Comparison of dialect training and adaptation results for different numbers of speakers.

we compare adaptation and training results we can conclude that adaptation significantly outperforms training for small amounts of sentences and small numbers of speakers. For example, when we performed training with thirty one speakers and 520 sentences, the results obtained were similar to those of adaptation experiments with as few as six speakers and only 200 training sentences. The performance of a system trained with thirty one speakers and 1 000 sentences was similar to that of a system trained with only six speakers and 500 sentences. Therefore, both the robustness and trainability of an adaptation-based system are highly increased, when compared with standard ML training.

18.3   The Multilingual Speech-Recognition System

In SLT-2 we developed a multilingual speech recogniser capable of decoding a word string in any of a given set of languages. In Chapter 16 we discussed the language-modelling issues arising in a multilingual recogniser. Here, we focus mainly on the acoustic-modelling aspects. In a multilingual recogniser, language identification is achieved simultaneously, as a result of observing the language identity of the majority of the hypothesised words. Our approach was to treat all words as equal tokens regardless of the languages they belong to. The statistics of the acoustic and language models were estimated using a multilingual speech database with orthographic transcriptions. Language-specific knowledge was incorporated into the system through the dictionary of pronunciations used by the HMMs and by specifying phoneme classes that could contain phonemes for different languages. In this initial system, the phoneme sets did not overlap across languages. The proposed approach has some interesting characteristics:

- HMMs of allophones (of any language) that belong to the same classes and share similar context, could potentially share the same Gaussian codebooks. This work investigates the effect of Gaussian sharing on recognition performance.
- Multilingual language models can be used for improving language identification performance. It allows us to incorporate a high-level knowledge source for language identification at the lexical level.
- The system is capable of recognising sentences spoken in more than one language. Mixing words from different languages, or code switching, is common within linguistic communities where there is general familiarity with more than one language.
- In real-time multilingual applications, a single decoder can be used. Alternative approaches usually do language identification followed by a language-specific recogniser or require multiple recognisers to run in parallel.

18.3.1 Multilingual Recognition Experiments

We constructed a series of bilingual (English/Swedish) recognisers for the ATIS domain. For rapid experimentation we limited and balanced the amount of training data to 4 000 male utterances per language. We organised our experiments based on the sharing of model parameters at the acoustic and language levels. For acoustic modelling, we used PTM models. The PTM phoneme classes were organised based on place of articulation for vowels and manner of articulation for consonants. The English and Swedish phonemes were grouped according to the following classes: front vowels, central vowels, back vowels, diphthongs, semivowels and glides, nasals, voiced fricatives, unvoiced fricatives, affricates, aspirated, voiced plosives, and unvoiced plosives. Swedish HMM allophones of a given class shared the same Gaussian codebook. We trained mono- and multilingual systems. Monolingual systems share no parameters across languages, while multilingual systems may share Gaussian codebooks. The multilingual PTM system with shared acoustic parameters used twelve phoneme classes. In this case, phonemes in the same classes shared the same Gaussian codebook. The nonshared PTM system was trained using twenty four classes. Each language-specific set of phonemes had a separate codebook. The shared system had twice as many Gaussian components as the nonshared system, to maintain a constant ratio of Gaussian components to training acoustic vectors.

Statistical grammars were constructed in the form of backoff bigram language models (Katz 1987). Monolingual language models were trained using text from a single language. As we saw in Chapter 16, we used two different multilingual

Table 18.2. *English/Swedish word-error rates of shared versus constrained LMs for various acoustic parameter sharing*

Test Language	Sharing Acoustic Model	Shared LM	Constrained LM
English	No	7.25	7.21
	Yes	7.12	6.93
Swedish	No	7.02	6.29
	Yes	7.02	6.08

language models trained using all the English and Swedish data pooled together: shared LM, which allows code switching through the backoff node, and constrained LM, which does not allow code switching.

The experimental results are summarised in Table 18.2. In the table, *sharing acoustic model* means that Gaussian codebooks are shared across languages. A first remark is that sharing acoustic parameters does not seem to affect the word-error rate. Sharing a backoff node in the language model results in significant degradation in performance for the Swedish test set. This result could be associated with the greater increase in perplexity in the Swedish test set compared with the English test set (see Table 18.3). The increase in error rate could also be explained by the imbalance in the amount of data used for training the language models.

18.3.2 Language Identification

We analysed the language-identification performance of the bilingual system. In Table 18.4, we show the percentage of words and sentences that contain a word in the other language. We observe that about 1 percent of the recognised words have the wrong language identity. Therefore, sharing the LM backoff node provides the flexibility of mixing languages in an utterance at the expense of an increase in error

Table 18.3. *Comparison of English and Swedish language models*

Test Language	Number of Training Sentences	Vocabulary Size	OOV (%)	Perplexity Nonshared LM	Shared LM
English	20 K	1 165	0.2	22.4	23.8
Swedish	11 K	1 266	0.3	14.9	17.7

Table 18.4. *Language-identification errors for words and sentences*

Test Language	Nonshared Acoustic Models		Shared Acoustic Models	
	Word Miss (%)	Sent Miss (%)	Word Miss (%)	Sent Miss (%)
English	0.3	2.5	0.9	5.0
Swedish	1.1	6.4	0.9	4.9

Table 18.5. *Language-identification errors after taking simple majority of words in hypothesis*

Test Language	Nonshared Acoustic Models Sent Miss (%)	Shared Acoustic Models Sent Miss (%)
English	0.0	0.2
Swedish	0.7	0.4

rate. Good language-identification performance can easily be obtained by taking a simple majority of the words of a hypothesis (Table 18.5).

18.4 Conclusions

In this chapter we discussed dialect and language issues for a multidialect, multilingual speech recogniser. In SLT-2 we found that there is a consistent degradation in performance across speakers when there is a dialect mismatch. We used transformation and combined transformation and Bayesian adaptation algorithms to adapt a Stockholm-trained system to the Scanian dialect. The results showed that adaptation is capable of improving the robustness of our system, using very small amounts of adaptation data. This robustness could be achieved even with a small number of adaptation speakers, which is not true for standard ML training. Hence, in terms of robustness and trainability, adaptation is a much better alternative than standard ML training for the development of dialect-specific systems.

To build a multilingual speech recogniser, we investigated the effect of sharing acoustic and language parameters. We showed that parameter sharing in the acoustic model did not hurt recognition performance. As a result, a compact bilingual recogniser was built that achieved very high language identification accuracy. We plan in the future to extend this approach to use more languages, and to investigate new approaches of sharing acoustic models across languages.

19   Common Speech/Language Issues

DAVID CARTER, MANNY RAYNER, ROBERT EKLUND,
JAAN KAJA, BERTIL LYBERG, PER SAUTERMEISTER,
MATS WIRÉN, LEONARDO NEUMEYER,
AND FULIANG WENG

T HIS chapter is concerned with issues pertaining to both speech- and language-processing aspects of SLT.[1] Section 19.1 starts by briefly describing the interface between the DECIPHER^{TM} recogniser and the CLE. Section 19.2 describes our approach to the problems posed for recognition by languages like Swedish, which permit productive formation of compound nominals. Finally, Section 19.3 describes initial attempts to make use of prosodic information in the input signal, including a simple version of prosody translation implemented for the Swedish-to-English language pair.

19.1   The Speech/Language Interface

The CLE converts N-best sentence hypothesis lists provided by DECIPHER^{TM} into word lattices. This is done by initialising the lattice to be the sequence of words in the first hypothesis, and then, for each subsequent sentence hypothesis in turn, adding as few edges as possible to it so as to provide a path corresponding to that hypothesis. As each edge is added, it is assigned the acoustic cost (represented as the shortfall from the score of the top hypothesis) of the current sentence hypothesis. This lattice forms the basis of the analysis chart; an illustrative example can be found in Section 1.3.

Usually, each new sentence hypothesis after the first can be handled by adding only one or two new word edges to the lattice. Thus, most of the redundancy inherent in the N-best list is factored out, allowing parsing to be much more efficient than if each sentence hypothesis were processed independently. Often, the word lattice will license a few paths not included in the N-best list; for example, an N-best list consisting of the three hypotheses "one way", "one day", and "some way" would give rise to a lattice in which either "one" or "some" could be followed by either

---

[1] Some related topics have already been discussed in earlier chapters. In particular, the use of acoustic scores in parsing and disambiguation is covered in Sections 4.2.3 and 4.3.3.

"way" or "day", thus licensing the sequence "some day". This extra generality, when it makes any difference at all, is usually an advantage, as sometimes one of the additional paths is the correct one, and an analysis is found and selected for it.

A number of subtleties arise in constructing the lattice. First, some sentence hypotheses can be ignored: if the words in a hypothesis have the same sequence of semantic word classes as a better-scoring hypothesis (e.g., "Show me flights to Oakland" when "Show me flights to Atlanta" scores better) then it cannot give rise to the winning analysis, so is pruned out at this early stage. Second, filled pauses ("um", "er") are simply deleted before the word sequence is added to the lattice. Third, for some languages, especially French, it is convenient for the recogniser to treat as words some units which syntactically are multiple words, and vice versa: for example, in French, *"d'American Airlines"* is recognised as the two units *"d'American"* and *"Airlines"*, whereas the CLE treats them as *"d'"* (a contraction of *"de"*) followed by the lexical item *"American Airlines"*. The necessary separating and joining of lexical items is done by applying the CLE's spelling-rule mechanism (see Chapter 7) just as for text input.

19.2   Split verses Unsplit Compounds in Speech Understanding

This section describes and evaluates a simple and general solution to the handling of compound nouns in Swedish and other languages in which compounds can be formed by concatenation of single words. The basic idea is to split compounds into their components and treat these components as recognition units equivalent to other words in the language model. By exploiting the principled grammar-based language-processing architecture of the CLE, it is then possible to accommodate input in split-compound format.

19.2.1   Introduction

In many languages, including German, Dutch, Swedish, Finnish, and Greek, compound nouns can be formed by concatenation of single nominals. (For more information on Swedish compounds, see Section 11.4.1). In most previously reported work, such as the widely publicised SQALE project, compounds have been treated in the same way as any other words. However, as the vocabulary size grows, the productive nature of compounding makes this kind of approach increasingly less feasible; the most obvious indication of the problem's seriousness is the magnitude of the out-of-vocabulary (OOV) rate. For example, in an experiment on SQALE training texts (Lamel, Adda-Decker, and Gauvain 1995), using 20 000-word lexicons for both German and English resulted in a 7.5 percent OOV rate for German and 2.5 percent for English. The German lexicon had to be extended to 64 000 words to obtain OOV rates similar to those of the 20 000-word lexicon for English.

Results like these strongly suggest that treating compounds in the same way as other words is not satisfactory. Two recent papers address this issue. Spies (1995) reports results on an isolated-word large-vocabulary German dictation application, in which the components of compounds, rather than the compounds themselves, were treated as units. Geutner (1995) describes a more elaborate method, also implemented for German, in which full morphological decomposition of words was used. Both authors report unspectacular but encouraging initial results.

This section describes and evaluates a simple and general solution to the handling of Swedish compound nouns, carried out in the spirit of the work reported in the Spies and Geutner papers. Syntactically, semantically, and prosodically, Swedish compound nouns are similar to English compound nominals except for the obvious difference: English orthography inserts spaces between components, whereas Swedish uses no such spaces. These observations suggested to us that Spies' strategy should be an appropriate way to attack the problem: splitting compounds into their components, and treating these components as recognition units equivalent to other words in the language model. In contrast to Spies, however, our recogniser is for continuous speech, and is embedded in a spoken language understanding system. It is thus necessary not only to recognise, but also to reassemble and make sense of the split compounds, the means to do this being provided by the language-processing modules of the system.

19.2.2 Speech Recognition Experiments

The experiments described here were performed using the Stockholm speech corpus (Section 17.1). This consisted of 11 275 sentences, of which 10 831 were used for training. The orthographic transcriptions of the sentences of the corpus were further processed to create two different versions of the corresponding text corpus. In the first, "split" version, all compound words, including numbers, were split into their components. In the second, "unsplit" version, only numbers were split. In both cases, the numbers were split because it would be futile to try to list them in the lexicon; the same approach was taken in the German SQALE experiments (Lamel et al. 1995, 186). The 444 held-out test sentences contained 3 758 words in the split version, and 3 584 in the unsplit version.

The split and unsplit versions of the corpus were used to train two different versions of the Swedish recogniser, which differed only in terms of vocabulary and language model. The recognition vocabulary consisted of the set of all surface words in the relevant version of the corpus. The bigram language model was calculated directly from the corpus, without, for example, backing off surface words to classes. The two recognisers were run on the held-out test set, producing the results shown in Table 19.1.

Since the total number of words is different in the split and unsplit cases, the WER with respect to compounds can be measured in two ways. More specifically, the following two methods for calculating the WER were used. In the first one,

Table 19.1. *Word-error rates obtained in*
Swedish compound-splitting experiments

	Split	Unsplit
WER with respect to compound components (method 1)	**7.9%**	8.2%
WER with respect to full compounds (method 2)	8.3%	**8.7%**

corresponding to the first row of 19.1, a splitting function, which (for the purpose of the experiments) is used for mapping compounds to their components, was applied to both the hypotheses from the recogniser and to the references. (This function modifies only the unsplit data.) We then compared the newly formed hypotheses and references to get the WER. Thus, in this case the WER was calculated with respect to the compound components.

In the second method, corresponding to the second row of the table, the same splitting function, but with mappings of numbers removed, was used in the reverse direction to map all the compound components in both hypotheses and references back to their compounds. The result was then used for computing the WER. Thus, in this case the WER was calculated with respect to the full compounds.

The WERs are lower for the split system according to both measures. However, from the point of view of language processing, it is the main (boldfaced) diagonal that is of primary relevance, since what we want to compare are recognisers that output either split or unsplit words. The other diagonal has been included to provide a fair comparison from the point of view of speech-recognition performance.

As for the unsplit case in method 1, we have the methodological problem that compound words, as well as their components, are in the recogniser lexicon. Thus, there is a good chance that the recogniser will output the components, whereas the reference contains the compound. This will then be counted as one substitution followed by one or more insertions. It can be argued that the confusion between a compound and its components is not a major error. Method 1, applied to the unsplit case, removes this ambiguity and gives a performance figure that can be compared with the split case.

Method 2 can be said to simulate a language-processing system in the sense of reassembling the compounds. In most cases, this reverse mapping is straight-forward, but there are cases in which a potential compound does not actually constitute a compound where it occurs in a sentence. For example, the temporal noun phrase "*måndag eftermiddag*" ("Monday afternoon") has a corresponding compound "*måndageftermiddag*". However, the two forms differ in meaning (and are also prosodically distinct). Since method 2 creates a compound from every sequence of words that in some context could be a compound, it does not take this

288   *The Spoken Language Translator*

difference into account, and in this sense the figures in the second row of 19.1 are imperfect.

As a comparison, the WER in the unsplit case *without* the reverse mapping is 9.3 percent. This number is relevant to tasks like dictation, where we are interested in the direct output from the recogniser and, thus, where a confusion between a compound and its components would be considered an error.

19.2.2.1 Language Processing for Split Compounds

The results in the previous section show that compound splitting produced a modest improvement in the recogniser's WER. In the context of a speech-*understanding* system like SLT, however, the most relevant criterion for success is the effect on end-to-end performance. Another question of practical importance is the extent to which the language-processing modules need to be altered to accommodate input in split-compound form.

The principled grammar-based architecture of the CLE made it simple to modify the speech/language interface to accommodate input in split-compound format. Since morphology and syntax rules have the same form (see the discussion in Section 2.4.2) all that was necessary was to change the status of compounding rules from "morphology" to "syntax". In a little more detail:

- Declarations were supplied to identify some morphology rules as specifically compounding rules.
- A switch was added, which, when on, allowed the designated morphology rules to be used as syntax rules.

After a little experimentation, it also turned out to be advantageous to add a few dozen lexicon entries, to cover words that could potentially be constructed as compounds, but in reality are noncompounds. These were automatically generated from the lexicon by using a simple algorithm. No other changes to the system were made, and the adaptation process required only two person-days of work.

19.2.2.2 End-to-End Performance Evaluation

To test the effect of compound splitting on end-to-end system performance, we processed the 444-sentence test set through two versions of the Swedish-to-English configuration of SLT, which only differed with respect to whether or not compound splitting was used in the recogniser. Of the 444 utterances, 41 gave rise to different translations when compound splitting was introduced. These 41 utterances were examined by three independent judges, who were all native speakers of English and fluent in Swedish. Each utterance was presented together with the two candidate translations produced by the split and unsplit versions of the system, respectively:

Table 19.2. *End-to-end evaluation comparison, giving each judge's preferences for utterances where the translation was affected by compound splitting*

	Split Better	Unsplit Better	Unclear
Judge 1	19	12	10
Judge 2	24	11	6
Judge 3	19	10	12

each judge was asked to state whether translation 1 was better or worse than translation 2, or alternatively that neither translation was clearly better than the other. The order in which the two translations were presented – that is, split before unsplit or vice versa – was decided randomly in each case.

The results are summarised in Table 19.2. Agreement among the judges was good: there were only five sentences out of the forty one for which a pair of judges gave opposite rulings, one marking the split version as better and the other marking it as worse. It is interesting to note that although the unsplit version was in several cases better than the split one, the errors in the split translations were never actually caused by failure on the part of the CLE to reassemble a split compound.

19.2.3 Conclusions

To summarise the results of the experiments in this section, we found that compound splitting introduced an undramatic but tangible improvement in both WER and end-to-end system performance. It decreased the vocabulary size for both speech and language processing, and required no substantial modification of any part of the system. Our overall conclusion is that compound splitting is a clear winner.

Nonetheless, we were somewhat disappointed to find that the improvement resulting from compound splitting was not larger. We believe that one reason for this lack of improvement was the very small number of translators used to create the four-translator text corpus (TC) (cf. Section 8.4), which led to unnaturally uniform and homogeneous data; in particular, the OOV rate on the test portion, even without compound splitting, is only about 0.5 percent.

Preliminary results on the email corpus (EC) support this hypothesis. As described in Section 8.4, this corpus was created using a much larger number of translators, and the result is a much more reasonable approximation of a real Swedish ATIS corpus. We merged the TC and EC, taking half of EC as test data and the remaining material as training. Examining this new data, about 5 percent of all tokens in the test set are compounds, and the OOV rate of the full test set is 3.0 perceent. In contrast, the OOV rate measured just on compounds is nearly 23 percent. However, if compounds are split, OOV falls from 3.0 percent to 2.1 percent (30 percent relative) on the whole test set, and from 23 percent to 7 percent (70 percent relative) on compounds only. These statistics give us reason to expect that the effect of compound splitting on WER and end-to-end performance would be rather greater on a more realistic corpus.

19.3   Prosody Translation

To attain the goal of natural-sounding, high-quality speech translation, prosody will ultimately have to be taken into account. This section describes one step towards this long-term goal, namely, translation of focal accent (main stress) for the language pair Swedish to English.[2] We consider two cases. First, the focal accent may be used to highlight (contrastively) a particular element of a sentence. This is realised more or less in the same way in Swedish and English; hence, in this case it is sufficient to realise the prosodic prominence at the corresponding word(s) in the target language. Second, prosodic prominence in the source language may be realised at the lexical or syntactic level in the target language, though this occurs infrequently in our domain. The only common example concerns the Swedish word *"en"* (*"ett"* in neuter gender), which like French *"un/une"* can be used as either an indefinite article (English "a"/"an") or a number (English "one"). In general, both readings are available; if *"en"* or *"ett"* is prosodically prominent, however, only the number reading is possible.

The rest of the section describes how we handle the two cases above. The process is naturally divided into three steps: detection of prosodic prominence in the source language (Section 19.3.1), transfer to the target language (Section 19.3.2), and, finally, realisation – that is, lexical choice and/or generation of the prosodic manifestation – in the target language. For our purposes, the last step is trivial; it was achieved simply by having the system generate the relevant prominence markup to the input of the synthesiser (TrueTalk from Entropic Systems), and is hence omitted here.

19.3.1   Detection of Focal Accent

This section describes an implemented system for detection of focal accent in Swedish, which works in connection with the DECIPHER[TM] speech recogniser. The input to the system is the speech signal of an utterance supplemented by information provided by the recogniser, namely, an orthographic representation of

---

[2] For related work with respect to the language pair German to English, see Strom et al. (1997) and Lieske et al. (1997).

the utterance and an alignment of the phonemes and words along the time axis. The output from the system is the word that is judged to carry the focal accent.

19.3.1.1 Overview

In general, all major aspects of prosody – fundamental frequency (F_0), intensity, and duration – may contribute to the manifestation of focal accent. However, F_0 is generally regarded as the primary cue for detecting focal accent in Swedish (Bruce 1977; Sautermeister and Eklund 1997).[3] As an approximate solution, we have therefore based our focal-accent detector on acoustic information only pertaining to F_0. Another design consideration concerns whether the system works purely bottom-up in the sense that only acoustical information is used, or whether additional top-down information is taken into account. The latter might include information about syllables that are likely candidates for carrying focal accent in Swedish; other options are information about phrase boundaries or sentence mode (Elsner 1997). In this sense, our current system is restricted to a pure bottom-up approach.

The system works as follows. First, the F_0 contour is extracted from the speech signal using a standard algorithm. In order to obtain a normalised F_0 contour, a semitone scale is used, and the estimated frequency declination through the utterance is subtracted from the F_0 contour. The actual detection of focal accent is then carried out by looking for the maximum rise just before the maximum peak of the normalised F_0 contour, and by relating this to the alignment information provided by the recogniser. The following sections describe this procedure in more detail.

19.3.1.2 Extracting and Normalising the F_0 Contour

Many algorithms for F_0 extraction have been developed (Bagshaw 1994; Hess 1991), but none have so far turned out to work robustly and accurately for all conditions. We have adopted an algorithm known as *Enhanced Super Resolution F_0 Detector* (eSRFD) (Bagshaw 1994). This has proven to work well for high-quality speech, which is what we have been using in SLT. In addition, we postprocess the estimated F_0 contour with a nonlinear smoothing filter (Rabiner, Sambur, and Schmidt 1975), in order to remove irregularities produced by the F_0 extractor as well as other small perturbations not needed here.

Next, we map the contour to a musical scale in order to obtain a representation that is more natural to display and work with from the point of view of human perception. More specifically, the F_0 values are converted to a semitone scale using

---

[3] For example, it has been argued that a related phenomenon such as prolonged duration may largely be a secondary effect resulting from the fact that the production of a particular F_0 gesture will require a certain minimal time interval (Lyberg 1979; Lyberg and Lindström 1993).

the following equation (excluding F_0 values equal to zero, which correspond to unvoiced speech):

$$F_{0,\text{semitone}} = 12.0 \log_2 \left(\frac{F_{0,Hz}}{50.0} \right).$$

In order to obtain a continuous curve, the contour is then linearly interpolated across intervals that have F_0 values equal to zero. The interpolation is followed by a smoothing process to make the derivative continuous as well.

The actual normalisation is thus performed by using the semitone scale and by estimating and subtracting the declination of the F_0 contour. We assume that the declination is linear within an utterance and that it passes through the minima of the F_0 variations. To find the local minimum points of the contour, we use the derivative of the curve. In addition, the first nonzero value of the contour is considered to be a minimum. The set of local minimum points is then modified by excluding points that are larger than the median of the curve. To be able to estimate a linear declination we need at least two minimum points. If the set of local minimum points contains less than two points we take the first nonzero point of the curve along with the minimum nonzero point to be valid minimum points.

The declination is estimated using least-mean-squares regression analysis on the calculated local minimum points. The declination is then subtracted from the F_0 contour. Finally, the contour as a whole is adjusted by making the minimum point of the curve equal to zero to avoid negative values.

19.3.1.3 Detecting the Focal Accent

The focal accent is clearly related to the maximum peak of the normalised F_0 contour. More specifically, we take the focal accent in Swedish to be located at the phoneme corresponding to the maximum rise before the peak (Bruce 1977). To determine this point, we analyse the interval of the normalised curve from the preceding minimum point up to the peak. For each phoneme in this interval, a value R is calculated as follows:

$$R = [F_{0,\text{norm}}(n_{\text{end}}) - F_{0,\text{norm}}(n_{\text{start}})] \sum_{n=n_{\text{start}}}^{n_{\text{end}}} F_{0,\text{norm}}(n).$$

Here, n_{start} and n_{end} are the first and last F_0 samples of the phoneme, respectively. However, for the first phoneme, n_{start} corresponds to the sample of the minimum point, and for the last phoneme n_{end} corresponds to the sample of the maximum point. The phoneme that maximises R is thus considered to be the phoneme where the focal accent is realised. This is usually a syllable nucleus, that is, a vowel. Alternatively, it may be located within an unvoiced phoneme since we have a continuous, interpolated contour. Although such a virtual rise lacks a fundamental frequency, we have chosen not to treat it differently from a normal rise. Finally, by making use of the alignments provided by the recogniser we can pick out the word carrying the focal accent.

No extensive evaluation of the implemented system has been carried out. However, a preliminary test was made with ten subjects, each being instructed to read two isolated sentences; each of the sentences was read five times with varying focal-accent positions. The first sentence consisted of voiced phonemes only, whereas the other sentence included many unvoiced segments. For 93 of the 100 utterances, the system was able to pick out the word at which the subjects had been instructed to put the focal accent. We take this as a preliminary indication that our approach to detecting focal accent in Swedish is feasible at least for read speech.

19.3.2 Prosody Transfer

Once the focal accent has been located, information about it is passed through to the CLE by means of annotations on the words in the N-best list. Each such word has associated with it an integer in the range 0 to 3; currently, we only use 0 (for unaccented words) and 3 (for the word carrying the focal accent in each hypothesis).

For cases such as Swedish *"en"* or *"ett"* and French *"un"* or *"une"*, where prosodic prominence determines the possible meanings of a word, it is straightforward to introduce a mechanism whereby a lexical entry for such a word is only activated when the accent has a suitable value. This in turn constrains the sentence meanings that may be constructed, and hence the translations produced.

Our other case, that of realising the focal accent in the target language on the word corresponding to the accented source word, is also straightforward if we can reliably pair up corresponding words once the translation, and the source string from which it arose, have been determined. Of course, in general, working out this correspondence is not a well-formed problem because the translation relation is not one to one between words; a word in the source sentence may correspond to any number of target words, including zero.

We recognise this by calculating an optimal alignment between source and target: that is, we use the word-to-word transfer rules (see Section 2.2) to pair stretches of the source and the target strings (each corresponding to zero or more words) so that all words in both sentences are covered, and so that a cost function is minimised.

Pairing two nonempty stretches licensed by a word-to-word transfer rule incurs no cost, so this is the most preferred option. A small cost is incurred for an empty word sequence on either side in a pair licensed by a word-to-word rule, and a larger one for crossovers between pairs (i.e., if stretch S1 is paired with T2, and S2 with T1, where S1 precedes S2 on the source side and T1 precedes T2 on the target side); this recognises that differences in word order do occur, but assumes they are best avoided if possible. A still larger cost is incurred for stretches on either side not accounted for by word-to-word rules at all.

Once the optimal pairing has been found, the target word(s) corresponding to the accented source word can easily be read off. If there are no such target words, no nondefault accent is assigned to the target sentence. If there are such words, however, the accent is placed on all of them. Realising the accent, whether default, or assigned to a single word, or to a sequence of adjacent words, is the task of the synthesis process.

PART IV

Evaluation and Conclusions

20 Evaluation

DAVID CARTER, MANNY RAYNER, ROBERT EKLUND, CATRIONA MacDERMID, AND MATS WIRÉN

T
HIS chapter presents a detailed empirical evaluation of the SLT system. We start in Sections 20.1, 20.2, and 20.3 by discussing methodological issues and our evaluation framework. The heart of the chapter is Section 20.4, which describes a speech-to-text evaluation of several versions of the system, carried out on previously unseen speech data. We have two distinct goals in mind here. First, we simply want to give a fair picture of how well the system works in practice. Second, we compare performance of the main system with that of variants created by replacing selected components or changing the values of critical parameters. This enables us to evaluate objectively how important some of our design choices turn out to be in practise. Section 20.5 presents another and somewhat different evaluation, specifically designed to investigate the phenomenon of *pipeline synergy*; in a pipeline spoken language processing architecture like that of SLT, probabilities of failure of the different components are not independent, but in fact turn out to be strongly correlated.

20.1 Methodological Issues

There is still no real consensus on how to evaluate speech translation systems. The most common approach is some version of the following. The system is run on a set of previously unseen speech data; the results are stored in text form; someone judges them as acceptable or unacceptable translations; and finally the system's performance is quoted as the proportion that is acceptable. This is clearly much better than nothing, but still contains some serious methodological problems. In particular:

1. There is poor agreement on what constitutes an acceptable translation. Some judges regard a translation as unacceptable if a single word choice is suboptimal. At the other end of the scale, there are judges who will accept any translation that conveys the approximate meaning of the sentence, irrespective of how many grammatical or stylistic mistakes it contains.

Without specifying more closely what is meant by "acceptable", it is difficult to compare evaluations.

2. Speech translation is normally an interactive process, and it is natural that it should be less than completely automatic. At a minimum, it is clearly reasonable in many contexts to feed back to the source-language user the words the recogniser believed it heard, and permit him or her to abort translation if recognition was unacceptably bad. Evaluation should take account of this possibility.

3. Evaluating a speech-to-speech system as though it were a speech-to-text system introduces a certain measure of distortion. Speech and text are in some ways very different media: a poorly translated sentence in written form can normally be reexamined several times if necessary, but a spoken utterance may be heard only once. In this respect, speech output places heavier demands on translation quality. On the other hand, constructions that would be regarded as unacceptably sloppy in written text can often pass unnoticed in speech.

We have investigated redesigning our translation evaluation methodology to take account of all of the above points. Currently, most of our empirical work treats the system as though it produced text output; we describe this mode of evaluation in Section 20.2, and present results of experiments that use it in Section 20.4. We have also experimented with a novel method that evaluates the system's actual spoken output, which we describe in Section 20.3.

20.2   Evaluation of Speech-to-Text Translation

In speech-to-text mode, evaluation of the system's performance on a given utterance proceeds as follows. The judge is first shown a text version of the correct source utterance (what the user actually said), followed by the selected recognition hypothesis (what the system thought the user said), and finally a text version of the translation.

The judge is first asked to decide whether the recognition hypothesis is acceptable. Judges are told to assume that they have the option of aborting translation if recognition is of insufficient quality; judging a recognition hypothesis as unacceptable corresponds to pushing the "abort" button. After this, they are asked to classify the quality of the translation along a seven-point scale; the points on the scale have been chosen to reflect the distinctions judges most frequently have been observed to make in practise. When selecting the appropriate category, judges are instructed only to take into account the actual spoken source utterance and the translation produced, and ignore the recognition hypothesis. The possible judgment categories are the following; the headings are those used in Tables 20.2 to 20.5.

Fully acceptable Fully acceptable translation.

Unnatural style Fully acceptable, except that style is not completely natural. This is most commonly due to overliteral translation.

Minor syntactic errors One or two minor syntactic or word-choice errors, otherwise acceptable. Typical examples are bad choices of determiners or prepositions.

Major syntactic errors At least one major or several minor syntactic or word-choice errors, but the sense of the utterance is preserved. The most common example is an error in word order produced when the system is forced to back up to the robust-translation method.

Partial translation At least half of the utterance has been acceptably translated, and the rest is nonsense. A typical example is when most of the utterance has been correctly recognised and translated, but there is a short false start at the beginning which has resulted in a word or two of junk at the start of the translation.

Nonsense The translation makes no sense. The most common reason is gross misrecognition, but translation problems can sometimes be the cause as well.

Mistranslation The translation makes some sense, but fails to convey the sense of the source utterance. The most common reason is again a serious recognition error.

Results are presented by simply counting the number of translations in a run that fall into each category. We have sometimes found it useful to group the categories into a coarser classification. The first three ("fully acceptable", "unnatural style", and "minor syntactic errors") we class as "clearly useful"; the next two ("major syntactic errors" and "partial") as "borderline"; the final two categories are labelled "useless". By taking account of the "unacceptable hypothesis" judgments, it is possible to evaluate the performance of the system either in a fully automatic mode, or in a mode where the source-language user has the option of aborting misrecognised utterances.

20.3   Evaluation of Speech-to-Speech Translation

Our intuitive impression, based on many evaluation runs in several different language pairs, is that the fine-grained style of speech-to-text evaluation described in the preceding section gives a much more informative picture of the system's performance than the simple acceptable/unacceptable dichotomy. However, it raises an obvious question: How important, in objective terms, are the distinctions drawn by the fine-grained scale? The preliminary work we now go on to describe attempts to provide an empirically justifiable answer, in terms of the relationship between translation quality and comprehensibility of output speech. Our goal, in other words, is to measure objectively the ability of subjects to understand the content of speech output. This must be the key criterion for evaluating a candidate translation: if apparent deficiencies in syntax or word choice fail to affect subject's ability to understand content, then it is hard to say that they represent real loss of quality.

The programme sketched above is difficult or, arguably, impossible to implement in a general setting. In a limited domain, however, it appears quite feasible to construct a domain-specific form-based questionnaire designed to test a subject's understanding of a given utterance. In ATIS, a simple form containing about twenty questions extracts enough content from most utterances that it can be used as a reliable measure of a subject's understanding. The assumption is that a normal domain utterance can be regarded as a (full or partial) database query involving a limited number of possible categories: these are concepts like flight origin and destination, departure and arrival times, choice of airline, and so on. A detailed description of the evaluation method follows.

The judging interface is structured as a hypertext document that can be accessed through a Web browser. Each utterance is represented by one Web page. On entering the page for a given utterance, the judge first clicks a button that plays an audio file, and then fills in an HTML form describing what he or she heard. Judges are allowed to start by writing down as much as they can of the utterance, so as to keep it clear in their memory as they fill in the form.

The form is divided into four major sections. The first deals with the linguistic form of the enquiry, for example, whether it is a command (imperative), a Y-N question, or a WH question. In the second section the judge is asked to write down the principal object of the utterance. For example, in the utterance "Show flights from Boston to Atlanta", the principal object would be "flights". The third section lists some fifteen constraints on the object explicitly mentioned in the enquiry, like "... one-way from New York to Boston on Sunday". Initial testing proved that these three sections covered the structure and content of most enquiries within the domain, but to account for unforeseen material the judge is also presented with a "miscellaneous" category. Depending on the character of the options, form entries are either multiple choice or free text. All form entries may be negated ("No stopovers") and disjunctive enquiries are indicated by means of indexing ("Delta on Thursday or American on Friday"). When the page is exited, the contents of the completed form are stored for further use.

Each translated utterance is judged in three versions, by different judges. The first two versions are the source and target speech files; the third time, the form is filled in from the human-transcribed *text* version of the source utterance. (The judging tool allows a mode in which the text version is displayed instead of an audio file being played.) The intention is that the source text version of the utterance should act as a baseline with which the source- and target-speech versions,

Table 20.1. *Relative comprehensibility of source and target speech for English → French test on 200 unseen utterances.*

	Source	Target	Difference	Quality
Precision	97.6%	86.0%	11.6%	88.4%
Recall	97.5%	84.0%	13.5%	86.5%

respectively, can be compared. Comparison is carried out by a fourth judge. Here, the contents of the form entries for two versions of the utterance are compared. The judge has to decide whether the contents of each field in the form are compatible between the two versions.

When the forms for two versions of an utterance have been filled in and compared, the results can be examined for comprehensibility in terms of the standard notions of precision and recall. We say that the recall of version 2 of the utterance with respect to version 1 is the percentage of the fields filled in version 1 that are filled in compatibly in version 2. Conversely, the precision is the percentage of the fields filled in version 2 that are filled in compatibly in version 1.

The recall and precision scores together define a two-element vector, which we will call the *comprehensibility* of version 2 with respect to version 1. We can now define C_{source} to be the comprehensibility of the source speech with respect to the source text, and C_{target} to be the comprehensibility of the target speech with respect to the source text. Finally, we define the quality of the translation to be $1 - (C_{source} - C_{target})$, where $C_{source} - C_{target}$ in a natural way can be interpreted as the extent to which comprehensibility has degraded as a result of the translation process.

In a preliminary experiment, we used this measure to evaluate the quality of translation in the English → French version of SLT. A set of 200 previously unseen English utterances was translated by the system into French speech, using the same kind of subjects as in the previous experiments. Source-language and target-language speech was synthesised using commercially available, state-of-the-art synthesisers (TrueTalk from Entropic Systems and CNETVOX from ELAN Informatique, respectively). The subjects were allowed to hear each utterance only once. The results were evaluated in the manner described, to produce figures for comprehensibility of source and target speech, respectively. The figures are presented in Table 20.1.

When asked for a subjective impression of the SLT system's quality, a common response we have received is that "the system gets it right at least three-quarters of the time". The above evaluation represents our most ambitious attempt so far to lend substance to this claim.

20.4   Speech-to-Text Evaluation Results

Although speech-to-speech evaluation is obviously desirable for a speech-to-speech system, such evaluations are in practise very time consuming compared to ones performed on speech-to-text. We have therefore carried out the bulk of our experiments in the latter mode, which is able to give a good impression of the performance of the recognition and language-processing parts of the system.

We evaluated thirteen configurations of the English-to-French version of the system and three of the English-to-Swedish version by applying the classification described in Section 20.2 to a 400-utterance unseen test set.[1] The configurations, with the abbreviations used for them in Tables 20.2 to 20.7 below, were as follows.

> **Main** The main or default configuration, which this book has described so far and which we use for our demonstrations. All the available ATIS training data (some 22 180 utterances, consisting of the ATIS-2 and ATIS-3 training data and the ATIS-2 test data) were used to train the system components, all of which were switched on during processing. All the other configurations described in this list differed from the main one in the ways that will be given for each.
>
> **LexT** Only transfer at the surface and lexical levels (not the phrasal or full QLF levels) was carried out.
>
> **LPT** Transfer at the surface, lexical, and phrasal QLF levels, but not the full QLF level, was carried out.
>
> **1 000** Only 1 000 training utterances were used. These were chosen by selecting speakers at random from the training data and then including all the utterances they produced, rather than by selecting the utterances themselves at random, a method that would have given an artificially wide spread of speaker characteristics for this number of utterances.
>
> **5 000** As for **1 000**, but 5 000 training utterances were used.
>
> **Ref** The speech recogniser was not used; instead, the language-processing parts of the system were applied to reference input, thus simulating perfect speech recognition.
>
> **N = 1** Only the top item of the N-best list produced by the speech recogniser was used (instead of the usual top five items).
>
> **N = 2** Only the top two items of the N-best list produced by the speech recogniser were used.
>
> **NoPr** Constituent pruning was switched off.
>
> **Flat** The derived grammar was produced using flat cutting-up criteria with special treatment of phrasal rules (see Section 3.4).
>
> **FlatNoP** The derived grammar was produced using flat cutting-up criteria without special treatment of phrasal rules (see Section 3.4).

---

[1] The same test set was used for the experiments described in Section 3.4.

Table 20.2. *Speech-to-text results, main system and first two variants,*
all utterances, for English → Swedish and English → French

	Main	LexT	LPT	Main	LexT	LPT
Target language	Swe	Swe	Swe	Fre	Fre	Fre
Recognition OK	80.2	76.2	74.8	71.0	67.5	68.0
Fully acceptable	59.8	25.5	35.0	29.5	4.0	15.8
Unnatural style	6.0	9.0	8.2	9.0	1.5	5.0
Minor syntactic errors	9.2	25.8	18.5	26.8	13.0	20.5
Clearly useful	**75.0**	**60.3**	**61.7**	**65.3**	**18.5**	**41.3**
Major syntactic errors	7.5	11.8	12.8	5.5	23.0	19.5
Partial translation	8.5	13.0	10.5	1.0	17.8	10.8
Borderline	**16.0**	**24.8**	**23.3**	**7.0**	**40.8**	**30.3**
Nonsense	4.0	9.2	8.2	22.8	39.0	24.8
Mistranslation	4.5	5.2	6.2	5.0	1.2	3.2
No translation	0.5	0.5	0.5	0.5	0.5	0.5
Clearly useless	**9.0**	**14.9**	**14.9**	**27.8**	**40.7**	**28.5**

TwoL The derived grammar was produced using two-level cutting-up criteria with special treatment of phrasal rules (see Section 3.4).

MultiNoP The derived grammar was produced using multilevel cutting-up criteria without special treatment of phrasal rules (see Section 3.4).

The results were as follows. All figures are percentages; the "Recognition OK" line is the percentage of utterances for which recognition was judged good enough that a user with an "abort" button would have refrained from using it.

Table 20.2 compares performance of the main systems for English → Swedish and English → French, together with versions for each language pair in which one or two levels of translation were switched off. The first and fourth columns indicate that the main system produced clearly useful Swedish and French translations for 75 percent and 65 percent of the utterances, respectively. The remaining columns show that all three main levels of translation (surface/lexical, phrasal, and full) make important contributions. For English → French, an additional 20 percent of the utterances get a clearly useful translation for every one of these phases that is switched on. The effect is not as pronounced for English → Swedish; English word order is closer to Swedish than to French, and surface-processing methods are correspondingly more effective. Mainly for the same reasons, the Swedish scores are generally higher than the French ones. Due to shortage of time, and since it seemed rather the more interesting language pair, the remaining versions of the system were only evaluated for English → French.

A comparison of the first and fourth columns in Table 20.3 (main system and perfect speech recognition, respectively) suggests that recognition problems were

Table 20.3. *Speech-to-text results, main system and variants 4–8, English → French, all utterances*

	Main	1 000	5 000	Ref	N = 1	N = 2
Recognition OK	71.0	67.0	69.2	(all)	69.5	72.2
Fully acceptable	29.5	21.2	28.0	34.8	27.2	29.0
Unnatural style	9.0	9.0	8.2	5.5	9.2	9.0
Minor syntactic errors	26.8	27.8	25.2	34.2	26.2	26.8
Clearly useful	**65.3**	**58.0**	**61.4**	**74.5**	**62.6**	**64.8**
Major syntactic errors	5.5	6.0	7.0	14.2	6.0	6.0
Partial translation	1.0	1.0	1.0	0.2	2.8	2.2
Borderline	**6.5**	**7.0**	**8.0**	**14.4**	**8.8**	**8.2**
Nonsense	22.8	30.0	25.2	9.8	24.2	22.0
Mistranslation	5.0	4.5	4.8	0.8	3.8	4.5
No translation	0.5	0.5	0.5	0.5	0.5	0.5
Clearly useless	**28.3**	**35.0**	**30.5**	**11.1**	**28.5**	**27.0**

responsible for around 10 percent of the utterances failing to produce clearly useful translation. The low figure for "clearly useless" in column four supports the hypothesis that speech-recognition problems are responsible for most of the outright failures in translation. Of the suboptimal configurations in this table, reducing the training set to 5 000 lost us 4 percent at the "clearly useful" level; reducing to 1 000 lost another 3.5 percent. Considering only the top two items in the N-best list lost us only 0.5 percent, while looking only at the top item lost another 2 percent.

Table 20.4 compares different versions of pruning and grammar specialisation. The second column shows that pruning is extremely useful for a grammar with special treatment of phrasal rules (cf. Chapter 3). Switching it off causes performance to drop by nearly 5 percent at the "clearly useful" level; the most important effect, however, is on processing speed, which, as shown in Table 20.9, is slowed down by approximately an order of magnitude. To our surprise, however, Table 20.9 and the last column suggest that a multilevel specialised grammar with no special treatment of phrases is only marginally inferior to the main system in terms of processing speed and accuracy. Pruning, in other words, can be replaced by grammar specialisation with only a moderate loss of performance. Of the variant EBL chunking criteria considered in columns 3 to 6, only FlatNoP (flat specialised grammar with no special treatment of phrases) was markedly worse than the one used in the main system in terms of its effect on end-to-end performance.

When only the acceptably recognised utterances are considered (Tables 20.5, 20.6, and 20.7), we see that language processing produces clearly useful results 87.8 percent of the time for the main system, with other conditions showing similar

Table 20.4. *Speech-to-text results, main system and variants 9–13,*
English → French, all utterances

	Main	NoPr	Flat	TwoL	FlatNoP	MultiNoP
Recognition OK	71.0	70.2	70.8	70.8	68.0	72.0
Fully acceptable	29.5	27.2	28.2	29.5	28.8	28.2
Unnatural style	9.0	7.2	8.8	8.8	5.8	7.0
Minor syntactic errors	26.8	26.2	28.0	27.0	21.2	26.0
Clearly useful	**65.3**	**60.6**	**65.0**	**65.3**	**55.8**	**61.2**
Major syntactic errors	5.5	4.2	5.5	5.8	10.0	7.0
Partial translation	1.0	3.0	1.2	1.2	6.5	4.2
Borderline	**6.5**	**7.2**	**6.7**	**7.0**	**16.5**	**11.2**
Nonsense	22.8	24.2	22.8	22.5	23.0	21.8
Mistranslation	5.0	5.2	5.0	4.8	4.2	5.2
No translation	0.5	2.5	0.5	0.5	0.5	0.5
Clearly useless	**28.3**	**31.9**	**28.3**	**27.8**	**27.7**	**27.5**

improvements. The figure of 87.8 percent is well above the 74.5 percent we got for the whole corpus when we assumed perfect speech recognition; the reason is that the utterances that survive speech recognition tend to be shorter and/or more within the domain, and are therefore easier for language processing to deal with. This is an example of pipeline synergy, discussed in Section 20.5.

Table 20.5. *Speech-to-text results, main system and versions with*
one or two levels of translation switched off, for English → Swedish
and English → French, acceptably recognised utterances only

	Main	LexT	LPT	Main	LexT	LPT
Target language	Swe	Swe	Swe	Fre	Fre	Fre
Fully acceptable	73.7	33.2	46.5	39.9	5.9	22.3
Unnatural style	7.1	11.7	11.0	11.5	1.1	5.8
Minor syntactic errors	9.9	32.2	22.6	36.4	18.4	27.7
Clearly useful	**90.7**	**77.1**	**80.1**	**87.8**	**25.4**	**55.8**
Major syntactic errors	6.5	12.7	13.3	7.0	32.0	25.2
Partial translation	1.5	4.2	1.3	0.0	20.2	7.7
Borderline	**8.0**	**16.9**	**14.6**	**7.0**	**52.2**	**32.9**
Nonsense	0.0	3.6	2.0	4.5	21.3	9.1
Mistranslation	0.6	1.6	2.7	0.0	0.4	1.5
No translation	0.6	0.7	0.7	0.7	0.7	0.7
Clearly useless	**1.2**	**5.9**	**5.4**	**5.2**	**22.4**	**11.3**

Table 20.6. *Speech-to-text results, main system and variants 4–8, English → French, acceptably recognised utterances*

	Main	1 000	5 000	N = 1	N = 2
Fully acceptable	39.9	30.7	38.7	37.9	38.5
Unnatural style	11.5	10.4	10.8	11.8	11.0
Minor syntactic errors	36.4	40.0	35.8	36.8	36.4
Clearly useful	**87.8**	**81.1**	**85.3**	**86.5**	**85.9**
Major syntactic errors	7.0	7.8	8.2	7.9	7.6
Partial translation	0.0	0.7	0.0	0.4	0.7
Borderline	**7.0**	**8.5**	**8.2**	**8.3**	**8.3**
Nonsense	4.5	9.6	5.7	4.6	5.2
Mistranslation	0.0	0.0	0.0	0.0	0.0
No translation	0.7	0.7	0.7	0.7	0.7
Clearly useless	**5.2**	**10.3**	**6.4**	**5.3**	**5.9**

We also evaluated the conditions relative to each other by asking a judge to decide, for each pair of differing translations of a given input, whether one was better and, if so, which. Over the set of thirteen different conditions, this amounted to the judge specifying a partial ordering on up to thirteen (though usually fewer) different translations. From this partial ordering we were able to read off, for any desired pair of conditions, the number of inputs for which the first translation produced a better translation, and the number for which the second did better. A simple statistical test, using the null hypothesis of a binomial distribution with

Table 20.7. *Speech-to-text results, main system and variants 9–13, English → French, acceptably recognised utterances*

	Main	NoPr	Flat	TwoL	FlatNoP	MultiNoP
Fully acceptable	39.9	36.4	38.2	40.0	41.6	37.9
Unnatural style	11.5	8.9	11.6	11.2	8.4	7.9
Minor syntactic errors	36.4	35.1	38.6	37.2	29.2	35.9
Clearly useful	**87.8**	**80.4**	**88.4**	**88.4**	**79.2**	**81.7**
Major syntactic errors	7.0	5.5	6.7	6.7	10.6	8.3
Partial translation	0.0	0.7	0.4	0.4	2.2	2.4
Borderline	**7.0**	**6.2**	**7.1**	**7.1**	**12.8**	**10.7**
Nonsense	4.5	10.0	3.9	3.9	7.3	6.9
Mistranslation	0.0	0.0	0.0	0.0	0.0	0.0
No translation	0.7	3.4	0.7	0.7	0.7	0.7
Clearly useless	**5.2**	**13.4**	**4.6**	**4.6**	**8.0**	**7.6**

Table 20.8. *Comparison of main version with each variant*

Variant	Main Better	Variant Better	SDs
Ref	35	109	**−6.17**
N = 2	27	32	−0.65
Flat	20	23	−0.46
Main	0	0	0.00
TwoL	10	10	0.00
N = 1	49	46	0.31
5 000	53	42	1.13
MultiNoP	67	52	1.38
NoPr	65	42	**2.22**
1 000	97	58	**3.13**
FlatNoP	151	81	**4.60**
LPT	225	101	**6.87**
LexT	309	58	**13.10**

$p = \frac{1}{2}$, then indicated whether one of the conditions was significantly better or whether the differences could have been random.

Table 20.8 gives the figures for the main version of the system compared to each of the twelve variants (and, trivially, to itself). Thus, for example, when the main version was compared to the version with no constituent pruning, the main version was found to be better for sixty five utterances, and the no-pruning one for fourty two. Using a normal approximation, this represented a divergence of 2.22 standard deviations from the expected difference of zero under the null hypothesis that the two versions were equally good. Such a divergence is significant at the 5 percent level (two-tail), so that it is shown in boldface.

In fact, these figures, and the corresponding ones (not shown here) comparing variants with each other, happen to induce a partial ordering on the different conditions, where condition A is placed before condition B in the ordering if, and only if, A performed significantly better than B under our criterion.[2] The equivalence classes so defined are indicated by the double horizontal lines in the table. Thus, it is not surprising that the "Ref" case (of perfect speech recognition) was significantly better than any other condition. Then there followed a set of seven conditions – the majority of those tested, including the main system – whose

---

[2] Such an ordering is not guaranteed; it could happen that A is significantly better than C, but not significantly better than B, which in turn is not significantly better than C.

Table 20.9. *Processing times*

	Source	Target	Total
Main	2.327	2.507	4.834
1 000	1.309	2.656	3.965
5 000	1.178	2.639	3.817
Ref	1.704	2.714	4.418
N = 1	1.008	2.516	3.524
N = 2	1.228	2.562	3.790
NoPr	39.942	3.129	43.071
Flat	1.408	2.531	3.939
FlatNoP	0.742	1.526	2.268
TwoL	1.633	2.546	4.179
MultiNoP	3.003	2.479	5.482
LexT	0.524	0.039	0.563
LPT	0.677	0.915	1.592

performance could not be distinguished by this test. The no-pruning, 1 000-sentence training set, and "FlatNoP" (simplest possible EBL) conditions were significantly worse than all of these, but comparable to each other. In turn, they were better than the variant that only translated at the lexical and phrasal levels, which itself was better than the lexical-level-only variant. One could summarise these results with the following points:

- Perfect speech recognition, not surprisingly, would be very useful.
- Grammar-based processing is also very useful.
- Corpus data is needed for training, but for this kind of domain its effect tops out at or before 5 000 sentences.
- Constituent pruning is useful, largely because it renders many sentences processable inside a reasonable time, although the same effect can in part be achieved through suitable use of EBL.
- The system is not very sensitive to the length of the N-best list or to the differences between (sensibly chosen) EBL chunking criteria.

Linguistic processing times under the thirteen conditions are presented in Table 20.9, as mean numbers of seconds over the 400 sentences on a 450MHz Pentium II running SICStus Prolog. A timeout of 180 seconds was used; only a very small number of utterances timed out. Here, the key points appear to be the following:

- Linguistic-processing time is typically about four or five seconds per utterance, divided evenly between source-language processing (linguistic analysis) and target-language processing (transfer and generation).
- Linguistic analysis using a 5-best speech hypothesis list is only a little more than twice as slow as using a single speech hypothesis.

(Target-language processing is not substantially affected by the length of the N-best list, since the same number of hypotheses is passed to the transfer process).

- Pruning makes a difference to analysis-processing time of more than an order of magnitude in cases where it is applicable.

20.5 Pipeline Synergy

Most spoken language translation systems developed to date, including SLT, rely on a pipelined architecture, in which the main stages are speech recognition, linguistic analysis, transfer, generation, and speech synthesis. When making projections of error rates for systems of this kind, it is natural to assume that the error rates for the individual components are independent, making the system accuracy the product of the component accuracies. We have often heard versions of the above argument advanced as criticisms of the basic pipeline architecture of the SLT system; in this final section, we will produce experimental evidence suggesting that the simple model leads to serious overestimates of system error rates, since there are, in fact, strong dependencies among the components. For example, if an utterance fails recognition, then, had it been recognised, it would have had a higher-than-average chance of failing linguistic analysis; similarly, utterances that fail linguistic analysis because of incorrect choice in the face of ambiguity are more likely to fail during the transfer and generation phases if the correct choice is substituted. Intuitively, utterances that are hard to hear are also hard to understand and translate; this effect is sometimes referred to as *pipeline synergy*.

The experiments reported were carried out on an earlier version of SLT, using the 1 001-utterance set of ATIS data provided for the December 1993 ARPA Spoken Language Systems evaluations. This corpus was unseen data for the present purposes. Processing was split into four phases, and the partial results for each phase evaluated by skilled judges. Where feasible (for example, for recognition), a correct alternative was supplied when a processing phase produced an incorrect result, and processing restarted from the alternative. This made it possible to perform statistical analysis contrasting the results of inputs corresponding to correct and incorrect upstream processing.

The results showed that dependencies, in some instances quite striking, existed among the performances of most pairs of phases. For example, the error rates for the linguistic analysis phase, applied to correctly and incorrectly recognised utterances, respectively, differed by a factor of about 3.5; a chi-squared test indicated that this was significant at the $P = 0.0005$ level. The dependencies existed at all utterance lengths, and were even stronger when evaluation was limited to the portion of the corpus consisting of utterances of one-to-ten–words. Predicting the system error rate on the independence assumption by simple multiplication resulted in a 16 percent proportional overestimate for all utterances, and a 19 percent overestimate for the one-to-ten–word utterances.

We used a version of the system in which only the full translation processing phase was switched on; utterances that failed to receive a full QLF-level analysis thus produced no translation. Since the other processing phases are mainly aimed at error recovery, and the evaluation here is based on a dichotomy between correct and incorrect processing, this is appropriate. We focussed our investigations on four conceptual functionalities: speech recognition, source-language analysis, grammar specialisation, and transfer and generation. The above breakdown was motivated partially by the expense and tedium of judging intermediate results by hand; ideally, we would have preferred a more fine-grained division, for example, splitting transfer and generation into two phases. The results however, seem, adequate to illustrate our basic point. The error rate for each functionality was defined as follows:

Speech recognition Portion of utterances for which the preferred N-best hypothesis is not an acceptable variant of the transcribed utterance. "Acceptable variant" was judged strictly: thus, for example, substitution of "a" by "the" or vice versa was normally judged unacceptable, but "all the" instead of "all of the" would normally be acceptable.

Source-language analysis Portion of input utterance hypotheses that do not receive a semantic analysis. This neglects the problem that some semantic analyses are incorrect; other studies (Agnäs et al. 1994, Appendix A) indicate that of sentences for which some analyses are produced, around 5 to 10 percent are assigned only incorrect analyses.

Grammar specialisation Portion of input utterance hypotheses receiving an analysis with the normal grammar that receive no analysis with the specialised grammar.

Transfer and generation Portion of input utterance hypotheses receiving an analysis with the normal grammar that do not produce an acceptable translation.

The basic method for establishing correlations among processing functionalities was to contrast results between two sets of inputs, corresponding to (i) correct upstream processing and (ii) incorrect but correctable upstream processing, respectively. In the second case, the input was substituted by input in which the upstream errors had been corrected. The expectation was that in cases where an upstream error had occurred the chance of failure in a given component would be higher even if the upstream error were corrected; this indeed proved to be the case.

The simplest example is provided by the linguistic processing phase. Of the 1 001 utterances, 789 were recognised acceptably, and 212 unacceptably. In the first group, 706 of the utterances received a QLF (89.5 percent); when the 212 misrecognised utterances were replaced by the correctly transcribed reference versions, only 135 (63.7 percent) received a QLF. Thus, one can conclude that utterances failing recognition would anyway be 3.5 times as likely to fail linguistic processing as well. According to a standard chi-squared test, this result is significant at the $P = 0.0005$ level.

Moving on to the grammar specialisation phase, there are two possible types of upstream error for a given utterance: recognition can fail, or the utterance can be out of coverage for the general (unspecialised) grammar. Only the first type of error is correctable. So the meaningful population of examples is the set of $706 + 135 = 841$ utterances for which a QLF is produced assuming correct recognition. Of the 706 correctly recognised examples, 653 (92.5 percent) still produced a QLF when the specialised grammar was used instead of the general one. Of the 135 incorrectly recognised examples, only 101 (74.8 percent) passed grammar specialisation. The ratio of error rates, 3.4, is similar to the one for linguistic analysis, and is also significant at the $P = 0.0005$ level.

For the transfer-and-generation phase, the population of meaningful examples is again 841, but this time there are two types of correctable upstream error: either recognition or grammar specialisation can fail. Of the 653 examples with no upstream error, 539 (82.5 percent) produced a good translation; of the $841 - 653 = 188$ examples with a correctable upstream error, 119 (63.3 percent) produce a good translation. The ratio of error rates, 2.1, is lower than for the linguistic analysis and grammar specialisation phases, but is still significant at the $P = 0.0005$ level.

If we calculate error rates for each phase over the whole population of meaningful examples (correct upstream processing + correctable upstream errors), we get the following figures.

Recognition 1 001 examples; 789 successes; error rate $= 21.2$ percent.

Linguistic analysis 1 001 examples; $706 + 135 = 841$ successes; error rate $= 15.9$ percent.

Grammar specialization 841 examples; $653 + 101 = 754$ successes; error rate $= 10.3$ percent.

Transfer and generation 841 examples; $539 + 119 = 658$ successes; error rate $= 21.8$ percent.

On the naive model, the error rate for the whole system should be $(1 - (1 - 0.212)(1 - 0.159)(1 - 0.103)(1 - 0.218)) = 0.535$. In actual fact, however, the error rate is $(1 - 539/1\,001) = 0.462$. Thus the naive model overestimates the error rate by a factor of $0.535/0.462 = 1.16$.

It is not immediately clear why these strong correlations exist. One hypothesis that we felt needed investigation is that they are a simple consequence of the known fact that accuracy in general correlates strongly with utterance length, with long utterances being difficult for all processing stages. If this were so, one would expect the effect to be less pronounced if the long utterances were removed. Interestingly, this does not turn out to be true. We repeated the experiments using only utterances of one to ten words (688 utterances of the original 1 001): the new results, in summary, were as follows. All of them were significant at the $P = 0.0005$ level.

Speech recognition 577 utterances (83.9 percent) were acceptably recognised.

Linguistic analysis 531 of the 577 acceptably recognised utterances (92.0 percent) received a QLF; 75 of the 111 unacceptably recognised utterances (67.6 percent) received a QLF. The ratio of error rates is 4.1.

Grammar specialisation 497 of the 531 correctly recognised utterances receiving a QLF (93.6 percent) passed grammar specialisation; 54 of the 75 relevant incorrectly recognised utterances did so (72.0 percent). The ratio of error rates is 4.4.

Transfer and generation 428 of the 497 utterances with no upstream error received a good translation (86.1 percent); 67 of the 109 utterances with a correctable upstream error did so (61.5 percent). The ratio of error rates is 2.8.

The naive model predicts a combined error rate of 45.1 percent; the real error rate is 37.8 percent. Thus, the naive model overestimates the error rate by a factor of 1.19, an even larger difference than for the entire set.

A more plausible explanation for the correlations is that they arise from the fact that all the components of the system are trained on, and therefore biased towards, rather similar data. This training may be automatic, or it may arise from system developers devoting their efforts to more frequently occurring phenomena (cf. Section 8.6). Even if training and test sentences formally outside the domain are excluded from consideration, some sentences will still be more typical than others in that they employ more frequently occurring words, word sequences, constructions, and concepts. It is quite probable that typicality at one level – say, that of word N-grams, making correct recognition more likely – is strongly correlated with typicality at others – say, source language grammar coverage, especially when specialised.

There are several interesting conclusions to be drawn from the results presented above. First, pipelined systems are clearly doing better than the naive model predicts. More interestingly, the experiments clearly show that the whole concept of evaluating individual components of a pipelined system in isolation is more complex than one at first imagines. Since all the components tend to find the same utterances difficult, the upstream components act as a filter that separates out the hard examples and passes on the easy ones. Thus, a test that measures the performance of a component in an ideal situation, assuming no upstream errors, will in practice give a more or less misleading picture of how it will behave in the context of the full system. In general, downstream components will *always* have a lower error rate than a test of this type suggests.

In particular, the performance of the language processing component of a pipelined speech-understanding system is not something that can meaningfully be measured in isolation. A clear understanding of this fact allows development effort to be focussed more productively on work that improves system performance as a whole.

21 Conclusions

MANNY RAYNER, DAVID CARTER,
PIERRETTE BOUILLON, MATS WIRÉN,
AND VASSILIS DIGALAKIS

I N A MUCH-QUOTED DICTUM, Drew McDermott once said that the field of AI was starving for want of a few well-documented failures. We do not think that the SLT project has been a failure. However, since it has not yet resulted in a functioning, commercially available speech translation system, we cannot claim that it is an objective success either. It seems most reasonable to say that it falls into the large class of projects that don't really solve the problem they set out to solve, mainly because that problem is so difficult. While attempting to build a general grammar-based speech translation system, we have attacked many interesting and important subproblems; some of these subproblems have been clear success stories. In this chapter, we briefly list the parts of the project in which things went the way we wanted them to, and in which we feel we made real progress. In general, we have tried to describe both the successful and the less successful parts of the project in an honest way, and we hope that other researchers will find this account of our experiences useful.

So: our successes. As noted in the first chapter of the book, approaches based on general hand-coded grammars are currently unfashionable. To our minds, the most significant contribution of the book has been to demonstrate that it is in fact quite feasible to use these methods in serious applications. The techniques described in Chapters 3, 4, and 5 show how parsed corpora can be rapidly created by graphical disambiguation, and used to train efficient versions of a general grammar specialised to the particular characteristics of the training corpus. The key ideas developed here are grammar specialisation through Explanation-Based Learning, discriminant-based statistical preferences for language processing, and discriminant-based constituent pruning. All of these ideas were thoroughly worked out during the project and feel very solid to us.

We also think that we have made progress on the task of building large unification-based linguistic descriptions. In particular, Chapters 10 and 11 provide general recipes for converting grammars for English into corresponding grammars for French and Swedish. It seems plausible that similar methods would work for most other European languages. We have also shown in Chapter 13 that it can be practically feasible to write a single large grammar valid for two closely related languages. Chapter 7 described an implemented formalism that makes feasible rapid development of morphological descriptions for new languages. Putting all this together, we have a framework that allows us quickly to implement large-scale unification-based grammars by efficient reuse of existing resources.

With regard to the translation task itself, our work lends support to the idea of multi-engine translation first suggested by Frederking and Nirenburg (1994). We have presented in Chapters 1, 2, and 12 a hybrid transfer architecture based on Quasi Logical Form transfer and trainable preferences, which we believe represents a good tradeoff between the opposing positions of pure grammar-based transfer on the one hand, and pure statistical translation on the other. We have done some nontrivial work on the problem of evaluating spoken language translation systems. In particular, the experiments of Section 20.5 are, as far as we are aware, the first formal description of the phenomenon of pipeline synergy.

On the speech-recognition side, the demands made by the SLT system have encouraged us to develop a number of interesting new techniques, in particular, the discrete-mixture HMMs described in Section 15.4. Discrete-mixture HMMs run two to three times faster than state-of-the-art continuous HMMs with similar recognition performance and have better bandwidth characteristics as well, a surprising and significant result. We have also made useful progress on the tasks of estimating language models from small amounts of data (Chapter 16), making recognisers robust to dialectal variation (Section 18.2), and building recognisers that can robustly handle multiple languages (Section 18.3).

It's time to say goodbye. We have enjoyed doing this project and writing this book. Thank you for reading it.

A   Appendix: The Mathematics of Discriminant Scores

DAVID CARTER

Suppose we assume that the probability p_d that a given occurrence of a datum d will be good is itself distributed uniformly at random as d varies. That is, if we take a particular datum for which we have not yet seen any occurrences at all, then any probability between 0 and 1 that a given occurrence of d will be good is equally likely (but all occurrences of the same d are governed by the *same* value p_d). In other words, d is as likely to be a reliably good discriminant ($p_d = 0.99$, say) as to be a fairly uninformative one (e.g., $p_d = 0.48$) or a reliably bad one (say, $p_d = 0.02$). This (we assume) is the prior distribution for p_d: its density function is $f_d(p) = 1$ for all p from 0 to 1. The expected value of p_d (i.e., our estimate of the probability that a new occurrence of d will be good) is $\frac{1}{2}$.

Now suppose we observe G good occurrences of d and B bad ones. The density function $g_d(p)$ for the posterior distribution for p_d is given by the following standard formula, which is related to Bayes' rule:

$$g_d(p) = \frac{f_d(p)P(G, B \mid p)}{\int_0^1 f_d(x)P(G, B \mid x)\,dx}. \tag{A.1}$$

The expected value of $g_d(p)$ is given by the formula

$$E(g_d) = \int_0^1 x g_d(x)\,dx \tag{A.2}$$

$$= \frac{\int_0^1 x^{G+1}(1-x)^B dx}{\int_0^1 x^G(1-x)^B dx}, \tag{A.3}$$

since $P(G, B \mid x)$, the probability of getting G good outcomes and B bad ones from a binary distribution with probability x of a good outcome, is $x^G(1-x)^B$ times a combinatorial constant, which can be ignored here as it is the same for numerator and denominator of Equation A.1.

A standard result is that

$$\int_0^1 x^M y^N dx = \frac{M!N!}{(M+N+1)!}. \tag{A.4}$$

The formula for $E(g_d)$, therefore, reduces to

$$E(g_d) = \frac{(G+1)!B!/(G+B+2)!}{G!B!/(G+B+1)!} \tag{A.5}$$

$$= \frac{G+1}{G+B+2}, \tag{A.6}$$

which is our posterior estimate for the probability that a new occurrence of d will be good, given a uniform prior, G good observations and B bad ones.

It can be seen that for nonnegative G and B, Equation A.6 gives $0 < E(g_d) < 1$, and $E(g_d)$ strictly increasing in G and strictly decreasing in B. These are desirable properties: no matter how many bad occurrences we observe, the possibility of the next one being good is never quite ruled out, but it is viewed as increasingly unlikely. In terms of pruning, this means that a datum with no good occurrences and 100 bad ones scores worse than one with no good occurrences and 10 bad ones, and is therefore viewed as a better candidate for pruning.

However, our initial conservative assumption of a uniform prior distribution turns out not to fit our population of data very well. Examination of training data suggests that there are relatively few data d, such that p_d is near the middle of the range; values close to 0 and 1 (especially to 0) are much more common. The effect of this can be seen by comparing two hypothetical data, say d_1 with $(G, B) = (0, 8)$ and d_2 with $(G, B) = (9, 89)$. These both give $E(g_d) = 0.1$ according to Equation A.6, but in practice d_2 would be rather more likely to yield a good outcome on the next observation (after all, it has already done so nine times) than d_1, whose true underlying probability is likely to be closer to 0.

Equation A.6 can be interpreted as saying that to estimate the probability that the next occurrence of d will be good, we should use the maximum likelihood estimate not for the events that we have actually observed (G good and B bad) but for a set of $G' = G + 1$ good and $B' = B + 1$ bad: that is, the set we observed plus one more good event and one more bad (the symmetry reflecting the uniform prior). If we apply this strategy, but take as our prior distribution what until now has been our posterior one, we get

$$G' = G + \lambda \frac{G+1}{G+B+2}$$

$$B' = B + \lambda \frac{B+1}{G+B+2},$$

where λ is the number of extra events assumed. Setting λ arbitrarily to one and substituting into the maximum likelihood formula $\frac{G'}{G'+B'}$ we get an estimate of

$$\frac{G(G+B+3)+1}{(G+B)(G+B+3)+2} \tag{A.7}$$

for the expected value of the (new) posterior distribution, that is, for the probability that the next observed occurrence of d will be good. This formula has the desirable properties noted above (never 0, strictly increasing in G and decreasing in B) but seems to do better with cases like d_1 and d_2 above: if d_1 has $(G, B) = (0, 8)$ then a d_2 with $(G, B) = (1, 89)$, rather than $(9, 89)$, will be given a similar estimate. This looks intuitively better: training data with counts like these tend in practice to be about equally likely to yield a good outcome on the next trial. Furthermore, to fall below the threshold of $\frac{1}{200}$ required for pruning to occur, if $G = 0$ we need $B \geq 13$; for nonzero G, $B \geq 200 * G$ is approximately sufficient, and these values also seem to work well in practise.

B   Appendix: Notation for QLF-Based Processing

MANNY RAYNER

We have throughout the book rationalised the representation of QLFs and grammar rules in the interests of expositional clarity. The concrete notation used in the implemented system, and its relationship to the rationalised representation, are defined here.

B.1   QLFs

The design of QLF was originally motivated by semantic considerations not generally relevant to its use in machine translation, and we have in this book revised QLF format accordingly. There are five main points:

1. Extra slots. term and form constructs in the implemented version of QLF contain some extra slots, which are intended to be used in semantic interpretation. The values of these slots play no part in the processing described here, and we have consequently omitted them altogether.
2. Vacuous lambda abstraction in forms. The implemented version of QLF also requires that the bodies of forms must have the syntactic form of a lambda abstraction. In nearly all cases, this restriction is realised by wrapping the body in a vacuous lambda abstraction of the form $\lambda P.P(B)$, where B is the real body. We have consistently omitted these vacuous wrappers.
3. Lambda abstraction in terms. Similarly, the implemented version of QLF requires that the restriction in a term must be a lambda-bound form, and that the lambda-bound variable must be distinct from the variable occurring in the term's second argument position. Since the distinction between these two variables can at best be said to be unclearly motivated, we have conflated them and removed the formal lambda binding.
4. Representation of PPs. For historical reasons, the implemented version represents PPs as forms. We have replaced them throughout with simple predicate applications.
5. Shortening of QLF constants. QLF word-sense constants in the current implemented version are generally atoms consisting of the surface form

of the word followed by a paraphrase. In order to save space, we have reverted to an earlier version of the notation, which used the simpler convention that a word-sense constant consists of the surface form followed by a number. We have also made diverse minor changes in the print forms of other QLF constants.

Figure B.1 contrasts the book and implemented versions of a QLF chosen to illustrate all the points listed above.

Book version:

```
[imp,
  form(verb(no,no,no,imp,yes),E,
      [show1,E,
         term(ref(pro,you,_),X,[personal,X]),
         term(q(_,bare,plur),Y,
             [and,
              [flight1,Y],
              [to1,Y,
               term(proper_name,Z,
                    [name_of,Z,boston1])]])])]
```

Implemented version:

```
[imp,
  form(_,verb(no,no,no,imp,y),E,
      P^
      [P,
        [show_Reveal,E,
         term(_,ref(pro,you,_,1([])),X,
             X1^[personal,X1],_,_),
         term(_,q(_,bare,plur),Y,
             Y1^
             [and,
              [flight_AirplaneTrip,Y1],
              form(_,prep(to),_,
                  Q^
                  [Q,Y,
                   term(_,proper_name(_),Z,
                       Z1^[name_of,Z1,boston_City],
                       _,_)],
                  _)],
             _,_)]],
      _)],
```

Figure B.1. Book and implemented versions of QLF for "show flights to Boston".

320 *The Spoken Language Translator*

B.2   Grammar Rules

The implemented CLE notation for grammar rules diverges from that used in Chapter 2 in two main respects. First, there are several differences in the concrete syntax used. The implemented version of the grammar formalism writes a rule as a list consisting of the mother category followed by its daughters; also, for reasons that are mostly historical, the feature set is split into subsets consisting of syntactic and semantic features, respectively, and the qlf feature is marked specially in the semantic part. Each rule is associated with a rule identifier, a rule-group identifier, and a documentation field; the rule identifiers are used to link the syntactic and semantic halves of the rule. The same syntactic rule can be linked with multiple semantic rules, yielding one full rule for each semantic rule. Each semantic rule consequently has a secondary identifier.

Figure B.2 presents an example, contrasting the book and implemented versions of the notation. Here, num and gen have been treated as syntactic features, and qlf and arg are considered as semantic. Each category in the semantic part of the rule is written in the form

```
(QLF, <cat>:<features>)
```

where <cat> is the category name, QLF is the value of the qlf feature, and <features> are the remaining semantic features. np_det_nbar is the rule identifier, np_group the rule-group identifier, and sem_rule1 the semantic rule

```
Book version:

np:[qlf=term(Det, X, Nbar), num=N, gen=G] -->
    det:[qlf=Det, num=N, gen=G],
    nbar:[qlf=Nbar, arg=X, num=N, gen=G].
```

```
Implemented version:

syn(np_det_nbar, np_group,
    doc("[un grand fauteuil]",[],
        "NP consisting of DET and NBAR"),
    [np:[num=N, gen=G],
    det:[num=N, gen=G],
    nbar:[num=N, gen=G]]).
```

```
sem(np_det_nbar, sem_rule1,
[(term(Det, X, Nbar), np:[]),
 (Det, det:[]),
 (Nbar, nbar:[arg=X])]).
```

Figure B.2. Book and implemented versions of first grammar rule in Figure 2.11.

identifier. As far as normal grammar rules and lexical entries are concerned, it is trivial to map the implemented notation into the variant of Definite Clause Grammar we have used. Unfortunately, the CLE formalism also includes one construct, the *rule schema*, which cannot be carried over in a straightforward way to the compact notation. Specifically, it is possible to make the body of the rule into an open list, whose tail is set from the value of a feature in one of the categories; this provides an elegant way of describing subcategorisation constructions. Figure B.3 illustrates how the rule schema notation can be used to rewrite two rules into a single schema, which will in fact be able to deal with any kind of subcategorisation pattern defined by a verb entry. The large grammars presented in Chapters 9, 10, and 11, each contain two or three instances of use of rule schemas, all of which are structurally similar to the example just presented.

Original rules:

```
vp:[subject=Subj, qlf=V, gapsin=In, gapsout=In]) -->
  v:[qlf=V, verbform=finite,
     subject=Subj, complements=[],
     gapsin=In, gapsout=In].

vp:[subject=Subj, qlf=V, gapsin=In, gapsout=Out]) -->
  v:[qlf=V, verbform=finite,
     subject=Subj,
     complements=[np:[qlf=NpQ, case=object,
                      rel=NpR, arg=NpX,
                      gapsin=In, gapsout=Out]]
     gapsin=In, gapsout=Out],
  np:[qlf=NpQ, case=object,
      rel=NpR, arg=NpX,
      gapsin=In, gapsout=Out].
```

Version in implemented notation using rule schema:

```
syn(vp_v_complements, vp_group,
[vp:[gapsin=In, gapsout=In],
  v:[verbform=finite, syncomps=SynComps,
     gapsin=In, gapsout=In] |
  SynComps]).

sem(vp_v_complements, sem_rule1,
[(V, vp:[subject=Subj]),
 (V, v:[subject=Subj, semcomps=SemComps] |
 SemComps]).
```

Figure B.3. Two rules from Figure 2.13 rewritten into a rule schema.

B.3   Lexicon

Lexicon entries in the implemented system are separated into syntactic and semantic halves in the same way as the grammar rules discussed in the preceding section, and a similar surface notation is used. Figure B.4 presents an illustrative example. Here, the lex denotes the syntactic half of the rule, and sense the semantic half.

Book version:

```
det:[qlf=ref(def,le,sing), num=s, gen=m] --> [le].
```

Implemented version:

```
lex(le, [det:[num=s, gen=m]]).

sense(le, (ref(def,le,sing), det:[])).
```

Figure B.4. Book and implemented versions of lexicon entry from Figure 2.11.

References

H. Abramson. A logic programming view of relational morphology. In *Proceedings of COLING-92*, pages 850–854, Nartes, France, 1992.

M.-S. Agnäs, H. Alshawi, I. Bretan, D. Carter, K. Ceder, M. Collins, R. Crouch, V. Digalakis, B. Ekholm, B. Gambäck, J. Kaja, J. Karlgren, B. Lyberg, P. Price, S. Pulman, M. Rayner, C. Samuelsson, and T. Svensson. Spoken language translator: First year report. Technical Report SRI Technical Report CRC-043, SRI, Cambridge, England, 1994.

A.V. Aho, R. Sethi, and J.D. Ullman. *Compilers, Principles, Techniques and Tools*. Addison-Wesley, Reading, Massachusetts, 1986.

L. Ahrenberg. A grammar combining phrase structure and field structure. In *Proceedings of COLING-90*, volume 2, pages 1–6, Helsinki, Finland, 1990.

H. Alshawi, editor. *The Core Language Engine*. MIT Press, Cambridge, Massachusetts, 1992.

H. Alshawi, D.J. Arnold, R. Backofen, D.M. Carter, J. Lindop, K. Netter and, S.G. Pulman, J. Tsujii, and H. Uszkoreit. Eurotra ET6/1: Rule formalism and virtual machine design study. Technical report, Commission of the European Communities, Luxembourg, 1991.

H. Alshawi, C.G. Brown, D.M. Carter, B. Gambäck, S.G. Pulman, and M. Rayner. Joint research report R91011 and CCSRC-018. Technical report, SICS and SRI International, Stockholm, Sweden and Cambridge, England, 1991.

H. Alshawi and D.M. Carter. Training and scaling preference functions for disambiguation. *Computational Linguistics*, 20(4):635–648, 1994.

H. Alshawi and S.G. Pulman. Ellipsis, comparatives and generation. In H. Alshawi, editor, *The Core Language Engine*, pages 251–275, MIT Press, Cambridge, Massachusetts, 1992.

R. Amalberti, N. Carbonell, and P. Falzon. User representations of computer systems in human–computer speech interaction. *International Journal of Man–Machine Studies*, 38:547–566, 1993.

M. Bäckström, K. Ceder, and B. Lyberg. Prophon – an interactive environment for text-to-speech conversion. In *Proceedings of European Conference on Speech Communication and Technology*, pages 144–147, Paris, France, 1989.

P.C. Bagshaw. *Automatic Prosodic Analysis for Computer Aided Pronunciation Teaching*. PhD thesis, University of Edinburgh, Edinburgh, Scotland, 1994.

L.R. Bahl, F. Jelinek, and R.L. Mercer. A maximum likelihood approach to continuous speech recognition. *IEEE Transactions Pattern Analysis and Machine Intelligence*, 5:179–190, 1983.

J.K. Baker. The Dragon system – an overview. *IEEE Transactions on Acoustics, Speech and Signal Processing*, 23(1):24–29, 1975.

L.E. Baum, G. Soules, T. Petrie, and N. Weiss. A maximization technique in the statistical analysis of probabilistic functions of finite state Markov chains. *Annals of Mathematical Statistics*, 41:164–171, 1970.

J.R. Bellegarda and D. Nahamoo. Tied mixture continuous parameter modeling for speech recognition. *IEEE Transactions on Acoustics, Speech, and Signal Processing*, 38(12):2033–2045, 1990.

G. Bès and C. Gardent. French order without order. In *Proceedings of 4th European Association for Computational Linguistics*, pages 249–255, Manchester, England, 1989.

T. Bowden. Cooperative error handling and shallow processing. In *Proceedings of 7th European Association for Computational Linguistics*, pages 297–300, Dublin, Ireland, 1995.

I. Bretan, R. Eklund, and C. MacDermid. Approaches to gathering realistic training data for speech translation systems. In *Proceedings from the Third IEEE Workshop on Interactive Voice Technology for Telecommunications Applications, IVTTA-96*, pages 97–100, Basking Ridge, New Jersey, September 30–October 1, 1996.

I. Bretan, A.-L. Ereback, C. MacDermid, and A. Waern. Simulation-based dialogue design for speech-controlled telephone services. In *Proceedings of CHI'95*, pages 145–146, Denver, Colorado, 1995.

P. Brown, S.A. Della Pietra, V.J. Della Pietra, J.C. Lai, and R.L. Mercer. Class-based n-gram models of natural language. *Computational Linguistics*, 18(4):31–40, 1992.

G. Bruce. *Swedish Word Accents in Sentence Perspective*. Number XII in Travaux de l'Institute de Linguistique de Lund. CWK Gleerup, Lund, Sweden, 1977.

G. Bruce and E. Gårding. A prosodic typology for Swedish dialects. In *Proceedings of Nordic Prosody*, pages 219–228, Dept. of Linguistics, Lund University, Lund, Sweden, 1978.

T. Bub, W. Wahlster, and A. Waibel. Verbmobil: The combination of deep and shallow processing for spontaneous speech translation. In *Proceedings of ICASSP 97*, pages 71–74, Munich, Germany, 1997.

J. Carbonell, T. Mitamura, and E.H. Nyberg 3rd. The Kant perspective: a critique of pure transfer (and pure interlingua, pure statistics, ...). In *Proceedings of Fourth International Conference on Theoretical and Methodological Issues in Machine Translation*, pages 225–235, Montreal, 1992.

D.M. Carter. *Interpreting Anaphors in Natural Language Texts*. Ellis Horwood, Chichester, England, 1987.

D.M. Carter. Lattice-based word identification in CLARE. In *Proceedings of Association for Computational Linguistics-92*, pages 159–166, Columbus, Ohio, 1992.

D.M. Carter. Rapid development of morphological descriptions for full language processing systems. In *Proceedings of 7th European Association for Computational Linguistics*, pages 202–209, Dublin, Ireland, 1995.

D.M. Carter, R. Becket, M. Rayner, R. Eklund, C. MacDermid, M. Wirén, S. Kirchmeier-Andersen, and C. Philp. Translation methodology in the spoken language translator: An evaluation. In *Proceedings of Association for Computational Linguistics Workshop on Spoken Language Translation*, pages 73–82, Madrid, Spain, 1997.

D.M. Carter, J. Kaja, L. Neumeyer, M. Rayner, F. Weng, and M. Wirén. Handling compound nouns in a Swedish speech-understanding system. In *Proceedings of International Conference on Spoken Language Processing*, volume 1, pages 26–29, Philadelphia, Pennsylvania, 1996.

K. Church. A stochastic parts program and noun phrase parser for unrestricted text. In *Proceedings of the First Conference on Applied Natural Language Processing*, pages 136–143, Austin, Texas, 1988.

M. Cohen, H. Murveit, J. Bernstein, P. Price, and M. Weintraub. The DECIPHER speech recognition system. In *Proceedings of IEEE International Conference on Acoustics, Speech and Signal Processing*, pages 77–80, Albuquerque, New Mexico, 1990.

M. Cohen, Z. Rivlin, and H. Bratt. Speech recognition in the ATIS domain using multiple knowledge sources. In *Proceedings of ARPA Spoken Language Systems Technology Workshop*, pages 257–260, Austin, Texas, 1995.

D. Cutting, J. Kupiec, J. Pedersen, and P. Sibun. A practical part-of-speech tagger. In *Proceedings of the Third Conference on Applied Natural Language Processing*, pages 133–140, Trento, Italy, 1992.

I. Dagan and A. Itai. Word sense disambiguation using a second language monolingual corpus. *Computational Linguistics*, 20(4):563–596, 1994.

S.B. Davis and P. Mermelstein. Comparison of parametric representations for monosyllabic word recognition in continuously spoken sentences. *IEEE Transactions on Acoustics, Speech, and Signal Processing*, 28(4):357–366, 1980.

T. Dean and M. Boddy. An analysis of time-dependent planning. In *Proceedings of AAAI-88*, pages 44–54, St. Paul, Minnesota, 1988.

C.G. DeMarcken. Parsing the LOB corpus. In *Proceedings of 28th Association for Computational Linguistics*, pages 243–251, Pittsburgh, Pennsylvania, 1990.

A.P. Dempster, N.M. Laird, and D.B. Rubin. Maximum likelihood estimation from incomplete data. *Journal of the Royal Statistical Society (B)*, 39(1):1–38, 1977.

S. DeRose. Grammatical category disambiguation by statistical optimization. *Computational Linguistics*, 14:31–39, 1988.

P. Diderichsen. *Elementær Dansk Grammatik*. Gyldendahl, Copenhagen, Denmark, 1946.

V. Digalakis, P. Monaco, and H. Murveit. Acoustic calibration and search in SRI's large vocabulary speech recognition system. In *Proceedings of IEEE, ASR workshop*, pages 44–46, Snowbird, Utah, 1993.

V. Digalakis, P. Monaco, and H. Murveit. Genones: Generalized mixture tying in continuous hidden Markov model-based speech recognizers. *IEEE Transactions Speech and Audio Processing*, 281–289, 1996.

V. Digalakis and L. Neumeyer. Speaker adaptation using combined transformation and Bayesian methods. *IEEE Transactions Speech and Audio Processing*, 294–300, 1996.

V. Digalakis, L. Neumeyer, and M. Perakakis. Quantization of cepstral parameters for speech recognition over the World Wide Web. *IEEE Journal on Selected Areas in Communications*, 17(1):82–90, January 1999.

V. Digalakis, L. Neumeyer, and D. Rtischev. Speaker adaptation using constrained reestimation of Gaussian mixtures. *IEEE Transactions Speech and Audio Processing*, 357–366, September 1995.

V. Digalakis, S. Tsakalidis, and L. Neumeyer. Reviving discrete HMMs: The myth about the superiority of continuous HMMs. In *Proceedings of European Conference on Speech Communication and Technology*, pages 2433–2466, Budapest, Hungary, 1999.

R.O. Duda and P.E. Hart. *Pattern Classification and Scene Analysis*. J. Wiley and Sons, New York, Chichester, Brisbane, Toronto, Singapore, 1973.

E. Ejerhed, G. Källgren, O. Wennstedt, and M. Åström. *The Linguistic Annotation System of the Stockholm–Umeå Corpus Project. Description and Guidelines*. Report No. 33, Department of General Linguistics, Umeå University, Sweden, 1992.

R. Eklund and A. Lindström. Pronunciation in an internationalized society: A multidimensional problem considered. In *FONETIK 1996, Papers presented at the Swedish Phonetics Conference*, Nässlingen, 29–31 May, 1996, volume 2 of *TMH-QPSR*, pages 123–126, 1996.

R. Eklund and A. Lindström. How to handle "foreign" sounds in Swedish text-to-speech conversion: Approaching the 'xenophone' problem. In *Proceedings of International*

Conference on Spoken Language Processing, volume 7, pages 2831–2834, Sydney, Australia, 1998.

C.-C. Elert. Indelning och gränser inom området för den nu talade svenskan – en aktuell dialektografi. In L.-E. Edlund, editor, *Kulturgränser – myt eller verklighet*, pages 215–228, Diabas, Umeå University, Umeå, Sweden, 1994.

A. Elsner. Focus detection with additional information of phrase boundaries and sentence mode. In *Proceedings of Eurospeech*, pages 227–230, Rhodes, Greece, 1997.

S. Engelson and I. Dagan. Minimizing manual annotation cost in supervised training from corpora. In *Proceedings of 34th Annual Meeting of the Association for Computational Linguistics*, pages 319–326, Santa Cruz, California, 1996.

D. Estival. Generating French with a reversible unification grammar. In *Proceedings of COLING-90*, pages 106–111, Helsinki, Finland, 1990.

R.E. Fikes and N.J. Nilson. Strips: A new approach to the application of theorem proving to problem solving. *Artificial Intelligence*, 3:251–288, 1971.

R. Frederking and S. Nirenburg. Three heads are better than one. In *Proceedings of Fourth Conference on Applied Natural Language Processing*, pages 95–100, Stuttgart, Germany, 1994.

S. Fries. Dialektgränser och kulturgränser. In L.-E. Edlund, editor, *Kulturgränser – myt eller verklighet*, pages 189–198, Diabas, Umeå University, Umeå, Sweden, 1994.

V. Fromkin, editor. *Errors in Linguistic Performance: Slips of the Tongue, Ear, Pen and Hand*. New York, Academic Press, 1980.

B. Gambäck. *Processing Swedish Sentences: A Unification-Based Grammar and Some Applications*. PhD thesis, Royal Institute of Technology, Department of Computer and System Sciences, Kista, Sweden, 1997.

B. Gambäck and M. Rayner. The Swedish Core Language Engine. In *Proceedings of 3rd Nordic Conference on Text Comprehension in Man and Machine*, pages 71–85, Linköping, Sweden, 1992.

E. Gårding. Toward a prosodic typology for Swedish dialects. In K.-H. Dahlstedt, editor, *The Nordic Languages and Modern Linguistics*, pages 466–474, 1975.

J.L. Gauvain, L.F. Lamel, G. Adda, and M. Adda-Decker. The LIMSI continuous speech dictation system: Evaluation on the ARPA Wall Street Journal task. In *Proceedings of IEEE International Conference on Acoustics, Speech and Signal Processing*, pages I-125–I-128, Adelaide, Australia, 1994.

M. Gavaldà, L. Mayfield, Y.-H. Seo, B. Suhm, W. Ward, and A. Waibel. Parsing real input in Janus: a concept based approach. In *Proceedings of Sixth International Conference on Theoretical and Methodological Issues in Machine Translation*, pages 196–205, Leuven, Belgium, 5–7 July 1995.

G. Gazdar and C. Mellish. *Natural Language Processing in Prolog*. Addison-Wesley, Reading, Massachusetts, 1989.

P. Geutner. Using morphology towards better large-vocabulary speech recognition systems. In *Proceedings of ICASSP 95*, pages 445–448, Detroit, Michigan, 1995.

M. Grevisse. *Le Bon Usage*. DeBoeck Duclot, 13th edition, Paris-Gembloux, 1993.

J. Grimshaw. On the lexical representation of Romance reflexives. In J. Bresnan, editor, *The Mental Representation of Grammatical Relations*. MIT Press, Cambridge, MA, 1982.

R. Grishman and M. Kosaka. Combining rationalist and empiricist approaches to machine translation. In *Proceedings of Fourth International Conference on Theoretical and Methodological Issues in Machine Translation*, pages 263–274, Montreal, Canada, 1992.

T. van Harmelen and A. Bundy. Explanation-based generalization = partial evaluation (research note). *Artificial Intelligence*, 36:401–412, 1988.

P. Hedelin, A. Jonsson, and P. Lindblad. Svenskt uttalslexikon. Technical report, Dept. of Information Theory, Chalmers University of Technology, Göteborg, Sweden, 1987.

C.T. Hemphill, J.J. Godfrey, and G.R. Doddington. The ATIS spoken language systems pilot corpus. In *Proceedings of DARPA Speech and Natural Language Workshop*, pages 96–101, Hidden Valley, Pennsylvania, 1990.

W.J. Hess. Pitch and voicing determination. In S. Furui and M. M. Sondhi, editors, *Advances in Speech Signal Processing*, pages 3–98, Marcel Dekker, 1991.

I.L. Hetherington and V.W. Zue. New words: Implications for continuous speech recognition. In *Proceedings of Eurospeech 93*, volume 3, pages 1533–1536, Berlin, 1993.

L. Hirschman, M. Bates, D. Dahl, W. Fisher, J. Garofolo, D. Pallett, K. Hunicke-Smith, P. Price, A. Rudnicky, and E. Tzoukermann. Multi-site data collection for a spoken language corpus. In *Proceedings of ARPA Speech and Natural Language Workshop*, pages 19–24, Plainsboro, New Jersey, 1993.

J.R. Hobbs and J. Bear. Two principles of parse preference. In *Proceedings of COLING-90*, volume 3, pages 162–167, Helsinki, Finland, 1990.

X.D. Huang and M.A. Jack. Semi-continuous hidden Markov models for speech signals. In A. Waibel and K.F. Lee, editors, *Readings in Speech Recognition*, pages 340–346, Morgan Kaufmann Publishers, San Mateo, CA, 1990.

R.M. Iyer, M. Ostendorf, and J. Rohlicek. Language modeling with sentence-level mixtures. In *Proceedings of Human Language Technology Workshop*, pages 82–87, Plainsboro, New Jersey, March 1994.

E. Jackson, D. Appelt, J. Bear, R. Moore, and A. Podlozny. A template matcher for robust NL interpretation. In *Proceedings of Speech and Natural Language Workshop*, pages 190–194, Plainsboro, New Jersey, 1994.

F. Jelinek. Continuous speech recognition by statistical methods. In *IEEE Proceedings*, volume 64:4, pages 532–556, 1976.

G. Källgren. "The first million is hardest to get": Building a large tagged corpus as automatically as possible. In H. Karlgren, editor, *Proceedings of COLING-90*, volume 3, pages 168–173. University of Helsinki, Helsinki, Finland, 1990.

G. Källgren. Storskaligt korpusarbete pa dator: En presentation av SUC-korpusen. In H., Karlgren, editor, *Förhandlingar vid Tjugonde sammankomsten för svenskans beskrivning*, number 18, pages 168–173. Lund University Press, Lund, Sweden, 1991.

G. Källgren. Några icke-lingvistiska aspekter av arbetet med SUC. In *Förhandlingar vid tjugonde sammankomsten för svenskans beskrivning*, number 20, pages 218–232. Lund University Press, Lund, Sweden, 2–3 December 1993.

R.M. Kaplan and M. Kay. Regular models of phonological rule systems. *Computational Linguistics*, 20(3):331–378, 1994.

F. Karlsson, A. Anttila, J. Heikkilä, and A. Voutilainen, editors. *Constraint Grammar*. Mouton de Gruyer, Berlin, Germany and New York, New York, 1995.

L. Karttunen. D-PATR: A development environment for unification-based grammars. In *Proceedings of COLING-86*, pages 74–80, Bonn, Germany, 1986.

L. Karttunen, R.M. Kaplan, and A. Zaenen. Two-level morphology with composition. In *Proceedings of COLING-92*, pages 141–148, Nantes, France, 1992.

S.M. Katz. Estimation of probabilities from sparse data for the language model component of a speech recognizer. *IEEE Transactions on Acoustics, Speech and Signal Processing*, ASSP-35, pages 400–401, 1987.

M. Kay. Non-concatenative finite-state morphology. In *Proceedings of European Association for Computational Linguistics*, pages 2–10, Copenhagen, Denmark, 1987.

G. Kiraz. Multi-tape two-level morphology. In *Proceedings of COLING-94*, pages 180–186, Kyoto, Japan, 1994.

K. Koskenniemi. *Two-level morphology: a general computational model for word-form recognition and production*. Number 11 in University of Helsinki Publications. University of Helsinki, Department of General Linguistics, Helsinki, Finland, 1983.

328   *The Spoken Language Translator*

H.-C. Kwon and L. Karttunen. Incremental construction of a lexical transducer for Korean. In *Proceedings of COLING-94*, pages 1262–1266, Kyoto, Japan, 1994.

L. Lamel, M. Adda-Decker, and J.L. Gauvain. Issues in large vocabulary, multilingual speech recognition. In *Proceedings of Eurospeech*, pages 185–188, Madrid, Spain, 1995.

C.J. Leggetter and P.C. Woodland. Maximum likelihood linear regression for speaker adaptation of continuous density hidden Markov models. *Computer Speech and Language*, 9(2):171–185, 1995.

C. Lieske, J. Bos, M. Emele, B. Gambäck, and C.J. Rupp. Giving prosody a meaning. In *Proceedings of Eurospeech*, pages 1431–1434, Rhodes, Greece, 1997.

A. Life and I. Salter. Data collection for the mask kiosk: WOZ vs prototype system. In *Proceedings of International Conference on Spoken Language Processing*, volume 3, pages 1672–1675, Philadelphia, Pennsylvania, 1996.

A. Lindström and R. Eklund. [jà:mes] or [dʒɛImz] or perhaps something in-between? Recapping three years of xenophone studies. In *Proceedings of Fonetik 99, The Swedish Phonetics Conference*, number 81 in Gothenburg Papers in Theoretical Linguistics, pages 109–112, Gothenburg University, Gothenburg, Sweden, 1999a.

A. Lindström and R. Eklund. Xenophones revisited: Linguistic and other underlying factors affecting the pronunciation of foreign items in Swedish. In *Proceedings of International Conference of Phonetic Sciences 99*, volume 3, pages 2227–2230, San Francisco, California, 1999b.

P. Linell. Speech errors and the grammatical planning of utterances. In W. Koch, C. Platzack and G. Tottie, editors, *Textstrategier i tal och skrift*, pages 134–151, Almqvist and Wiksell, Stockholm, Sweden, 1981.

Linguistic Data Consortium Web site, available at: http://www.ldc.upenn.edu, accessed 1999.

B. Lyberg. Final lengthening – partly a consequence of restrictions on the speed of fundamental frequency change? *Journal of Phonetics*, 7:187–196, 1979.

B. Lyberg and A. Lindström. Will the time required to perform a certain fundamental frequency change restrict possible segment duration values? In *Proceedings of Nordic Prosody VI*, pages 151–158, Stockholm, Sweden, 1993. Almqvist and Wiksell International.

C. MacDermid and C. Eklund. Simulering av en automatiserad översättningstjänst för resebokningar. Technical report, Telia Research AB, Haninge, Sweden, 1996.

C. MacDermid and C. Eklund. Report on the first WOZ simulation for the SLT-DB project. Technical report, Telia Research AB, Haninge, Sweden, 1997.

C. MacDermid and M. Goldstein. The 'storyboard' method: Establishing an unbiased vocabulary for keyword and voice command applications. In *Adjunct Proceedings of Human–Computer Interaction 96*, pages 104–109, London, England, 1996.

M. Marcus, B. Santorini, and M.A. Marcinkiewicz. Building a large annotated corpus of English: the Penn Treebank. *Computational Linguistics*, 19(2):313–330, 1993.

M. McCord. Heuristics for broad-coverage natural language parsing. In *Proceedings of 1st ARPA Workshop on Human Language Technology*, pages 127–132, Plainsboro, New Jersey, 1993.

C.S. Mellish. Implementing systemic classification by unification. *Computational Linguistics*, 14(40):40–51, 1988.

E.A. Meyer. Die intonation im Schwedischen, i: Die Sveamundarten. *Stockholm Studies in Scandinavian Philology*, number 10. University of Stockholm, Stockholm, 1937.

E.A. Meyer. Die intonation im Schwedischen, ii: Die norrländischen Mundarten. *Stockholm Studies in Scandinavian Philology*, number 11. University of Stockholm, Stockholm, 1954.

P. Miller and I. Sag. French clitic movement without clitics or movement. Technical report, Center for the Study of Language and Information, Stanford, California, 1995.

T.S. Mitchell, S. Kedar-Cabelli, and R. Keller. Explanation-based generalization: A unifying view. *Machine Learning*, 1(1):47–80, 1986.

R.C. Moore and H. Alshawi. Syntactic and semantic processing. In H. Alshawi, editor, *The Core Language Engine*, pages 129–148, MIT Press, Cambridge, Massachusetts, 1992.

H. Murveit, J. Butzberger, V. Digalakis, and M. Weintraub. Large vocabulary dictation using SRI's DECIPHER(TM) speech recognition system: Progressive search techniques. In *Proceedings of International Conference on Acoustics, Speech and Signal Processing*, pages 319–322, Minneapolis, Minnesota, 1993.

L. Neumeyer, V. Digalakis, and A. Sankar. A comparative study of speaker adaptation techniques. In *Proceedings of European Conference on Speech Communication and Technology*, pages 1127–1130, Madrid, Spain, 1995.

K. Oflazer. Two-level description of Turkish morphology. In *Proceedings of European Association for Computational Linguistics*, page 472, Utrecht, Netherlands, 1993.

K. Oflazer. Spelling correction in agglutinative languages. available at: http://www.cmp-lg.lanl.gov. (Computational Linguistics Archieve), 1994 (accessed 1998).

H.S. Park. *The Korean Core Language Engine*. PhD thesis, Cambridge University Computer Laboratory, Cambridge, England, 1998.

D.B. Paul. The Lincoln robust continuous speech recognizer. In *Proceedings of IEEE International Conference on Acoustics, Speech and Signal Processing*, pages 449–452, Glasgow, Scotland, 1989.

F.C.N. Pereira. Extraposition grammars. *Computational Linguistics*, 7:243–256, 1981.

F.C.N. Pereira and S. Shieber. *Prolog and Natural-Language Analysis*. Center for the Study of Language and Information, Stanford, California, 1987.

G.D. Plotkin. A note on inductive generalization. *Machine Intelligence*, 5:153–163, 1970.

C. Pollard and I. Sag. *Head-Driven Phrase Structure Grammar*. Center for the Study of Language and Information and University of Chicago Press, Stanford, California and Chicago, Illinois, 1994.

S. Pulman. Passives. In *Proceedings of 3rd Conference of the European Chapter of the Association for Computational Linguistics*, pages 306–313, University of Copenhagen, Copenhagen, Denmark, 1987.

S.G. Pulman and M.R. Hepple. A feature based formalism for two-level phonology. *Computer Speech and Language*, 7:333–358, 1993.

L.R. Rabiner, S.E. Levinson, B.H. Juang, and M.M. Sondhi. Recognition of isolated digits using hidden Markov models with continuous mixture densities. *Bell Systems Technical Journal*, 64(6):1211–1234, 1985.

L.R. Rabiner, M.R. Sambur, and C.E. Schmidt. Applications of non-linear smoothing algorithms to speech processing. *IEEE Transactions on Acoustics, Speech and Signal Processing*, 23:552–557, 1975.

M. Rayner and P. Bouillon. Hybrid transfer in an English-French spoken language translator. In *Proceedings of IA '95*, pages 153–162, Montpellier, France, 1995.

M. Rayner, P. Bouillon, and D.M. Carter. Using corpora to develop limited-domain speech translation systems. In *Proceedings of Translating and the Computer*, volume 17, London, England, 1995. ASLIB.

M. Rayner, P. Bouillon, and D.M. Carter. Adapting the Core Language Engine to French and Spanish. In *Proceedings of NLP-IA*, pages 224–232, Moncton, New Brunswick, Canada, 1996.

M. Rayner, I. Bretan, M. Wirén, S. Rydin, and E. Beshai. Composition of transfer rules in a multi-lingual MT system. In *Proceedings of Workshop on Future Issues for Multilingual Text Processing, 4th Pacific Rim International Conference on Artificial Intelligence (PRICAI 96)*, pages 60–68, Cairns, Australia, August 1996.

M. Rayner and D.M. Carter. Fast parsing using pruning and grammar specialization. In

Proceedings of 34th Annual Meeting of the Association for Computational Linguistics, pages 223–230, Santa Cruz, California, 1996.

M. Rayner and D.M. Carter. Hybrid language processing in the spoken language translator. In *Proceedings of ICASSP 97*, volume I, pages 107–110, Munich, Germany, 1997.

M. Rayner, D.M. Carter, P. Price, and B. Lyberg. Estimating the performance of pipelined spoken language translation systems. In *Proceedings of International Conference on Spoken Language Processing*, volume 3, pages 1251–1254, Yokohama, Japan, 1994.

M. Rayner, V. Digalakis, D.M. Carter, and P. Price. Combining knowledge sources to reorder N-best speech hypothesis lists. In *Proceedings of 2nd ARPA Workshop on Human Language Technology*, pages 217–221, Princeton, New Jersey, 1994. Morgan Kaufmann. Also SRI Technical Report CRC-044.

M. Rayner and C. Samuelsson. *Corpus-based grammar specialization for fast analysis*. In Agnäs et al. *Spoken language translator: First year report*. SRI Technical Report CRC-043, SRI, Cambridge, England, 1994.

G. Ritchie, G.J. Russell, A.W. Black, and S.G. Pulman. *Computational Morphology*. MIT Press, Cambridge, Massachusetts, 1992.

J.A. Robinson. A machine-oriented logic based on the resolution principle. *Journal of the Association for Computing Machinery*, 12(1):23–41, 1965.

J.R. Ross. *Constraints on Variables in Syntax*. PhD thesis, MIT, Cambridge, MA, 1967.

H. Ruessink. Two level formalisms. *Utrecht Working Papers in Natural Language Processing*, no. 5, Utrecht, Netherlands, 1989.

C. Samuelsson. *Fast Natural-Language Parsing Using Explanation-Based Learning*. PhD thesis, The Royal Institute of Technology and Stockholm University, Stockholm, Sweden, 1994a.

C. Samuelsson. Grammar specialization through entropy thresholds. In *Proceedings of Association for Computational Linguistics 94*, pages 188–195, Las Cruces, New Mexico, 1994b.

C. Samuelsson and M. Rayner. Quantitative evaluation of explanation-based learning as an optimization tool for a large-scale natural language system. In *Proceedings of 12th IJCAI*, pages 609–615, Sydney, Australia, 1991.

A. Sankar and C.-H. Lee. A maximum likelihood approach to stochastic matching for robust speech recognition. *IEEE Transactions Speech and Audio Processing*, 190–202, 1996.

P. Sautermeister and R. Eklund. Some observations on the influence of F_0 and duration to the perception of prosodic prominence by Swedish listeners. In *FONETIK 97*, number 4 in PHONUM, Reports from the Department of Phonetics Umeå University, pages 121–124. Umeå University, Umeå, Sweden, May 1997.

P. Sautermeister and B. Lyberg. Detection of sentence accents in a speech recognition system. In *Journal of the Acoustical Society of America*, volume 99:4, page 2493, 1996.

R.C. Schank and R. Abelson. *Scripts, Plans, Goals and Understanding*. Lawrence Erlbaum, Hillsdale, New Jersey, 1977.

S.M. Shieber, G. van Noord, F.C.N. Pereira, and R.C. Moore. Semantic-head-driven generation. *Computational Linguistics*, 16:30–43, 1990.

K. Sima'an. *Learning Efficient Disambiguation*. Number 2. ILLC Dissertation Series, Amsterdam, The Netherlands, 1999.

M. Spies. A language model for compound words in speech recognition. In *Proceedings of Eurospeech '95*, pages 1767–1770, Madrid, Spain, 1995.

D. Stallard and R. Bobrow. The semantic linker – a new fragment combining method. In *Proceedings of 1993 ARPA Human Language Technology Workshop*, pages 37–42, Princeton, NJ, 1993.

V. Strom, A. Elsner, W. Hess, W. Kasper, A. Klein, H.U. Krieger, J. Spilker, H. Weber, and G. Görz. On the use of prosody in a speech-to-speech translator. In *Proceedings of Eurospeech '97*, pages 1479–1482, Rhodes, Greece, 1997.

D. Tannen. Oral and literate strategies in spoken and written narratives. *Language*, 58(1):1–21, 1982.

M. Tomita. *Efficient Parsing for Natural Language*. Kluwer Academic Publisher, Dordrecht, 1986.

H. Trost. The application of two-level morphology to non-concatenative German morphology. In *Proceedings of COLING-90*, pages 371–376, Helsinki, Finland, 1990.

H. Trost. X2MORF: A morphological component based on augmented two-level morphology. In *Proceedings of IJCAI-91*, pages 1024–1030, Sydney, Australia, 1991.

H. Trost and J. Matiasek. Morphology with a null-interface. In *Proceedings of COLING-94*, pages 141–147, Kyoto, Japan, 1994.

S. Tsakalidis, V. Digalakis, and L. Neumeyer. Efficient speech recognition using subvector quantization and discrete-mixture HMMs. In *Proceedings of IEEE International Conference on Acoustics, Speech and Signal Processing*, Phoenix, Arizona, 1999.

A. Waibel, M. Finke, D. Gates, M. Gavalda, T. Kemp, A. Lavie, M. Maier, L. Mayfield, A. McNair, I. Rogina, K. Shima, T. Sloboda, M. Woszczyna, P. Zhan, and T. Zeppenfel. Janus II – advances in spontaneous speech translation. In *Proceedings of ICASSP 96*, volume 1, pages 409–412, Atlanta, Georgia, 1996.

F.L. Weng, H. Bratt, L. Neumeyer, and A. Stolcke. A study of multilingual speech recognition. In *Proceedings of European Conference on Speech Communication and Technology*, pages 359–362, Rhodes, Greece, 1997.

F.L. Weng and A. Stolcke. Partitioning grammars and composing parsers. In *Proceedings of 4th International Workshop on Parsing Technologies*, pages 271–272, Prague, the Czech Republic, 1995.

F.L. Weng, A. Stolcke, and A. Sankar. Efficient lattice representation and generation. In *Proceedings of International Conference on Spoken Language Processing*, volume 6, pages 2531–2534, Sydney, Australia, 1998.

E. Williams. Across-the-board application of rules. *Linguistic Inquiry*, 8:419–423, 1977.

P.C. Woodland, J.J. Odell, V. Valtchev, and S.J. Young. Large vocabulary continuous speech recognition using HTK. In *Proceedings of IEEE International Conference on Acoustics, Speech and Signal Processing*, pages II-125–II-128, Adelaide, Australia, 1994.

W. Woods. Language processing for speech understanding. In W. Woods and F. Fallside, editors, *Computer Speech Processing*. Prentice-Hall International, Englewood Cliffs, NJ, 1985.

D. Yarowsky. Decision lists for lexical ambiguity resolution. In *Proceedings of 32nd Annual Meeting of the Association for Computational Linguistics*, pages 88–95, Las Cruces, New Mexico, 1994.

S.J. Young. A review of large-vocabulary continuous speech recognition. *Signal Processing Magazine*, volume 13:5, pages 45–57, 1996.

Index